HUMANISTIC PSYCHOLOGY

This book provides a thought-provoking examination of the present state and the future of Humanistic Psychology, showcasing a rich international contributor line-up.

The book addresses head-on the current state of a world in crisis, not only placing the current conjuncture within a wider evolutionary context, but also demonstrating the specifically humanistic-psychological values and practices that can help us to transform and transcend the world's current challenges. Each chapter looks in depth at a variety of issues: counselling and psychotherapy, creativity and the humanities, post-traumatic stress, and socio-political movements and activism.

The book amply confirms that Humanistic Psychology is as alive, and as innovative and exciting, as it ever has been, and has tremendous relevance to the uncertainties that characterize the unprecedented individual and global challenges of the times. It celebrates the diverse and continuing significance of Humanistic Psychology by providing a robust and reliable roadmap for a new generation of counsellors and psychotherapists. In these richly diverse chapters will be found inspiration, pockets of resistance, mature critical reflexivity and much much more – a book accurately reflecting our present situation, and which is an invaluable addition to the psychology literature.

Richard House, PhD, C. Psychol. is a Chartered Psychologist, an educational consultant, a political activist, and long-time campaigner on childhood issues and Steiner education. Formerly senior lecturer in psychotherapy (Roehampton University) and education studies (Winchester), a counsellor-psychotherapist and editor of *Self & Society* journal, his eleven previous books include *Therapy Beyond Modernity* (2003) and *Too Much, Too Soon? Early Learning and the Erosion of Childhood* (2011).

David Kalisch, MA (Cantab), UKCP, UKAHPP (Aff. Memb.) is a psychotherapist, supervisor and trainer with nearly 30 years' experience in gestalt, humanistic and core process therapies. David has been co-editor of *Self & Society* journal since 2011, and co-edited (along with Richard House and Jennifer Maidman) *The Future of Humanistic Psychology* (PCCS, 2013). He is Director of CHPC Training.

Jennifer Maidman, (Dip Couns, MBACP) is a British musician, singer, producer and songwriter who has worked extensively with many well-known groups and artists, including Paul Brady, Van Morrison, Bonnie Raitt, Mark Knopfler, Robert Wyatt and Annie Whitehead. She was a key member of the Penguin Café Orchestra. She also trained as a humanistic counsellor with Noreen Emmans and Jimmy McGhee, and has written for *Therapy Today*, *Asylum* and *Self & Society*. She co-edited *The Future of Humanistic Psychology* (PCCS, 2013) with Richard House and David Kalisch.

HUMANISTIC PSYCHOLOGY

Current Trends and Future Prospects

Edited by Richard House, David Kalisch and Jennifer Maidman

Routledge
Taylor & Francis Group

LONDON AND NEW YORK

First published 2018
by Routledge
2 Park Square, Milton Park, Abingdon, Oxon OX14 4RN

and by Routledge
711 Third Avenue, New York, NY 10017

Routledge is an imprint of the Taylor & Francis Group, an informa business

British Library Cataloguing in Publication Data
A catalogue record for this book is available from the British Library

Library of Congress Cataloging in Publication Data
A catalog record for this title has been requested

ISBN: 978–1–138–69886–4 (hbk)
ISBN: 978–1–138–69891–8 (pbk)
ISBN: 978–1–315–39294–3 (ebk)

Typeset in Bembo
by Keystroke, Neville Lodge, Tettenhall, Wolverhampton

Printed and bound in Great Britain by
TJ International Ltd, Padstow, Cornwall

CONTENTS

NOTES ON CONTRIBUTORS

About the editors

Richard House, PhD, C. Psychol. is an educational and left-green political campaigner in Stroud, UK. Formerly a practising therapist, senior university lecturer in Early Childhood (Winchester) and in psychotherapy (Roehampton) and former co-editor of *Self and Society* journal, Richard co-founded the Independent Practitioners Network, the Alliance for Counselling and Psychotherapy and several early childhood campaigns. Richard is author or editor of eleven books, including *In, Against and Beyond Therapy* (PCCS, 2010), *Therapy Beyond Modernity* (Karnac, 2003), and *Against and For CBT* (PCCS Books, 2008, co-ed. Del Loewenthal). A trained Steiner teacher and childhood campaigner, in 2006, 2007, 2011 and 2016 Richard co-organized four influential multiple-signatory press letters on the state of childhood in modern culture. He loves John McLaughlin's Mahavishnu Orchestra; and trying (and, to date, failing) to work less hard. Email: richardahouse@hotmail.com

David Kalisch, MA (Cantab). After working initially in social work and education, David trained in Gestalt therapy and then in Core Process psychotherapy, and subsequently established The Centre for Humanistic Psychology and Counselling (CHPC) in Exeter, Devon, where he and his colleagues have run courses in Humanistic Psychology, humanistic counselling, gestalt psychotherapy, gestalt groupwork and personal development for over 25 years. David also has private practices in Exeter and Taunton and has written numerous articles for *Self & Society* journal, which he now co-edits, having formerly served on the editorial board for many years. He lives with his long-term partner, Christine, in Devon, and has an adult son and daughter, three adult step-children and seven grandchildren.

Jennifer Maidman, Dip.Couns, MBACP. Jennifer has made music for over 40 years, performing with Joan Armatrading, Gerry Rafferty, David Sylvian,

Robert Wyatt, The Proclaimers, Bonnie Raitt and Van Morrison, among others. She wrote for Boy George and Sam Brown, and produced albums for Paul Brady, Murray Head, Linda McCartney, and her partner Annie Whitehead. She was a key member of the original Penguin Café Orchestra, and her solo album 'Dreamland' will be released in 2017. Jennifer has been involved with human potential work since the 1970s, has written for *Therapy Today* and *Self & Society*, and was formerly co-editor of the latter. She trained as a humanistic counsellor with Noreen Emmans and Jimmy McGhee. Jennifer lives with her partner, by the sea, in Birchington, Kent, UK and in the mountains near Woodstock in Upstate New York, USA. Website: www.jennifermaidman.com

About the contributors

Manu Bazzano is a psychotherapist and supervisor in private practice, primary tutor at Metanoia Institute, London, and visiting lecturer at the University of Roehampton, London and various other schools and colleges. Among his books are: *Buddha is Dead* (2006); *Spectre of the Stranger* (2012); *After Mindfulness: New perspectives on psychology and meditation* (2013); *Therapy and the Counter-tradition: The edge of philosophy* (co-edited with Julie Webb); and the forthcoming *Zen and Therapy* (Routledge) and *Nietzsche and Psychotherapy* (Karnac). He is editor of *Person-Centered and Experiential Psychotherapy*, and book review editor for *Self & Society*. He has studied Eastern contemplative practices since 1980 and in 2004 was ordained a Zen monk in the Soto and Rinzai traditions. Website: www.manubazzano.com

Caroline Brazier is course leader of the Tariki Psychotherapy Training Programme and the Ten Directions ecotherapy training, and author of seven books on Buddhism, psychotherapy and ecotherapy. She has practised and taught psychotherapy for more than 25 years, and has been involved in developing a Buddhist therapeutic model known as the other-centred approach (www.buddhistpsychology.info). Her forthcoming book, *Ecotherapy in Practice: A Buddhist Model*, will be published by Routledge in August 2017. Caroline lives and works with her partner in a Buddhist centre run by Tariki Trust in Leicestershire. She has three children and four grandchildren.

Alexandra Chalfont practises as a psychotherapist, supervisor, trainer and executive coach in West London. Her specialisms have included mixed-culture relationships and intergenerational trauma, based on a lifelong interest in intercultural understanding. She has served, inter alia, as Chair of the Neuro-Linguistic Psychotherapy and Counselling Association, Co-Chair of the Association for Humanistic Psychology in Britain, Chair of the United Kingdom Council for Psychotherapy's Book Editorial Board and editor of *Self & Society*. Alexandra is currently setting up EngAgeingOnline, an initiative to provide online relational therapy and support to older people suffering from the effects of isolation and loneliness. Contact Chalfont7@icloud.com

Mick Cooper is a Professor of Counselling Psychology at the University of Roehampton and a chartered counselling psychologist. Mick is author and editor of a range of texts on person-centred, existential, and relational approaches to therapy. His latest book is *Existential Psychotherapy and Counselling: Contributions to a pluralistic practice* (Sage, 2015). Mick has also led a range of research studies exploring the process and outcomes of humanistic counselling with young people.

Windy Dryden is Emeritus Professor of Psychotherapeutic Studies at Goldsmiths University of London, and is a Fellow of the British Psychological Society. He has authored or edited more than 215 books, including the second editions of *Counselling in a Nutshell* (Sage, 2011) and *Rational Emotive Behaviour Therapy: Distinctive features* (Routledge, 2015). In addition, Windy edits 20 book series in the area of counselling and psychotherapy, including the *Distinctive Features in CBT* series (Routledge) and the *Counselling in a Nutshell* series (Sage). His major interests are in rational emotive behaviour therapy and Cognitive Behaviour Therapy (CBT); single-session interventions; the interface between counselling and coaching; pluralism in counselling and psychotherapy; writing short, accessible self-help books for the general public; and demonstrating therapy live in front of an audience.

Nick Duffell is a psychotherapy trainer and author of *The Making of Them* (2000) and *Wounded Leaders* (2014); he co-authored *Sex, Love and the Dangers of Intimacy* (2002), *Trauma, Abandonment and Privilege* (2016), and *The Simpol Solution* (2017). As a psycho-historian, he promotes a depth-psychology perspective of issues that affect our public life, such as identity and emotions, fear and vulnerability.

Colin Feltham is Emeritus Professor of Critical Counselling Studies, Sheffield Hallam University. His recent publications include *Failure* (Acumen, 2012), *The Sage Handbook of Counselling and Psychotherapy*, 3rd edn (ed. with Ian Horton, Sage, 2012), and *Counselling and Counselling Psychology: A critical examination* (PCCS Books, 2013). Colin lives and teaches in Denmark, and is an external examiner for training courses and doctoral projects in the UK. He has a regular 'interview' feature in *Therapy Today* and is on the boards of the *British Journal of Guidance and Counselling*, the *Irish Journal of Psychology*, and *Self & Society*.

Harris L. Friedman, PhD, is Research Professor (Retired) of Psychology at University of Florida, Professor Emeritus at Saybrook University, and on the faculty at Goddard College. He is senior editor of the *International Journal of Transpersonal Studies* and associate editor of *The Humanistic Psychologist*. He can be contacted at harrisfriedman@hotmail.com.

Dina Glouberman, PhD, is the visionary Co-founder and Director, since 1979, of Skyros Holidays, world leader in holistic holidays and trainings. She is also the author of the classic books *Life Choices, Life Changes* and *Joy of Burnout*. Formerly senior lecturer in Psychology and a consultant editor, she leads Imagework training courses internationally, is Honorary President of the International Imagework Association and a psychotherapist. Her focus now is on understanding and guiding people through turning points and new beginnings. Her latest book is called *You Are What You Imagine* (Watkins, 2014). Websites: www.dinaglouberman.com; www.skyros.com

Jill Hall was born in South Africa into an environment of extreme inequality and oppression, and cannot remember a time when she was not disturbed, puzzled and fascinated about what it means to be a human being. She moved to London in her late teens, working as an actress until becoming a mother and philosophy student. Attracted to the arena of self-development in the early days of Humanistic Psychology, she later became a tutor at the Institute of Biodynamic Psychology. She now runs weekend residential groups in Norwich, UK, and has been a guest lecturer for various professional bodies and universities. She is the author of *The Reluctant Adult* (Prism Press, Bridport, 1993).

James T. Hansen is a professor at Oakland University in the Department of Counseling. His primary scholarly interests are philosophical and theoretical issues in counselling and critical examination of contemporary mental health culture. Jim has published about 50 refereed articles in leading counselling journals. He is co-editor of an award-winning book on humanism, and his book on philosophical issues in counselling was published in early 2014. Jim has over 25 years of experience as a practitioner, supervisor and consultant.

Peter Hawkins has been involved in Humanistic Psychology for over 40 years, as a psychotherapist, Executive Coach and Leadership Team Coach, consultant, trainer, author, researcher and international speaker and workshop leader. He was founder of the Bath Centre for Psychotherapy and Counselling (1984), and co-founder of the Centre for Supervision and Team Development (1979) and Bath Consultancy Group (1986), and the first Chair of the Humanistic and Integrative section of the United Kingdom Council for Psychotherapy. Peter is currently Professor of Leadership at Henley Business School, Chairman of Renewal Associates and author of many best-selling books, including: *Leadership Team Coaching* (2011, 2014 and 2017); *Leadership Team Coaching in Practice* (2014); *Supervision in the Helping Professions* (with Robin Shohet 1989, 2000, 2006, 2012); *Coaching, Mentoring and Organizational Consultancy: Supervision and development* (with Nick Smith 2006, 2013); *Creating a Coaching Culture* (2012); and *Wise Fool's Guide to Leadership* (2005). Peter has been a consultant supervisor and trainer in over 50 countries.

John Heron is a Co-director of the South Pacific Centre for Human Inquiry in New Zealand. He was formerly Founder and Director of the Human Potential Research Project, University of Surrey, UK; Assistant Director, British Postgraduate Medical Federation, University of London; and Director, International Centre for Co-operative Inquiry, Volterra, Italy. John was also a co-founder in the UK of the

Association of Humanistic Psychology Practitioners (AHPP), Co-counselling International, the Institute for the Development of Human Potential, the New Paradigm Research Group, and the Research Council for Complementary Medicine. He is a researcher, author, facilitator and trainer. His books include *Feeling and Personhood* (1992), *Group Facilitation* (1993), *Co-operative Inquiry* (1996), *Sacred Science* (1998), *The Complete Facilitator's Handbook* (1999), *Helping the Client* (2001), and *Participatory Spirituality* (2006).

Louis Hoffman, PhD, is a faculty member at Saybrook University. He has eleven books to his credit, including *Existential Psychology East-West*. Louis is a past president of the Society for Humanistic Psychology and the current president of the Rocky Mountain Humanistic Counseling and Psychological Association. Due to his contributions to the profession, Louis has been recognized as a Fellow of the American Psychological Association as well as Division 10 (Society for the Psychology of Aesthetics, Creativity, and the Arts), Division 32 (Society for Humanistic Psychology), and Division 52 (International Psychology). Along with his academic work, Louis maintains a private practice in Colorado Springs, Colorado. He remains active in advocacy for and service to people experiencing homelessness and other marginalized groups, including serving on the board for the Coalition for Compassion and Action.

Lois Holzman, PhD, is a passionate advocate for conceptual tools and practices that empower people to transform the alienation and passivity of our culture. As a developmental psychologist and activist scholar, she promotes postmodern, culture-change approaches to human growth and learning. Lois is Director of the East Side Institute (www.eastsideinstitute.org), an international training and research centre for new approaches to therapeutics, education and community building; and a founder of the biennial *Performing the World* conference, which brings together hundreds of practitioners, scholars, researchers and activists for whom theatrical performance and the creative arts are essential for personal and social–political transformation. With colleague Fred Newman, the late public philosopher and founder of social therapy, Lois has advanced social therapeutics, a 'psychology of becoming' that incorporates play, performance and practical philosophy to inspire lifelong human development through group creativity. Her *Vygotsky at Work and Play* and Newman and Holzman's *Lev Vygotsky, Revolutionary Scientist* (2013, Classic Text Edition) have introduced psychologists, educators and helping professionals the world over to an activist take on the methodological writings of psychologist Lev Vygotsky.

Gaie Houston M.A.[Oxon] Dip. App. BSc lives in London. She works as a trainer and Emeritus Advisor for The Gestalt Centre, and as a supervisor, and less now as a therapist. She was trained in America in group and organizational behaviour, and in London as a therapist. She wrote her first book on group behaviour for the BBC in 1975, and has since published nine books on group and individual psychotherapy.

She has worked in many countries, from Japan, Russia and Kyrgyzstan to the USA and Scandinavia. Recently she has had to curtail her overseas work to look after her husband. Her last work abroad was in Paris, the weekend of the dreadful Bataclan attack, which began very close to where she was staying.

Stanley Krippner, PhD, is Professor of Psychology at Saybrook University in Oakland, California. He has been president of both the Association for Humanistic Psychology and the Society for Humanistic Psychology, and has received the Pathfinder Award for his contributions to this field, as well as the Ashley Montagu Peace Award and the Lifetime Achievement Award from the International Association for the Study of Dreams. In 2002, he received the American Psychological Association Award for Distinguished Contributions to the International Advancement of Psychology. His books include *Personal Mythology*, *Demystifying Shamans and Their World*, *Haunted by Combat*, and *The Voice of Rolling Thunder*.

Katherine McArthur is a Research Associate at Strathclyde University, a humanistic counsellor working with adults and young people in private practice, and a volunteer supervisor with Cruse Bereavement Care Scotland. Her PhD focused on school-based humanistic counselling, and she recently authored *The School-Based Counselling Primer* (PCCS, 2016). She currently coordinates the Glasgow Intergenerational Mentoring Network, a research and development project exploring social inequality in education.

Olivia Merriman-Khanna is a Chartered Psychologist (BPS), an HCPC Registered Counselling Psychologist and a BABCP-accredited CBT psychotherapist. Olivia completed her doctorate in counselling psychology at Roehampton University and undertook her post-doctoral training in cognitive behavioural therapy at Kings College London. Olivia has a particular interest in working with trauma and she is also a trained EMDR practitioner. She currently works as a clinician and supervisor for Wandsworth Improving Access to Psychological Therapies service where she is the Improving Access lead and Perinatal lead.

Seamus Nash is a UKCP-registered psychotherapist and supervisor working within end of life care. His doctoral thesis at the University of Huddersfield is based on research into practitioners' meanings of person-centredness. His practice is informed by being a father and a partner. Seamus is learning to play the piano and to enjoy music in all its forms. Family, friends, spirituality and nature help Seamus remain grounded and he is optimistic about people, the planet and life.

Maureen O'Hara, PhD, is Professor of Psychology at National University in La Jolla, California and CEO of International Futures Forum–US. Maureen worked closely with Carl Rogers, facilitating large group events and training counsellors in many countries. Maureen's current work with the International Futures Forum takes the lessons learned from humanistic practice into the public policy, community and organizational spheres, and explores the impact of global cultural shifts on emotional development and well-being. Maureen was President of the Association for Humanistic Psychology, and President of Division 32 of the American Psychological Association, recently receiving their Distinguished Lifetime Achievement Award. Her recent books include *Handbook of Person-Centered Psychotherapy and Counseling*, 2nd edn (2013) (with M. Cooper, P. Schmid and A.C. Bohart) and *Dancing at the Edge: Competence, culture and organization in the 21st century* (2012) (with G. Leicester).

Daniel B. Pitchford, PhD, is a professor at Northcentral University in Prescott Valley, Arizona. He has worked extensively as an educator, psychotherapist, and clinical supervisor in the Pacific Northwest. He has co-developed and co-led the Certificate Specialization in Trauma Studies at Saybrook University and provided policy and practice of trauma treatment on the Intergovernmental Council for Trauma and Homelessness for King County in Seattle, Washington, as well as sitting on the board for Trauma Policy and Healthcare Practice in Oregon State. He is co-author of *PTSD: Biography of a disease.*

Steven Pritzker is Director of the MA and PhD Creativity Studies Specialization and The Creativity Studies Certificate at Saybrook University. He is co-editor-in-chief of *The Encyclopedia of Creativity* published by Academic Press. Steven is a Fellow of the American Psychological Association and president-elect of Division 10 (Psychology of Aesthetics, Creativity and the Arts). His research has examined creativity and film; collaborative creativity in writing and business; creativity and spirituality; audience flow; comedians and longevity; and the creative process in high-achieving writers. Steven is a writer and creativity coach who has written and produced over 200 episodes of network television.

Ruth Richards is Professor of Psychology at Saybrook University, in the College of Social Sciences, and works in areas of consciousness, spirituality, integrative health, and in creativity studies. She does qualitative research on subjective experiences of creative process in arts and science and in everyday life, with interest in ways creative activity might contribute to health and can at times even change *us*, all else being equal, for the better. There are potential implications both for individuals and for cultures. Ruth also works with www.ahimsaberkeley.org, an interfaith and social action organization. She is currently in Brooklyn, NY, with activities including participation with www.bwac.org, the largest non-profit, volunteer artists' organization in Brooklyn, with major gallery and performance space, furthering the voice of New York and the local community. Ruth's numerous publications include the edited *Everyday Creativity and New Views of Human Nature*, and she is winner of the Rudolf Arnheim Award from Division 10 of the American Psychological Association for outstanding lifetime accomplishment in psychology and the arts. Her many interests include healthy benefits of the creative process for individuals and cultures, for personal, ethical, and spiritual development, issues of empathy and relational creativity in a troubled world, questions of beauty and awareness, and applications of chaos theory to an emerging worldview and view-of-self in the 21st century.

Andy Rogers trained at the University of East Anglia in the late 1990s and has worked in and written about the therapy field ever since. He now coordinates a counselling service in a large college of further and higher education, and is an active participant in the Alliance for Counselling & Psychotherapy. Andy is also a father, contemporary music obsessive, occasional blogger and keen home cook.

John Rowan joined the AHP(B) in 1970, and in 1972 was Chair. He pursued Humanistic Psychology largely by going to groups. Then in 1976 the first edition of *Ordinary Ecstasy* came out. It is now in its third edition. John is a Fellow of the BPS, BACP and UKCP. He is now pursuing Dialogical Self Theory, and his book on that, called *Personification*, came out in 2010. He lives in Chingford, London with his wife Sue and their dog James.

Andrew Samuels is Professor of Analytical Psychology at the University of Essex and holds visiting Chairs at New York, Roehampton and Goldsmiths College, London. A Jungian training analyst, he also works internationally as a political consultant. He is a member of the Association for Humanistic Psychology and has been a long-standing member of the Editorial Board of *Self & Society* journal. Andrew is the former Chair of the UK Council for Psychotherapy (UKCP), and former Honorary Secretary of the International Association for Analytical Psychology. He is also Co-founder of Psychotherapists and Counsellors for Social Responsibility (PCSR) and of the Alliance for Counselling and Psychotherapy, and a Founder Board Member of the International Association for Relational Psychoanalysis. His many books have been translated into 21 languages. Website: www.andrewsamuels.com

Kirk J. Schneider, PhD, is a licensed psychologist and leading spokesperson for contemporary existential-humanistic psychology. Kirk is past president (2015–2016) of the Society for Humanistic Psychology of the American Psychological Association, recent past editor of the *Journal of Humanistic Psychology* (2005–2012), president-elect of the Existential-Humanistic Institute (EHI), and adjunct faculty at Saybrook University and Teachers College, Columbia University. A Fellow of the American Psychological Association (APA), Kirk has published over 100 articles and chapters and has authored or edited eleven books, including *The Paradoxical Self, Horror and the Holy, The Psychology of Existence* (with Rollo May), *The Handbook of Humanistic Psychology* (2nd edn) (with Fraser Pierson and James Bugental), *Rediscovery of Awe, Existential-Integrative Psychotherapy, Existential-Humanistic Therapy* (with Orah Krug – accompanying APA video also available), *Humanity's Dark Side: Evil, destructive experience, and psychotherapy* (with Art Bohart, Barbara Held, and Ed Mendelowitz), *Awakening to Awe, The Polarized Mind, The Essentials of Existential-Humanistic Therapy Supervision* (with Orah Krug), and in press, *The Wiley World Handbook of Existential*

Therapy (with Emmy van Deurzen et al.). *The Spirituality of Awe: Challenges to the robotic revolution* is in preparation.

Robin Shohet is co-author of *Supervision in the Helping Professions* (4th edn, 2012) and editor of *Passionate Supervision, Supervision as Transformation* and *Supervision in the Medical Profession*. He co-founded the Centre for Supervision and Team Development (www.cstdlondon.co.uk) in 1980 and lectures in supervision worldwide.

Keith Tudor is a Certified Transactional Analyst (psychotherapy) and a Teaching and Supervising Transactional Analyst (psychotherapy). He is Professor of Psychotherapy and Head of the School of Public Health & Psychosocial Studies at Auckland University of Technology, Auckland, Aotearoa New Zealand. Keith retains his voluntary professional registration with the UK Council for Psychotherapy, which he has held since 1994, for ten years of which (1999–2008) he was, additionally, a registered group psychotherapist and facilitator through full membership of the Association of Humanistic Psychology Practitioners (UKAHPP). Keith is the author/editor of 13 books, is editor of *Psychotherapy and Politics International*, the co-editor of *Ata: Journal of Psychotherapy Aotearoa New Zealand*, and an associate editor of *Self & Society*.

David Wasdell is a partially dyslexic polymath, with degrees in mathematics, physics and theology and a lifetime spent in consultancy research in behavioural and physical sciences. He is the Founding Director of the Unit for Research into Changing Institutions (URCHIN) (founded in 1981), an educational research charitable trust registered in the UK. Since 1987 he has been the International Coordinator of the Meridian Programme (formerly the Manhattan Project of Behavioural Science). He has specialized in consultancy research with a wide range of institutions and organizations undergoing rapid change in conditions of low resource and high stress. For the last ten years he has directed the Apollo-Gaia Project, a worldwide action-research initiative focused on the feedback dynamics of the global climate system and the effective human response.

FOREWORD TO
THE NEW EDITION

Manu Bazzano

Conceived in the flirty, contagious good spirits of the post-war years; propelled at birth by the universal sigh of relief that accompanied a hallowed moment of truce; cradled in an experiential playground that was cheerfully shielded from the strains of the Cold War, Humanistic Psychology had it all. And, it must be said, it made very good use of its privileged upbringing. With an egalitarian spring in its step, it got down to setting things straight. It saw through and bravely denounced the doctrinaire stuffiness of a reified and capitalized unconscious. It presciently recognized the menace implicit in the behavioural and cognitive reprogramming of humans. It brought the exploration of *psyche* into the open, outside the analyst's vault of curiosities and outside the brutalist rewiring of brains and refitting of bodies and minds for the assembly line and the traffic jam.

It shouted its truths and half truths from the rooftops of communes and organic farmhouses; it sang and beat its djembe drum; it hugged, catharted, laughed and wept; it progressed by regress: to childhoods, foetal life, and even past lives. It took up existentialism and succeeded egregiously in creating the rosy version that is now all the rage. It promoted spirituality and socio-political change; it embraced otherness in all its facets. True, it paid little or no attention to the non-human, and it did leave humans at the very centre of it all, confirming, even with its forays into the trans-human and ecology, its terminal anthropocentrism. But its inclusivity and openness to the new are indisputable. Above all, Humanistic Psychology spoke to the world congruently, empathically, and holding this frail blue planet with unconditional positive regard. Did the world listen? Did it notice? As I'm writing this, the geopolitical landscape keeps tilting towards opposite values: intolerance, divisiveness, hatred of otherness, the worship of supremacy, easy money, and war. The few public figures who at present speak out for humanness, justice and equality are increasingly ridiculed by a hostile media and ostracized by a mounting wave of reactionary populism.

Does Humanistic Psychology have a future? I am tempted to say that there is no future for Humanistic Psychology, and that's precisely where its hope lies. Or, that there is no hope for Humanistic Psychology, and that's where its future lies. These two complementary statements are not born out of cynicism but on the consideration that to bank on a future and live on hope in this uncertain world is to set oneself up for disappointment. However, Humanistic Psychology never got over its happy childhood and, on balance, the incurable optimism that typifies this influential third force can be seen at times as counterproductive.

While we are busy pondering the future of Humanistic Psychology, the sweeping, uncontested neoliberal take-over of the humanities has meanwhile already entered a new phase. The few remaining instances of unaudited human communication (between trainers and trainees, clients and therapists, or in the production of psychology literature itself) are being nimbly and swiftly co-opted. Here I must confess my secret admiration for the amazing skill and dexterity with which corporate and state power has cloned the language, style and manners of Humanistic Psychology. Some practitioners suggested that they wouldn't have been as effective if some humanistic psychologists themselves were not so eager to lend a helping hand. I had my doubts about this position until the following incident gave me food for thought.

A couple of years ago I was introducing Rogers' six conditions for positive change to first year trainees on a humanistic counselling course. By the time I got to the fifth condition, empathy, one of the participants objected: 'This is all very well, but how do you *measure* something like empathy? We need to measure empathy, don't we? Otherwise how do we know that it is *really* happening?' A lively conversation followed, and what emerged was that another humanistic tutor at the very same course had strongly emphasized the need to accurately measure congruence, unconditional positive regard and empathy. Understandably, the trainee was confused.

Depending on one's view, the above can be read as either a gleaming example of the refreshing multiplicity of views within Humanistic Psychology, or as a sure sign of its being neutered and incorporated within the neopositivist, neoliberal project. Some would say that an open-minded, inclusive modality that is anchored in a fluid clinical philosophy still needs a strong central ethos if it wants to keep plurality from becoming either Babel or bland endorsement of diversity. Whether one sees this as appealing or unsettling, multiplicity of views is what this book offers in profusion. This in itself is an expression of inclusivity and generosity, two of the most appealing attributes of Humanistic Psychology – visibly present here in the open-handedness with which the three editors have put this book together.

Readers will find in these very diverse chapters inspiration and encouragement, pockets of resistance and instances of abdication: the book accurately reflects our present situation and is invaluable for that reason. The receptive reader may feel touched by some of these offerings. Borrowing from 13th century mystical realist Dōgen Zenji, I would say that all it takes for a tradition to remain dynamically alive in a fast-changing world is that somewhere, someone's heart is touched. He or she may then be able to divine glimmers of a future, and find the courage to dream the dream further. That's the only way, I believe, that Humanistic Psychology has a future. And that's our only hope.

FOREWORD TO
THE FIRST EDITION (2013)

Andrew Samuels

Only in the therapy field could a celebratory book carry so many anxieties! But what's wrong with that? After reading the chapters of this book, I felt I had a pretty good idea of what was on people's minds, and this Foreword is both my digestion of those concerns and a critical discussion of them. What I write is informed by my personal history in connection with Humanistic Psychology and by a set of parallel concerns in my own professional community (I am a Jungian analyst). I will return to these aspects later. Then there's a lifetime of involvement in the professional politics and 'cut and thrust' of theory-making in the psychological field. Finally, I developed a huge respect for the admixture of rigour and passion to be found in these pages, which I hope comes through in what follows.

First, let's look at the context that contributed to the content of the book, as well as being the public space into which it enters. In the United States and Britain, with resonances in other Western countries, a full-scale war has broken out regarding emotional distress (and 'illness'): how we talk about it, whether we try to measure it or not, and – crucially – what we do about it. Behind this battle for ownership of the soul lies contemporary culture's profound ambivalence regarding psychotherapy and counselling. Many countries have now opted for what they believe to be a quick and effective form of therapy, Cognitive Behaviour Therapy (CBT), which, proponents say, has been scientifically measured to have proven effects in relation to sufferers of anxiety and depression.

But if you read my last sentence again, you will see just below its surface the main grounds upon which the war is being fought. Are there really separate illnesses or diseases called 'anxiety' and 'depression'? No one in the field seriously believes that, hence the coinage 'co-morbidity'. And whether or not you can measure either the illness or the cure is such a hot topic that it will be keeping university philosophy of science departments busy for years. Is there such a thing as an 'effective' therapy? Don't people keep coming back?

Recently, a further front opened up in connection with the fifth version of the *Diagnostic and Statistical Manual of Mental Disorders* of the American Psychiatric Association (or DSM-V). Many established professional bodies are concerned that 'the psychiatrists' bible' adopts an over-easy pathologization of what are really ordinary – if difficult and painful – human experiences, such as grief. Others have protested that DSM-V isn't scientific enough, failing to consider genetic determinants of mental illness. At the time of writing it seems that the DSM psychiatrists have seen off the opposition. What is your problem, they say, with taking a systematic approach to mental illness? How can that fail to help? The media agreed.

But will they actually win? The stock-in-trade of psychiatry remains drug treatments and, recently, a series of books and scholarly papers have appeared (notably Irving Kirsch's *The Emperor's New Drugs: Exploding the Antidepressant Myth*) that cast doubt on the reliability of the research that seems to support such treatments. Kirsch's point is that the methodology that underpins such research – randomized controlled trials (RCTs) – is liable to many kinds of distortion. For example, if a patient is given a placebo with a mild irritant in it, she/he will assume they have been given the actual drug being trialled (all drugs have side-effects, don't they?) and, Hey Presto! – they get better.

In Britain, there is great interest now in discussing the pros and cons of RCTs because they are used to ration therapy on the British National Health Service (NHS). Well-established approaches, such as humanistic, integrative, family systemic and psychodynamic therapies, are vanishing from the NHS. Either CBT, or a watered-down version of it that I call 'state therapy', get the funding. This has led some to say that we (the humanistic field) should do RCTs of our own.

Others point to the fact that there is a huge amount of *non-RCT* evidence for the efficacy of psychotherapy and counselling. But the government agency that draws up guidelines for treatments on the NHS does not recognize the methodologies that underpin this research. At times, this National Institute for Health and Care Excellence (NICE) does seem to have been captured by the proponents of RCTs and – due to the way in which it has been researched via RCTs – CBT. The UK Department of Health claims that NICE is beyond its control, which has left many observers gobsmacked. Still others, notably my old friend John Rowan [see Chapters 1 and 19 below – eds], say it is all pointless.

To say that nothing in this 'battle for the soul' is encouraging to the future prospects of Humanistic Psychology is to understate the position. But people and groups respond to challenges, and that is one way to understand the rationale and purpose of this book.

Humanistic Psychology has, traditionally, eschewed many of the features of other traditions within psychotherapy. It has not valorized theory. It has not sought to adopt a highly professional persona or set of personae. It has not attempted to align itself with the social 'now' and with the powerful. Maybe this went too far, and a humanistic therapist caricature can easily be imagined. But the key problem is how to fix the problems with the easy-going approach without getting into what Heraclitus called an *enantiodromia* – a total swing from one extreme position to the polar opposite. In this swing to do research, work out more theory and seek professional acceptance, Humanistic Psychology – to put it in a nutshell – wants the prizes it sees others as having, and adopts the tactics and tropes it understands – rightly or wrongly – these other groups as having adopted. Hence the 'purity' of the humanistic approaches might be lost. I actually think that this is a legitimate concern. *Enantiodromias* lead to totalizing outcomes.

But I am equally worried that adherence to an ideal of so-called 'pluralism' will be deployed to justify these innovations in the direction of greater acceptance, *aka* 'integration'. Pluralism does not simply mean 'the Many' or many new add-ons. Rather, pluralism, in all serious uses of the term, means *the relations between the One and the Many*. For Humanistic Psychology, that would mean not just reaching out to other ways of doing things, but, rather, holding the tension between there being One humanistic way of doing things, and there being Many ways.

Most of the authors in the book do agree that Humanistic Psychology needs to change (or has changed for better or, more usually, for worse), but they don't want to lose the good bits. Baby and bathwater . . .. What I'd like to do here is signpost a number of areas within Humanistic Psychology, not all of them written about herein, to see how the changes that people desire might come about – but in a spirit of what Walter Bagheot (the British parliamentarian) called 'animated moderation' rather than fuelled by Anna Freud's 'identification with the aggressor'.

I've selected the following areas for what will have to be a few quite informal comments: (i) clinical ethos; (ii) diversity and equalities; (iii) aggression, lust and other difficult emotions; (iv) the past in the present (trauma and resilience); (v) the body; (vi) social responsibility and engagement, including ecopsychology; and (vii) spirituality.

Clinical ethos. 'It's the relationship, stupid!' was recently seriously suggested as a slogan to advertise psychotherapy. Humanistic Psychology and psychotherapy can be seen as more than incidental precursors of what the pioneering relational psychoanalyst Stephen Mitchell called 'the relational turn' in psychotherapy. Naturally, as one who has become institutionally involved in relational psychoanalysis, I think that the psychoanalytic bit does offer some added value, especially when it comes to the algebraic intricacies of intersubjectivity. But the fact remains: unconditional positive regard (and, crucially, the perception of it by the client) and authentic relating have played an identifiable role in breaking the ground for these developments in psychoanalysis. Taking the field as a whole, I think it is reasonable to say that human-istic psychotherapists are *the* experts in the therapy relationship – and maybe in the therapeutic/working alliance as well. I must add that to achieve this, they have had to learn from relational psychoanalysis with regard to therapist self-disclosure, acknowledgement (of therapist mistakes) and enactments. It's a good example of cross-fertilization.

Diversity and equalities. I didn't find enough meaty attention in the book to questions of inclusivity and exclusivity in the field. It is not enough to say that 'we are not homophobic' or that Humanistic Psychology (like the Ritz Hotel) is open to all. Nor is it enough to claim that many humanistic trainings are in the van when it comes to diversity and equalities. There is still a problem concerning who gets therapy and who gets to train as a therapist. What is needed is a raft of strategies and educational approaches applied systematically over time, making use of the expertise that already exists. Only then will we stop reading that 'the client was a 47-year-old Lesbian', or hearing a therapist say that she has immersed herself in the culture of a particular client and so understands where they are coming from.

Aggression, lust and other difficult emotions. For some, the positive and life-affirming nature of Humanistic Psychology is its strong point (and they can quite easily distinguish this from positive psychology). But for years now people have wondered whether the impression that humanistic therapists don't 'do' aggression is accurate. Do they always look on the bright side of life? I would argue (as would many, I think) that aggression, and even destructiveness, are a crucial part of self-actualization. As to sexual behaviour, my perception is that many aspects of what sexual minorities do tends to produce a moralistic response in a substantial number of humanistic practitioners (and probably other psychotherapists as well). For example, many are all at sea when confronted by promiscuity and infidelity in their clinical work, and tend to be rather conventional (and hence inadvertently condemning) in response.

The past in the present (trauma and resilience). The job is to allow for the influence of the past on the present without indulging in parent-bashing and evading personal responsibility, isn't it? And, concerning trauma and abuse, to find ways to move forward, based on facilitating the client's resilient capacities. Terms like post-traumatic growth and adversity-activated development are still foreign to most psychoanalytically oriented practitioners. Yet they seem to be congruent with most of the core values of humanistic psychotherapy.

The body. This is a highly personal view, but I am no longer persuaded that to consider the body in its imaginary or imaginal sense (the 'subtle body') is a good-enough perspective for a clinician. The actual, sweaty, fleshy body is there, in the relationship, in the room, and those therapists that know how to touch the client's body, or how to set it in motion, have much to teach others. And closely allied to body is *imagination*, which means that one path for future evolution is to strengthen and enhance the relationships between humanistic psychotherapy and all the arts therapies. It's no accident that [the late] Natalie Rogers was such an influential figure in the creative arts therapies.

Social responsibility and engagement, including ecopsychology. Humanistic Psychology has been at the forefront of using 'therapy thinking' in social contexts, and in contributing to deeper understandings of how it is that Western, capitalistic societies contribute to a suppression of human potential. More recently, developments in ecopsychology have emerged from within the humanistic (and other) traditions. These ideas are directly clinically relevant. Clients are irradiated with their negative experiences of living on a despoiled planet.

Spirituality. There is a place within humanism for the spiritual, and, I would suggest, for a religious attitude. Spirituality is also about persons – Jung said 'the mysteries of life are always hidden between Two', and 'the soul is the very essence of relationship'. There's something I call 'social spirituality', as well. People come together in groups to achieve something in the social world, and a kind of spiritual dew descends on them, transforming what they do from being only a social movement into something concerned with the great spiritual-existential issues of meaning and purpose. Recent developments in Transpersonal Psychology are not only inspiring in themselves. Once again, we see how clinically vital they are. What brings two people (therapist and client) into such close psychological proximity that their hearts, minds and psyches inter-penetrate, thus helping the therapy along, if not their transpersonal connection?

I'll conclude the Foreword to this epic book by delivering on my promise to talk about my personal involvements, and bring in some parallels from the experiences of the Jungian community.

Back in the early 1970s, I was in training to be an encounter group conductor and a Jungian analyst – at the same time! I chose the Jungian route because of my intense personal need to bring my troubles to a protected setting where I was the only 'client'. But I kept up my interests in Humanistic Psychology and psychotherapy, as you can see from my biography in the book. In 2014, I am organizing (with others) a conference on the relationships between Jungian analysis and humanistic psychotherapy [see *Self and Society*, 43 (3), 2015 for this conference's full proceedings – eds]. We want to call it 'Beyond the two Carls', to use Brian Thorne's celebrated phrase. It's never too late to heal a split, I guess.

Jungians have struggled with professionalization. In the old days, you became a Jungian analyst if Jung agreed you were one. I think we have lost something with the growth of all the accoutrements of a profession such as rules and regulations about training. Nevertheless, Jungian psychology does resemble Humanistic Psychology in that there is more to it than the actual practice of therapy and analysis. Notably, there are the 'Jung Clubs' which are open to all, rather like the Association for Humanistic Psychology in Britain.

Jungians also have grievances that they have been overlooked in their prescience. For example, Jung saw that the mother was being neglected in Freudian psycho-analysis and so sought to rectify this – decades before Klein, Winnicott and object relations. We – the Jungians – don't know whether to go on complaining about this or not. Humanistic psychotherapists and psychologists have the same problem.

I'll return at the last to the book as a whole. Here is a field in ferment, assailed by self-doubt yet proud of past attainments. The editors and the contributors have produced what diplomats call a *tour d'horizon*, a survey that does not pretend to be neutral or cohesive, is not predictive or admonishing – yet will inspire discussion and debate for many years to come.

ACKNOWLEDGEMENTS AND DEDICATIONS

We would like to offer our heartfelt thanks to all our contributors, who have gone many an extra mile to help us bring this book successfully to publication. Thanks also to our esteemed Foreword writers, Manu Bazzano and Andrew Samuels, and to the production editor and team at Routledge for their professionalism and efficiency in bringing this book to fruition.

The chapters in this book have been specially written for this volume, with the following chapters being updated and extended versions of articles, the original versions of which first appeared in *Self & Society* journal:

Chapter 2 first appeared in *Self & Society: International Journal for Humanistic Psychology*, 40 (1), 2012, pp. 10–15

Chapter 3 first appeared in *Self & Society: International Journal for Humanistic Psychology*, 40 (1), 2012, pp. 7–9

Chapter 7 first appeared in *Self & Society: International Journal for Humanistic Psychology*, 40 (1), 2012, pp. 21–5

Chapter 11 first appeared in *Self & Society: International Journal for Humanistic Psychology*, 40 (3), 2013, pp. 34–6

Chapter 14 first appeared in *Self & Society: International Journal for Humanistic Psychology*, 40 (2), 2013, pp. 21–5

Chapter 15 first appeared in *Self & Society: International Journal for Humanistic Psychology*, 40 (3), 2013, pp. 37–9

Chapter 18 first appeared in *Self & Society: International Journal for Humanistic Psychology*, 40 (2), 2013, pp. 18–20

Chapter 20 first appeared in *Self & Society: International Journal for Humanistic Psychology*, 40 (3), 2013, pp. 40–1

Chapter 22 first appeared in *Self & Society: International Journal for Humanistic Psychology*, 40 (1), 2012, pp. 30–1

Chapter 23 first appeared in *Self & Society: International Journal for Humanistic Psychology*, 40 (1), 2012, pp. 26–9

Chapter 24 first appeared in *Self & Society: International Journal for Humanistic Psychology*, 40 (2), 2013, pp. 26–30

Chapter 26 first appeared in *Self & Society: International Journal for Humanistic Psychology*, 40 (4), 2013, pp. 53–7

Warm thanks to the authors, and to *Self & Society* journal, for permission to reproduce updated and extended versions of the above-listed chapters in this volume.

David would like to dedicate this book to his partner Christine for her patience during this, and several other time-consuming projects recently, and to his children who have taught him what being 'humanistic' really means.

Jennifer: I dedicate this book to my partner Annie, with heartfelt thanks for her boundless love, support and kindness, and to my late parents, Beryl and Brian, who were endlessly tolerant, loving and 'humanistic' without ever having heard the word. Thanks also to dear comrades in Birchington, Kent and Woodstock NY for their honesty, love and fellowship (you know who you are), and to all my wonderful friends in the worlds of music, art and therapy. 'Don't Let the Moonlight Fade Away.'

Richard would like to dedicate this book to his daughter Shanice, who shows every sign of helping to keep the flame of these vital ideas and practices alive for this and the next generation.

Exeter, Birchington and Stroud, UK
December 2016

EDITORIAL INTRODUCTION

Richard House, David Kalisch
and Jennifer Maidman

What a difference four years can make! When we published the first edition of this book in 2013, Barack Obama was still US President, Britain was still committed to the European Union, and 'alt-right' was a relatively unknown term. Now, post-Trump, post-Brexit, and even 'post-truth', with critical European elections still ahead as we write, the skies suddenly look a lot darker than they did just a few years ago. Many of the apparently consensual assumptions of the previous sixty years arguably lie shattered in pieces, while the mainstream commentariat – the same folk who so conspicuously failed to see Brexit and Trump coming (and, for that matter, left-wing political leaders Bernie Sanders and Jeremy Corbyn) – vainly attempt to make sense of what seem to be era-defining moments. It is a veritable 'bonfire of the certainties' (Authers, 2016), to mis-quote Tom Wolfe, as everything solid melts into thin air.

These are without doubt highly challenging times for all of us, then – not least for Humanistic Psychology; but as we will argue, at the same time multiple opportunities may be opening up for the humanistic project, too. Never, arguably, has the humanistic perspective in psychology been so desperately needed, as we are everywhere surrounded, if not engulfed, by the relentless 'March of the Inhuman' (Sim, 2001).

It is perhaps appropriate, therefore, that this extensively revised and augmented new edition is in many ways a new book – with a new title – representing more of a consolidation and celebration of Humanistic Psychology in all its richness and expansiveness, secure in the strength of its history and continuing influence (explicit and implicit) and confident in its humanistic critique of capitalism's out-of-control accelerationism and pathological 'annihilation of space by time' (Noys, 2014; Wajcman, 2015) – in contrast to the uncertain, even anxious concern about its imminent demise that was suggested by at least some of the contributors to our first edition.

So what has changed in this expanded and updated edition? Apart from the re-configuration of the book, with more emphasis on its history and current strengths, as well as the challenges it faces, the unfolding, consensus-shattering global events of the past four to five years have, we maintain, heightened rather than reduced Humanistic Psychology's relevance in today's world. As multiple stresses associated with neoliberalism and austerity precipitate a burgeoning epidemic of mental health problems and a chronic loss of certainty, and attitudes and values which Humanistic Psychology (and other liberalizing movements) have long espoused appear to be under threat – universalism, human rights, women's and minority rights, anti-racism and anti-fascism, care for the Earth, distributional fairness, freedom from intrusive surveillance, and so forth – the need to revisit and re-assert humanistic principles may be greater than ever.

What also gives more gravitas to this current collection are major new contributions from three great elders of Western Humanistic Psychology – John Rowan and Dina (Zohar) Glouberman from Britain and Maureen O'Hara from the USA – alongside several other entirely new and substantial contributions, with John and Dina looking back panoramically over our history, and Maureen more forward-looking – but both facing outwards to the wider socio-historical context in which Humanistic Psychology is situated. In short, the conditions that made Humanistic Psychology so relevant and vital in the 1960s and 1970s are with us again – and, it seems, in intensified form.

So with an awareness that any attempt to make sense of things at a 'big picture' level at this stage could come back to haunt us, and an accompanying awareness that suggests challenging one's own hype rather than doubling down on it might be a sensible way to proceed, we nonetheless venture forth to attempt to set Humanistic Psychology, and the publication of this book, in context.

In order to start to consider what Humanistic Psychology might contribute to the new, disquieting and rapidly emerging socio-economic-cultural terrain facing us, it is useful to take a step back and consider the cultural conditions in which Humanistic Psychology emerged in the first place. Humanistic Psychology, like any cultural phenomenon, developed in a particular socio-historic context. It has been some fifty years since the humanistic 'brand' first began to enter the cultural mainstream in North America, where it was widely hailed as a 'Third Force' to counterbalance the perceived reductionist excesses of behaviourism and the pessimistic outlook of psychoanalysis. Its optimistic ethos and emphasis on human potential, rather than on deficiency and a dehumanizing 'psychopathology' discourse, perfectly suited the 1960s *Zeitgeist* of expansiveness, creativity and abundance and, for a while at least, it went from strength to strength. Yet here we are in 2017 when, despite considerable propagation of humanistic *ideas* into the wider society, the humanistic approach, within both Psychology and within the psychological therapies, seems to have a definite visibility (if not credibility) problem – as some of our contributors argue in this book. Has something gone wrong, or have we missed a trick and been outwitted by more ruthlessly power-aware approaches? Or was this always the inevitable outcome for an approach whose common ground rested largely upon shared values and progressive but, crucially, *diverse* attitudes, rather than on a single, sharply defined (tribalist?) theoretical doctrine?

After the carnage and atrocities of the Second World War, which followed hard upon the Great War and subsequent Great Depression, there had been not only a widespread desire for a more equal society (witness the surprise landslide election of Atlee's progressive Labour government in Britain in 1945), but also a thirst for a deeper understanding of human nature and the existential human condition. Pioneering (and sometimes maverick) humanistic psychologists such as Rollo May, Abraham Maslow, Carl Rogers, Eric Berne and Fritz Perls were soon making an impact on conventional psychological thinking and practices, and rapidly became virtual celebrities in their time, with the 'movement' they collectively founded beginning to recast psychology and therapy in less professionalized and more democratic terms, as something that could be 'all things to all people', and which no longer necessarily needed to be considered as lying purely and exclusively within the realm of experts (e.g. Mair, 1997). To 'know oneself' was no longer to be the preserve of a privileged and fortunate few – anyone could have a go.

Though it can sound quite passé and unexceptional today, in its time this was indeed revolutionary stuff. You did not have to be 'neurotic' or 'broken' to seek therapy, which came increasingly to be seen as being about self-discovery, personal growth and the healing of society's problems from the inside out, rather than simply 'curing' an individual's psychological disease or psychopathology. The emphasis was on individual *autonomy*, taking personal responsibility for oneself, and being fully alive in the moment. Carl Rogers went on to question whether 'professionals' were even needed any more in his seminal lecture on the helping professions, in which he had a telling section entitled, 'Dare we do away with professionalism?' (Rogers, 1973; see also *Self & Society*, 2013a). Tellingly, today Rogers' profound question still remains largely unanswered (though it has been exhaustively explored within the humanistic literature); and sadly, in our view – and notwithstanding many notable and admirable exceptions keeping the humanistic flame alive – since the 1990s the pendulum seems to have swung back toward both the 'professionalization of helping', and a psychiatrically oriented, pathology-based model of human functioning (Parker *et al.*, 1995). Therapy these days, at least in the mainstream, is once again for those who are defined as sick or deficient in some way – and at worst, might be deployed as a means for getting the disadvantaged (back) into a low-paid and demeaningly alienating jobs market (e.g. Thomas, 2016). As we put it in the title of a theme issue of the *Self & Society* journal which we co-edited, 'Welcome to the paradigm war' (*Self & Society*, 2013b).

Still, back in its halcyon days, Humanistic Psychology seemed, for a while at least, to be an unstoppable force that found common cause with other left/green cultural movements of the time. Well-known therapists appeared on television, and popular therapy books such as Eric Berne's *Games People Play* (1964 – over 5 million copies sold to date), Carl Rogers' *On Becoming a Person* (1961), and Arthur Janov's *The Primal Scream* (1970) became best-sellers, with the latter being read by tens of thousands of Americans, in the process bringing Janov considerable popular success and acclaim. The sheer scale of the movement around that time, both in North America and beyond, is staggering by today's standards, with Rowan (2004) reporting that the fifth European Association for Humanistic Psychology (EAHP) Congress in Rome in 1981 attracted some 500 participants, and with the sixth Congress, held in Paris, attracting 800 participants – only to be aced by the March 1985 quarter-century celebration in San Francisco, which attracted a mega-gathering over 1,000 strong (Rowan, 2004: 231–3).

John Rowan also describes several other extraordinary events in the history of Humanistic Psychology. For example, there was the conference held in Easton, Maryland State in 1979, at which some 120 leading government officials from virtually every government department assembled for three days to explore the implications of humanistic values and practices for social change. Perhaps it is no coincidence that this occurred during the presidency of arguably one of the most progressive and unjustly unrecognized US presidents of recent decades, Jimmy Carter. According to then AHP President, Jean Houston (quoted in Rowan, 2004: 229), 'We in the AHP were asked by a number of key officials to continue to assist and consult with their departments . . . The *Washington Post* featured a long editorial applauding the conference.' Notwithstanding the pioneering work of figures such as Susie Orbach and Andrew Samuels in bringing emotional awareness into the British political world via their Antidote work, remembering such extraordinary initiatives can only evoke a mixture of awe and desperate yearning for such progressive thinking helping to heal our broken political system today (cf. Palmer, 2011). Across its mixed history, Humanistic Psychology has repeatedly (though perhaps not always) been 'ahead of its time' and ahead of the game, in all manner of rich and creative ways.

During the heady late 1960s, therapists and 'alternative' psychiatrists, such as R.D. (Ronnie) Laing, Thomas Szasz and Arthur Janov, became as much the spokespeople of the 'counter-culture' as were the hippy poets, rock stars and novelists, and the new 'celebrity' political philosophers such as Herbert Marcuse, Jean-Paul Sartre, Paul Goodman (*Self & Society*, 2016) and Noam Chomsky. Those were the days when Ronnie Laing questioned the very foundations of mainstream psychiatric thinking (routinely attracting hissing whenever his name was mentioned at orthodox psychiatry conferences), took LSD, went to India, and wrote poetry. Laing's *Politics of Experience and The Bird of Paradise* (1967) became a cult classic; and Arthur Janov helped John Lennon exorcise his inner demons, leading to a best-selling album about the experience – the 1970 release, 'Plastic Ono Band'.

Many of us post-war 'baby-boomers' were instinctively drawn to the values of the humanistic approaches (we use the plural advisedly), and perhaps above all by the belief that they offered a route to greater *authenticity* (cf. Jackson, 2013). The desire to be *real* and *authentic* – keywords in the new humanistic lexicon – resonated deeply with the rock and roll generation, tired of what many saw, like James Dean's *Rebel without a Cause*, as their parents' generation's 'uptight' artifice and sexual repression. Humanistic Psychology seemed like a major step in the right direction, toward the kind of egalitarian, person-centred, forward-looking world that many longed for, conveniently lacking any of the totalitarian conformity of state communism – still a force to be reckoned with back then – without having to engage too much with the frustrations, compromises and general 'square-ness' of increasingly satirized mainstream politics. Rather like Dylan and the Rolling Stones, then, for a while at least Humanistic Psychology was *cool, far out*, and above all counter-cultural and exciting.

It has been said by some that the 1960s really ended, not on 1 January 1970, but on 8 December 1980 when John Lennon was shot in New York. One of the editors of this book (J.M.) was in a large Primal group at Art Janov's Institute in Los Angeles, California that very night. Many in the group spent the evening screaming and crying out in inconsolable shock, horror and disbelief. How could this have happened? Lennon's hugely influential art, irreverence for authority and persona had brought many to this 'therapeutic Mecca' in the first place. How could the figurehead of the 'revolution' who had imagined 'all the people living life in peace' be shot in cold blood? Our optimistic *humanistic* philosophy maintained that people were basically good – that the human organism could be trusted; if we allowed its inherent wisdom to prevail all would be well. To many it seemed as if the egalitarian dream of the sixties was really over, and as political progressives struggled with the ascendancy of the neoliberal right's champions, Reagan and Thatcher, many baby-boomers arguably sought refuge from what they saw as a dehumanizing, free-market ideology by immersing themselves in an increasingly individualistic and introspective therapy culture.

We could draw parallels with recent political developments. Another dream at least appears to be coming to an end. The day after Donald Trump was elected, many young progressives were seen crying inconsolably in the streets. Similarly, with Brexit, there was an outpouring of grief and disbelief. These events seem to represent the 'how-could-this-happen?' moments of a whole new generation. This time around though, with a global swing toward right-wing populism, authoritarianism and intolerance, perhaps the fear runs deeper and the stakes seem higher, particularly for those who grew up in, and perhaps took for granted, the sense of 'progress-toward-a-more-tolerant-future' ethos of the nineties and noughties. The great financial crisis of 2008 seems to have changed everything, and even eight years later, it is unclear which way the world is heading. Are we really going backwards? As we write this, nobody really knows.

The 'Woodstock generation' was to encounter bewilderment and the shattering of their hopes and dreams again and again as the 1980s unfolded, and ruthless Darwinian market forces, given free rein by Friedman- and Hayek-inspired Reaganomics and Thatcherism, raged across the Western world. 'Self-actualization', the Holy Grail of the early humanistic movement, also began to manifest a darker, shady side: self-obsession and an insatiable appetite for 'stuff' (see, for example, Lasch, 1979; Wallach and Wallach, 1983; Furedi, 2004; Gerhardt, 2010). The advertising industry, never slow to jump on a trend, also co-opted the humanistic message of authenticity and freedom. Authenticity now became something that could be attributed to a product, and with psychology manipulatively exploited to increase sales (Roberts, 2015) – 'It's the *real* thing'; and as the Coke Generation 'taught the world to sing in perfect harmony', the message was clear: self-liberation could now be achieved through conspicuous consumption.

The nineties and the noughties continued in much the same individualistic and materialistic vein, and, notwithstanding the occasional recession, a whole new generation was invited to join in the party. In the UK, Tony Blair's Centrist New Labour was elected in a landslide to the optimistic strains of 'Things Can Only Get Better'. With hindsight, that seems rather naive, not unlike, some might argue, the 'All You Need is Love' ethos of the late 1960s. And meanwhile, as the neoliberal world view became increasingly mainstream, normalized and taken-for-granted, and as the 'haves' pulled up the economic ladder and left the 'have nots' behind, much mainstream 'therapy', humanistic or otherwise, seemed to be moving away from (perhaps it had little choice?) a 'human potential' model, and increasingly toward ministering to the emotional and spiritual wounds of those who had fallen by the wayside in what had become, despite the smokescreen of 'touchy-feely' messages, a fiercely competitive and sometimes soul-destroying culture.

In his 2008 invocation of 'Yes we can' discourse, US President Barack Obama sought to re-awaken and re-connect with an optimistic humanistic ethos. As Obama realized, a *humanistic* generation of baby-boomers does still exist, who still, despite everything, want to believe that a just, progressive society is a real possibility. We are still here, and it appears a majority of young people also share similar values and aspirations for a more tolerant and inclusive society. Yet the democratic left has self-evidently failed to connect with many of those who feel they have been left behind by globalism, or that their anxieties about a rapidly changing world have been dismissed or even ridiculed. Enter the New Populism of Nigel Farage, Donald Trump *et al.*

In terms of age, all three of us editors are part of that idealistic generation which now finds itself taking stock and asking – despite the inequality, the wars, the fundamentalism, the rampant capitalism, the terrorism, the political corruption, 'post-truth' anti-ethics and hate-speech, and the other ills that continue to plague the human race – to what extent might those of us who have been drawn to and aligned ourselves with humanistic ideas have succeeded in realizing at least some of the humanistic dream? And is that dream still valid in current cultural-historical circumstances, or do we need a new one (or, at the very least, and given recent events, a realistically updated one)? There are, perhaps, tentative signs of a renewed interest in the history of our field, from those who were not there first time around. For instance, David Tennant (the renowned actor best known for playing Doctor Who) is soon to star in a major film about R.D. Laing and Kingsley House. Still, no matter how much we might revisit and even revere the past, we are where we are now.

This brings us to the book you now have in your hands, which broadly seeks to answer that question, 'Where are we now?' Has Humanistic Psychology fulfilled some, or any, of its early promise and potential? Has it floundered along the way, and turned into something that its founders, among others, might fail to recognize, were they alive today? Further, as at least one of our distinguished contributors

(Peter Hawkins) suggests, has Humanistic Psychology actually contributed negatively to some of the mess we currently find ourselves in? And might it be so that, notwithstanding the somewhat tainted humanistic dream, Humanistic Psychology's comparative failure to make significant inroads into modern academic and cultural discourses and practices is an argument for *redoubling* our efforts to assert the human against the inhuman, both within mainstream positivistic Psychology and in present-day culture more generally, rather than to give up in despair?

Perhaps it is also time to fearlessly consider Humanistic Psychology's current condition, the pathway of its development over the past half century, and what this suggests about its future – as addressed by many of our contributors, especially in Part IV of this book. What are its distinctive achievements, and what might it have surrendered or compromised in the process of becoming more respectable, 'professional' and mainstream? Are what seem to some to be unacceptable compromises actually signs of adaptation and a coming of age, and therefore to be welcomed, or at the least accepted? Again, you will find a diverse and sometimes conflicting range of opinions in these pages on this very issue – a key issue in any overall assessment of Humanistic Psychology's contribution with which we invite readers to engage.

This thoroughly revised and re-titled new edition, augmented by a number of newly written contributions by major figures in the field, originally developed from a series entitled 'The Future of Humanistic Psychology' first published in *Self & Society* journal, the quarterly journal of the Association for Humanistic Psychology in Britain. Moreover, in keeping with the international flavour of both *Self & Society* and of Humanistic Psychology itself, we are delighted to welcome contributions from some of the leading figures in the field from North America and Australasia as well as from the UK.

In the trajectory of Humanistic Psychology, especially but not exclusively in the UK, while counselling and psychotherapy have without question enjoyed a boom period of increased social acceptance (so much so that it is indeed as if Philip Rieff's 'Triumph of the Therapeutic' has finally come to pass – Rieff, 1966), within that trend many if not most counsellors and psychotherapists espouse at least *some* humanistic values and practices. And yet affiliation to overtly 'humanistic' professional organizations is everywhere either at a standstill, or on the wane. Why might this be? Is there perhaps a failure of 'branding'? For whatever reason, many long-standing humanistic organizations continue to experience alarming declines in membership.

There are clearly issues of professional identity and affiliation here in the UK, with the centre of gravity of humanistic work having shifted through the 1980s and 1990s from the 'Growth Centres' to the territory of the practitioner, training and accreditation lobbies. In this changed context, the question of affiliation – and the simple economic calculus that militates against belonging to more than one or two professional organizations – has become a more pragmatic one, rather than necessarily a statement of core values, possibly thereby eroding the rather loose and ill-defined sense of affiliation and kinship that somehow held the 'humanistic movement' together so well in previous decades.

Does this even matter though, when many adherents of both the Psychodynamic and Cognitive Behavioural approaches embrace many core Humanistic Psychology values, such as the centrality of the therapeutic relationship and Carl Rogers' 'core conditions' of empathy, congruence and unconditional positive regard? Perhaps we should all be happy, given that 'imitation is the sincerest form of flattery'! With the importance of the late Dan Stern's 'present moment in psychotherapy' recognized (*aka* 'the here and now'; Stern, 2004; Owens, 2013), notions of 'embodied presence' and the 'embodied mind' fast becoming ubiquitous (e.g. Corrigall *et al.*, 2006), and *awareness* – another of the 1960s' humanistic buzzwords – now commercially repackaged as 'mindfulness' (e.g. Bazzano, 2013), is it perhaps time to at least celebrate these successes of influence, and to reframe Humanistic Psychology as a once revolutionary movement that is now being so comprehensively absorbed into the mainstream that it will soon no longer have anything distinctive to offer in terms of its own differentiated 'brand'?

Putting this another way, and as some argue in this collection: was the term 'humanistic' *always* going to be too broad an umbrella-term for its constituent parts? And perhaps, thinking more widely, what are the characteristics of, and is there still a place for, humanistic values in a psychology field becoming dominated by 'audit mindedness' (e.g. Power, 1997; King and Moutsou, 2010) and 'bang for buck' thinking in the delivery of services increasingly standardized into protocol-driven and (supposedly) 'evidence-based' 'treatments' (e.g. Marzillier, 2004; Holmes *et al.*, 2006; Elkins, 2007; House and Bohart, 2008)?

Some of the writers in these pages imply that humanistic values are essentially little more than a relic of the hedonistic and overly optimistic 1960s' mind-set. However, there is a strong counter-argument, also made in these pages, that on the contrary, humanistic values might represent the clearest expression thus far, within the field of Psychology at least, of that great, liberalizing swathe of ideas and sensibility called 'humanism' (broadly defined), and that those values remain the strongest bulwark that we have against the triumph of technocratic scientism, soulless materialism, and the march of the inhuman, and are therefore now needed more than ever (see Maureen O'Hara's chapter for a particularly passionate argument very much along these lines). But if the latter is true, then is humanism itself still sufficiently relevant in the world of post-modernity – and if not, what adaptations must it make to be so? And is there a potential third, more middle-ground position emerging, which honours both sides of the argument while transcending their apparently binary, either/or form? Again, several chapters in this collection start to sketch what such a tendency might look like.

However, it would be short sighted and naive in the extreme to pursue these questions at the philosophical level alone, and not to question also the influence of far broader and deeper underlying tectonic shifts that all societies, and the global system itself, are undergoing, at breathtaking and increasingly accelerating speed (see, for example, Bauman, 2007; Gilding, 2012; Mason, 2016; Wallerstein *et al.*, 2013; Žižek, 2014). Although inevitably the jury is out on what exactly is driving this end-of-cycle trend – take your pick from end of the world/end of capitalism/ new phase of neoliberalism/rise of authoritarian capitalism/terminal decline of the

West, and more – it seems already safe to suggest that business-as-usual assumptions are not going to work in the emerging situation.

Thus, in order to succeed, attempts at understanding the present (and the future) might need to transcend the simplistic – and moralistic – binaries of 'progressives' versus 'regressives', 'left' versus 'right', 'goodies' versus 'baddies', head versus heart, so beloved of ideologues of both left and right. On this basis, Humanistic Psychology, founded on values of mutual respect, integrity, honouring of difference and diversity and the willingness and ability to embrace uncertainty, could have a vital role to play by *not* coming down on one side or another in the aforementioned binaries, and by *not* becoming polarized itself into its own version of the above binaries (to use a useful concept developed by one of our distinguished US contributors, Kirk Schneider – see Schneider, 2013); but by finding the middle ground where both sides in these (apparent?) conflicts can meet as openly and non-defensively as possible in their full humanness.

In publishing this new and extensively revised and updated edition and by taking a broader overview in it of what the humanistic movement is, how it emerged, its many contributions to the psychology and therapy fields and to the wider culture, its current foci of interest, as well as some thoughts about its future trajectory, we are strongly asserting, collectively depicting and fulsomely celebrating the influence of Humanistic Psychology as a substantial, enduring and broadly liberating one – and one with, as we have argued, quite possibly increased relevance and vitality in these difficult times.

There will always be tensions within any field. Currently in the UK, and at the risk of over-simplification, there is considerable debate taking place between, on the one hand, those who feel that humanistic approaches need to be more pragmatic and do whatever is expedient to further their penetration into the mainstream; and on the other, those who feel that humanistic values, if authentically expressed, must always and *necessarily* embody a strong counter-cultural, even revolutionary quality. Both sides in these debates are well represented in many of the chapters in this book, and it is certainly not our job as editors to referee or lend our weight to one set of arguments over another. As already noted, you will also find emerging in these pages a potential middle-ground position that consciously strives to honour both sides of the polarities, and searches for the common ground between them – a common ground that we who still proudly identify ourselves as 'humanistic' can still find, connecting us far more than dividing us.

To quote from just one such chapter: 'The highest and best role for our humanistic community should be to recover our roots as a cultural movement – not as a counter-cultural movement but a cultural growth movement aimed at facilitating the emergence of a vision of personhood adequate to the complexity of the times' (Maureen O'Hara, p. 85). You will find these arguments, different perspectives and attempts at an overarching and inclusive narrative and a great deal more, discussed and dissected with passion and intelligence in the pages of this book.

The book is divided into four parts – History and context; Socio-political-cultural perspectives; Current applications, tensions, and possibilities; and Future prospects. Rather than use this already over-long introduction to showcase the book's twenty-six engaging chapters, we will leave those summary tasters to our introductions to each part.

We hope, finally, you enjoy reading the book as much as we have enjoyed putting it together. It can be read as either a breathless cover-to-cover read, or a 'source-book' to be selectively dipped into, to suit readers' own particular interests. And having immersed yourself in such a rich and diverse collection of humanistically oriented material, perhaps you will find yourself wondering – as we have – if the dream really is over – or at least, whether it might have changed beyond all historical recognition? Or might, as several contributors suggest, Humanistic Psychology have a continuing and indeed increasingly important role to play in these difficult times? And is it still conceivable that a fundamental paradigm shift might lead to academic Psychology degree courses openly embracing the kind of avowedly critical (Parker, 2007), human-centred theories and ethos that Humanistic Psychology at its best represents and champions – or the kind of consciousness perspectives proposed by the likes of Stan Grof (2000) and Jill Hall (this volume); or even the kind of transpersonal *heart-centred psychology* championed by leading-edge thinkers like Robert Sardello (2015) and Nick Duffell in this volume?

While we have our own views on all these issues (which we will be exploring in our Editorial Conclusion), until then we naturally wish to leave it to you to formulate your own answers to these self-searching questions.

References

Authers, J. (2016) Donald Trump and the Bonfire of the Certainties. Accessible at www. ft.com/content/89757a34-a5e2-11e6-8898-79a99e2a4de6 (retrieved 25/11/2016).
Bauman, Z. (2007) *Liquid Times: Living in an Age of Uncertainty*. Cambridge: Polity Press.
Bazzano, M. (2013) 'In praise of stress induction: mindfulness revisited', *European Journal of Psychotherapy and Counselling*, 15 (2): 174–85.
Berne, E. (1964) *Games People Play: The Psychology of Human Relationships*. New York: Grove Press (latest edition, Penguin, 2010).
Corrigall, J., Payne, H. and Wilkinson, H. (eds) (2006) *About a Body: Working with the Embodied Mind in Psychotherapy*. London: Routledge.
Elkins, D.N. (2007) 'Empirically supported treatments: the deconstruction of a myth', *Journal of Humanistic Psychology*, 47 (4): 474–500.
Furedi, F. (2004) *Therapy Culture: Cultivating Vulnerability in an Uncertain Age*. London: Routledge.
Gerhardt, S. (2010) *The Selfish Society: How We All Forgot to Love One Another and Made Money Instead*. New York: Simon & Schuster.
Gilding, P. (2012) *The Great Disruption: How the Climate Crisis Will Transform the Global Economy*. London: Bloomsbury.
Grof, S. (2000) *Psychology of the Future: Lessons from Modern Consciousness Research*. Albany: SUNY Press.
Holmes, D., Murray, S.J. and Perron, A. (2006) 'Deconstructing the evidence-based discourse in health sciences: truth, power and fascism', *International Journal of Evidence-Based Healthcare*, 4: 180–6.

House, R. and Bohart, A.C. (2008) '"Empirically supported/validated treatments" as modernist ideology, II: alternative perspectives on research and practice'. In R. House and D. Loewenthal (eds), *Against and For CBT: Towards a Constructive Dialogue?* (pp. 202–17). Ross-on-Wye: PCCS Books (2nd edition in preparation).

Jackson, C. (2013) 'Something more to say . . .', *Therapy Today*, 24 (5): 10–13.

Janov, A. (1970) *The Primal Scream – Primal Therapy: The Cure for Neurosis*. New York: G.P Putnam's (latest edition, Abacus, 1990).

King, L. and Moutsou, C. (eds) (2010) *Rethinking Audit Cultures: A Critical Look at Evidence-based Practice in Psychotherapy and Beyond*. Ross-on-Wye: PCCS Books.

Laing, R.D. (1967) *The Politics of Experience and The Bird of Paradise*. Harmondsworth: Penguin (latest edition, 1990).

Lasch, C. (1979) *The Culture of Narcissism*. New York: Norton.

Mair, K. (1997) 'The myth of therapist expertise'. In R. House and N. Totton (eds) *Implausible Professions: Arguments for Pluralism and Autonomy in Psychotherapy and Counselling* (pp. 87–98). Ross-on-Wye: PCCS Books (abridged from C. Feltham and W. Dryden (eds), *Psychotherapy and Its Discontents* (pp. 135–60). Buckingham: Open University Press, 1992).

Marzillier, J. (2004) 'The myth of evidence-based psychotherapy', *The Psychologist*, 17 (7): 392–5.

Mason, P. (2016) *Postcapitalism: A Guide to our Future*. London: Penguin.

Noys, B. (2014) *Malign Velocities: Accelerationism and Capitalism*. Winchester: Zero Books.

Owens, P. (2013) 'The humanistic scientist: an appreciation of the work of Daniel N. Stern', *Self & Society: International Journal for Humanistic Psychology*, 40 (3): 46–51.

Palmer, P.J. (2011) *Healing the Heart of Democracy: The Courage to Create a Politics Worthy of the Human Spirit*. San Francisco, CA: Jossey-Bass.

Parker, I. (2007) *Revolution in Psychology: Alienation to Emancipation*. London: Pluto Press.

Parker, I., Georgaca, E., Harper, D., McLaughlin, T. and Stowell-Smith, M. (1995) *Deconstructing Psychopathology*. London: Sage.

Power, M. (1997) *The Audit Society: Rituals of Verification*. Oxford: Oxford University Press.

Rieff, P. (1966) *The Triumph of the Therapeutic: Uses of Faith after Freud*. London: Chatto & Windus.

Roberts, R. (2015) *Psychology and Capitalism: The Manipulation of Mind*. Winchester: Zero Books.

Rogers, C.R. (1961) *On Becoming a Person: A Therapist's View of Psychotherapy*. Boston: Houghton Mifflin; London: Constable.

Rogers, C. (1973) 'Some new challenges', *American Psychologist*, 28 (5): 373–87.

Rowan, J. (2004) 'Some history of humanistic psychology', *The Humanistic Psychologist*, 32 (Summer): 221–38.

Sardello, R. (2015) *Heartfulness*. Gainesville, TX: Goldenstone Press.

Schneider, K.J. (2013) *The Polarized Mind: Why It's Killing Us and What We Can Do about It*. Colorado Springs, CO: University Professors Press.

Self & Society (2013a) Issue 41 (2): Special Theme Issue on 'Carl Rogers and the Helping Professions – 40 Years On'.

Self & Society (2013b) Issue 40 (4): Special Theme Issue – 'Psychiatry, Big Pharma and the Nature of Distress: welcome to the paradigm war'.

Self & Society (2016) Issue 44 (4): Special Theme Issue – 'Paul Goodman'.

Sim, S. (2001) *Lyotard and the Inhuman*. Cambridge: Icon Books.

Stern, D.N. (2004) *The Present Moment in Psychotherapy and Everyday Life*. New York: W.W. Norton.

Thomas, P. (2016) 'Psycho politics, neoliberal governmentality and austerity', *Self & Society: International Journal for Humanistic Psychology*, 43: 382–93.

Wajcman, J. (2015) *Pressed for Time: The Acceleration of Life in Digital Capitalism*. Chicago, IL: University of Chicago Press.

Wallach, M.A. and Wallach, L. (1983) *Psychology's Sanction for Selfishness: The Error of Egotism in Theory and Therapy*. San Francisco, CA: W.H. Freeman.

Wallerstein, I., Mann, M., Collins, R., Derluguian, G. and Calhoun, C. (2013) *Does Capitalism Have a Future?* Oxford and New York: Oxford University Press.

Žižek, S. (2014) *Trouble in Paradise*. London: Allen Lane.

PART I

History and contexts

EDITORS' INTRODUCTION
TO PART I

Richard House, David Kalisch and
Jennifer Maidman

Humanistic Psychology tends to be forward-looking rather than past-focused, but in order to understand and locate its current state and future possibilities, it is important to connect with our roots and examine the historical trajectory of the humanistic project within psychology and the psychological therapies. In their keynote opening chapter, respected elders of Britain's Humanistic Psychology movement John Rowan and Dina (Zohar) Glouberman pose the fundamental question 'What is Humanistic Psychology?', casting light on some of the core principles and values underpinning psychology's 'Third Force', and exploring the historical background and some of the key events associated with the evolution of the humanistic approach.

In Chapter 2 on 'Creativity in the evolution of Humanistic Psychology', Louis Hoffman, Ruth Richards and Steven Pritzker look at the place of creativity as an important emergent theme within humanistic writing, with particular reference to its relevance for theory, research and practice. The authors also seek creatively to engage Humanistic Psychology to move beyond simply retelling the same, familiar stories and narratives, in the process setting out some exciting new areas for development, and offering practical suggestions for increasing creativity's presence and influence in the field.

In a typically sharply argued third chapter, Colin Feltham then considers Humanistic Psychology's past and future. Feltham declares his personal sympathy with aspects of Humanistic Psychology, considering its strengths and critiquing what he sees as its weaknesses – namely, its lack of realism, lack of engagement with contemporary, harsh socio-economic realities, and the extent to which it might have failed to live up to its early promise. Feltham considers whether Humanistic Psychology might, in time, become a barely significant set of nostalgic theories and practices, or whether it might yet find ways to bring its important focuses on birth, education, feelings, spirituality and patriarchal civilization to a new readership and public. Colin Feltham is one of several 'critical friends' of Humanistic Psychology represented in the book, and the cogency, openness and integrity of his contribution constitute an admirable model for anyone aspiring to deepen our critical reflexivity, and constructively to challenge our taken-for-granted humanistic assumptions.

Finally in Part 1, Seamus Nash looks in Chapter 4 at the place of person-centred counselling in Humanistic Psychology, drawing on his doctoral research to focus on what precisely person/client-centred practitioners mean when they use the terms 'person-centred' and 'client-centred' to describe their therapeutic work, and how they perceive their own practice. In attempting to understand what it is like to be a person/client-centred therapist, and in mapping what practitioners understand to be their espoused theory, what the theory means to them personally, and what are the main elements of this theory that they operationalize in their practice, Nash provides an admirable model for locating and interrogating this core therapeutic approach within the wider context of humanistic therapy praxis.

Taken together, these four positioning chapters provide a fitting and authoritative backdrop for our subsequent foray into the rich and diverse dimensions of the field, in all its variegated and untamed breadth and depth. Certainly, it is vitally important that as the elders of Humanistic Psychology age and pass on, the extraordinary and *daring* history of the movement is faithfully recorded, both for posterity and the History of Ideas, and also for a younger generation currently showing a welcome upsurge in the principled idealism and passion for social justice that fuelled Humanistic Psychology in its formative period. The 'Roots and History of Humanistic Psychology' occasional series in the humanistic journal *Self & Society* is just one way in which this vital history of the movement is being documented for those who will follow and keep the flame alive.

1

WHAT IS HUMANISTIC PSYCHOLOGY?

John Rowan and Dina Glouberman

Humanistic Psychology is a psychological perspective that rose to prominence in the mid-20th century partly as a response to the limitations of Sigmund Freud's psychoanalytic theory and B. F. Skinner's behaviourism. Considered a 'third force', this approach emphasized individuals' inherent drive toward self-actualization, the process of realizing and expressing one's own capabilities and creativity. It moved away from a medical model to a democratic and holistic one, based on fostering communication, creativity, and personal development throughout life for everyone.

Some of the underlying assumptions were that we are constantly evolving beings, that we need to take a holistic approach to being human which is an integration of the physical, the mental, the emotional and the spiritual, that self-exploration, creativity, free will, authenticity, and positive human potential were important for everyone, and that self-development could be done in an essentially democratic way through self-exploration and group work as much as through professional consultation.

Humanistic Psychology was an important part of a worldwide surge of interest in what human beings could be and could become, which started in the 1940s, grew slowly in the 1950s, grew much faster in the 60s and finally reached its full flowering in the 1970s. Today it is consolidating itself, and becoming much more widely accepted.

In the process of change and development, a number of different names and titles have been used for this humanistic approach. Sometimes it has been called 'third force psychology'; sometimes the 'self-awareness movement' (because awareness seemed to be quite a key word); sometimes the 'human potential movement' (because of its insistence that the average and the normal are actually less than average and less than normal); and sometimes just 'personal growth', because of its belief that people could continue to grow beyond their usual limits, if they were allowed to. Today it is less of a movement and more of a tendency or approach within the whole field of self-development. The full story can be followed in books such as de Carvalho (1991), Moss (1999), Rowan (2001) and Whitton (2003).

In the early days, one man was the pioneer of this way of looking at the world: Abraham Maslow. He was an academic psychologist who later became president of the American Psychological Association. He put forward the key idea of self-actualization: the idea that our purpose in life is to go on with a process of development that starts out in early life but which often gets blocked later (Maslow 1987). He was joined by others such as Carl Rogers (another president of the APA), Charlotte Buhler, Roberto Assagioli, Fritz Perls, Virginia Satir, Kurt Goldstein, Sidney Jourard, Rollo May, Clark Moustakas, Ira Progoff, Jean Houston, Alvin Mahrer and others. Although Humanistic Psychology is sometimes seen as synonymous with the work of Maslow and Rogers, all of these thinkers and clinicians contributed to the full development of the humanistic approach.

One of the most characteristic features of this approach is that it lays a great deal of stress upon personal experience: it is not enough to read about it in books. This personal experience did not need to happen in a professional setting of the therapist/patient relationship, but rather could happen in groups and communities which were essentially democratic and where people could be authentically themselves.

To this end, a number of different methods emerged including Psychodrama, Gestalt, Encounter, Breathwork and Dance Therapy, which helped people in a group or community become intimate and open with each other quickly, and to explore issues in more dramatic ways. These methods tended to utilize movement, drama, imagination, and other verbal and non-verbal ways to open up, shed light upon, and often resolve issues that had not responded to highly professionalized and verbally based therapies such as psychoanalysis.

Open and honest communication was considered key to creating honest, loving and essentially democratic groups that could be a crucible for healthy personal development and transformation.

And so this movement produced a unique kind of institution which had never existed before – the growth centre. A growth centre is a place where you can go and be encouraged to meet other people and meet yourself. This idea of meeting yourself is unique. No one had ever talked about that before, except in a rather forbidding way connected with illness or personal problems, or perhaps as part of a religious group.

But the growth centre is for everyone who feels that there is more – there does not have to be anything wrong with them. And there they find an encouraging environment. If you go to one, you will find yourself in an atmosphere that enables you to open up and trust the situation enough so that you can move forward – maybe even sometimes leap forward – in self-understanding and human relationships. It is open to all – you do not have to be sick or troubled in order to go. In the USA the Esalen Institute (www.esalen.org) and the New York Open Center (www.opencenter.org) among others are still going, and so is the Open Centre (www.opencentre.com) in England and the Skyros Centre (www.skyros.com)in Greece.

In the year 2000 there was a big humanistic conference, called Old Saybrook 2, and this led to a bursting forth of new books and new thinking about the humanistic approach. The *Handbook of Humanistic Psychology* (2nd edition 2015) put together 800 pages of new thinking covering vast ranges of the psychological landscape; the *Handbook of Action Research* (Reason & Bradbury, 2001) is not entirely humanistic, but does include important humanistic and transpersonal material; *Humanistic Psychotherapies* (Cain & Serlin, 2002) comprised another 700 pages of research and practice.

Theory in Humanistic Psychology

Because all the pioneers of Humanistic Psychology were very individual people, there is no one single accepted theory that we can lay out and say – this is it. But there are some very consistent themes running through all the material put forward by the people mentioned above.

The first is that, deep down underneath it all where it really counts, you are OK. This goes against many other and much older theories which say that people are fundamentally bad, selfish, narrow and nasty. By saying that people are fundamentally OK, we do not at all mean that people are not sometimes destructive, or that there is no evil in the world. What we mean is that if someone will agree to work with us on his or her destructive actions or evil wishes, in an atmosphere of trust and acceptance, that person will discover that the evil and destructiveness are just as phoney and just as forgettable as the false niceness of other people, which apparently causes no problems.

In other words, we believe that personal nastiness and personal niceness are most often, in both cases, masks and illusions, put on for reasons that seemed good at the time, but which have now become stuck and rigid, and out of our control. In that sense, if you want to use labels, we are all neurotic. By working on ourselves to unstick the rigidities and loosen the masks, we can eventually learn how to live without needing masks at all – though it might still be useful to put one on occasionally, as we might have a dress suit or an evening gown.

So when we talk about self-actualization, about getting in touch with what is the deepest truth within us, and allowing that to come out, we are not saying something fearful or dangerous. People do often say – 'How do I know I won't hate my deepest self when I come across it?' But this is an unrealistic fear, and it is up to the therapist, group leader, or guide to represent the trust we have that our deepest truth is ultimately life enhancing.

The second thread that runs all through Humanistic Psychology is an emphasis on the whole person. If we say that human beings exist on at least five levels – body, feelings, intellect, soul and spirit – then we have to do justice to all five of those levels in all our efforts at realizing human potential. Ken Wilber (2000) spells out all the implications of this more clearly than anyone else. If I want to be that self which I truly am, then I have to be it on all five of those levels – I must not leave any of them out. Any theory, any therapy, which leaves out one or more of these must be inadequate to deal with the full human being who has to be met and responded to. It was Maslow who taught us to think in terms of levels, and to ignore all this is to live in Flatland.

Now today there is much more interest in the body – diet, exercise and so on – but much of that interest seems to us very external. It is as if we were supposed to be somewhere outside our bodies, disciplining them and making them do things, sometimes under protest. But the humanistic approach is to say that I *am* my body. If you touch my hand, you are touching *me*. So I am just as responsible for my body as I am for my thoughts, feelings, mental pictures or whatever – it is me doing it. This total responsibility for our own bodies, feelings, ideas and intuitions is very characteristic of Humanistic Psychology, and theoreticians such as Mahrer (1989) and Schutz (1979) have made it clear exactly how this works.

This means that we are interested in integration. By integration we mean that the splits in the person can be healed, and that the holes in the personality can be filled. The various parts of the person can get to know each other better, accept each other more, and change in that process. This is not a process of subordinating all the various tendencies in the person to one overall control, like some kind of totalitarian ego – it is more like a harmony of contrasts (Rowan, 2010).

The third thread we can follow all through the humanistic approach is the emphasis on change and development. Human beings are seen not as static victims or villains, but as people in a process of growth, which is natural and needful. All through our infancy, childhood and adolescence we are going through very substantial changes, involving our most basic attitudes and how we see ourselves. Maslow said that we grow through six main levels of development. His rather speculative theory has now been researched by people such as Lawrence Kohlberg (1981), Clay Alderfer (1972) and Jane Loevinger (1976) in many different countries of the world.

However, the implications of having a 'ladder' approach, with its implicit hierarchy needs a great deal more thought. This is particularly so because much of the theory and research ends by favouring the middle class urban male (Glouberman, 1977).

While levels are a useful concept, it is best if they do not categorize a person but rather a state of being. It is important to note that at any point, people are operating on many different levels. This becomes clear, for example, when you work with imagery and dreams, and it turns out that an image might have a meaning on a physical, mental, emotional, or spiritual level. Which level comes to the fore can vary from time to time. Similarly, a dream might represent the unconscious or the superconscious (Glouberman, 2010, 2014).

In this sense, much development is about getting glimpses of another level, and eventually more and more valuing and living at that level, eventually following its lead, while maintaining one's connections with past and future levels. We begin to put the higher or deeper levels in charge, rather than the child's emotions or the mind's control mechanisms. As Thich Nhat Hanh, a Vietnamese Zen Monk, put it in one of his talks, 'We are all part time Buddhas'.

This process of evolution can continue, if we let it, in adulthood, too. What Humanistic Psychology says is that we could all continue to grow if we did not limit ourselves and sell ourselves short. All the humanistic methods are designed to enable us to take off our self-imposed limitations, and continue to grow into our full potential as human beings.

Indeed, when we are on an evolutionary path of personal development, we cannot simply rest on our laurels because we are constantly changing. If we stop ourselves from listening to our real self because our old identity is tied up in attitudes and actions that are no longer healthy for us, we can become emotionally disturbed, burnt out, even physically ill. This can happen at work, in relationships, or in any other aspect of life. Thus one could argue that personal growth should carry a health warning: Keep listening to your real self, keep evolving, keep opening to your new possibilities. Getting stuck is dangerous for your health (Glouberman, 2007).

One more idea that is important in Humanistic Psychology is abundance motivation. Most other psychology says that our actions are basically motivated by deficiency – that is, a lack of something. We might lack food and look for it, or lack safety and look for it, or lack company and look for it. This is to treat human beings as if they were basically something like a thermostat, only acting when something moves them outside their proper limits. But human beings also have an achievement motivation, and a need for varied experience, and an enormous curiosity, which takes them out of this deficiency-oriented realm into an abundance-oriented world of experience. So when we seek to realize our potential, we are not repairing some deficiency, we are entering a world where being can sometimes be more important than having or doing.

Most of us normally think that if we have enough worldly goods, then we can do what we want to do, and then we can be happy. The sequence is HAVE – DO – BE. But what we in Humanistic Psychology say is that it is exactly the other way round. If we can be who we really are, we will find ourselves doing things that genuinely satisfy us and give us enjoyment, and then we shall have all we really want. The sequence for us is BE – DO – HAVE.

This begins to sound religious or spiritual, and it is one of the characteristics of Humanistic Psychology, which distinguishes it very sharply from secular humanism, that it has a place for the spiritual though not usually conventional religion. Maslow always laid great stress on the importance of peak experiences and the experience of transcendence.

So when we say that Humanistic Psychology is concerned with the whole person, we really do mean it in a very particular way. We have developed a number of direct and effective ways of working, most particularly those labelled as humanistic or existential (Schneider & Krug, 2010). We assume that people are whole, and we treat them as if they are whole, and we encourage them to act as if they are whole.

The real self

The notion of the real self is one of the most characteristic of humanistic concepts. But it is not unique to us. Table 1.1 demonstrates that numerous writers have expressed some version of this idea.

TABLE 1.1 Inner and outer

Writer	Central	Peripheral
C.G. Jung	Self	Persona
A. Adler	Creative self	Guiding fiction
P. Federn	Id	Ego-states
F.S. Perls	Self	Self-image
R. Assagioli	I	Subpersonalities
D. Winnicott	True self	False self
H. Guntrip	Primary libidinal ego	Internal objects
R.D. Laing	Real self	False self
A. Janov	Real self	Unreal self
J. Love	Primal intent	Conscious will
R.E. Johnson	Real self	Symbolic self
P. Koestenbaum	Transcendental ego	Empirical ego

What all these investigators are saying is that the ordinary ego which is presented to the world, and which other people know us by, is false. It is a made-up thing, a mask, a fiction. We might have spent many years building it up, and have invested a lot of energy in it, but it is unreal. Benson (1974) calls it the Public Relations Personality, and emphasizes how desperately it depends upon other people's opinions. It essentially arises out of an attempt to protect the real self from pain. It puts up boundaries and walls between the various parts of ourselves, so that pain will not be felt, or so that familiar pains are held on to lest they turn into something worse. A common way of representing this is by way of the concentric ring diagram (see Figure 1.1). This diagram can be made much more complex. Lowen has one

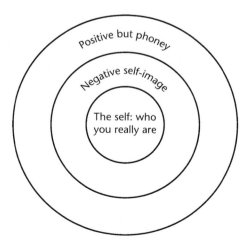

FIGURE 1.1 Circles of the self

with four rings, Perls one with five, and Elliott has one with ten, but the basic principle can be well illustrated with these three.

Most of us are quite conscious, as soon as it is pointed out, that our positive self-image is an illusion, but our next thought is that underneath this we are bad. Each person has a different notion of what this badness is, but the three most common feelings about this are:

1. If they knew how nasty (evil, bad, horrible, hating) I really am, they would all hate me.
2. If they knew how inadequate (weak, worthless, inept) I really am, they would all reject me.
3. If they knew how needy (insatiable, sucking in and then destroying, attracting and then devouring) I really am, they would all avoid me.

In extreme cases, we might even believe all three of these things at the same time! All three of them pertain to the false self and its definitions of the world.

It is because we believe (perhaps vividly, perhaps only vaguely) that we are bad or pathetic behind our façade of goodness, that we resist therapy. The discoveries we might make, once we start questioning our false front, might be too terrible to bear. The false self defends itself against such discoveries. And so people put off therapy like they put off going to the dentist – until the pain gets to be too much to bear.

But Humanistic Psychology says that underneath all this positive and negative stuff there is the real self, which is perfectly OK. We will have to work through the good and bad stuff to get there, but this will be all right, because the bad stuff is just as illusory as the good stuff. It, too, was just a story we made up and lived out for neurotic reasons. It is no more fundamental, no more basic, than the positive self-image that it balances.

Our primary aim, then, in humanistic psychotherapy, is to enable the person to get in touch with their real self – to gain an actual experience of the real self. And so we encourage clients all the time to question all – all, without exception – of the taken-for-granted images of themselves, having only quite a limited degree of respect for their defences.

Defences

This question of defences is one of the key areas where Humanistic Psychology differs from psychoanalysis. Psychoanalysis, as put forward by Freud, has no notion of the real self (though this is not true of some of the later people such as Horney (1950) and Winnicott (1975)). Consequently it takes the negative self-image as being the basic truth about the person, and sees the person as a permanent battle-ground for good and evil. The good Ego must be strengthened and buttressed against the evil Id. Certainly the way of doing this is not a blind suppression, but a much more sophisticated 'know your enemy' investigative weakening process that involves getting to know the Id much better; but still defences are going to be necessary, only perhaps healthy ones like sublimation or suppression rather than unhealthy ones, such as projection and repression.

However, we do not have any need for defences in the humanistic system, because the person would only be defending themselves against their own real self – and there is obviously no point in that. So our policy in regard to defences is continually to chip away at them, in a manner and at a speed that is only limited by the need to maintain rapport between therapist and client. We obviously do not want to be hurtful to the point where the client breaks off therapy. And in this respect we are exactly like the psychoanalysts: we pay a lot of attention to the quality of the relationship. We suspect that the same is true of a good behaviourally oriented or cognitive psychotherapist, and nowadays many of these practitioners and theorists are acknowledging it. For example: 'ACT therapists assume that it is neither possible nor healthy to attempt to rescue clients from the difficulty and challenge of growth' (Hayes, 2004, p. 651). However, the humanistic attitude is not the same as acceptance. Humanistic psychotherapy is a process of questioning all that is false in the person, and its object in doing that is to lay bare what is true in the person, in the confidence that what is true in the person is always OK.

The real self

To understand the real self it is necessary to revisit the concept of levels. As already mentioned, Maslow introduced the idea of levels of development. The idea is that we are all on a path of psychospiritual development, whether we know it or not and whether we like it or not. And this path has certain well-defined way-stations, which Maslow named and described. One of these is called self-actualization. The self-actualized person has finally discovered and owned his or her own real self. Later, however, Ken Wilber expanded the notion of levels by referring to the great spiritual traditions of the world. In a striking piece of research (Wilber, 2000) he showed that the Maslow levels were only the lower rungs on a much longer ladder that includes the transpersonal.

So what is this real self, and what does it feel like to open it up? Broughton (1975) in his research found that this stage was one where 'mind and body are both experiences of an integrated self'. And Wilber (1980, p. 45) who calls this the 'centaur level' says: 'This integrated self, wherein mind and body are harmoniously one, we call the "centaur". The centaur: the great mythological being with animal body and human mind existing in a perfect state of at-one-ment.'

What this achievement of integration brings with it is a great sense of what the existentialists have called 'authenticity'. And indeed the existentialist thinkers have done a great deal to outline this stage in some detail. According to general existential thought, when an individual's self is taken fully as autonomous, he or she can assume responsibility for being-in-the-world. And if we do this we can, as Sartre put it, choose ourselves. Here are some other existentialist texts to give the flavour:

The 'I' casts off its shells, which it finds untrue, in order to gain the deeper and authentic, infinite, true self.

(Jaspers, 1931; quoted in Friedman 1964, p. 150)

Before his death, Rabbi Zusya said: 'In the coming world, they will not ask me: "Why were you not Moses?" They will ask me: "Why were you not Zusya?"'

(Buber, 1975, p. 251)

Free and alone, without assistance and without excuse.

(Sartre, 1959, p. 275)

Rogers is one of the great fathers of Humanistic Psychology, and he certainly saw the matter in this way, as can be seen in all his writings. Here is a passage in which he is most explicit about this:

I have been astonished to find how accurately the Danish philosopher Søren Kierkegaard pictured the dilemma of the individual more than a century ago, with keen psychological insight. He points out that the most common despair is to be in despair at not choosing, or willing, to be one's self; but that the deepest form of despair is to choose 'to be another than himself'. On the other hand 'to will to be that self which one truly is, is indeed the opposite of despair', and this choice is the deepest responsibility of man.

(Rogers, 1961, p. 110)

Wilber argues that Humanistic Psychology and existentialism belong to the same level, the centaur. There is a set of concepts that goes with this; Authenticity, or knowing who you really are (Bugental, 1981); Seeing through your own eyes, rather than through the eyes of others; Autonomy, or self responsibility; Intentionality, or being in charge of our own lives; Choice, the inevitability and necessity of choice as a human being. That is why humanistic psychologists refuse to talk about human behaviour, and insist on talking about human action. The term 'action' implies responsibility in a way that 'behaviour' does not. If we do not take responsibility for our own actions, we are not living a fully human life.

The real self that we are aiming at in humanistic psychotherapy is not something very abstract and hard to pin down – it is situated very concretely both in the empirical realm of psychological research and in the conceptual realm of philosophy. It is contrasted very sharply and clearly with the aims of other forms of therapy, though it is closest to existential psychotherapy, as described by Friedenberg (1973, p. 94):

The purpose of therapeutic intervention is to support and re-establish a sense of self and personal authenticity. Not mastery of the objective environment; not effective functioning within social institutions; not freedom from the suffering caused by anxiety – though any or all of these may be concomitant outcomes of successful therapy – but personal awareness, depth of real feeling, and, above all, the conviction that one can use one's full powers, that one has the courage to be and use all one's essence in the praxis of being.

And this means that there are certain things that the real self certainly is not. It is not the transpersonal self, the higher self described by Assagioli (1975) and others. It is not the ultimate all-embracing God of Christianity, Judaism or Islam. It is not the ultimate formless void of Eastern mysticism and the perennial philosophy. It is simply the real self – that which was buried and put away as being too weak and too vulnerable for everyday life, as Winnicott (1975) well described. We put it away – very often in a moment of panic or terror because that seemed the only way to survive. We developed enormously effective systems of blocking it off and pretending it was not there. But at certain moments – often called peak experiences – we get back that freshness of experience, that marvellous sensitivity to the world.

When we get close to the real self in therapy it feels awfully dangerous to go any further. This is for two different reasons: first, the way in lies through all our most negative self-images, which have been experienced as painful and shocking, and so we are scared of meeting even more, even dirtier secrets as we dig down further; and second, there seems to be something 'ultimate' about the real self, so that when we get to it, it seems like a breakthrough into a whole different world. We are promised that this different world will be better, but it is the difference that appals us. It seems that we almost have to die to get there. In fact, Alvin Mahrer (1996) has been quite explicit about this.

Getting close to the real self, then, almost inevitably brings with it feelings that have to do with extreme good and extreme evil, with Heaven and Hell, with death and destruction as well as with life and growth. And in fact, contact with the real self is often experienced as a breakthrough. Finding suddenly that we are able to let go of all those false pictures of ourselves that the mental ego took for granted, can bring feelings of bliss or ecstasy. An example from an anonymous group member:

> Then one cold Saturday in February we had an all-day [primal] marathon and I had the most profound experience of my life. On that day I fell in love for the first time. It was the first time because my head, heart and body were involved. I was no longer stone cold rigid and unavailable. I experienced my own beauty that day, as a woman, as a person. I really felt it on the inside. I loved everyone as they were. With each person and with each moment I was different. I saw their perfection and I also saw their limits. I was not judging. I was just appreciating. I went through a door to a place I could only call whole, clear vision. A sight that sees all undisturbedly. The endless self judgements had quieted. I was. I felt very young, open, vulnerable, not afraid and at peace.

It does not have to happen that way, but we have seen this sort of thing happen many times in therapy, and it is genuinely impressive when it does take place.

The earlier experiences of the real self – which tend to last for short periods only, which is why they are called peak experiences – are often more ecstatic; the later experiences of the real self become more ordinary, partly because ecstasy becomes more ordinary, and partly because we are getting ready for our next breakthrough.

Is there a real self?

There is a question that Humanistic Psychology has to answer. It has to do with the challenge of social constructivism, social constructionism, deconstruction and postmodernism. Its most acute point, it seems to us, is at the question of the self. All of these challenges say in their different ways that there is no 'real self' in the sense usually proposed by humanistic psychologists. Therefore, there is no such thing as being authentic (true to oneself) or autonomous (taking charge of one's life) or self-actualization (being all that one has it in oneself to be). If this is true, then Humanistic Psychology is obsolete, overtaken by a postmodern wave that has passed it by.

Ernesto Spinelli, the eminent existential thinker, has a problem with the humanistic idea of the real self:

> I would argue that humanistic theory's greatest weakness (and, significantly, its major divergence with existential-phenomenological theory) lies precisely in its somewhat unquestioning and advocacy of a Western notion of a singular, intrapsychic, real self that can be distinguished from any number of 'false selves'. I would further suggest that it is this adherence to such a notion that provoked the solipsistic excesses of the 1960s and 1970s to which Rowan refers and that continues to maintain an isolationist divide between 'self and other' as understood and practised by humanistic therapists.
>
> *(Spinelli, 2001, pp. 469–70)*

Of course the notion of a real self is not unique to Humanistic Psychology. It is quite common, particularly in psychotherapy, for theorists to distinguish between a centre and the periphery of the person. None of these are guilty of solipsistic excesses, even though they hold to this distinction.

Coming back to specifically humanistic theory, however, the idea of a real self seems necessary to any valid notion of authenticity, choice and responsibility. These concepts are central to the humanistic outlook, and we should have thought to the existential standpoint, too. It would be a strange existentialism that abandoned such central concepts.

At a certain point in psychospiritual development the person has to take responsibility for his or her own growth, and cannot rely on the pressure of society to carry them on. In that sense it must be an individual journey. But to assume that the real self is a solipsistic self is a misunderstanding of the nature of being human.

The fact that the individual has to make the choice does not mean that it is taken in isolation. In fact, the more we are in touch with our real self, the less likely we are to engage in neurotic, driven, competitive, power hungry or co-dependent relationships, and the more authentically loving we can be.

The real self is also a loving self, and a social self. Development takes place in a social context that includes a wide variety of relationships to other people and to the society. This is why growth groups and communities became such an important part of Humanistic Psychology, as did movement toward social change. It was always understood in most humanistic circles and publications that we needed to find ourselves, but we also needed to find the other, and that to do this, we needed to create a healthy, loving, and honest world.

The transpersonal

How does all this relate to the transpersonal? There is a very close connection between the humanistic and the transpersonal; it was Maslow who was the prime mover in initiating Humanistic Psychology, and it was Maslow who was the prime mover in initiating Transpersonal Psychology. And at present there is a very close relationship between the Association for Humanistic Psychology and the Association for Transpersonal Psychology.

Transpersonal Psychology is now a well-defined field in its own right, with two international journals and a multitude of excellent texts. But it need not be seen as a school of counselling with a separate identity but rather as a dimension of all counselling which can be given a chance or ignored. It is a human dimension available to all, which most of us have come across in one way or another. In this sense, it is not something strange or marginal, but a readily available resource.

Petruska Clarkson (2003) showed that the transpersonal relationship has its place alongside the working alliance, the transference-countertransference relationship, the authentic relationship and the developmentally needed relationship. It needs just as much attention, just as much respect, as any of these other and more widely accepted relationships.

Many of the people who are reading this, for example, will probably have had what Maslow (1973) calls a peak experience. One's reactions while watching a beautiful sunset or listening to an especially moving piece of music, for example, can lead to peak experiences. Tanzer (1967) found that childbirth could be a potent source of peak experiences, if the mother (in suitable circumstances) allowed it to be, and ways were found of teaching mothers how to have such experiences. Instead of having a painful and distressing time, these mothers often had 'a great and mystical experience, a religious experience if you wish – an illumination, a revelation, an insight' (Maslow, 1973, p. 183).

According to the classic psychological account from the work of Abraham Maslow, peak experiences tend to be triggered by intense, inspiring occurrences. 'It looks as if any experience of real excellence, or real perfection . . . tends to produce a peak experience' (Maslow, 1973, p. 175). The lives of most people are filled with long periods of relative inattentiveness, lack of involvement or even boredom.

In contrast, in their broadest sense, peak experiences are those moments when we become deeply involved in, excited by, and absorbed in the world.

The most powerful peak experiences are relatively rare. For Maslow, the highest peaks include 'feelings of limitless horizons opening to the vision, the feeling of being simultaneously more powerful and also more helpless than one ever was before, the feeling of great ecstasy and wonder and awe, the loss of placing in time and space' (Maslow, 1970, p. 164). This now ties in with our understanding of the transpersonal. We can say that a peak experience of this latter kind might give us a glimpse at least of the transpersonal realm. And such glimpses can be genuinely helpful, as Anthony, Ecker and Wilber (1987) make clear.

Ken Wilber (1983) noted that in the process of psychospiritual development there are three broad phases: the prepersonal, where we have not yet achieved full rationality; the personal, where we have been fully initiated into language, and mathematics and science; and the transpersonal, where we go beyond the conventional bounds of time and space and do not find ordinary notions of rationality enough to encompass our experience. To put it another way, there is the personal unconscious as described by Freud and others; there is the conscious and the preconscious, which are much more accessible and familiar; and there is the superconscious, as described in psychosynthesis (Assagioli 1991), as well as the collective unconscious, as described by Jung (1968). The transpersonal is the realm of the superconscious.

Ken Wilber (1997) also points to four great divisions within the realm of the transpersonal: the Centaur (the first level of the transpersonal, still partly in the personal, but characterized by a mystical experience called the discovery of the real self, as we have seen above); the Psychic/Subtle or the Subtle (the great realm of symbols and images and archetypes and big dreams and deity figures described by people such as Jung, Hillman and Cortright); the Causal (the deep water of spirituality, where all the symbols disappear, and we are alone with the infinite divine); and the Nondual, where all categories disappear, and the self too – the ultimate mystical experience.

If we accept this broad schema, it becomes clear that Humanistic Psychology has taken possession of the Centaur stage, because all of the therapies described as humanistic believe in the real self, and in the kind of ecstasy that can be described as a peak experience. This is perhaps only the foothills of mysticism, but it does have a place for the kind of experience that James Horne (1978) describes as 'casual extraverted mysticism'. Gestalt therapy talks about the 'mini-satori', psychodrama talks about the 'cathartic breakthrough', primal integration talks about 'personal transformation', person-centred therapy talks about 'becoming real', humanistic-existential therapy talks about 'being authentic', and so forth. But this is all on the edges of the transpersonal proper, because it still retains the 'skin-encapsulated ego' described by Alan Watts and referred to by Joanna Macy (1991).

If we want to go to the heartland of the transpersonal as it reveals itself in therapy, we have to move on to the Subtle level. It is here that we find the phenomena that truly go beyond the personal. It is here we find what Henri Corbin (1969) has called the 'imaginal world', what Schwartz-Salant (1986) has called 'the subtle body', what Whitmont (1987) has called 'the guidance self', what Assagioli (1975)

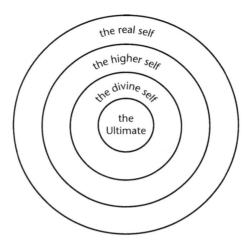

FIGURE 1.2 Deeper circles of the self

has called 'the higher self', what Hillman (1997) has called 'the soul', what Jung (1968) has called 'the high archetypes', what Buddhists (Govinda, 1973) have called 'the *sambhogakaya*', and what, more recently, Cortright (2007) has described as 'the *antaratman*'.

If we visualize the real self as previously discussed as the centre of a series of concentric circles, comprising the various false selves in daily use, all we then need to do is to visualize the Subtle self as inside that, and the Causal self as inside that again (see Figure 1.2).

Thus experiencing the real self can be seen as a possible springboard toward further levels of the transpersonal self and, ultimately, the Nondual where the self itself disappears.

Is Humanistic Psychology still needed?

In many ways, Humanistic Psychology is now part of the mainstream, rather than being something new and unfamiliar. It is no longer unfashionable to admit that you are interested in understanding yourself and what you might be or become. In fact the 'new' positive psychology movement (Snyder & Lopez, 2002) has much in common with Humanistic Psychology, and the 'new' approaches to coaching (Cox, Bachkirova & Clutterbuck, 2010) have taken much from the humanistic tradition, particularly when working with organizations.

Today there are fewer growth centres than there were, partly because the approach has been adopted much more widely. Certainly, most courses that are concerned with training people to deal with others now include some emphasis on understanding yourself, and they use humanistic thinking and humanistic methods – often unacknowledged. They have to, because any attempt to understand or work with others on any kind of emotional level has to involve some self-understanding, some self-awareness. And this is the heartland of Humanistic Psychology.

But the decline in growth centres can also be related to the increase in professionalization and of teaching people how to fit better into the status quo. Thus while much has been absorbed into the mainstream from Humanistic Psychology, many of the more radical assumptions of Humanistic Psychology have been left behind. Humanistic notions such as the importance of self-development for its own sake, of evolution throughout life, of the wholeness of the individual, of creating democratic groups and communities with open and honest communication, indeed of the idea that authenticity and the real self matter more than success, have in many cases fallen by the wayside.

It might, therefore, be more necessary than ever that Humanistic Psychology become the standard bearer for a radical vision of what it means to be human.

References

Alderfer, C.P. (1972) *Existence, Relatedness, Growth*, New York: Collier-Macmillan.

Anthony, Dick, Ecker, Bruce & Wilber, Ken (1987) *Spiritual Choices*, New York: Paragon House.

Assagioli, R. (1975) *Psychosynthesis: A Manual of Principles and Techniques*, London: Turnstone Books.

Assagioli, R. (1991) *Transpersonal Development: The Dimension beyond Psychosynthesis*, London: Crucible.

Benson, L. (1974) *Images, Heroes and Self-perception: The Struggle for Identity – From Mask-wearing to Authenticity*, Englewood Cliffs, NJ: Prentice-Hall.

Broughton, J.M. (1975) 'The development of natural epistemology in adolescence and early adulthood', Harvard, unpublished doctoral dissertation.

Buber, Martin (1975) *Tales of the Hasidim*, New York: Schocken Books.

Bugental, J.F.T. (1981) *The Search for Authenticity (enlarged edition)*, New York: Irvington.

Cain, David J. & Serlin, I (eds) (2002) *Humanistic Psychotherapies: Handbook of Research and Practice*, Washington, DC: APA.

Clarkson, Petruska (2003) *The Therapeutic Relationship (2nd edition)*, London: Whurr.

Corbin, Henri (1969) *Creative Imagination in the Sufism of Ibn 'Arabi*, Princeton, NJ: Princeton University Press.

Cortright, Brant (2007) *Integral Psychology: Yoga, Growth and Opening the Heart*, Albany: SUNY Press.

Cox, Elaine, Bachkirova, Tatiana & Clutterbuck, David (eds) (2010) *The Complete Handbook of Coaching*, London: Sage.

de Carvalho, Roy José (1991) *The Founders of Humanistic Psychology*, New York: Praeger.

Friedenberg, E.Z. (1973) *Laing*, London: Fontana/Collins.

Friedman, M. (ed.) (1964) *The Worlds of Existentialism: A Critical Reader*, Chicago, IL: University of Chicago Press.

Glouberman, D. (1977) 'A study of psychological differentiation', Brunel University, unpublished doctoral dissertation.

Glouberman, D. (2007) *The Joy of Burnout: How the End of the World Can Be a New Beginning*, London: Skyros Books.

Glouberman, D. (2010) *Life Choices, Life Changes: Develop Your Personal Vision with Imagework*, London: Skyros Books.

Glouberman, D. (2014) *You Are What You Imagine: Three Steps to a New Beginning Using Imagework*, London: Watkins Publishing Ltd.

Govinda, L. (1973) *Foundations of Tibetan Mysticism*, New York: Weiser.

Hayes, Steven C. (2004) 'Acceptance and Commitment Therapy, relational frame theory and the third wave of behavioral and cognitive therapies', *Behavior Therapy* 35: 639–665.

Hillman, James (1997) *The Soul's Code*, New York: Bantam Books.

Horne, J.A. (1978) *Beyond Mysticism*, Waterloo: Canadian Corporation for Studies in Religion.

Horney, K. (1950) *Neurosis and Human Growth*, New York: Norton.

Jung, Carl Gustav (1968) *The Archetypes and the Collective Unconscious (2nd edition)*, London: Routledge.

Kohlberg, Lawrence (1981) *The Philosophy of Moral Development*, San Francisco, CA: Harper & Row.

Loevinger, J. (1976) *Ego Development*, San Francisco, CA: Jossey-Bass.

Macy, Joanna (1991) *World as Lover, World as Self*, Berkeley: Parallax Press.

Mahrer, Alvin R. (1989) *Experiencing: A Humanistic Theory of Psychology and Psychiatry*, Ottawa: University of Ottawa Press.

Mahrer, Alvin R. (1996) *The Complete Guide to Experiential Psychotherapy*, New York: John Wiley & Sons.

Maslow, Abraham H. (1970) *Religions, Values and Peak-experiences*, New York: The Viking Press.

Maslow, Abraham H. (1973) *The Farther Reaches of Human Nature*, London: Penguin.

Maslow, Abraham (1987) *Motivation and Personality (3rd edition)*, New York: Harper & Row.

Moss, Donald (1999) *Humanistic and Transpersonal Psychology: A Historical and Biographical Sourcebook*, Westport, CT: Greenwood Press.

Reason, Peter & Bradbury, Hilary (eds) (2001) *Handbook of Action Research: Participative Inquiry and Practice*, London: Sage.

Rogers, C.R. (1961) *On Becoming a Person*, London: Constable.

Rowan, John (2001) *Ordinary Ecstasy: The Dialectics of Humanistic Psychology (3rd edition)*, London: Routledge.

Rowan, John (2010) *Personification: Using the Dialogical Self in Psychotherapy and Counselling*, Hove: Routledge.

Sartre, J.-P. (1959) *The Age of Reason*, New York: Bantam.

Schneider, Kirk J. & Krug, Orah T. (2010) *Existential-Humanistic Therapy*, Washington, DC: American Psychological Association.

Schneider, Kirk J., Bugental, J.F.T. & Pierson, J.F. (eds) (2015) *The Handbook of Humanistic Psychology*, London: Sage.

Schutz, Will C. (1979) *Profound Simplicity*, London: Turnstone Books.

Schwartz-Salant, Nathan (1986) 'On the subtle-body concept in clinical practice', in N. Schwartz-Salant & M. Stein (eds) *The Body in Analysis* (pp. 19–58), Wilmette, IL: Chiron.

Snyder, C.R. & Lopez, Shane J. (eds) (2002) *Handbook of Positive Psychology*, Oxford: Oxford University Press.

Spinelli, E. (2001) 'A reply to John Rowan', in K.J. Schneider, J.F.T. Bugental & J.F. Pierson (eds) *The Handbook of Humanistic Psychology: Leading Edges in Theory, Research and Practice* (pp. 465–471), Thousand Oaks, CA: Sage.

Tanzer, D.W. (1967) 'The psychology of pregnancy and childbirth', Brandeis University, unpublished doctoral dissertation.

Whitmont, Edward (1987) 'Archetypal and personal interaction in the clinical process', in N. Schwartz-Salant & M. Stein (eds) *Archetypal Processes in Psychotherapy* (pp. 1–26), Wilmette, IL: Chiron.

Whitton, Eric (2003) *Humanistic Approach to Psychotherapy*, London: Whurr.

Wilber, Ken (1980) *The Atman Project: A Transpersonal View of Human Development*, Wheaton: The Theosophical Publishing House.

Wilber, Ken (1983) *Eye to Eye*, Garden City, NY: Anchor.

Wilber, Ken (1997) *The Eye of Spirit*, Boston, MA: Shambhala.

Wilber, Ken (2000) *Integral Psychology*, Boston, MA: Shambhala.

Winnicott, D.W. (1975) *Through Paediatrics to Psychoanalysis*, London: Hogarth Press.

2

CREATIVITY IN THE EVOLUTION OF HUMANISTIC PSYCHOLOGY

Louis Hoffman, Ruth Richards and Steven Pritzker

Humanistic Psychology in recent years has too often focused on the same themes without bringing forth enough new perspectives, applications, and voices. Creativity has two important roles in addressing this issue and advancing Humanistic Psychology. First, creativity is an important and emergent theme in humanistic writing with relevance for theory, research, and practice. Second, it is important to creatively engage Humanistic Psychology to move beyond a retelling of the same old stories and themes. This chapter illustrates some exciting new areas and offers several practical suggestions for increasing creativity's presence and influence in Humanistic Psychology.

> . . .of the song-clouds my breath made
> in cold air
> a cloak has grown
> white and,
>   where here a word
>   there another
> froze, glittering,
> stone-heavy.
> A mask I had not meant
> to wear, as if of frost,
> covers my face.
>   *(Levertov, 1970, p. 42)*

Humanistic Psychology emerged at a time when change was the *Zeitgeist*, offering a fresh voice and perspective on the human condition and psychological theory. Since its inception, however, the creative voices have too often grown into a chorus of familiar themes. If Humanistic Psychology is to retain its status as a force in psychology, it will be necessary to unfreeze its voice, shed its cloak, and find a new voice. This does not require a shedding of the basic principles and values of Humanistic Psychology. Rather, it advocates the need for new interpretations, experiences, and applications of Humanistic Psychology that meet the needs and energy of contemporary times.

Creativity is essential to the renewal of Humanistic Psychology. Its very nature is change, adaptation, and renewal. It is a vehicle for our higher human possibilities. We are advocating for Humanistic Psychology to embrace the study of creativity, in general, but more importantly to apply it within the humanistic paradigm for the purposes of human betterment and changing the world.

Creativity and Humanistic Psychology

Even today, many see human creativity as an optional extra. To some, it is not even worthy of serious study – it is a frill, a lark, an avocation for a rainy Sunday afternoon. Some think it is for a special few, or see it as largely about art (and perhaps science and leadership). It is common to hear phrases such as, 'I can't paint a picture; I am not creative!' For these people, they cannot do it, and that is the end. They have turned their back on their birthright – and ours.

In the future, we see all this changing dramatically. We see creativity, 'the originality of everyday life', becoming ever more obviously about ways of functioning more consciously and fully in all of life – or even as a way of life – relevant to personal change, social change, psychological and mental health, awareness, presence in the moment, a rich attention to our many options, and for those so inclined, part of a spiritual path. It is 'natural' in Humanistic Psychology. This certainly resonates with Maslow's *self-actualizing creativity*.

Thematic analysis of a recent book, *Everyday Creativity and New Views of Human Nature* (Richards, 2007a), revealed 12 themes, typically process-related, that cut across the chapters: *dynamic, conscious, healthy, non-defensive, open, integrating, observing actively, caring, collaborative, androgynous, developing, brave*. Note also similarities to past writings about creativity by humanistic psychologists including Maslow, Rogers, and May. Mike Arons and others have also addressed varied links between aspects of creative process and Humanistic Psychology (e.g., Arons, 2007; Arons & Richards, 2001; Combs & Krippner, 2007; Schneider, 2004). An *everyday creative* product can be identified after Frank Barron (1969) in terms of only two criteria, *originality* and *meaningfulness*, and it can be applied broadly to individual lives at work and leisure. It is universally available, although often underdeveloped. It is not so much about *what* one does as *how* one does it. Hence, creative process again becomes key. A highly creative participant in one study (Richards et al., 1988) was an auto mechanic who devised his own tools. Many have probably known an uncreative auto mechanic! One can be creative (or not) in how one teaches a class, organizes an office, landscapes their home, rears a child, or creates a special banquet on a tight budget. Creativity can literally save someone who is lost, starving, endangered, or otherwise at risk. But it is not just about survival or coping; it also can be about learning what one is *surviving for*.

Increasingly, for many in this field, interest is less in the *creative product*, described by these two criteria, than the *creative process* that leads to this rich ability to change, adapt, and move forward along a path of development, and even cultural evolution. This is a major change in focus: to turn the camera around from the creative product – the usual concern – to look back at who is creating it, and how they are affected, a humanistic concern. Whenever a person is changing, shifting, flexibly adapting to their environment (or adapting it to us), improvising, or having a hunch or intuition, they are being everyday creative. One becomes a mindful agent of the future, rather than an automaton, running through preset routines, habits, and duties. One comes alive.

We also believe we are not looking at only a cognitive skill or set of rules and procedures, but at complex holistic capabilities that engage all aspects of the person including cognitive and affective functions, intentionality, conscious and unconscious, and at various points in the process different states or alterations in consciousness (see Richards, 2007a, 2010). It is also very much worth remembering that Maslow saw, ultimately, that self-actualizing in general, and self-actualizing creativity, were not all that different (Maslow, 1971).

It can even be asked whether creativity is good for those engaging in it. One finds increasingly more evidence of health benefits, including work on expressive writing (even including boosted immune function) to a possible protective effect (or 'compensatory advantage') of high creativity in certain persons at risk for major psychiatric problems (Kinney & Richards, 2011; Richards et al., 1988). Highly creative people accept changes of aging more comfortably, and there are initial suggestions people may actually live longer. One's ability to use mental imagery in creative healing creates a mind–body bridge that, for instance, can change patterns of local blood flow and other parameters. Uses of arts in cancer, HIV, and coping with loss and trauma are just a few other examples (Richards, 2007a; Runco & Pritzker, 2011). New writing also looks at complex issues in the ethics of creativity (Moran et al., 2014), and hopeful possibilities, including ways that creative activity, all else being equal, can even help us to become better people (Richards, 2014). These are complex topics, and hopefully it is evident that what are being dealt with are the powerful potentials of mind–body–spirit that can reach into all aspects of one's lives.

Why then are more people not emphasizing creativity, for instance, in the schools? Remember, creativity is also about change, and the creator is a threat to the status quo. We are talking new values and new priorities. There is typically a resistance to the new, whether at work, at school, at home, or internally as one defends against the sorts of self-knowledge that can emerge when truly open to unconscious sources (Runco & Pritzker, 2011). It might be, in part, that unacknowledged fear of one's irrational mind, unconscious, or Shadow, may be one factor in pathologizing the highly creative person (Richards, 2010).

It is possible to work for a future that brings a *new definition of normalcy*, one that incorporates and cherishes the diversity of inspiration (and of many other things) and that accepts the sometimes odd-ball deviancy as part of the rich human range of possibility, rather than pathologizing it, or displacing a fear of one's depths onto certain vulnerable groups (certain psychiatric patients).

In fact, creativity and psychology have been intimately linked since Sigmund Freud, although the healthier implications emerged later with Humanistic Psychology. Freud proposed that creativity was the result of individuals' 'repression of instinctual libidinal energy' (Lemire, 1998, p. 109). Jung (archetypes), Kris (primary process), May (the daimonic), and other psychologists made significant contributions to the understanding of creativity in the early 20th century. Finally, in the 1950s and 60s, humanistic psychologists brought a fresh perspective to the field by focusing on the individual in an idealistic positive fashion that was symbolic of the optimistic post World War II American ethos.

Humanistic psychologists looked at creativity as a much more common human experience. For example, Abraham Maslow (1962) proposed that creativity was not limited to the traditional arts but could be a part of everyday life. He stated that almost everybody had the potential to be creative in their lives: 'we are dealing with a fundamental characteristic, inherent in human nature, a potentiality given to all or most human beings at birth, which most often is lost or buried or inhibited as the person gets enculturated' (p. 133). Maslow, based on his research, stated that the attributes of a creative individual include being able to be childlike at times while at the same time having a strong ego that allows the integration of opposing ideas into unity. He discussed the importance of education in art, poetry, and dancing, arguing that it could help students learn 'to accept and integrate the primary processes into conscious and preconscious life' (p. 136). Maslow's goal was to encourage the development of self-actualizing, flexible, and spontaneous individuals who func-tion in the world in a way that makes them psychologically and physically healthier, as well as attuned to higher needs in a culture. Loye (2007), in a key volume on the overlooked Darwin (regarding Darwin's views on prosocial and collaborative motives for humans), characterized humans as moving from defense to growth and caring (as per Darwin's *Descent of Man*) and on to a metamotivational stage related to Maslow's (1971) self-actualizing individual.

Carl Rogers (1963), elaborating on Maslow's vision, proposed that a self-actualizing person would be a non-conformist with a strong sense of self who could make valuable contributions to society. Rogers suggested that this ability to continu-ally evolve would provide the opportunity to develop leaders who would be 'likely to adapt and survive under changing environmental conditions . . . He would be a fit vanguard of human evolution' (p. 23). Rogers statement appears particularly prescient in view of our current environmental challenges.

Rollo May (1975) argued in *The Courage to Create* that we are living in an 'age of limbo' where constant change requires the courage to 'leap into the unknown' (p. 12). He proposed the theory that artistic creativity is an encounter in which the artist or writer engage subjectively with the objective world. The result is a unique expression that can influence the audience as well as the creator.

Prominent humanistic psychologists, including Rogers and May, along with others including Harvard's Gordon Allport and Henry Murray, attended the 1964 conference in Old Saybrook Connecticut, now seen as the landmark event in the establishment of Humanistic Psychology as a field and a third force in psychology (Taylor, 1994). Subsequently, several humanistic programs or institutions were established, including The Humanistic Psychology Institute in San Francisco (now called Saybrook University), which recently celebrated its 40th anniversary. May, whose books include the remarkable *Courage to Create* (1975), taught at Saybrook during the early years.

At Saybrook today, the spirit of Humanistic Psychology's connection to creativity continues to advance with new graduate programs. Saybrook was one of the first schools in the world to offer a Creativity Studies Certificate, a Masters in Psychology with a Specialization in Creativity Studies, and has just added a Doctorate in Psychology with a Specialization in Creativity Studies. The Creativity Studies curriculum is grounded in Humanistic Psychology with a commitment to help develop healthy self-actualizing students who in turn take their skills and intentions into the world to help others. Examples of unique emphases include, from Carl Rogers' daughter Natalie Rogers (2011), a rich program in expressive arts for personal and social change, from Stanley Krippner (Feinstein & Krippner, 2006), work in personal mythology and dreamwork (allowing conscious rewriting of unconscious personal and social scripts), and from Steven Pritzker (2007), work with creative expression and on the receiving end, with 'audience flow', whence we can help people become active creators in what might seem to be passive activity.

Saybrook's various programs are becoming popular with students, as seen in a recent article by a professor and ten students/alumni (Richards et al., 2011); as one sees, Saybrook students often want to change something significant in the world – or in themselves. They want to apply innovative approaches to clinical work, education, organizational development, self-improvement, and more.

Although creativity can be used for 'evil', all else being equal, creative *process* can further one's openness, lack of defensiveness, and general mental health. Indeed, creativity can change everything! Who we are. What we want in life. It can open doors to our higher potential. We hope, increasingly, at Saybrook and in general, to facilitate this journey.

Creativity in Humanistic Psychology

There are some notable examples of creativity in contemporary Humanistic Psychology. Kirk Schneider's existential-integrative psychology (Schneider, 2008; Schneider & Krug, 2009) provides a model for existential psychology to work with other psychological theories, including mainstream psychology, utilizing creativity through an integrative process. Schneider's model was praised by Wampold (2008), a leading therapy outcome researcher, who stated that 'an understanding of the principles of existential therapy is needed by all therapists, as it adds a perspective that might . . . form the basis of all effective treatments' (p. 6). David Elkins (2009), in his book *Humanistic Psychology: A clinical manifesto*, took on some of the most important and controversial issues in contemporary psychology with a deeply humanistic voice.

In particular, Elkins challenged attempts to narrowly regulate psychotherapy practice in ways antagonistic to Humanistic Psychology while providing an important evidence-based defense of humanistic approaches to therapy. Mendelowitz (2008), in *Ethics and Lao Tzu: Intimations of character*, embraced creativity on multiple levels. In his book, he integrated the arts into a story of his work with a client, who was herself an artist. The style as well as the content exudes creativity while also speaking to the power of creativity to impact the human condition. While these represent important creative contributions to Humanistic Psychology, and show the potential to open possibilities in Western mental health, more applications are still needed.

Diversity, creativity, and Humanistic Psychology

Great opportunities for creativity arise when one opens oneself up to that which is different. In a world that is becoming increasingly diverse, and increasingly international, opportunities for creativity are prominent. Even more, creativity is necessary in order to enter into dialogues that honor the history, traditions, and values of cultures while advancing the collective wisdom and scholarship. Too often, as critiqued by Ren (2009), international dialogues quickly turn into attempts to impose one culture's values and approaches upon the other culture. It requires creativity, and a loosening of one's ideals, to engage in international dialogue in a manner that is respectful of differences and allows for something new to emerge.

As an illustration, beginning in 2007, a series of dialogues on existential psychology began in China (see Hoffman et al., 2009). Existential psychology emerged from a Western paradigm and, although it challenged much of the status quo of Western thought, it retained many Western values, such as individualism, that do not fit well with Chinese culture. In order to minimize the possibility of the imposition of Western values, several principles were utilized that encouraged a more creative approach:

1. Prioritizing relationship building as the foundation of dialogue.
2. The sharing of Western approaches to existential psychology was always accompanied by the encouragement of cultural critique, or critically thinking about how these ideas and approaches did not fit or needed to be adapted to be utilized in China in a culturally sensitive manner.
3. The conversations sought to identify *indigenous Chinese approaches to existential psychology*, which were understood as approaches to understanding human nature and change that shared many, but not all, of the values of existential psychology.
4. Encouraging dialogue between indigenous Chinese worldviews and approaches to psychology with the Western existential perspectives (see Yang & Hoffman, 2011).

Relational creativity becomes important here, where creative process is applied to interaction (see Richards, 2007b). These dialogues would not have achieved the success that has been attained without several applications of creativity. First, the relational foundation provided the safety for participants to share different perspectives and openly critique the Western approaches to existential psychology. This created the space for creative new expressions and applications of existential psychology to emerge. Second, being intentional in identifying and exposing differences and points of discomfort was necessary to begin exploring creative resolutions to the challenges of using an existential paradigm in Chinese culture. Third, dialogue across differences pushed individuals to use creativity in recognizing similarities and seeking ways to integrate ideas that emerged from very different cultures.

Moats, Claypool, and Saxon (2011) provide a beautiful illustration of how growth and creativity can emerge from the natural tension of cross-cultural dialogue. These three authors participated in existential dialogues in China, originally as students and later as professionals. Their article reflects upon how their experiences in China dislodged them from their personal and professional comfort zones, often challenging deeply held beliefs. Partially because of the relationships they were developing, it was not easy to discard the sources of discomfort, resulting in the necessity of finding creative resolutions to dealing with their discomfort. The result was a shift in their beliefs that has significantly impacted the way they apply and practice psychology.

As a second example, Cleare-Hoffman (2009) utilized an existential framework to explore the meaning of Junkanoo, a Bahamian festival. This festival originated with the African slaves brought to the Bahamas, as a way of retaining aspects of their spiritual and cultural beliefs. Cleare-Hoffman illustrates that Junkanoo began as a celebration of freedom while the celebrants were still bound in slavery. This is a very different understanding of freedom compared to what is commonly held in many Western cultures. This, again, illustrates the potential for new, creative interpretations of foundational humanistic principles and values through engagement with diversity.

Creativity can also be illustrated in ways that existential and Humanistic Psychology engage cultural movements, such as the contemporary protest movements. Protest movements, such as Black Lives Matter and the Occupy movement in the United States, represent creative ways of channeling pain, trauma, and oppression into movements for change (Hoffman et al., 2016a, 2016b). In many ways, these exemplify the creative use of what May refers to as the daimonic. The daimonic, according to May (1969), refers to anything natural in the person that has the potential to consume or take over the entire personality. In the contemporary protest movements, organizers are helping channel the pain from difficult experiences into advocacy for change. This serves two important purposes. First, these advocate for needed social changes. Second, they illustrate the creation of individual and collective meaning that help sustain people experiencing the suffering while also helping maintain the energy and motivation to advocate for change. Humanistic psychologists are helping to provide a frame for understanding and enhancing these movements (Hoffman et al., 2016a, 2016b).

Using art and Humanistic Psychology for change and healing

Thus far we have advocated for ways of applying creativity extending beyond the creative arts. In addition to these approaches to creativity, Humanistic Psychology continues to provide leadership in the application of the creative arts in therapy and healing processes. Ilene Serlin has been using a humanistic foundation for applications of the dance and movement therapy in various international contexts. For instance, Serlin (2012, 2014) has used dance and movement therapy with individuals from Israel who have experienced trauma, including what is often persistent, complex trauma. Additionally, Serlin has been providing systematic training in dance and movement therapy in China in conjunction with the China Institute of Psychotherapy.

Several recent books incorporate a humanistic perspective to explore the use of poetry for healing, growth, and even advocacy. *Stay Awhile: Poetic narrative on multiculturalism and diversity* by Hoffman and Granger (2015) examines the use of poetry with multicultural issues. Hoffman and Granger explore how poetry can be used to promote cultural empathy and healing at the cultural level, particularly in response to traumas that impact a cultural group. Additionally, they address how poetry can be used to advocate for social change.

In another book in the same series, Hoffman and Moats (2016) address the use of poetry with grief and loss. In the book, the existential-humanistic framework for using poetry with grief and loss is explicated. Considerations are given to the meaning-making process, preserving memories and emotions through poetry, and changing how people *experience* their painful emotions, instead of simply trying to overcome them. A third book in the series uses poetry to explore spiritual struggles, again incorporating a strong humanistic perspective (Hoffman & Fehl, 2016). Emphasis is placed on learning to embrace spiritual struggles and recognizing these as an integral part of spiritual development. Additionally, Hoffman and Fehl recognize the importance of limitations in knowing, mystery, and awe as important aspects of spirituality, and note their importance in the creative process.

A recent video called *Creativity in the Classroom* (American Psychological Association, 2016) was prepared by the educational coalition of the American Psychological Association. The purpose is to use research-based information to encourage teachers to use more creativity in lesson planning, encourage creativity in their students, and enhance their own creativity.

Conclusion

Creativity should be recognized and celebrated as having an honored place in Humanistic Psychology. From its origins, Humanistic Psychology has been open to the humanities, literature, and the arts. Many humanistic practitioners have long integrated the arts into the healing and change process. However, what is needed now are broader ways of understanding and applying creativity that can permeate throughout the Humanistic Psychology field and cross cultural divides. These creative engagements have the potential to not only change Humanistic Psychology, but to change the person, and even to begin to transform the world.

References

American Psychological Association. (2016, April 14). *Creativity in the classroom.* (Video file) Retrieved from www.apa.org/education/k12/creativity-module.aspx

Arons, M. (2007). Standing up for humanity: Upright body, creative instability, and spiritual balance. In R. Richards (Ed.), *Everyday creativity and new views of human nature: Psychological, social, and spiritual perspectives* (pp. 175–193). Washington, DC: American Psychological Association.

Arons, M., & Richards, R. (2001). Two noble insurgencies: Creativity and Humanistic Psychology. In K. J. Schneider, J. F. T. Bugental, & J. F. Pierson (Eds.), *Handbook of Humanistic Psychology: Leading edges in theory, research, and practice* (pp. 127–142). Thousand Oaks, CA: Sage Publications.

Barron, F. (1969). *Creative person and creative process.* New York: Holt, Rinehart, and Winston.

Cleare-Hoffman, H. P. (2009). Junkanoo: A Bahamian cultural myth. In L. Hoffman, M. Yang, F. J. Kaklauskas, & A. Chan (Eds.), *Existential psychology east-west* (pp. 363–372). Colorado Springs, CO: University of the Rockies Press.

Combs, A., & Krippner, S. (2007). Structures of consciousness and creativity: Opening the doors of perception. In R. Richards (Ed.), *Everyday creativity and new views of human nature: Psychological, social, and spiritual perspectives* (pp. 131–149). Washington, DC: American Psychological Association.

Elkins, D. N. (2009). *Humanistic Psychology: A clinical manifesto. A critique of clinical psychology and the need for progressive alternatives.* Colorado Springs, CO: University of the Rockies Press.

Feinstein, D., & Krippner, S. (2006). *The mythic path (3rd edition).* Santa Rosa, CA: Energy Psychology Press.

Hoffman, L., & Fehl, S. (2016). *Journey of the wounded soul: Poetic companions for spiritual struggles.* Colorado Springs, CO: University Professors Press.

Hoffman, L., & Granger, N. Jr. (2015). *Stay awhile: Poetic narratives on multiculturalism and diversity.* Colorado Springs, CO: University Professors Press.

Hoffman, L., & Moats, M. (2016). *Capturing shadows: Poetic encounters along the path of grief and loss.* Colorado Springs, CO: University Professors Press.

Hoffman, L., Granger, N. Jr., & Mansilla, M. (2016a). Multiculturalism and meaning in existential and positive psychology. In P. Russo-Netzer, S. E. Schulenberg, & A. Batthyany (Eds.), *Clinical perspectives on meaning: Positive and existential psychology* (pp. 111–130). New York, NY: Springer.

Hoffman, L., Granger, N. Jr., Vallejos, L., & Moats, M. (2016b). An existential-humanistic perspective on Black Lives Matter and contemporary protest movements. *Journal of Humanistic Psychology.* Advance online publication. doi: 10.1177/0022167816652273 (Special Issue on Cultural and Social Justice Issues in Humanistic Psychology; M. E. Lemberger-Truelov, Special Issue Editor).

Hoffman, L., Yang, M., Kaklauskas, F. J., & Chan, A. (Eds.) (2009). *Existential psychology east-west.* Colorado Springs, CO: University of the Rockies Press.

Kinney, D., & Richards, R. (2011). Bipolar mood disorders. *Encyclopedia of Creativity (2nd edition).* San Diego, CA: Academic Press.

Lemire, D. (1998). Individual psychology and innovation: The de-Freuding of creativity. *The Journal of Individual Psychology, 54*(1), 108–118.

Levertov, D. (1970). *Poems 1968–1972.* New York, NY: New Directions Books.

Loye, D. (2007). *Darwin's lost theory.* Carmel, CA: Benjamin Franklin Press.

Maslow, A. H. (1962). Creativity in self-actualizing people. In A. Maslow (Ed.), *Toward a psychology of being* (pp. 127–137). Princeton, NJ: D Van Nostrand. doi:10.1037/10793-010

Maslow, A. H. (1971). *The farther reaches of human nature.* New York: Penguin.

May, R. (1969). *Love and will.* New York, NY: Delta.

May, R. (1975). *The courage to create.* New York, NY: Norton.

Mendelowitz, E. (2008). *Ethics and Lao Tzu: Intimations of character.* Colorado Springs, CO: University of the Rockies Press.

Moats, M., Claypool, T., & Saxon, E. (2011). Therapist development through international dialogue: Students' perspectives on personal and professional life changing interactions in China. *The Humanistic Psychologist, 39,* 276–282.

Moran, S., Cropley, D., & Kaufman, J. (Eds.) (2014). *The ethics of creativity.* London, UK: Palgrave Macmillan.

Pritzker, S. (2007). Audience flow. In R. Richards (Ed.), *Everyday creativity and new views of human nature: Psychological, social, and spiritual perspectives* (pp. 109–129). Washington, DC: American Psychological Association.

Ren, Z. (2009). On being a volunteer at the Sichuan earthquake disaster area (translated version). *Hong Kong Journal of Psychiatry, 19*(3), 123–125.

Richards, R. (2007a). *Everyday creativity and new views of human nature: Psychological, social, and spiritual perspectives.* Washington, DC: American Psychological Association.

Richards, R. (2007b). Relational creativity and healing potential: The power of Eastern thought in Western clinical settings. In J. Pappas, B. Smythe, & A. Baydala (Eds.), *Cultural healing and belief systems* (pp. 286–308). Calgary, Alberta: Detselig Enterprises.

Richards, R. (2010). Everyday creativity in the classroom: A trip through time with seven suggestions. In R. A. Beghetto & J. C. Kaufman (Eds.), *Nurturing creativity in the classroom* (pp. 206–234). New York: Cambridge University Press.

Richards, R. (2014). A creative alchemy. In S. Moran, D. Cropley, & J. Kaufman (Eds.), *The ethics of creativity* (pp. 119–136). London, UK: Palgrave Macmillan.

Richards, R., Kinney, D. K., Lunde, I., & Benet, M. (1988). Creativity in manic depressives, cyclothymes, their normal relatives, and control subjects. *Journal of Abnormal Psychology, 97,* 281–288.

Richards, R., Kolva, J., Atkin, M., Cheatham, H., Crocker, R., Ockuly, M. D., et al. (2011). Creativity revalued: How professors, students, and an innovative university are turning the tide. *NeuroQuantology, 9*(3), 468–493.

Rogers, C. R. (1963). The concept of the fully functioning person. *Psychotherapy: Theory, Research & Practice, 1*(1), 17–26. doi:10.1037/h0088567

Rogers, N. (2011). *Creative Connection for groups: Person-centered expressive arts for healing and social change.* Palo Alto, CA: Science and Behavior Books.

Runco, M., & Pritzker, S. (2011). *Encyclopedia of creativity (2nd edition).* San Diego, CA: Academic Press.

Schneider, K. J. (2004). *Rediscovery of awe: Splendor, mystery, and the fluid center of life.* St. Paul, MN: Paragon House.

Schneider, K. J. (Ed.) (2008). *Existential-integrative psychotherapy: Guideposts to the core of practice.* New York: Routledge.

Schneider, K. J., & Krug, O. T. (2009). *Existential-humanistic psychology.* Washington, DC: American Psychological Association.

Serlin, I. A. (2012). The courage to move. In S. Schwartz, V. M. Speiser, P. Speiser, & M. Kossak (Eds.), *Arts and social change: The Lesley University experience in Israel* (pp. 117–124). Netanya, Israel: Porat Publishing.

Serlin, I. A. (2014). Kinesthetic imaging. In B. E. Thompson & R. A. Neimeyer (Eds.), *Grief and the expressive arts: Practices for creating meaning* (pp. 116–119). New York, NY: Routledge.

Taylor, E. (1994). Transpersonal psychology: Its several virtues. In F. Wertz (Ed.), *The humanistic movement: Recovering the person in psychology* (pp. 170–185). Lake Worth, FL: Gardner Press.

Wampold, B. E. (2008, February 4). Existential-integrative psychotherapy: Coming of age [Review of Existential-integrative psychotherapy: Guideposts to the core of practice]. *PsycCRITIQUES: Contemporary Psychology: APA Review of Books, 53*(6). doi: 10.1037a 0011070

Yang, M., & Hoffman, L. (2011). Introduction to the special section on the First International Conference on Existential Psychology. *The Humanistic Psychologist, 39*, 236–239.

3

THE PAST AND FUTURE OF HUMANISTIC PSYCHOLOGY

Colin Feltham

In this chapter I declare my personal sympathy with aspects of Humanistic Psychology and state what I consider its strengths to be. I also critique what I regard as its weaknesses – its lack of realism, lack of engagement with contemporary, harsh socio-economic realities, and discuss some of its failures to live up to its early promise. Humanistic Psychology might, in time, become a barely significant set of nostalgic theories and practices, or could yet find ways to bring its important focus on birth, education, feelings, spirituality, and patriarchal civilization to a new readership and public.

I do not want to spend too long on any tedious, definitional preamble. Instead, let me recount briefly what some of my associations with Humanistic Psychology are. Born in 1950, I grew up within the late hippie era. Throughout my searching, late-teenage years, academic psychology seemed disappointingly about anything but human experience, Anglo-American philosophy was far too analytical, and even much existentialist philosophy felt too wordy and escaped my grasp. Pacifist protest, rock music and drugs on the other hand, were everywhere. I was loosely involved, or interested in, yoga, meditation, existentialism, Zen Buddhism, Gandhi, Krishnamurti, Hermann Hesse, Timothy Leary, Alan Watts, the Continuum Concept, peace, primal therapy, primal integration and (later) Mahrer's experiential psycho-therapy. I attended nude massage workshops, and others on dance and singing. But I never quite belonged to the light and the good, reading Thomas Hardy (especially *Jude the Obscure*), Kafka, Camus, Henry Miller and others with rather too much negative pleasure. I was also never a joiner as such, but a loner and an outsider.

I wonder if Humanistic Psychology, like many similar movements and discip-lines, has had its heyday of impact and its spike of optimism, but is now in decline? I realize that I am in favour of many of the things Humanistic Psychology and therapy stand for, but I am also against some. I am doubtful about many of its explanations even while I might broadly support its aims. I still believe that we inhabit a damagingly patriarchal society that needs more female influence and under-standing of, and respect for feelings, the body, children and the environment. But I do not share the optimistic belief that human beings are deeply and intrinsically autonomous, self-actualizing and trustworthy. In Feltham (2007, 2012 and 2015) in particular, I have outlined views about the ways in which I consider we are also subject to entropic forces, negative evolutionary and genetic inclinations, and capitalist threats. I think some practitioners of the humanistic therapies are perhaps stuck in a 1960s mind-set of naivety and romantic optimism, and exhibit a knee-jerk rejection of anything they see as positivistic and/or authoritarian. If enough people trust their own organismic valuing process, primal or discharge away their inner distress, raise their children in a child-centred way, create local solidarity groups, meditate, dance, practise idiosyncratic spiritualities, eat the right things and recycle waste conscient-iously, then, goes the thinking, all shall be well. Although I am obviously caricaturing here (and some, perhaps fairly, will think me cynical), there is some truth in the idea that most Humanistic Psychology/therapy is underpinned by a simple set of optimistic values akin to religious faith, and is not characterized by a great deal of radical, rigorous critical thinking. Indeed, the place of serious intellectual thought in Humanistic Psychology is uncertain, though Grogan (2013) and Milton (2002) among others have brought critical-cultural thinking to bear on it.

One significant speculation is warranted here. Let us note Adorno *et al.* (1950), following Erich Fromm's work, as a milestone publication in the attempt of psycho-logy to both critique 20th-century political character and to suggest new ways forward. This has also been regarded as reinforcing 'cultural Marxism' and its 'long march through the institutions' which is now often labelled the social justice movement, or political correctness. Add to this the exodus of Jews from Europe to the USA in the early 20th century and the emergence of so-called 'Jewish psycho-logical evangelism' (Heinze, 2004), seen concretely in the key figures of Maslow, Perls, Reich, Moreno, Berne, Assagioli, Frankl, Janov, Yalom and many others, all from a Jewish background and all prominent leaders of Humanistic Psychology models. Not only psychoanalysis, which some called the 'Jewish science', but also CBT, with Jewish leaders such as Ellis and Beck, emerged from this cultural back-ground. The total Jewish population currently stands at approximately 14 million (0.2% of world population), with almost 7 million living in the USA; statistics that suggest a disproportionate influence in academia and even more so in the psycho-therapy domain. The Holocaust undermined belief in God and understandably prompted an anti-fascist 'never again' movement which in part prompted and under-pinned the search for goodness within human beings and an attendant psychological evangelism.

In an unconnected and 'non-Jewish' development, Rogers' personality and work riled against (initially religious) authority and asserted the trustworthy inner resources of the individual. The 1960s saw a huge youth movement against war and materialism in the counterculture. The Vietnam War of 1955 to 1975, and intimations of the false consciousness of the American Dream (as portrayed for example in Arthur Miller's 1949 play *Death of a Salesman*), illustrate some of the social factors being protested against here. The authority figure, 'the Man', the patriarchy, all these and the associated hate objects of the Establishment, neoliberalism, medical psychiatry, Big Pharma, New Public Management, and so on, are targets of the essentially left-wing psychotherapy world.

But social and economic developments since the 1960s have not fostered the same level of fiery discontent. Standards of living have gradually increased. While total equality remains unfulfilled as a political aim, women experience much greater freedoms, as do ethnic minorities in mainstream white cultures, gay marriage is established, and Paralympic events attest to greater levels of respect for disabled people. Therapy is now part of the mainstream, albeit often in a brief CBT format. The anti-capitalism movement challenges the free market and its socio-economic consequences, but related anarchist groups usually have little time for therapy, which is often suspected of being collusive or irrelevant. The USA may be regarded by many as the source of much psychosocial distress but it remains the fount of most new therapeutic theory. Oddly enough, although original Humanistic Psychology was antagonistic toward formal religion, spiritual or transpersonal elements of theory and practice have flourished, while psycho-political awareness has diminished among humanistic practitioners over the past few decades. Multiculturalism has increased and with it the growth of Islam has taken place, about which Humanistic Psychology is relatively silent. All these phenomena suggest that the movement born in the middle of the 20th century has not kept pace with social trends and world events.

Probably, some of my opposition to Humanistic Psychology – and all things bright and beautiful – results from deep incurable attitudinal pathologies of my own, as well as my ageing process. Not for nothing have I been attracted to writers such as Schopenhauer, Camus, Cioran, Beckett and Houellebecq. Temperamentally I am somewhat more Freudian (pessimistic) than Rogerian. I do not accept Rogers' concept of an actualizing tendency, or at least not in its uncritical form: Schopenhauer's concept of 'Will' better explains to me the negative forces of human expansion as seen in population growth and climate change. Neither can I accept Yalom's warm, American, optimistic portrayal of therapy as an answer to Schopenhauerian pessimism (in his novel *The Schopenhauer Cure*; Yalom (2005)) and Nazi psychopathology (in *The Spinoza Problem*; Yalom (2012)), although it is encouraging to see such links being made with philosophy. Just how broad a church, or how much a psychological anthropology, Humanistic Psychology might perhaps be can be determined by comparing Rowan (2014) with Yalom (2008) and Feltham (2016) in which we are, respectively, regarded as spiritual beings with infinite resources, as finite humans who can overcome the fear of death, and members of a species who anxiously face complete and meaningless annihilation on death.

I have to some extent 'done my own thing' in life but I have also compromised extensively, and wrestled only half-successfully with intimate relationships, satisfying work and peace of mind in the face of mortality. But my opposition also comes from disappointment, ongoing observations and wide reading. Primal therapy, which I had in Los Angeles in the late 1970s, was in my view not nearly as successful as was claimed at the time, and its original proponents have not shown humility by revising theories or outcome claims. Transactional analysis did not remain simple and accessible for very long. Jackins' re-evaluation co-counselling did not really transform people or societies, and his biography casts serious doubts on him. On reflection, grandiose claims by humanistic therapists such as Will Schutz, for example asserting psychogenic causes of cancer and cures by psychotherapy, seem not only dubious but reprehensible. Biographies about Jiddu Krishnamurti too cast some doubts on the extent of his authenticity. My sons, raised in a positive, child-centred way, for all their good points, did not become anything like entirely non-problematic, 'fully functioning' adults. It is not uncommon to hear criticisms of 'old hippies' who had a good time themselves but have not demonstrably helped to create a better world for their descendants. The romantic idea that *living in the now* (promoted by Zen, illegal drugs, Gestalt, Tolle, *et al.*) would help to rectify all personal and social ills has begun to look extremely naive.

To my mind, a great deal of writing on evolutionary psychology and deep history render the shallow, ahistorical account of all psychologies suspect. The positive psychology and mindfulness movements in CBT seem to have hijacked part of the Humanistic Psychology agenda. Every other person I meet in the counselling/therapy field claims to be on a spiritual journey and yet remains inarticulate about what that actually means. People involved for many years in humanistic therapy (indeed, in all therapies) did not stand out as significantly different from others in terms of freedom from neuroses, vanity and folly. Petruska Clarkson killed herself. But I have never entirely shaken off the influence of Krishnamurti's simple, sincere teaching, nor of primal therapy's focus on feelings. Years in academia exercised my head but not my feelings, my attention to detail but not to large, obvious human problems. My current 'position' is roughly, highly concisely, as follows.

Human beings are evolved animals; many people still find this either unpalatable, or they do not really understand or accept it. In a nutshell, we humans retain all animals' need for food, and most of us also retain some tendencies to be somewhat territorial, kin-protective and xenophobic, driven toward sex, with some inflexible behavioural habits, and so on. The advent of complex human consciousness, symbolism and language led to something like a 'Fall' (Feltham, 2007) or marked alienation from our original nature. For Ken Wilber this is a necessary dip, as it were, on the way to an awaited inevitable upward trend. For others, such as the primitivist-anarchist John Zerzan, our fall into agriculture, territoriality, patriarchy, symbolism, religion, etc. merely intensified via industry and technology in the last few thousand years, to the point where it remains an open question whether we will destroy ourselves. Layers of self- and other-deception have not been greatly overturned by the psychotherapies, in spite of this being one of psychotherapy's main foci and proudest claims. Many people remain in the grip of irrational religions, New Age fads and other dubious systems of thought; and this problem is compounded by political correctness and postmodernism which fetishize and promote 'difference' and tend to silence deep investigation and authentic dialogue. What is called 'capitalist realism' (the thick milieu of monetary illusion, economic inequalities, addictive consumerism, dehumanizing work and technologization of the mind) shows no real sign yet of being much modified or overturned. As individuals (all seven billion plus of us) we are probably far less autonomous and free than we like to think, being shaped by ancient historical forces and continuing political and economic factors that are, arguably, too big and complex for most of us to truly grasp and change. Now we are faced with potentially catastrophic climate change and international economic and military threats that we might well fail to meet effectively.

All the psychotherapies promote a concentration on the individual and the view that he or she can make effective changes in self and society. But this is not borne out by observation. No counselling or psychotherapy training course genuinely addresses in any depth the evolutionary, genetic, neurological, socio-economic, environmental and entropic forces stacked against us. Indeed, it is as if Darwin has no relevance, and evolutionary psychology has nothing to teach us; and only pop-neurology is entertained where it appears to fit with humanistic and psychodynamic theories of attachment and therapeutic relating. Our field seems much happier moving in a hazy spiritual or transpersonal direction than tackling 'real world' and scientific domains. Science still tends to be regarded with suspicion by humanistic psychologists, which suggests to me a perception that science is just another aspect of authority to be uncritically rejected. I think it is true that some of the deeper humanistic therapies address aspects of human dysfunction untouched by others, but not necessarily with great understanding or success, more often slipping into romantic and esoteric practices. What I would like to see is much greater willingness to address all such themes, along with identifying what, if anything, is durable and genuinely promising about Humanistic Psychology.

To my mind, recognition of the damaging effect of patriarchy is one such theme, to include the dangers of suppressing bodily and emotional needs. Others include consolidation of research on childbirth, birth trauma and its long-term effects; the damage done by competitive mass education; the psychology of greed and violence; the notion of 'radical honesty' (put forward by the Gestalt therapist Brad Blanton) that promotes the values of authenticity and *parrhesia*; wider experimentation in dialogue in the manner of David Bohm; the possibility that something like an 'anthropathology-free' consciousness might be real and available to more than a handful of individuals like the Buddha, Jiddu Krishnamurti and U.G. Krishnamurti, Eckhart Tolle *et al.* (all of whom might or might not have embodied such states). Humanistic Psychology still has some valuable proposals to bring to the table of research, practice and argument, but to do so it must be willing to think critically, to engage in interdisciplinary dialogue and to discard whatever is anachronistically redundant. And ultimately, do we need labels like 'Humanistic Psychology' any more than we need the labels of pathology?

One useful example of forward-moving quantitative psychology is Steven Pinker's (2012) book *The Better Angels of our Nature*, in which he demonstrates fairly convincingly that human violence of all kinds has declined significantly across the centuries, for diverse reasons. Pinker has some background in evolutionary psychology and uses statistics heavily in this book – factors that might alienate many

Humanistic Psychology readers. Yet his message is extremely hopeful. It might take much longer than we would like but we are apparently becoming demonstrably more empathic and less violent as a species. Hopefully we will also gradually become less deceptive and greedy, and as much ashamed of these characteristics as we now are of violence against women and children, torture and capital punishment. Recent anti-capitalist protests focusing on bankers' excessive pay and politicians' alienation from ordinary people's concerns is one sign that deception and greed might be becoming significantly more shameful.

Are there within the ranks of Humanistic Psychology people who can take on the challenge of research into radical human transformation? By this I refer to discoveries in the domain of freedom from anthropathology. Are there, as I intuit, links to be made between LSD, primal therapy, and the kind of embodied 'mystical' states associated with Krishnamurti and others? I believe Janov, Reich and similar others took a wrong turn and came to premature conclusions about deep emotional and somatic access issues. I suspect that 'successful' deep primalling into an irreversibly innocent (pre-deceptive) state of human consciousness is currently a fortuitous reality granted only to a few gifted individuals, though I know that Tolle and some primal practitioners are much more optimistic about success in this area. Although I am sceptical about the claims of research on both meditation and primal phenomena, I think that here we potentially have Humanistic Psychology's equivalent of medicine's cancer research. Are these experiences real? Do they actually transform some people? Why do they fail with others? How can we learn from these questions? Can we put across such information in a way that scientists, politicians and the public cannot ignore?

As things stand, Humanistic Psychology and therapy no doubt have some sort of future, but probably not one that is massively influential. However, those who have played an active part in its development and retain faith in its potency might well regard it as thriving. On the pessimistic side, I think we have to consider the possibility that it is now a relatively weak, minority-interest subject and practice sustained mainly by its committed or nostalgic elders *keeping the faith* and a handful of romantic enthusiasts. To some extent it acts as a challenge to the cognitively biased clinical psychology profession. But it has been eclipsed by the jargonized-mesmerized intellectuals and the economically motivated technocrats and medicine men (e.g. proponents of postmodernist, social constructivist and Lacanian therapies, online therapy, CBT, psychopharmacology). Person-centred therapy and its tenets remain popular within some sections of the counselling world for mixed reasons: (1) because it appears to be 'easy' and 'nice' (my apologies at these observations, which I recognize as harsh but which I believe are necessary); and (2) because it appears to offer a form of attitudinal resistance to oppressive authoritarian trends and institutions.

I know this has been done before, but is there not perhaps a need for a new humanistic (psychology) manifesto, spelling out values and aims for 2017 and beyond? The distinction between the confusing secular connotation of 'humanism' and Humanistic Psychology and psycho-practice might finally be made clear. The precise relationship between Humanistic Psychology and the human potential movement likewise, but also consideration of views on the human condition, human nature, trans/post-humanism and the multiplicity of (not only Western) relevant anthropologies, might be focused upon. Acceptance of Humanistic Psychology as a noble-enough ragbag of alternative lifestyles and modestly anti-establishment politics (if this is what it is) could be made explicit. Clarification of what still holds together the range of diverse therapies – Gestalt, Reichian, psychodrama, person-centred, Transactional Analysis, psychosynthesis, primal, existentialist, ecotherapy, etc. – under one identity could be a challenging task (Totton, 2010). It might also be accepted that in the irresistible mêlée of pluralism and entropy (what I think of as *neophilia within moribundancy*), some parts of Humanistic Psychology are moribund, some thriving, and some transmuting, even perhaps joining past enemies in new enterprises.

We cannot forget the trauma of the Holocaust from seventy years ago. In spite of the freedom from world-scale wars since 1945, we have continued to experience many serious regional conflicts and we are hardly nuclear-free. We certainly need some pro-humanizing wedge between the dehumanizing and irrational forces currently shaping our collective future in a complex and information-overloaded world. But in order to establish this we need a deeper and more thoughtful, more fully 'human condition'-oriented Humanistic Psychology than we have at present. Perhaps Schneider *et al.* (2014) go some way toward this but a wide-ranging critical Humanistic Psychology is still awaited. It should, I think, be a source of concern that no humanistic psychologists, not even Maslow, appear in a tome on human nature such as Downes and Machery (2013).

References

Adorno, T.W., Frenkel-Brunswik, E., Levinson, D.J. & Sanford, R.N. (1950) *The Authoritarian Personality*. New York: Norton.

Downes, S.M. & Machery, E. (eds) (2013) *Arguing about Human Nature: Contemporary Debates*. New York: Routledge.

Feltham, C. (2007) *What's Wrong with Us? The Anthropathology Thesis*. Chichester: Wiley.

Feltham, C. (2012) *Failure*. London: Routledge.

Feltham, C. (2015) *Keeping Ourselves in the Dark*. Charleston, WV: Nine-Banded Books.

Feltham, C. (2016) Depressive realism: what it is and why it matters to humanistic psychology. *Self & Society: An International Journal for Humanistic Psychology*, 44(2): 88–93.

Grogan, J. (2013) *Encountering America: Humanistic Psychology, Sixties Culture and the Shaping of the Modern Self*. New York: Harper Perennial.

Heinze, A.R. (2004) *Jews and the American Soul: Human Nature in the 20th Century*. Princeton, NJ: Princeton University Press.

Milton, J. (2002) *The Road to Malpsychia: Humanistic Psychology and Our Discontents*. San Francisco, CA: Encounter Books.

Pinker, S. (2012) *The Better Angels of our Nature: A History of Violence and Humanity*. London: Penguin.

Rowan, J. (2014) The transpersonal in individual therapy. In W. Dryden & A. Reeves (eds) *The Handbook of Individual Therapy (6th edn)*. London: Sage.

Schneider, K.J., Pierson, J.F. & Bugental, J.F.T. (eds) (2014) *The Handbook of Humanistic Psychology and Practice: Theory, Research, and Practice (2nd edn)*. Thousand Oaks, CA: Sage.

Totton, N. (2010) *The Problem with Humanistic Therapies*. London: Karnac.

Yalom, I. (2005) *The Schopenhauer Cure*. Scranton, PA: HarperCollins.

Yalom, I. (2008) *Staring at the Sun: Overcoming the Dread of Death*. London: Piatkus.

Yalom, I. (2012) *The Spinoza Problem*. New York: Basic Books.

4

THE PLACE OF PERSON-CENTRED COUNSELLING IN HUMANISTIC PSYCHOLOGY

Seamus Nash

Introduction

This chapter is about sharing research findings, learnings and thoughts regarding a research project I conducted for my doctorate. The project focused on what precisely person/client-centred practitioners mean when they use the terms 'person-centred' and 'client-centred' to describe their therapeutic work. The research was about attempting to understand and map what these practitioners understood to be their espoused theory, what that theory meant to them, what the main elements of this theory are, i.e. the elements they operationalize in their practice, and how they perceived their practice. The overall aim was to elicit a sense of 'what it is like to be a person/client-centred counsellor and psychotherapist in the 21st century'. The work was largely inspired by the writings of the philosopher-practical theologian Peter Schmid (1997, 1998, 2003, 2012), who, writing from within the approach, I feel has given person/client-centred counselling and psychotherapy (PCPC) a new framework for a solid philosophical, anthropological, ethical, epistemological and political praxis.

We are living in exciting times currently within the Humanistic community in the UK. A new United Kingdom Council of Psychotherapy (UKCP) Chair with Humanistic Psychology leanings may be a portent for resurgence, and a re-grouping to look at developing a 'new message': that humanistic thinking and practice are not 'dated'; that in the UK Humanistic Psychology (HP) is dynamic, changing *and* has something to offer; that we have a burgeoning, active and effective research base; that we are taking on board other psychological 'roots' and theories to expand our base, hence keeping 'in touch' with the mainstream in psychological discourse. Person-centred therapy, however, has something HP as a whole can learn from: it has been advancing and evolving (Cooper *et al.*, 2013), providing a therapeutic space and conditions that allow the client to encounter themselves in some way, and for unknown options to emerge – options that might, however, sometimes appear 'negative' if viewed via a more 'outcome'-based or manualized model.

It is my contention that HP faces an identity crisis. The term 'Humanistic Psychology' is an umbrella concept for humanistic psychotherapies – even the term Humanistic Psychology is a loose pick-and-mix framework for holding what might be seen as an even more diverse philosophical paradigm. So, who are 'we' in the context of HP? Are we a psychology, a method of psychotherapy or counselling; what do we believe, how do we practise? Are we developing? Can we survive? In this chapter I will share, from a client/person-centred perspective, some responses and findings I have discovered that might assist with such questions.

What is HP? A brief consideration

HP was not well established as the 'third force' in modern psychology until the early 1960s. Its origins go much further back, with the emergence of the *humanist* tradition, the psychological influence of Eastern cultures, and reaction to the image of the person inherent in the prevailing behavioural and psychoanalytical Western psychologies of the early 20th century. Behavioural psychology viewed man as a biological organism reacting to environmental stimuli, conditioned by learning and past experience, which could potentially be reconditioned: 'Give me the specifications and I'll give you the man!' (Skinner, 1948: 343).

By contrast, the psychoanalytical perspective saw human beings as reacting to internal drives, motives and instincts, with the fulfilment and/or frustration of these instincts, particularly sex, libido, death and aggression, determining past, present and future perceptions of the self. Consequently, the core of man's being was seen as inherently leading to conflict, even to its own destruction, unless some means of control were employed.

HP was also influenced by post-Freudian theory. For example, Alfred Adler had proclaimed that aggression was the single basic human motivational instinct. However, by 1933 he was endorsing a very different view: 'There can no longer be any doubt that everything we call a body shows striving to become whole' (Adler, 1933; cited in Rogers, 1980: 113). A new paradigm was emerging, where individuals were considered as being essentially trustworthy, of having potential control of their destiny, as being proactive, conscious, creative, future-oriented, and possibly good.

Person-centred psychotherapy pre-dates HP, yet they share a common evolution (Barrett-Lennard, 1998; Kirschenbaum, 2007; Wilkins, 2003). Person-centred psychotherapy theory greatly informed the philosophical underpinning of HP, and once established as the 'third force' in psychology, person-centred psychotherapy was recognized as one of several new psychotherapy approaches within this new paradigm. Carl Rogers himself emphasized that 'one cannot engage in psychotherapy without giving operational evidence of an underlying value orientation and view of human nature' (Rogers, 1957b: 199), and which must include an understanding of positive mental health and distress.

The American Psychiatric Association's *Diagnostic and Statistical Manual of Mental Disorders* (APA, 2013; orig. 1952) has become the international 'bible' for the classification of mental disorders. Now in its fifth edition, it seems to include an entry for nearly every psychologically upsetting or unpleasant human condition. And though it asserts considerable influence across the entire mental health field, it offers no real understanding of what might constitute positive mental health other than the elimination, relief or adjustment to so-called unpleasant or pathological symptoms. It would seem that mainstream psychiatric medicine has little understanding of *positive* mental health.

Jahoda (1950) recognized that 'there exists no psychologically meaningful description of what is commonly understood to constitute mental health'. In 1958 she reviewed the existing literature (notably Allport, Benedict, Erikson and Goldstein) and proposed a criterion based on the following: attitudes toward self; growth, development and self-actualization; integration; autonomy; perception of reality; and environmental mastery. Smith's (1950/1959; cited in Patterson, 1985) criteria also relied heavily on predetermined assumptions of competence and effectiveness, and did not quite bridge the gap. A broad definition was required, with a single goal or motivation for life, which transcended all social, cultural, gender and time constraints (Patterson, 1985; Patterson and Hidore, 1997). The concept of *self-actualization* seemed to fit the bill. A term first used by American psychiatrist and neurologist Kurt Goldstein in his work with war veterans, Goldstein used the term to describe how humans, and indeed all living organisms regardless of their limitations, are 'governed by a tendency to actualize, as much as possible, its nature in the world' (Goldstein, 1939: 196). Further studies by Maslow (1956, 1970) and Rogers (1951, 1957c, 1959, 1963) affirmed the concept of self-actualization as one of the fundamental tenets of HP.

Shaffer (1978) outlines the central emphases within HP:

1. Humanistic Psychology is strongly phenomenological or experiential: its starting point is conscious.
2. Humanistic Psychology insists on man's essential wholeness and integrity.
3. Humanistic Psychology, while acknowledging that there are clear-cut limits inherent in human existence, insists that human beings retain an essential freedom and autonomy.
4. Humanistic Psychology is anti-reductionist in its orientation.
5. Humanistic Psychology, consistent with its strong grounding in existentialism, believes that human nature can never be fully defined experience (man cannot be understood except in its own terms – through the individual's frame of reference).

Drawing on the concepts of self-actualization and the actualizing tendency, the basic tenets of HP emerged. These have been modified over the years, and sadly the original source reference is long lost:

1. The individual is **unique**
2. An interactive **whole** (mind body spirit) – the self . . .
3. . . . With an **actualizing tendency**, with potential for growth – **self-actualization** . . .

4. ...Which is constantly unfolding – in a state of **becoming**
5. Human **needs** are healthy – primarily good, or at least neutral in nature
6. Need attainment is exercised within an intra/interpersonal **relational** and **experiential** field ...
7. ...In the form of reciprocal **love, understanding** and **choice**
8. **Human distress** is the product of need frustration and or deprivation, which thwarts the actualizing tendency and significantly inhibits self-actualization
9. Human behaviour can be **motivational** or **expressive**
10. Individuals have the capacity to draw on an **internal frame of reference** to determine a moral sense, and to ascribe **meaning** and **direction** to their life.

(Basic Tenets of Humanistic Psychology. Original source unknown; modified by Derek Lawton, 1990, unpublished)

Such ideas regarding the uniqueness of the individual, the sovereignty of the client and the quality of the therapeutic relationship between the person of the client and the person of the therapist, constitute the foundational premise of Humanistic Psychotherapy – as Rogers (1961) puts it: 'If I can provide a certain type of relationship the other person will discover within himself the capacity to use that relationship for growth, and change and personal development will occur' (Rogers, 1961: 33).

The relationship that is fostered departs from the notion that the client has to surrender their autonomy to the figure of an expert therapist who applies treatment interventions in accordance with some predetermined plan, so as to relieve client suffering. Instead the client is offered the opportunity to integrate incongruent experience into awareness and experience change in the immediacy of their experience – not according to some predetermined outcome prescribed by the therapist. This is a theory of change outlined in Rogers (1961) *Process Conception of Psychotherapy* and which forms the basis of Klein *et al.*'s (1969, cited in Greenberg and Pinsof 1986) *The Experiencing Scale*.

Personal perspective

I joined the United Kingdom Association for Humanistic Psychology Practitioners (UKAHPP) in 2006 having finished a postgraduate diploma/Masters course in client-centred psychotherapy. I have been a long-term member of the British Association for the Person-Centred Approach (BAPCA) and the World Association for Person Centered and Experiential Psychotherapies and Counselling (WAPCEPC). Until last year I was an active board member of UKAHPP.

In the United Kingdom, UKAHPP was one of the founding members of the UKCP. I was, for a considerable time, a UKAHPP delegate to the Humanistic and Integrative Psychotherapy Section, being a part of and seeing the field within our section grow, seeing the politics emerge at first hand, being a part of the changes and challenges within a large UKCP section.

The HIPC were involved in the process of looking at national standards for psychotherapists and counsellors. The final version of the National Occupational

Standards (Fonagy, 2010) was approved for publication in June 2010, and sits alongside the *Professional Occupational Standards for Psychotherapists and Psychotherapeutic Counsellors* developed by the UKCP (UKCP, 2010). It is my recollection that UKAHPP played a major role in providing expert readers to feed back on these standards with many of their recommendations and revisions being accepted.

What the above illustrates is exactly what my research was attempting to uncover: the 'face' of a psychotherapy. However, then it was about the 'face' of humanistic and integrative psychotherapy (HIP), and how we as both a section and as individual practitioners were manifesting HIP. It would be absurd in my view to think that politics did not then, or does not now, come into contention within the psycho-therapy field. Based on my experiences as a delegate and then as a practising client-centred psychotherapist I have stated in a chapter (in 2006b) and followed by Schmid (2012), that any consideration of the client as a 'human being' and working *with* human beings is *inherently* political. I know there might be some within the UK person-centred community who viewed my research with suspicion *and* some who did not like the fact that person-centred psychotherapy and counselling was straying (as they saw it) from the classical, non-directive roots of Rogers. Our history is certainly important, but so is growth and renewal. It is essential in my view for practitioners to *reflect* on their practice and to give consideration to their beliefs, as *beliefs* do contribute to *behaviours*.

Finally, the concepts of 'integrative', 'integration' and 'pluralism' are increasingly now regarded by many as central aspects of current humanistic practice (Dryden, 2013; Cain, Keenan and Rubin, 2016).

The search for identity and coherence

'Client-' or 'person-centred'?

My research project asked practitioners about the essential skills they felt they used, what attitudes they felt were important and what mattered in a person-centred therapeutic encounter. The research also asked if they identified with a particular 'tribe' or 'school' and what, if any, other theories and techniques informed their practice.

'Person-Centred' Psychotherapy and Counselling (PCPC) also known as 'Client-Centred' Therapy (CCT) and formerly known as 'non-directive' therapy was devel-oped by Carl Rogers and his colleagues in the 1940s and 1950s in an attempt to locate the person/client at the centre of the therapeutic encounter and to chal-lenge the dominance of the medical model, particularly psychiatry, at this time (Kirschenbaum, 2007: 79–124; Wilkins, 2011: 5). Since then PCPC has now a recognized family of related therapies (Sanders, 2004, 2012); a World Association and a highly developed theory of psychopathology (Joseph and Worsley, 2005); a research base (Cooper *et al.*, 2010a, 2010b; Elliott *et al.*, 2013) and an established peer-led and reviewed journal.

Within the literature there has been an attempt to map what PCPC is. Lietaer (2002), Sanders (2000, 2013) and Schmid (1998, 2003) have each added academic papers regarding identity issues within PCPC. These papers focused on the meaning and identity characteristics of the terms 'person-centred therapy', 'client-centred therapy' and 'the person-centred approach'. This research project sought to explore these terms and issues of identity and 'coherence' further. I was essentially looking at what the practitioner thought about their work and if this was based on Rogers or on the many PCPC commentators and academics who, without doubt, have heightened the scope and appeal of PCPC. I wanted to know how the 'grass roots' thought and did, using a sample drawn from the world PCPC community.

The prominence of Carl Rogers

Carl Rogers is credited as both the leading figure and 'founder' of PCPC (Cooper *et al.*, 2013: 2). It is fitting to begin with Rogers whose last publication *A Way of Being* (1980) was essentially a summary of his position and views. Rogers saw this 'way of being' in the following terms:

- hearing and validating the experience of others; being clear (pp. 5–26);
- regarding the therapeutic relationship as an I–Thou encounter (pp. 27–42);
- opposition to medicalization and behaviourism (pp. 53–59);
- the provision of a 'defineable climate of facilitative psychological attitudes' which Rogers characterized as Empathy, Unconditional Positive Regard, and Congruence, and regarded as the foundation of the person-centred approach (pp. 114–117);
- upholding the 'Actualizing Tendency' (pp. 117–121);
- the primacy of empathy as part of a 'way of being' (pp. 137–163);
- power and politics (pp. 181–206);
- challenging professionalism (pp. 243–248);
- affirming person/student-centred education and its politics (pp. 263–316);
- the qualities of the 'person of tomorrow' (pp. 339–356).

As a psychologist in the USA during the 1940s, Carl Rogers had faced opposition in describing himself as a psychotherapist, as he was not medically trained. Rogers therefore adopted the term 'counselling' to describe his work, which subsequently formed the basis for the development of client-centred psychotherapy. Although Rogers' client-centred approach now has international recognition as a valid form of psychotherapy, the terms 'counselling' and 'psychotherapy' remain interchangeable. Traditionally the term 'client-centred' tends to be used when referring to psychotherapy, and 'person-centred' when referring to the application of the approach in other settings, but now 'person-centred psychotherapy' is also in common usage.

Sanders (2012: 6) writes that Rogers, after his seminal 1959 paper, 'never did revise the theory to any great extent'. I chose his 1959 paper as the basis of my exploration as it is widely acknowledged as being his fullest integration of PCPC theory.

Chicago 2000

At the WAPCEPC conference in Chicago in 2000 the questions of identity and coherence were brought into the open in a series of three papers: Sanders (2000), Lietaer (2002) and Schmid (2003). These commentator/practitioners outline their criteria in answer to the question 'what are the criteria that define "person-centred": who are "We"?'

'Criteria' comes from the Greek word Κριτικος (criterion = a distinguishing characteristic as a condition for given facts; a touchstone) which in turn originates from the Greek word Κνινω (to separate, sort out, distinguish, select, decide). Schmid explains that the distinguishing feature of being 'person-centred' is being called and related to as a '*person*'. The etymology of the word 'person' reveals it comes from the Greek word Προσωπον (prosopon) which means 'mask or face'. The research was attempting to discover what 'face' practitioners 'show' in the world of their practice.

Table 4.1 shows how each of these commentators defines 'person-centred' identity.

TABLE 4.1 Defining 'person-centred' identity: Lietaer/Schmid/Sanders Grid

Lietaer	Schmid	Sanders
First order characteristics • Focus on the experiencing self • Moment-by moment empathy • A high level of personal presence • An egalitarian dialogical stance • A belief in the Rogerian therapist conditions is *crucial*	**First order characteristics** • Image of the person, including focus on the experiential self • Coherence or congruence of the image of the person in the theory of personality development, 'disorders' and practice	**Primary principles** • Primacy of the actualizing tendency • Assertion of the necessity of Rogers' therapeutic conditions 1957 and 1959: therapy based on 'active inclusion' of these • Primacy of the non-directive attitude at least at the level of content but not necessarily of process
Second order characteristics • Holistic person-centredness • Emphasis on self-agency and self-actualizing process • Self-determination and free choice as human possibilities • Pro-social nature of the human being • Autonomy and solidarity as existential tasks • Primarily a process-oriented, person-centred approach	**Second order characteristics** • Schmid has no second order characteristics as the first order are in and of themselves: **primary** • Primarily a 'dialogic' approach, existentially informed person-centred approach	**Secondary principles** • Autonomy and the client's right to self determination • Equality and non-expertness of the therapist • Primacy of non-directive attitude – in its purest form: 'inherent non-directive' • Sufficiency of 1957 and 1959 principles • Holism • Primarily a 'classical' oriented person-centred approach

Nash (2006a) formerly explored this through a qualitative research project. In 2013 Bruce Allan shared his own enquiry with me. The primary research finding is that the meaning and understanding of the term 'person-centred' has two dimensions. First, it is understood as a theory and as a method of undertaking a particular practice of psychotherapy and counselling. Second, it is a way of being and living in the world, informed and rooted in the ethics and values that underpin PCPC. All the relevant domains acquired from the data flow from these two dimensions (Nash, 2006a).

The main *descriptor* used predominantly now is 'person-centred'; indeed Rogers favoured using this term widely from 1974 (Meador and Rogers, 1973). Rogers, however, frequently used the terms 'person-centred' and 'client-centred' interchangeably and he is, for me, a primary source of confusion regarding the use of these nomenclatures. However, a significant number of practitioners/others still use the descriptor 'client-centred', myself included, as defining their practice; although both come from the same source, both are held and *practised* differently – this is certainly something I found from my research respondents – and both are located within the 'tribes' of the person-centred 'nation'.

Research method and sample

The operational method or 'tool' was an online, electronic, self-complete questionnaire – in essence a survey. This covered a wider, international population. The questionnaire was a structured self-report survey that uncovered respondents' attitudes and meanings which they felt were relevant for the practice of PCPC in today's world.

The population for the study was counsellors and psychotherapists within the World Association of the Person-Centred and Experiential community, covering Europe, the Americas, the Russian federation and the Far East and Japan. The sample was accessed through contacts within the World Association and its related partners and all the relevant person-centred journals via adverts, asking for participants. The project lent itself to an integrated frameworks methodology as it complemented the extant study and brought it to a wider population and sample, gaining more data, depth, strength and validity. The online electronic questionnaire was a simple way to gather data from across the world.

Inclusion and exclusion criteria

As with the extant study the inclusion criteria for participation were:

- qualified counsellor/psychotherapist to diploma level
- espousing person-/client-centred as main practising modality.

Exclusion criteria were student counsellors/psychotherapists; non person/client-centred practitioners and retired practitioners.

Summary of online results

There were 185 respondents to the survey, which is a 61.7% response rate; this is considered 'good'

There were 113 female respondents (61.1%) and 72 male (38.9%)

There were 4 black respondents (0.5%), 168 white (90.8%), 5 mixed race (2.7%) and 8 other (4.3%)

128 respondents (69.2%) were professionally registered or accredited practitioners

57 respondents (30.8%) were not registered or accredited

43 respondents were person-centred psychotherapists (23.3%)

27 respondents were client-centred psychotherapists (14.6%)

102 respondents were person-centred counsellors (55.1%)

13 respondents were client-centred counsellors (7.0%)

The respondents exhibited:

* High responses on Likert rating scale (8–10) for allowing the client to make sense of and explore their experience
* High responses on rating scale for empathy, 8–10
* High responses on rating scale for unconditional positive regard, 8–10
* High responses on rating scale for therapist congruence, 8–10
* High responses on rating scale for the essentiality of the actualizing tendency, 7–10
* High responses on rating scale for explicit acknowledging of the power dynamic, 8–10

Respondents understood 'person-centred' bi-dimensionally as both:

1. a form of therapy/counselling; and
2. a way of being and living in the world.

Within this bi-dimensional framework a number of perceptions and understandings emerge:

* PCPC anthropology: practitioners see the client *as a person: as an autonomous individual and as an interconnected person with responsibility to Others.*
* PCPC is perceived as a theory of motivation – the Actualizing Tendency.
* PCPC is perceived as a relational theory and is also an 'encounter based' therapy – the therapist brings themselves into 'play'.
* Understandings of how to practise PCPC therapy are unique to each practitioner, so each practitioner will interact with clients and 'do' therapy in their own way: in a real sense therapy is an 'art' rather than a 'technique' (Schmid, 1997).
* The therapist or counsellor is important: their presence, availability, skill, passion, beliefs combine to offer a unique 'person-centred' relationship with the client.

- PCPC is also a 'spiritually informed' therapeutic practice: it enables meaning making and moving with the client through their 'big questions'. It is thus phenomenological and existential, not just the 'I-Thou' of Buber; it is also the 'We' of Levinas (Schmid, 1997: 2).
- PCPC disavows *expertism*. The therapeutic encounter is seen as moment to moment, client led, focusing on the client, the therapist resisting the temptation to lead or diagnose, in keeping with Schmid's description of PCPC as an 'im-media-te encounter without the use of techniques including the client-centred ones' (Schmid, 1997: 2).
- Respondents describe an epistemology based on phenomenology and existentialism yet also the world as *constructed* and a person's truth as their own. The PCPC then sees the equation of therapeutic power as fundamental in and to the encounter.
- PCPC acknowledges the political dimensions of therapy and politics in general, and sees both therapist/counsellor and client as having a responsibility to each other, to the society in which they are located and to the wider world of which they are part.

Other related findings

- There is a distinct reporting of difference or differentiation between 'person-centred' and 'client-centred', based on how closely respondents to both terms held to early 'Rogerian' philosophy, content and style.
- Rogers figured prominently in representing the 'foundation' of respondents' practice rather than the academic, or other commentators, the influence of Rogers informing their practice and their personal engagement with his ideas/theory.
- Overall a general acceptance of the PCPC academic/other commentators and a positive link to the new additions to PCPC theory.
- The most significant 'tribe' was 'person-centred counselling'.
- A non-dilution of PCPC principles, ethics, anthropology and philosophy across the 'schools', yet an acceptance that PCPC is differently constituted and practised across the tribes.
- The 'Applications' of the person-centred approach in education/social work/conflict resolution/healthcare and group encounter work feature prominently.
- The 'person-centred approach' does not necessarily denote therapy; there is evidence of practitioner confusion with this term.
- There is definite evidence of the existence of 'schools' or 'tribes' of the PCPC 'family'.

As a method of therapy the person/client-centred approach is characterized by respondents in terms of:

- A clearly identified philosophical base: prominently phenomenology and existentialism

- Empathy, Unconditional Positive Regard for the client, and high levels of therapist Congruence
- Trust in the person of the client for direction and healing; use of therapy
- Principled non-directivity
- The centrality and influence of Carl Rogers, especially his 1959 paper
- Belief in the Actualizing Tendency as essential
- The influence of 'person-centred integration' and 'person-centred pluralistic' ways of working – based upon PCPC values and rooted in a person-centred anthropology: 'value based integrative practice' as suggested by Cooper *et al.* (2013: 5) and the importance of knowing the difference in their practice between 'an incoherent mash up' and a 'potentially creative synergy'!
- PCPC practice actively choosing to use and be influenced by other theories, for example: dream work, attachment theory and other psychoanalytic theories – object relations, mindfulness and positive psychology, two chair, expressive techniques, cognitive and behavioural elements, bodywork, hypnosis, relaxation techniques

As a 'way of being' and living, the person-centred approach is characterized by:

- Embodying and integrating PCPC values in one's life
- Living ethically and taking anti-oppressive stances; the influence of eco-psychology and ecological politics
- Acknowledgement of the political dimension to the PCPC and to life
- Power 'with' (as opposed to 'over') the client/people; actively seeking to equalize the power dynamic both within the therapy room and without, in the world

Other themes that emerged included:

- Therapist trust in client process and client authority, based on principle not beneficence
- The importance of the values held by the therapist
- An emphasis on principled non-directivity, as opposed to instrumental non-directivity
- The centrality of the actualizing tendency – a key link to Humanistic Psychology, psychotherapy and counselling (HPPC)
- Carl Rogers' Core Conditions (1957a and 1959) as both 'necessary and sufficient' for facilitating client change
- Holism
- Practitioners use a broad range of skills and involve other theories in their practice (see above)

PCPC developments

Respondents stated that they were interested and engaged with the developments within PCPC over the last twenty-five years and are knowledgeable about them:

Pre therapy, configurations of self, relational theory, developments in psycho-pathology – severe and enduring distress, post trauma, hearing voices and psychotic process, counselling for depression, counselling in schools, to name some of the developments.

How does this research inform HP?

What does Humanistic Psychotherapy look like? What is our face? Cain, Keenan and Rubin (2016: 4–5) identify ten core variables and emphases:

> An optimistic view of clients as resourceful and inclined to develop their potential; the quality of the therapeutic relationship is important to create an optimal relationship for clients; empathy is the core role of the therapist; a phenomenological emphasis on the client's subjective world; a strong emphasis on the role of emotion in the client's world; a focus on the self and self concept of the client; meaning is constructed through one's culture, values, personal history, a view that people are essentially free to choose the manner and course of their lives; all people confront the existential givens of life, death, freedom, choice, responsibility, facing meaninglessness, etc.; a holistic view as people as unique; beings-in-the-world.

My research asks practitioners about these aspects and attempts to get a picture of what actually is 'out there' how the theory is adhered to, believed in and utilized. It outlines the views of practitioners internally and examines the views of these practitioners to see if they match up internally to what the academics and comment-ators outlined – there is a high level of consistency and consonance: PCPC does indeed have a 'face'. The research established the bases of practice within a current sample in a number of dimensions, including psychology, anthropology, ethics, epistemology and philosophy.

Cain *et al.*'s core variables stretch across the board of the HPPC. However, Dryden (2013: 119–124) urges HP to focus on agreeing internal consistency/broad beliefs by focusing on four 'tasks':

1.   carry out an inventory of strengths and weaknesses
2.   publish up-to-date texts on HP
3.   pluralism: to align or not?
4.   engaging with reality.

Dryden (2013: 120) citing Totton (2010), perceives the strengths of HP as:

• a focus on growth
• strong on empowerment
• contactful and nurturing relationships

- non-medicalizing stance
- positive response to emotions (Cooper & Joseph, 2016)
- acknowledging the spiritual dimension
- HP offers a coherent social critique
- HP favours an experiential paradigm of practice and research

These mirror findings in my research project. It is the underlying values and internal unity of the PCPC approach that gives it depth and strength in its diversity – together we are stronger. These can be utilized as a new basis for exploration, dialogue and research.

However there are negatives, or 'weaknesses' according to Dryden and Totton, for example, the Humanistic field:

- can still exhibit a 'Pollyanna' view of human nature
- tends to deny pathology
- can miss transferential issues
- retains a negative attitude to rationality and theory
- is prone to impulsiveness and 'mysticism'.

This is where the work lies. These challenges mirror the criticisms levelled at PCPC, yet as I have outlined, within PCPC both nationally and internationally we have made tremendous progress on praxis, theory and research. The theory is evolving and PCPC and its tribes are bringing Rogers into a new century. Is HP out of the mainstream in terms of dialogue, research and advancement? No. PCPC has given HP a framework to use as a means of evolving and growing.

Research

There is, however, compelling evidence that HP has a robust research tradition, and that humanistic practice built on empathy, acceptance, collaboration and a genuine therapeutic relationship 'support[s] the humanistic assumption that clients are the principle drivers of therapeutic change' (Cooper, 2008: 162). Thus, 'Meta-analyses of humanistic therapies, as a whole, support the hypotheses that they are efficacious and effective forms of therapy, with a large average pre-post effect size of 0.99, reducing down to 0.89 when compared against wait-list or no-therapy controls' (Elliott *et al.*, 2004; cited in Cooper, 2008: 162). Stiles *et al.* (1986, 2006, 2008) have also conducted research supportive of PCPC–HP therapies.

Lambert, Fidalgo and Greaves (2016) explain that there has been a 'renaissance' in HP research, and, using Elliott *et al.*'s (2013) analysis, conclude:

1. It is inappropriate for academicians and policy makers to consider HP treatments as ineffective or inferior.
2. Gains by clients in HP therapies are similar in effectiveness to those of clients participating in other treatments.

3. These gains, achieved in twenty or fewer sessions, are maintained after termination.
4. Studies that control for the passage of time (e.g., using waiting list controls) have also shown large to moderate treatment effects favouring humanistic therapies.

(2016: 59–60)

Lambert *et al.* also found 'substantial evidence for the correlation between therapist attitudes and the outcomes of Humanistic Psychotherapy, *including reliable estimates of the actual strength of these correlations*' (2016: 74). HPPC, therefore, deserves recognition in funding, research and location within the field of treatment offered to potential clients. Finally, Norcross and Wampold (2011) give HP some suggestions as to the gaps in research that it can tackle.

What makes HP 'appealing'?

It is time to build on our strengths. By 'engaging with reality' Dryden says HP needs to engage in the current programmes or risk exclusion entirely. Dryden might have a point in that it is no longer good enough to simply criticize CBT without showing how 'we' are presenting our own case. Engaging other modalities in 'a meaningful dialogue' is required. The future of HP is then in our own hands!

The pluralism conundrum

Work has already been undertaken, then, to attempt to explain 'integration' Norcross and Goldfried (2005) and 'pluralism' Cooper and McLeod (2011) and to incorporate this in the theory and in the practice of HP. Dryden asks 'Do we go with pluralism'? Integration and pluralism are now accepted features within HP (Cain *et al.*, 2016). As noted in my research findings within PCPC, integration and pluralism are constructed and moulded into the therapeutic encounter by practitioners adhering to the value base of the therapy and then using them in ways that are consistent and coherent with PCPC values *and* the therapy's anthropology, its ethical stance, its philosophical roots, its psychology and its epistemology. If HP is to move forward, the debate might need to take place about how coherent and consistent practitioners are with its core values, anthropology and epistemology: maybe a British Handbook of HP is needed; filled with new theory, new research, new issues for debate.

Toward a 'consensual' model of humanistic practice

Dryden feels that HP needs to publish more up-to-date texts, thus working toward an updated model, based on a consensus within the HP family. This would be an exciting development. Sanders has attempted this with his 'Tribes' books within PCPC (2004, 2012). Cooper and Joseph (2016) outline a list of suggestions regarding how humanistic practitioners can work and give their practice substance by linking up with other psychological theories and being informed by them, which is already happening within the HP community.

Conclusion

Wampold (2011) described 14 qualities of effective therapists: a perusal of which will indicate what PCPC and HP do well, i.e. form warm and effective relationships that are empirically proven to be effective with a range of clients:

1. Effective therapists have a sophisticated set of interpersonal skills, including:

    a. Verbal fluency
    b. Interpersonal perception
    c. Affective modulation and expressiveness
    d. Warmth and acceptance
    e. Empathy
    f. Focus on other

2. Clients of effective therapists feel understood, trust the therapist, and believe the therapist can help them.
3. Effective therapists are able to form a working alliance with a broad range of clients.
4. Effective therapists provide an acceptable and adaptive explanation for the client's distress.
5. The effective therapist provides a treatment plan that is consistent with the explanation provided to the client.
6. The effective therapist is influential, persuasive, and convincing.
7. The effective therapist continually monitors client progress in an authentic way.
8. The effective therapist is flexible and will adjust therapy if resistance to the treatment is apparent or the client is not making adequate progress.
9. The effective therapist does not avoid difficult material in therapy and uses such difficulties therapeutically.
10. The effective therapist communicates hope and optimism. This communication is relatively easy for motivated clients who are making adequate therapeutic progress.
11. Effective therapists are aware of the client's characteristics and context.
12. The effective therapist is aware of his or her own psychological process and does not inject his or her own material into the therapy process unless such actions are deliberate and therapeutic.
13. The effective therapist is aware of the best research evidence related to the particular client, in terms of treatment, problems, social context, and so forth.
14. The effective therapist seeks to continually improve.

In my research I have found that PCPC practitioners do have an integrated practice based on holding the central attitudes embodied in the core conditions, do put the client first ('the centrality of the client'), and do relate to the client as a 'person', using non-medicalizing and non-pathologizing ways of working, based on encounter philosophy. On that foundation, it is time now to find some answers to

Dryden and Totton's observations and challenges, and to develop, evolve and move forward.

Acknowledgements

I would like to acknowledge the support of the editors and also Derek Lawton in writing this chapter – and to thank him for his kindness, thoughtfulness and friendship. This chapter is for Francizka.

Seamus Nash

Professional Doctorate, University of Huddersfield;
Principal Supervisor: Dr Rob Burton, International Director, School of Human and Health Sciences, University of Huddersfield;
Supervisor: Dr Helen Gavin, Director of Graduate Education, University of Huddersfield.

References

APA (American Psychiatric Association) (2013). *Diagnostic and Statistical Manual of Mental Disorders – DSM-5,* Washington, DC: American Psychiatric Association.

Barrett-Lennard, G.T. (1998). *Carl Rogers' Helping System: Journey and Substance,* London: Sage.

Cain, D., Keenan, K. & Rubin, S. (2016). *Humanistic Psychotherapies: Handbook of Research and Practice,* Washington, DC: American Psychological Association.

Cooper, M. (2008). *Essential Research Findings in Counselling and Psychotherapy,* London: Sage.

Cooper, M. & Joseph, S. (2016). 'Psychological foundations for Humanistic psychotherapeutic practice'. In D. Cain, K. Keenan & S. Rubin (eds) *Humanistic Psychotherapies: Handbook of Research and Practice* (pp. 11–46), Washington, DC: American Psychological Association.

Cooper, M. & McLeod, J. (2011). *Pluralistic Counselling and Psychotherapy,* London: Sage.

Cooper, M., Watson, J.C. & Holldampf, D. (2010a). 'Key priorities for research in the Person-Centred and experiential field: If not now, when?' In M. Cooper, J.C. Watson & D. Holldampf (eds) *Person-Centred and Experiential Therapies Work: A Review of the Research on Counselling, Psychotherapy and Related Practices* (pp. 240–251), Ross-on-Wye: PCCS Books.

Cooper, M., Watson, J.C. & Holldampf, D. (eds) (2010b). *Person-Centred and Experiential Therapies Work: A Review of the Research on Counselling, Psychotherapy and Related Practices,* Ross-on-Wye: PCCS Books.

Cooper, M., O'Hara, M., Schmid, P.F. & Bohart, A. (eds) (2013). *The Handbook of Person-Centred Psychotherapy and Counselling* (second edition), Basingstoke: Palgrave MacMillan.

Dryden, W. (2013). 'Humanistic Psychology: Possible ways forward'. In R. House, D. Kalisch & J. Maidman (eds) *The Future of Humanistic Psychology* (pp. 119–124), Ross-on-Wye: PCCS Books.

Elliott, R., Greenberg, L.S., Watson, J., Timulak, L. & Freire, E. (2013). 'Research on humanistic-experiential psychotherapies'. In M.J. Lambert (ed.) Bergin and Garfield's *Handbook of Psychotherapy and Behaviour Change* (sixth edition; pp. 495–537), Hoboken, NJ: Wiley.

Fonagy, P. (ed.) (2010). *Skills for Health: National Occupational Standards for Psychological Therapies*, London: Department of Health.

Goldstein, K. (1939). *The Organism*, New York: Harcourt Brace Jovanovich.

Greenberg, L.S. & Pinsof, W.M. (eds) (1986). *The Psychotherapeutic Process: A Research Handbook*, New York: Guildford Press.

Jahoda, M. (1950). 'Toward a sociology of mental health'. In M.J.E. Senn (ed.) *Symposium on the Healthy Personality: Supplement II. Problem of Infancy and Childhood* (pp. 211–230), New York: Joseph Marcy Foundation.

Joseph, S. & Worsley, R. (eds) (2005). *Person-Centred Psychopathology: A Positive Psychology of Mental Health*. Ross-on-Wye: PCCS Books.

Kirschenbaum, H. (2007). *The Life and Work of Carl Rogers*, Ross-on-Wye: PCCS Books.

Klein, M.H., Mathieu, P.L., Gendlin, E.T. & Kiesler, D.J. (1969). *The Experiencing Scale: A Research and Training Manual Volume 1* (pp. 56–63), Wisconsin Psychiatric Institute.

Lambert, M.J., Fidalgo, L.G. & Greaves, M.R. (2016). 'Effective Humanistic Psychotherapy processes and their outcomes'. In D. Cain, K. Keenan & S. Rubin (eds) (2016). *Humanistic Psychotherapies: Handbook of Research and Practice*, Washington, DC: American Psychological Association.

Lawton, D. (1990). Unpublished paper.

Lietaer, G. (2002). 'The client-centred/experiential paradigm in psychotherapy: Development and identity'. In J.C. Watson, R.N. Goldman & M. Warner (eds) *Client-Centred and Experiential Psychotherapy in the 21st Century: Advances in Theory, Research and Practice* (pp. 1–15), Ross-on-Wye: PCCS Books.

Maslow, A. (1956). 'Self-actualizing people: A study of psychological health', in C.E. Moustakas (ed.) *The Self: Exploration in Personal Growth* (pp. 160–194), New York: Harper & Row.

Maslow, A (1970). *Motivation and Personality*, New York: Harper & Row.

Meador, B.D. & Rogers, C. (1973). 'Client-Centered Therapy'. In R. Corsini (ed.) *Current Psychotherapies* (pp. 119–165), Itasca, IL: F.G. Peacock.

Nash, S. (2006a). 'What does it mean to be person-centred? Researching practitioners' understandings', *Self & Society, 34* (3): 23–31.

Nash, S. (2006b). 'Is there a political imperative inherent within the person-centred approach?' In G. Proctor, M. Cooper, P. Sanders & B. Malcolm (eds) *Politizing The Person-Centred Approach* (pp. 29–36), Ross-on-Wye: PCCS Books.

Norcross, J.C. & Goldfried, M.R. (eds) (2005). *Handbook of Psychotherapy Integration* (second edition), Oxford: Oxford University Press.

Norcross, J.C. & Wampold, B. (2011). 'Evidence based therapy relationships: Research conclusions and clinical practices', *Psychotherapy, 48* (1): 98–102.

Patterson, C.H. (1985). *The Therapeutic Relationship: Foundations for an Eclectic Psychotherapy*, Northvale, NJ/Monterey, CA: Brooks/Cole.

Patterson, C.H. & Hidore, S. (1997). *Successful Psychotherapy: A Caring, Loving Relationship*, Northvale, NJ: Jason Aronson.

Rogers, C.R. (1951). *Client-Centred Therapy*, London: Constable.

Rogers, C.R. (1957a). 'The necessary and sufficient conditions of therapeutic personality change', *Journal of Consulting Psychology, 21*: 95–103.

Rogers, C.R. (1957b). 'A note on the nature of man', *Journal of Counselling Psychology, 4* (5): 199–203.

Rogers, C.R. (1957c). 'A therapist's view of the good life', *The Humanist, 17* (5): 291–300.

Rogers, C.R. (1959). 'A theory of therapy, personality and interpersonal relationships, as developed in the client-centered framework'. In S. Koch (ed.) *Psychology: A Study of a Science, Vol. 3: Formulations of the Person and the Social Context* (pp. 184–256), New York: McGraw-Hill.

Rogers, C.R. (1961) 'A process conception of psychotherapy', in *On Becoming a Person*, London: Constable.

Rogers, C.R. (1963). 'The concept of the fully functioning person', *Psychotherapy: Theory, Research and Practice, 1* (1): 17–26.

Rogers, C.R. (1980). *A Way of Being*, Boston, MA: Houghton Mifflin.

Sanders, P. (2000). 'Mapping person-centred approaches to counselling and psychotherapy', in *Person-Centred Practice, 8* (2) 62–74. PCCS Books.

Sanders, P. (ed.) (2004). *The Tribes of the Person-Centred Nation: An Introduction to the Schools of Therapy Associated with the Person-Centred Approach*, Ross-on-Wye: PCCS Books.

Sanders, P. (ed.) (2012). *The Tribes of the Person-Centred Nation: An Introduction to the Schools of Therapy Associated with the Person-Centred Approach*, Ross-on-Wye: PCCS Books.

Sanders, P. (2013). *Person Centred Theory and Practice in the 21st Century*, Ross-on-Wye: PCCS Books.

Schmid, P. (1997). 'Person Centred Therapy: State of the Art'. Invited plenary address, IVth ICCCEP, Lisbon (manuscript).

Schmid, P. (1998). 'On becoming a person-centred approach: A person-centred understanding of the person'. In B. Thorne & E. Lambers (eds) *Person-Centred Therapy: A European Perspective* (pp. 38–52). London: Sage.

Schmid, P. (2003). 'The characteristics of a person-centred approach to therapy and counselling: Criteria for identity and coherence', *Person-Centred and Experiential Psychotherapies, 2* (2), 104–120.

Schmid, P. (2012). 'Psychotherapy is political or it is not psychotherapy: The person-centred approach as an essentially political venture', *Person-Centred and Experiential Psychotherapies, 11* (2); 95–108, London: Routledge.

Shaffer, J.B.P. (1978). *Humanistic Psychology*, Englewood Cliffs, NJ: Prentice-Hall.

Skinner, B.F. (1948). *Walden Two*, New York: Macmillan.

Stiles, W.B., Shapiro, D.A. & Elliott, R. (1986). 'Are all psychotherapies equivalent?', *American Psychologist, 41*: 165–180.

Stiles, W.B., Barkham, M., Mellor-Clark, J. & Connell, J. (2008). 'Effectiveness of cognitive-behavioural, person-centred and psychodynamic therapies as practiced in UK primary-care routine practice: Replication in a larger sample', *Psychological Medicine, 38* (5): 677–688.

Stiles, W.B., Barkham, M., Twigg, E., Mellor-Clark, J. & Cooper, M. (2006). 'Effectiveness of cognitive-behavioural, person-centred and psychodynamic therapies as practiced in UK National Health Service settings', *Psychological Medicine, 36* (4): 555–566.

Totton, N. (2010). *The Problem with the Humanistic Therapies*, London: Karnac Books.

UKCP (2010). *Professional Occupational Standards: For Psychotherapists and Psychotherapeutic Counsellors*, London: United Kingdom Council for Psychotherapy.

Wampold, B.E. (2011). *Qualities and Actions of Effective Therapists*, United States: APA.

Wilkins, P. (2003). *Person-Centred Therapy in Focus*, London: Sage.

Wilkins, P. (2011). *Person-Centred Therapy: 100 Key Points*, London: Routledge.

PART II

Socio-political-cultural perspectives

EDITORS' INTRODUCTION TO PART II

Richard House, David Kalisch and Jennifer Maidman

From its very outset, Humanistic Psychology has engaged fulsomely and fearlessly with the social, cultural and political, in a way that much of mainstream 'scientific', positivistic psychology has sought to avoid. This is a proud history that owes a great debt to those over many decades who have not shied away from asking the big questions, challenging concentrations and abuses of power in all its dimensions, and above all trying to show how a deeply human psychology can and must move beyond narrowly circumscribed academic preoccupations that have little if any relevance to the functioning of the wider society and its constituent structures. In Part II we therefore showcase some of Humanistic Psychology's most eminent and incisive commentators on 'matters societal', illustrating what an enormous contribution leading-edge humanistic thinking and praxis can make in our troubled world.

In Chapter 5, one of Humanistic Psychology's most celebrated elders, Maureen O'Hara, takes us on an exciting journey into 'Humanistic cultural praxis for an emerging world', outlining how Humanistic Psychology might serve as a praxis such that a new consciousness might emerge, better adapted to the challenges of turbulent times. Post-positive science helped spawn a new view of personhood that has been core to Humanistic Psychology, and O'Hara (a previous collaborator of Carl Rogers) highlights how Rogers carefully articulated the qualities of 'persons of tomorrow'. O'Hara goes on to discuss and give examples of how contemporary Humanistic Psychology, incorporating concepts of autopoesis and the self-organizing capacities of living systems, might help us face the existential threats to human survival referred to by the Club of Rome.

In Chapter 6, 'The development community and its activist psychology', another of our prominent US writers, Lois Holzman, presents a case study of a US-based development community practising a unique humanistic-critical synthesis known as 'The psychology of becoming/social therapeutics'. Its central focus is that of re-initiating the human capacity to collectively transform and continuously reshape the unity that is *us-and-our environment*. The recognition that the human capacity *to perform* is the source of development for persons, communities and our species lies at the heart of this exciting activist work, creating a different kind of tool to break through powerful impediments to social development and social activism.

In Chapter 7, prominent US-based therapist and academic James T. Hansen then looks at the future of *humanism*, and ways in which the values and impulses we associate with Humanistic Psychology can be encouraged and cultivated in mainstream 'mental health' culture. For Hansen, certain orientations to helping can be categorized as humanities approaches because their focus is on human meaning systems. The dominant medical model, in contrast, purposefully eschews human meaning systems. He sees it as unfortunate that humanities approaches are generally disconnected from each other, thus weakening their ability to impact mental health culture. Humanism can have a bright future if it is conjoined with other humanities-based orientations, creating a powerful, unified humanities response to the technical approaches that currently dominate the helping professions.

In the penultimate chapter in Part II, psycho-social analyst and intrepid climate campaigner David Wasdell writes on 'Climate dynamics: a study in psycho-social analysis'. Drawing strongly on the much-neglected psychodynamics of social systems, Wasdell traces the origins of the paradigm change in applied psycho-analysis that emerged in the late 1970s, combining the prenatal world of foetal formation with the post-natal field of infant development. Primitive defences against anxiety are argued to be learned rather than innate, and Wasdell draws major implications for our understanding of the unconscious response to climate change. Recognition is needed that the psychotic level of current social anxiety does not emanate from future environmental disruption, but from the repressed boundary of the world of uterine regression. It follows that collective recovery from foetal phantasy is a prerequisite for the task of realistic problem-solving for a rapidly changing planet.

Finally in Part II, British psychohistorian Nick Duffell writes in Chapter 9 on 'Steps to a politics of heart'. Acknowledging that modern politics has taken a marked turn for the worse, Duffell argues that it is time for somatic psychological knowledge to leave the consulting room and support political maturity for a better world. As a starting-point for such a New Politics, if we are willing to hear, the human heart offers us lessons in wisdom, empathy, connection and feedback. For Duffell, the heart's self-regulatory function models the needed regulatory governance for our globalized world, within joined-up, democratically enforced international cooperation.

Part II offers just a comparatively small selection from the vast cornucopia of possibilities that innovative humanistic thinking can bring to modern society, and its many vicissitudes and struggles. One is reminded of the statement of that great humanitarian scientist, Albert Einstein, who famously maintained that 'We can't solve problems by using the same kind of thinking we used when we created them'. Humanistic Psychology at its best, along with its rich array of critical thinkers as represented here, offers precisely the kind of innovative, 'out-of-box' insight and indications for praxis that a world paralysed by business-as-usual thinking so desperately needs.

5

HUMANISTIC CULTURAL PRAXIS FOR AN EMERGING WORLD

Maureen O'Hara

> Humanity is cascading through a self-produced rupture in its history into an epoch of anthropo-transmutation . . . human actions changing basic features of human existence and its nature.
>
> *(Dror, 2015)*

> [T]he salvation of this human world lies nowhere else than in the human heart, in the human power to reflect, in human humbleness and in human responsibility.
>
> *(Havel, 1990)*

Challenging the limits

Humanistic Psychology is a child of cultural turmoil. Movements for civil rights, women's rights, anti-war, student rebellions, psychedelic drugs, new music, radical politics, critical intellectual movements and transgressive arts were pervasive enough in the 1960s to be considered a counter-culture (Roszak, 1969). Out of that turmoil, and responsible for some of it, came a worldview that put freedom and dignity of persons at its centre and sought methods of consciousness practice to expanded human potential. I use the term 'Humanistic Psychology' here as an umbrella for a loosely associated ecology of psychological theory and practices of change, that became known as the 'Third Force' (and Fourth Force). The participants did not always agree even on central points such as the existence of evil, science and religion, the use of psychedelic drugs or the relative virtues of particular economic systems; but what they did have in common from the beginning was the belief that the modernist techno-industrial paradigm had run its course and that a new mythos to guide human action was needed. In the light of two disastrous world wars and the invention of nuclear weapons, despite the wonders that modern civilization brought, the technocratic worldview had itself become a source of darkness.

In their diverse ways, humanistic psychologists sought a new cosmology for understanding ourselves and our world that broke with the limited conceptions of humanness inherited from the Enlightenment and earlier. Much influenced by ideas from Asian philosophy and a new physics, which replaced the atomistic Newtonian view with a view of reality as energy and flow, this new paradigm connected us to the wider cosmic story and widened our sense of what we might possibly become. So I ask forbearance, then, on lumping together as 'humanistic' approaches that, though they have significant differences, all seek to enhance our future as persons, to build humane societies and safeguard our wondrous planet without which the rest is moot.

Back to the future

In 1969 the American humanistic psychologist Carl Rogers gave a commencement address to Sonoma State University graduates in which he described his view of what he called 'Persons of Tomorrow for a World of Tomorrow' (Rogers, 1980). He and other humanistic colleagues, including Abraham Maslow, Rollo May, Allan Watts, Gregory Bateson, John Rowen, Erich Fromm, Paul Goodman, Virginia Satir and many psychological thinkers of the day, noted a 'paradigmatic shift' under way and 'new developments that alter our whole conception of the potentialities of the individual; that change our perception of "reality"; that change our ways of being and behaving; that alter our belief systems' (p. 348). The origin of the discipline was to try to make sense of what was happening and to offer a praxis for psychological emancipation. Humanistic Psychology founders saw themselves as cultural leaders at the service of the entire society struggling to cast off antiquated frames of thought and set people free from oppressive and dehumanizing social structures to find the possibilities and pathways to a new and more human world. Though some humanistic and New Age writers were high on inspirational speculation (among other things) and light on empirical evidence, there was a general consensus among humanistic thinkers at the time that a counter-cultural tsunami was under way that potentially represented a leap in consciousness for humanity.

Rogers did have evidence. He and his colleagues were conducting encounter groups across the world in troubled areas such as South Africa and Northern Ireland, on campuses, in retreat centres and in urban areas of America where diverse groups were gathering to address the pain and possibilities of their lives. From these experiences Rogers believed he was witnessing the emergence of a new kind of person – 'persons of tomorrow' (Rogers, 1980). Describing the personal qualities of these people, Rogers pointed to their openness to inner subjective experience and to the outer world; their desire for authenticity, their rejection of phoniness, hypocrisy and manipulation; their scepticism about the limits of science and technology; their desire for wholeness – integrating intellect, feelings and the body; their high priority on intimacy; their commitment to fairness; their view of life as a process; their genuine caring attitude but suspicion of professional helpers; their closeness to nature and their ecologically mindedness; their aversion to large bureaucratic institutions; their search for empowerment and justice; their self-directedness; their moral compass attuned to the welfare of others; their anti-materialist values and their openness to spirituality.

Rogers believed that their capacity to both express their own unique humanness and their alignment to a greater society represented a new step in psycho-social evolution – a step that went beyond individualism and embraced a new view of persons who were whole unto themselves, but were at the same time a conscious part of relationships and communities. Similar profiles of an emerging eupsychian consciousness were described by Maslow (1971) and Roszak (1969) among others. At the same time a sharp distinction was being made in the broader field of psychology in ideas about personhood. On one side were those who agreed with Skinner that 'freedom and dignity' were romantic fantasies and argued that human behaviour, like that of other animals, could be controlled through judicial application of rewards and punishment, and those who agreed with the humanists that human beings are born with an inherent desire for dignity and freedom, to connect, grow, make meaning and choose. These freedoms were the sine qua non of personhood.

The empire strikes back

While counter-culturals were on the side of beings-for-themselves, established institutions generally sided with Skinner. They wanted people who would be at home in the hierarchical bureaucracies of the industrial society. By the 1980s, a powerful backlash against the counter-culturals was taking shape especially but not exclusively from the political and religious right; and critics were mobilizing against the values of the human potential movement and accusing the 'me generation' of narcissism, moral relativism, sexual decadence – in short, a threat to established society.

There was also opposition from professional colleagues in mainstream psychology. There the critique was of questionable clinical practice, intellectual naivety and sloppy science. Clinical Psychology took a sharp turn in a biomedical direction with the publication of the DSM III, which changed the focus of diagnosis from psycho-social to individual pathology. Cognitivism replaced humanism and computers became the dominant metaphor for 'mind'.

In the USA, increasingly restrictive mental health licensing laws placed ideological and epistemological barriers to graduates of humanistic graduate programmes – especially those training adult learners. As transformative innovators left mainstream psychology departments to seek more space for intellectual autonomy, innovation and creativity, positivist science filled the space reasserting its dominant position with a vengeance. The humanities were banished from psychology curricula, and licensing exams were focused on biological and behavioural sciences. Politically the rise of neoliberal economic theory shifted the conversation away from an emphasis on social values and toward individualism as the then British Prime Minister Mrs Thatcher so famously declared, 'There is no such thing as society'. Love, fellow feeling and authenticity had no place in the Reagan–Thatcher world.

Humanistic Psychology did not help itself, as its research agenda dwindled and emphasis on the eupsychian devolved into an inward-looking focus on self, demonization of academia, especially positivist science (Grogan, 2013) and an acritical acceptance of pseudoscience and New Age myths, however flimsy the evidence (O'Hara, 1988). What had been a critical interdisciplinary psycho-social movement embracing philosophy, post-modern human sciences and the humanities gradually slid back into the narrow therapeutic frame which, once again, came to be dominated by medical models – this time neurobiological and cognitivist in nature (Grogan, 2013). Instead of an interdisciplinary focus on enabling human development, research became focused on demonstrating that humanistic psychotherapy was every bit as effective as more technical approaches and getting a seat at the medical funding table.

Nevertheless grounded firmly in their actual concrete experiences working with people around the world, and seeing for themselves their yearning for freedom and emancipation, and experiencing first hand their capacity for transformative action, Carl Rogers and his colleagues remained convinced that although the rising opposition to counter-cultural values might conceivably overcome them, if enough people came to share the values of the persons of tomorrow, they could become a transformative cultural force.

Global existential crisis

The call for new modes of consciousness did not start with Humanistic Psychology. It had been a perennial theme in twentieth-century thought. In 1946, reeling from the destruction caused by the first nuclear bombs Albert Einstein wrote, 'Our situation is not comparable to anything in the past. It is impossible, therefore, to apply methods and measures which at an earlier age might have been sufficient. We must revolutionize our thinking, revolutionize our actions' (Einstein, 1948/2003: 52). Forty years later, addressing a joint session of the US Congress, Vaclav Havel said that without a global revolution in the sphere of human consciousness, nothing will change for the better in the sphere of our Being as humans, and the catastrophe toward which this world is headed, whether it be ecological, social, demographic or a general breakdown of civilization, will be unavoidable (Havel, 1990).

Einstein and Havel were surely correct, but I suggest that, situated within the Western twentieth-century framework as they were, they underestimated the psychological work involved in such a revolution, and the inevitable resistance. A 'revolution' means that we must break with deep conceptual patterns from the past that give us our sense of reality and identity. We must let go of ways of thinking and acting that created the mess in which we now find ourselves. At the same time new modes of thinking and action more adequate to lives in the new circumstances of the twenty-first century must become our focus. To evolve new minds we must take a leap into novel emotional, conceptual and institutional spaces and develop *new minds for new times*. And we must do all this within an existing culture that has different ideas, and while keeping the world from the catastrophe Havel and many other futures thinkers warn of.

What makes changing minds on a cultural scale especially challenging is that consciousness and culture are not separable – they are two faces of the same phenomenon. Consciousness creates distinct cultures, and distinct cultures create distinct consciousness. The persons we become – our mentality, mind, psychology, mindset and behaviour – are emergent products of the relationship between biological givens and specific cultural experiential contexts. A wide range of psychological processes such as identity, sense of self, attention, perception, motivation, cognitive style, sense of opportunity, meaning-making, sense of transcendent realities, and even brain organization are moulded through experience within particular cultural contexts (Nisbett, 2003; O'Hara & Lyon, 2014; Shweder, 1991; Sundararajan, 2015). So when cultures are in turmoil, we can expect individual psychological turmoil too.

In stable times, most of us are not ordinarily aware of the way in which our sense of reality is given by our particular culture. The taken-for-granted view is that our way is 'the' way – others are deviations. But when familiar life patterns are upended and master narratives lose their psychological impact or shared assumptions no longer fit current conditions, as is the case today, cognitive dissonance increases, cultural anxiety rises and social harmony breaks down. It becomes more thinkable to people who do not like the status quo that things could be different, and dissident views from the margins gain support. As confusion intensifies, it becomes harder to agree, to make decisions, make sense of events or predict the future, so the capacity to plan and take wise action falters. Though a certain amount of cultural churn is necessary to promote cultural dynamism and creativity, if things become too incoherent, people become scared, alienated and disaffected, and health declines, especially mental health (Erikkson & Lindström, 2014). Collective and personal anxiety can become so great that it overwhelms both individual and existing institutional capacities, leading to repression, collapse or transformation (Diamond, 2005; Kauffman, 1992; Leicester, 2007; Leicester & O'Hara, 2009; O'Hara & Leicester, 2012; Pauchant, 1994; Tarnas, 1991; Tuchman, 1978).

In a real sense we are all immigrants – adrift in a world we do not understand and we cannot control, using strategies that have served us well in the past but which, in the new global contexts, are fast losing their effectiveness. In Zygmunt Bauman's words, we are in a state of 'liquid modernity', which he describes as a 'state of constantly changing circumstances and shifting priorities that make it difficult for individuals to have the time or frames of reference to organize their lives under conditions of extreme ambiguity' (Bauman, 2010). This is a global phenomenon.

The contemporary refugee crisis in Syria and Europe bears all the hallmarks of a cultural crisis wherein existing individual and collective capacities in both a war-torn Syria and an unprepared European Union have been swamped by a cascade of acute needs with which neither existing institutions nor ways of thinking were developed to cope. After women were assaulted by Muslim immigrants on New Year's Eve 2016 in Cologne, for instance, Czech leader Milos Zerman blamed cultural differences, and proposed an end to immigration from non-European (meaning non-Christian) societies. Nationalist and neo-fascist movements are on the rise worldwide, their rhetoric mostly aimed at the 'others' – poor people, minorities, immigrants and refugees. Fault-lines are widening, and factions are becoming more hostile within previously stable societies as culture wars threaten to boil over.

In the USA, denial of the continued existence of racism and the divisiveness of the 2016 election rhetoric fan the flames of xenophobia. The US Southern Poverty Law Center reports that the number of hate groups who attack racial, ethnic, religious and sexual minorities in the USA increased dramatically during the Obama presidency. Research on core values, preferred life styles and political narratives within the American 2016 electorate shows marked incoherence and fragmentation into alien tribes, with little common ground, and who are increasingly polarized and antagonistic (Taylor, 2016). The mental health costs of so much turbulence and uncertainty are at unprecedented levels, as the world suffers a global pandemic of mental distress (Hämäläinen, 2014; O'Hara & Lyon, 2012).

Although attention is (belatedly) being given to the environmental, political and economic consequences of this historical disruption, the implications of the equally momentous psychological ruptures under way are still not fully recognized, and leaders are still trying to solve twenty-first-century challenges with mentalities from an earlier age that are inadequate to the complexity we now face. Most of the solutions being offered to an unprepared society aim to address symptoms, but ignore the deeper cultural existential crisis. This leaves us with the troubling paradox that at a time in our history when humanity needs to make collective decisions to tackle problems that pose catastrophic risks, the pervasive incoherence and cognitive overload threaten to interfere with our collective mental fitness, and plausibly leave inhabitants of twenty-first-century societies less adaptive, less resilient and less creative than our ancestors.

Denial, collapse or transformation?

When our world liquefies we understandably reach for stability – even the false stability of denial and defensiveness. When experts, leaders, policy-makers and pundits – also caught up in the same uncertainties – seek solutions, it is understandable that they stay within the modernist frameworks they know best. They are as anxious as the rest of us. Faced with unfathomable complexity, people want simple answers, clear explanations and reassurance. Addressing the hugely complex public mental health issues, for instance, where personal history, cultural expectations, economic and political ideologies, class, gender, ethnicity, religion, values and scientific paradigms interact in multiply determined ways, it is understandable that leaders in technocratic societies want to simplify and look for treatment protocols that can be standardized and 'scaled'. So they fall back on abstractions such as well-being indices, happiness science, Cognitive Behaviour Therapy (CBT) and increasingly, behavioural economics tricks such as 'nudges' from marketing and smart phone apps. Although promising greater efficiency, these approaches are mostly pseudo-solutions, firmly embedded within the very techno-industrial frame of mind that got us here in the first place.

Yet if denial, defence and collapse were the only responses human beings had to crises we would probably all be living in small hunter-gatherer bands at the mercy of environmental circumstances. The history of human consciousness suggests that there is another equally human response – a creative response.

It's the paradigm

Most comparisons of the relative effectiveness of various forms of psychotherapy and counselling skip over deeper paradigmatic distinctions about the kind of reality they describe. Key to understanding Humanistic Psychology's theories and practice is the core assumption, based on observations of living beings, that despite the second law of thermodynamics which predicts that systems decay from higher orders to lesser, in local cases the opposite can occur, and more complex systems can emerge. Life expresses this emergent tendency, to transcend threats by becoming more flexible and adaptive, and to actualize an equally powerful inherent potential to evolve.

Carl Rogers, after Goldstein (1934), referred to this phenomenon as a formative tendency present in the universe, from atoms to galaxies. More recently Maturana and Varela's concept of 'autopoesis' has been used by person-centred psychologists to account for this emergent process (Kriz, 2008). The radical difference between humanistic and other systems of change is this faith in the self-healing and self-organizing capabilities of living systems. It shifts power to heal away from the expert and back to the inherent capacity for self-healing and growth wherein the therapist acts as caring supporter and authentic witness.

As anyone who has sat with a psychotherapy client through an existential crisis, led a team or facilitated an encounter group is well aware, there often comes a stage in the change process when no matter how much we resist, old mental models and behavioural patterns become inadequate, certainties collapse, and pain and confusion reign. The temptation is great to escape the pain, find distractions, and look for a quick solution. But with enough courage, internal resilience, the right kind of cultural support, the presence of an empathic and caring other, and sometimes just stubborn luck, human imagination and creativity may bring about a transformative response. The temptation on the facilitator is to become the expert, and take charge of the process to make things go more quickly or better. But if one has faith that life knows what it is doing and if, instead of avoiding the turmoil and pain by denying its seriousness or trying to deaden it with enticing intoxication, we are willing to sit with it, be present with it, lean into it and trust that life knows what it is doing, consciousness may sometimes rearrange itself, self-ordering conceptual and emotional capacities to a more integrated level capable of handling the complex new circumstances.

Human beings are an astonishingly adaptive species. As we have done many times before in our history, we have the ability to transform ourselves, our conceptual frameworks, and our habits of life in response to a changing environment. Whether our starting-point is hunter-gatherer in Ethiopia dealing with the challenges imposed by encroaching modernity, a New Yorker after the bombings of September 11, a tech meet-up with participants located on five continents, or a refugee arriving on the shores of a Greek island, we are all strangers in a new world, and like all immigrants before us we must learn how to think about things we have never before encountered.

How might that look like in the twenty-first century?

In 2001, former UK foreign service officer Graham Leicester convened the International Futures Forum (IFF) in Scotland to begin a two-year project (now in its 15th year) to explore the implications for sustainability, governance, the economy and consciousness of a world in which the cultural givens of the Enlightenment were liquefying, thrusting us into a world we can no longer understand nor control. Immodestly, the group set out to reconsider the ideas of the Scottish Enlightenment with a view to identifying the contours of a Second Enlightenment. Notwithstanding the hubris, it soon became clear to us that any prospect for a future that could sustain and enhance human well-being and aspiration under the new conditions of the twenty-first century would require not only new technologies and new institutions, but a new psychology. It needed Carl Rogers' persons of tomorrow, and it needed settings in which they could be nurtured and supported.

In *Dancing at the Edge: Competence, culture and organization in the 21st century* (O'Hara & Leicester, 2012), largely based on conclusions from the aforementioned IFF project, we conclude that the emerging 'future' is already here, and participation in this new culture does indeed lead to a new mentality, and ways of being that go beyond the ideals of twentieth-century Western psychology. In particular, capacities such as reason, abstraction, quantification, reductionism and scientific thinking, which emerged as an outgrowth of the Enlightenment, are still important, but are no longer all that people bring to the table. Today, in order to succeed, people augment their technical expertise with a range of Being capacities such as compassion, intuition, poetics, imagination, spirituality, somatics, holistic and systems thinking, and the science of qualities – capacities that had been left behind or marginalized by modernity.

One IFF project involved shadowing senior executives who were regarded by colleagues as exceptional leaders known for their personal maturity and wisdom, and who had created organizations that made great efforts to nurture the human potential in their staffs. Their ways of being were highly consistent with Rogers' definition of a 'person of tomorrow' or 'fully functioning person'. They were technically competent – experts at their jobs – but beyond that, they had highly attuned empathy, were authentic, non-judgemental, inclusive. Leaders like these bring out the best in others and demonstrate a high level of self-awareness and self-mastery. They balance a holistic view, sensing deeper patterns in the field with the ability to focus and analyze complex problems. They are hybrids, exhibiting qualities valued in Western psychology and those more revered in Asian and indigenous thought. They take risks to push boundaries and transgress established patterns. They integrate spiritual awareness with concrete pragmatism. Even in centres of excellence like a national theatre company where extraordinary levels of performance are expected, 'critique' is a process of mutual engagement, formative modelling and unconditional respect.

Transformative infrastructure

How did they get that way? Well, most of them did not credit their official education. And they did not get there by themselves. Most acknowledged the importance of love, close relationships with mentors; and most credited the privilege of working with psychologically aware colleagues and friends who shared the same humanistic values. They spoke of how important it is to take risks to try to make something new happen, even against the odds. They emphasized the importance of reflexive learning, and almost all participated in some kind of consciousness practice.

Despite the conservative backlash, fed by a cynical elite who make snarky comments about 'touchy feely' and 'kumbaya' of the human potential movement, the last half century has, in fact, seen an exponential growth in resources for people seeking ways to stay human and to function at higher levels in the new world. Much of this has been fuelled by entrepreneurial professionals who are no longer comfortable within bureaucratic systems and who have struck out on their own to offer services that feed hearts and minds, bodies and souls. Counselling, psychotherapy, yoga, martial arts, mindfulness, meditation, biofeedback, fitness, holistic health practices, massage, stress reduction, active listening, empathy, somatics, support groups and participation in the arts are just part of the array of resources readily available, even in the smallest towns. Workplaces offer coaching, leadership training, communications skills, empathy, diversity sensitivity and cultural competence labs, wellness programmes and self-care resources, and religious institutions teach contemplative practices and transformative ministries.

There is also a burgeoning 'festival' culture based around the arts, and incorporating humanistic values in their mission, organization and their relationships with participants. California's Burning Man festival, for instance, which was started in 1986 as a small arts ritual by San Francisco cultural creatives, now attracts over 50,000 participants to a barren site in a scorching desert to experiment in self-organizing, co-creative events, radical inclusion, new ritual and ecstatic experiences (with and without drugs), inquiry into possible futures, and bears a striking resemblance to the great humanistic gatherings of the 1960s. Though less focused on nuclear disarmament than Carl Rogers and friends, strategies for avoidance of planetary suicide show up in sustainability movement events, transition towns, and eco-fairs which each year draw hundreds of thousands of participants.

In 2007 entrepreneur-environmental activist Paul Hawken published *Blessed Unrest*, describing, as the book's subtitle says, 'how the largest social movement in history is restoring grace, justice, and beauty to the world' (Hawken, 2007). The book describes over a million organizations worldwide working on aspects of ecological sustainability and social justice. Of these, according to Hawken's keyword descriptors of the groups' missions, 32,000 focus on issues that reflect humanistic aspirations and consciousness. Participation, personal and community empowerment, authentic communication, dialogue, mutual respect, collective deliberation, talking across differences, active listening, empathy, egalitarian governance, transformative conversation, collective intelligence, respectful relationships, dignity and non-violent communication are just a sample of keywords that show up frequently. It is unlikely that participants of many of these groups have had direct contact with Humanistic Psychology per se, but the almost universal commitment to the principles that in the 1960s Rogers identified as persons of tomorrow suggests that the core ideas have gone viral, and become an open-source resource for individual empowerment, community development and social change.

I do not imply by this that these ideas originate with Humanistic Psychology, rather that they and Humanistic Psychology reflect cultural shifts under way in the direction of greater respect for an expanded view of the potential of all persons, and a faith in our collective capacity to surmount the challenges faced in the new twenty-first-century culture. These initiatives, events and services, along with an immense literature of books and other media, when considered together as a loosely associated network, amount to a *transformative infrastructure* that provides both conceptual scaffolding and rehearsal spaces where transformative initiatives can be attempted, and new views of personhood and organization can be nurtured.

Reframing Humanistic Psychology as cultural praxis

Though psychotherapy remains an important tool in helping individuals deal with personal pain and the stresses of 'liquid modernity' it is not and should not be the whole story. In my view it is time for Humanistic Psychology to be more public and assertive about its radical vision of human potential and to reframe humanistic practice as a path to transformative innovation. In the next decades, many events will occur where solutions will be offered based in the old modernist frames. When that happens, humanistic psychologists can come forward with alternative transformative perspectives. Do research if possible and when research is published authors and editors should send press releases to local news outlets, the way mainstream academic journals do. It might not be picked up – but it might be. When ministers and officials make public statements that offer a diminished 'Skinnerian'/behaviourist view of human potential, humanistic organizations need to have articles ready to counter them; and when commentators make snarky comments, snap back with a gentle letter to the editor. When we get an opportunity to speak to groups or classrooms, we should take it and explain why 'business as usual' is not adequate. When new voices emerge anywhere that speak about transformational ideas, support them, consider them 'us', look for common ground. Visit local classrooms, offer simple workshops, convene dialogues, build community. Write for the general public – not just for professional colleagues. Progressive publications such as *Huffington Post* are eager to publish lively and controversial views. We need to provide them.

This is cultural work. The world is in dire trouble – the future threats include planetary suicide, and as both Einstein and Havel say, survival depends on enough of us developing a higher stage of consciousness. Humanistic psychologists know a lot about how to do that. The highest and best role for our Humanistic Psychology community should be to recover our roots as a *cultural movement* – not a *counter-cultural* movement but a cultural *growth* movement – aimed at facilitating the emergence of a vision of personhood adequate to the complexity of the times. The mission should be to join up – as partners – with others seeking to address the consequences of the historical rupture Dror (2015) describes in ways that will safeguard our planet, our dignity as persons-for-themselves and our collective future.

As cultural leaders we can help humanity wake up, break through its denial, and understand its moment in history, as we move from an industrial mechanical world to an emergent living world, maintain its mental equilibrium and create the conditions needed to grow through this epochal transition. If framed as cultural leadership, Humanistic Psychology – psychotherapy, counselling, education, organizational, institutional and community practices and social policy – could be seen as a holistic praxis for social transformation, addressing the inevitable pain of tumultuous times and at the same time releasing the inherent creativity and untapped resources toward restoring hope and building a saner twenty-first-century society. Fromm (1955) suggests that the creation of that society requires that we resist becoming robots who fit into a society that is becoming ever more dehumanized by 'creating again the opportunity for people to sing together, walk together, admire together – together' (p. 349). Success is not guaranteed, but if we are right about the capacity to grow beyond present limitations we must try; and there is no time to waste.

References

Bauman, Z. (2010). *44 Letters from the Liquid Modern World*. Cambridge, UK: Polity.

Diamond, J. (2005). *Collapse: How societies choose to fail or succeed*. New York: Viking.

Dror, Y. (2015). Priming leaders for fateful choices. *Eruditio: E-Journal of the World Academy of Arts and Sciences, 1*(6): 40–49.

Einstein, A. (1948/2003). A message to intellectuals. In J. Green (Ed.), *Albert Einstein* (p. 52). Princeton, NJ: Ocean Press.

Erikkson, M. & Lindström, B. (2014). The salutogenic framework for well-being: Implications for public policy. In T. J. Hämäläinen & J. Michaelson (Eds), *Well-being and Beyond: Broadening the public and policy discourse* (pp. 68–97). Cheltenham: Edward Elgar.

Fromm, E. (1955). *The Sane Society*. New York: Henry Holt.

Goldstein, K. (1934). *The Organism: A holistic approach to biology derived from pathological data in man*. New York: Zone Books.

Grogan, J. (2013). *Encountering America*. New York: HarperCollins.

Hämäläinen, T. J. (2014). In search of coherence: Sketching a theory of sustainable well-being. In T. J. Hämäläinen & J. Michaelson (Eds), *Well-being and Beyond: Broadening the public and policy discourse* (pp. 17–67). Cheltenham: Edward Elgar.

Havel, V. (1990). Speech to a Joint Session of the US Congress. Washington, DC.

Hawken, P. (2007). *Blessed Unrest: How the largest movement in history is restoring grace, justice, and beauty to the world*. New York: Penguin.

Kauffman, S. A. (1992). The sciences of complexity and 'Origins of Order'. Principles of organization in organisms. In J. E. Mittenthal & A. B. Baskin (Eds), *Proceedings of the SFI Studies in the Sciences of Complexity*. Reading, MA: Addison Wesley.

Kriz, J. (2008). *Self-actualization: Person-centered approach and systems theory*. Ross-on-Wye: PCCS Books.

Leicester, G. (2007). Rising to the occasion: Cultural leadership in powerful times. *Mission Models Money*. London, UK: International Futures Forum.

Leicester, G. & O'Hara, M. (2009). *Ten Things to Do in a Conceptual Emergency*. London: Triarchy Press.

Maslow, A. H. (1971). *The Farther Reaches of Human Nature*. New York: Penguin.

Nisbett, R. E. (2003). *The Geography of Thought: How Asians and Westerners think differently . . . and why*. New York: The Free Press.

O'Hara, M. (1988). Science, pseudoscience and mythmongering. In B. Basil (Ed.), *Not Necessarily the New Age* (pp. 145–164). Buffalo, NY: Prometheus.

O'Hara, M. & Leicester, G. (2012). *Dancing at the Edge: Competence, culture and organization in the 21st century*. Axminster, Devon, UK: Triarchy Press.

O'Hara, M. & Lyon, A. (2012). Wellbeing and Wellbecoming: Reauthorizing the subject in incoherent times. Working paper, International Futures Forum.

O'Hara, M. & Lyon, A. (2014). Wellbeing and wellbecoming: Reauthorizing the subject in inchoherent times. In T. Hämäläinen & J. Michaelson (Eds), *Well-being and Beyond: Broadening the public and policy discourse* (pp. 98–123). Cheltenham, UK: Edward Elgar.

Pauchant, T. C. (Ed.). (1994). *In Search of Meaning: Managing for the health of our organizations, our communities and the natural world*. San Francisco, CA: Jossey-Bass.

Rogers, C. R. (1980). *A Way of Being*. Boston, MA: Houghton Mifflin.

Roszak, T. (1969). *The Making of a Counter Culture: Reflections on the technocratic society and its youthful opposition*. New York: Doubleday.

Shweder, R. A. (1991). *Thinking through Cultures: Expeditions in cultural psychology*. Cambridge, MA: Harvard University Press.

Sundararajan, L. (2015). *Understanding Emotion in Chinese Culture: Thinking through psychology* (International and Cultural Psychology). New York: Springer.

Tarnas, R. (1991). *The Passion of the Western Mind*. New York: Random House.

Taylor, P. (2016). *The Next America: Boomers, Millennials and the looming generational showdown*. New York Public Affairs.

Tuchman, B. W. (1978). *A Distant Mirror: The calamitous 14th century*. New York: Ballantine.

6

THE DEVELOPMENT COMMUNITY AND ITS ACTIVIST PSYCHOLOGY

Lois Holzman

I do not have much use for labels, categories or academic disciplines, except to disrupt them by playing and creating new ones with them. So, by way of introducing myself, let me use a label I created: I am a radically humanistic, practical-critical, postmodern Marxist developmentalist. I am a community organizer working to involve the masses in a global conceptual revolution, a researcher and scholar located outside the university. I work/play to bring together people and things and ideas – often ones (such as those with which I just described myself) that have been kept apart by ideology, politics or societal and cultural norms and traditions. That is when it is the most difficult, most fun and most gratifying. Great thinkers, great ideas and great movements need to be brought together and played with, in my experience, to be useful to people. In the following pages, I will share some of what my colleagues and I have brought together in creating *a psychology of becoming*, and what I see as its role in the emergence of an international progressive movement for the re-initiation of human development through performance and play. I will locate this new psychology and the performance activism movement within the changing dynamics occurring in the Humanistic and the Critical Psychology arenas in the USA, of which they have been a part.

The *psychology of becoming* and *performance activism* have their roots in the upheavals of the 1960s. Among the millions who were radicalized then was Fred Newman, a New York City working-class man who got his education when public universities in New York were free. In 1965 he received a Ph.D. from Stanford University in the philosophy of science and the foundations of mathematics, and for a few years taught philosophy at several colleges and universities. Newman resonated with the ways in which the cultural movements of the time were challenging the Western glorification of individual self-interest, and was excited by the grassroots communal experiments to transform daily life going on at the time. He felt the need to confront America's failure to honestly deal with its legacy of slavery and racism, as its African American population remained poor and shut out of America's prosperity.

Believing that profound social change would not come from the university campus, Newman stopped teaching philosophy and left academia. With a handful of student followers, he set up community organizing collectives in working-class neighbourhoods of New York City. Soon after, they became involved in welfare rights organizing. During the late 1970s two main organizing thrusts were developed: organizing in the poorest, mostly African American, communities of New York City to activate and empower people politically; and engaging the subjectivity of community organizing and the mass psychology of contemporary capitalism. Over four decades, the number and variety of projects led by Newman grew exponentially to encompass culture, health, mental health, education and politics (Friedman, 2013; Holzman, 1999).

Two guiding principles were there at the start, and remain to this day. First, to be independently funded and supported, and not take money or be constrained by government or other traditional funding sources. This involved reaching out to ordinary Americans for financial support and participation, initially by stopping them on street corners and knocking on the doors of their homes. What has evolved over the years is a new kind of partnership between middle-class and wealthy Americans and the poor. Second, to create new kinds of institutions that in their very design and activity challenge the foundations of their traditional 'counterparts'. Among these projects are:

- a labour union for welfare recipients who did not labour and, therefore, were at no point of production;
- a school for children that denied the individuated, knowledge-seeking model of learning that is the bedrock of schooling, East and West;
- therapy centres with an approach to emotional help that denies the individualism and medical model of mainstream psychotherapy;
- a 'university' that is free, open to everyone who wants to participate and has no grades or degrees;
- a national network of talent shows for youth that denies the conception of talent; and
- electoral political campaigns that are not concerned with winning, and political parties that exist to transform political culture – including the possibility of doing away with political parties as the mode of citizen participation.

Today, the organizations that comprise what is now called the 'development community' are the All Stars Project, Inc. and its youth development programmes, university-style development school (UX) and political theatre (Castillo Theatre); the East Side Institute for Group and Short-Term Psychotherapy, the research and education centre that is my home; the Social Therapy Group in NYC and social therapy affiliates in other cities; independent voting org; and the bi-annual Performing the World conferences. These organizations have national and international reach, with the direct participation of tens of thousands, who impact on hundreds of thousands. Along with their varied foci is a shared methodology that involves people of all ages in the ongoing collective activity of creating new kinds of environments where they can be active performers of their lives. This methodology 'practically-critically' engages the institution of psychology and its impact on people's daily lives (Holzman, 2009; Newman & Holzman, 1997, 2006/1996).

From the beginning it was clear to us that mainstream psychology – with its individualistic focus, claim to objectivity, emulation and imitation of the physical and natural sciences, and dualistically divided worldview – was a powerful impediment to ongoing social development and social activism. Along with many, many others at the time, we believed the personal and political to be intimately connected. We put this belief into practice in a new and radical therapy, social therapy. Created by Newman, social therapeutic methodology initially stemmed not from the tradition of Humanistic Psychology but, rather, from two other sources: analytic philosophy, philosophy of science and the foundations of mathematics, the area of Newman's doctoral studies; and Marxism, the area Newman began to study seriously when he left university teaching to become a community and political activist.

It was not until I joined Newman in the late 1970s that a form of Humanistic Psychology entered the scene via socio-cultural, cultural-historical activity theory (CHAT) and Vygotskian theory. My view was that this approach was humanistic *and* critical. At the time, I was not aware that there was a Critical Psychology critique of Humanistic Psychology as based in and fostering individualism. I considered humanistic approaches to be a form of Critical Psychology in that they were designed as alternatives to both behaviourism and psychoanalysis (and, to varying degrees, the 'inside–outside' dichotomy psychology embraces and perpetuates). Decades later, having been a player in the postmodern turn that a sizable portion of the Humanistic Psychology division of the American Psychological Association took in the 1990s, I still think so. I hope the following brief history of Critical Psychology in the USA helps illustrate the humanism of Newman's and my work.

Critical psychologies

In the USA 'Critical Psychology', as officially designated, is almost non-existent. There are no university departments and only a handful of courses devoted to Critical Psychology. Dennis Fox and Isaac Prilleltensky, authors of the first American college text on Critical Psychology (*Critical Psychology: An Introduction*, which first appeared in 1997 and was revised in 2009 by the two original authors and Stephanie Austin), characterize the field as an alternative to mainstream psychology, especially its practices toward the oppressed and vulnerable, and advocate for fundamental changes to existing social structures with the goal of materializing greater social justice and human well-being (Fox, Prilleltensky & Austin, 2009: 3–5).

In addition to what is formally termed Critical Psychology, however, there are dozens of approaches that critique and challenge, in theory and/or practice, the foundations of mainstream psychology. My exploration of the history of these approaches led me to characterize them as identity-based, ideology-based and epistemology-based.

Identity-based Critical Psychology

Here we find psychologies that are critical of how mainstream psychological theory and/or method exclude, ignore or misrepresent vast groupings of people by virtue of psychology's unquestioned allegiance to white European males as normative. In the USA these critical psychologies stem from the political movements of the 1960s, including the Black Power movement, La Raza (Latino power), women's liberation and gay liberation. Black, feminist and gay psychologies were developed (primarily by African American, women, and lesbians and gay men, respectively) with psychological conceptions, practices and research agendas specific to what were thought to be the unique characteristics, needs and societal restrictions of each grouping. Black psychologists and feminist psychologists successfully organized themselves and formed professional associations in 1968; for lesbian and gay psychologists, the road was a longer one.

The Association of Black Psychologists was founded 'to have a positive impact upon the mental health of the national Black community by means of planning, programmes, services, training, and advocacy' (goo.gl/nTGxzO). Still in existence today, the organization has chosen African identity as its mission and the heart of its alternative psychology (termed 'African psychology') (ibid.). However, most Black psychologists working on issues of race, class and ethnicity work within the mainstream, and many are part of the American Psychological Association's (APA) Society for the Psychological Study of Ethnic Minority Issues, established in 1986.

Feminist psychology arguably stems from Karen Horney's work in the 1920s and 30s critiquing Freud, but contemporary American feminist psychology began with Weisstein's essay, 'Psychology Constructs the Female' – again, in 1968 – and the founding a year later of the Association for Women in Psychology (AWP) during the annual APA convention. In response to the continuing challenges of feminist psychologists within its ranks, a Psychology of Women division within the APA was established in 1973. Since then, most psychology-of-women issues have been subsumed within the division. The AWP continues with a more activist agenda that links identity politics and identity psychology (www.awpsych.org/index.php?option=com_content&view=article&id=51&Itemid=65&limitstart=1"goo.gl/ek2KQD).

In the 1960s, gay activists in the United States directly confronted governmental and institutional discrimination and police violence targeting homosexuals. The famed 1969 Stonewall riots in New York City's Greenwich Village marked the spark of the gay liberation movement in the USA. For gay activists and their allies, challenging the ways that psychiatry and psychology institutionally oppressed gay people was next on the agenda. The APA included homosexuality as a mental disorder in its first *Diagnostic and Statistical Manual of Mental Disorders*, published in 1952. From the late 1960s gay activists, as well as gay psychiatrists within the professional association, aggressively pressured the establishment, and the diagnosis was removed from the manual in 1973. The APA established the Society for the

Psychological Study of Lesbian and Gay issues in 1985, now called the Society for the Psychological Study of Lesbian, Gay, Bisexual and Transgender Issues (goo.gl/PhT8rp). In the ensuing decades, the depathologizing of homosexuality has come a long way.

Ideology-based Critical Psychology

While fully supporting the empowerment and liberation of the above-mentioned identity groups, the critique of the ideology-based psychologies is from a political-ideological position, rather than from a particular identity position. All anti-capitalist ideologies fall into this category, including Marxist, Marxist-feminist and postcolonial critique and liberation psychology. The anti-capitalist ideological critique of psychology that has arisen in the USA is centred on how psychology supports the status quo by socializing its citizens to a capitalist ideology through dichotomizing the individual and society, with the result that individuals become asocial and ahistorical entities. The resulting practices are said to be devastating, because 'Following this ideological reasoning, solutions for human predicaments are to be found almost exclusively with the self, leaving the social order conveniently unaffected' (Prilleltensky, 1994: 34–5).

My bookshelves are filled with critiques of psychology, nearly all of which make the same point as Prilleltensky does. It is worth noting the nearly complete absence of Marx in writings by Americans; we find little reference to (let alone discussion of) Marxism in the works of other well-known ideologically based critics, such as Cushman (1996), Richardson, Fowers & Guignon (1999), Sampson (1993) and Sloan (2000).

Epistemology-based Critical Psychology

To the extent that the approaches already described include a critique of psychology's methodology, they do so in the service of their identity or ideology critique. In contrast, epistemology-based critiques take mainstream psychology's methodology straight on and offer alternative methodologies for how to understand, study and support human life.

At the core of epistemology-based critiques is mainstream scientific psychology's exclusion of the (inter)-subjectivity of human life – a mistake stemming from when psychology adopted and adapted the scientific mindset of the early twentieth century and promoted itself as an endeavour no different in kind from the natural and physical sciences. Psychology devised ways of relating to human beings as if we were no different from the fish in the sea and stars in the sky, and continues to do so with increasing technological sophistication (Danziger, 1990, 1997; Gergen, 2015; Newman & Holzman, 2006/1996). However, human beings have access to our subjectivity, are self-reflecting and self-reflexive, use language, and make meaning and sense of our world. Thus, a psychology whose knowledge-seeking excludes both the study of these characteristics and the incorporation of these characteristics into its methodology is not a science at all.

There are many alternative methodologies that are inherently critical of mainstream psychology's epistemology. Some, such as phenomenological and hermeneutic psychology, study human experience interpretively. Devised from the works of the early twentieth-century German philosophers Heidegger and Husserl, the two approaches in psychology are best known through the works of Gadamer (1976), Levinas (1998), Merleau-Ponty (1962) and Ricœur (1996). As developed in the USA, Humanistic Psychology has incorporated the seminal ideas from these European scholars in its theoretical and empirical research.

More recent epistemology-based Critical Psychology includes approaches that fall under the headings of 'social constructionism' and 'postmodern psychology'. It is noteworthy that in the USA the group that was open to social constructionist and postmodern theory and practice and helped to place them on a broad stage during the 1990s was the Humanistic Psychology division of the APA (now called the Society for Humanistic Psychology), primarily through the efforts of Ken Gergen (1994, 2001, 2006).

What is common to these approaches is the exploration of the very nature of knowledge, and how it is generated. There is a focus on language as the meaning-making tool through which human beings construct knowledge and understanding. Meaning-making is understood as a relational or social process that occurs between people, rather than within or by an individual. As Lock and Strong state in their recent volume tracing the historical roots of social constructionism,

> [Social constructionism] provides a more adequate framework than the dominant tradition for conceptualizing and then exploring the meaning-saturated reality of being human. Our meaningful reality is much 'messier' than the Cartesian heritage has had us believe, and much more mysterious.
> *(Lock & Strong, 2010: 353)*

Another target of these epistemological critiques is psychology's presumption of objectivity and Truth. Alternative subjectivist accountings of truth are put forth: for example, social constructionists search for forms of dialogue alternative to objectivist-based debate and criticism (McNamee & Gergen, 1992, 1999); narrativists work to expose the 'storiness' of our lives and help people create their own (and, most often, better) stories (McLeod, 1997; Monk et al., 1997; Rosen & Kuehlwein, 1996; White & Epston, 1990); and collaborative therapists emphasize the dynamic and co-constructed nature of meaning (e.g. Anderson, 1997; Paré & Larner, 2004; Strong & Paré, 2004).

Another group of psychologists critical of the epistemology of mainstream psychology are those within the socio-cultural and CHAT traditions, who draw their inspiration from Soviet activity theory and the writings of Vygotsky (1978, 1987, 1993, 1994, 1997) and Bakhtin (1981, 1986). The critique of mainstream psychology is that it relates to human beings not only as isolated from each other, but as isolated from culture and human history, too. For developers of socio-cultural and

CHAT approaches, what it means to develop, learn and live is to engage in human activity so as to become a member of a culture. Similar to the social constructionists and postmodernists, human life is understood as a social–cultural–historical pheno-menon, with language (conversation, dialogue) playing a key role in how human beings come to understand and act upon the world.

Where these two epistemological critical psychologies diverge is in their view of the human language making and using ability. For most socio-cultural and CHAT psychologists, language is understood and empirically studied as a cultural mediator, and so the emphasis in their work is not so much on how meaning is made, but rather on how meaning is appropriated from the culture, and the role that language plays as a 'psychological tool' in acculturation (e.g. Cole, 1996; John-Steiner, 1997; Kozulin, 2001; Rogoff, 2003; Wertsch, 1991). As will be dis-cussed next, the psychology of becoming of social therapeutics is another direction that has emerged as a CHAT perspective that focuses not so much on the use of tools for cultural appropriation, but on the making of tools for the transforming of culture.

Activating postmodernism and postmodernizing activity theory

As a player in the CHAT and postmodern psychology arenas, I see both of them as simultaneously critical and humanistic. Each is rooted in deep concerns and unhap-piness with the current state of the world's people and the seemingly intractable poverty and inequality, and the failure of the dominant institutions to promote the general welfare. Each implicates the institution of psychology in the mess we are in. Each has evolved a critique of mainstream psychology's core conceptions and has brought forth alternative conceptions and practices, which have at their core the understanding of human beings as social and cultural (and, to a lesser extent, as his-torical). Both, it seems to me, are potentially psychologies of becoming. Newman's and my work and the activities of the development community are, methodologi-cally speaking, a synthesis of CHAT and postmodern psychology, fusing postmodern psychology's philosophical critique of psychology with Vygotsky's dialectical method and his understanding of development, learning and play to yield a *performatory process ontology* (Holzman, 2006).

Our synthesis begins with Karl Marx. His early philosophical writings speak to the fundamentality of human beings as social and active in creating themselves and the world simultaneously (his dialectical methodology): (1) 'As society itself produces man as man, so it is produced by him. Activity and mind are social in their content as well as in their origin: they are social activity and social mind' (Marx, 1967: 129); (2) 'The coincidence of the changing of circumstances and of human activity or self-changing can be conceived and rationally understood only as revolutionary practice' (Marx, 1974: 121). Revolutionary practice is not so much the organizing toward a specific goal, as it is a new conception of method that involves a unity of human beings and the world we have created/are re-creating.

Bringing this Marxist conception into psychology, Vygotsky posited a new conception of method, one that prefigured postmodernism in capturing the always emergent, or 'becoming-ness', of human beings:

> The search for method becomes one of the most important problems of the entire enterprise of understanding the uniquely human forms of psychological activity. In this case, the method is simultaneously prerequisite and product, the tool and the result of the study.
>
> *(Vygotsky, 1978: 65)*

Tool-and-result points the way out of the objective–subjective and theory–practice dichotomies that permeate psychology and social movements. Tool use is a main focus of CHAT researchers, who are primarily concerned with the relation between culture and cognition, and how children appropriate the culture of which they are part. But Vygotsky's tool-and-result suggests that we human beings are not only tool-users, but that we are also collective creators of new tool-and-results. We create culture. To the extent that contemporary human beings can become world historic or revolutionary, they must exercise this power (Newman & Holzman, 2003, 2013).

Vygotsky showed how little children learn and develop through tool-and-result activity. Describing play, he said; 'It is as though a child is a head taller than he is. Play is a leading factor in development' (Vygotsky, 1978: 102). He is telling us that in play, we are who we are *and* who we are becoming *at the same time*. He noted that children learn by playing with the adults and older children around them, creating performances of learning. Looking at the organizing work we and our colleagues were doing in therapeutics, youth organizing, theatre-building and independent politics, Newman and I came to realize that human development happens – not just with children, but with people of all ages – when we relate to people as 'a head taller' – that is, as who they are becoming. Just as a baby and mother perform conversation before the baby speaks correctly, school-age children can perform reading or arithmetic (maths) or science before they know how, and adults can learn how to run their world by performing power (Holzman, 1997, 2009; Newman & Holzman, 2013).

We all have the capacity to play as children do, to do what we do not yet know how to do, to be who we are and other than who we are at the same time. The babbling baby, the actor on the stage, the student in a school play, the researcher singing her data, and all of us – are capable of creating new performances of ourselves continuously if we choose to. In this way, performance is a new ontology, a new understanding of how development happens – through the social-cultural activity of people together creating new possibilities and new options for how to be in, relate to, understand and change the world – which, of course, includes ourselves.

Mainstream psychology is designed as the study of *product* – the isolated individual at different points in time. It is incapable of seeing, let alone understanding, *process*. In this way, mainstream psychology contributes mightily to alienation, i.e. relating to the products of production severed from their producers and from the process of their production – that is, as commodities. This way of relating is not limited to cars, loaves of bread and computers. It is, rather, the normal way of seeing and relating to everything in contemporary Western culture. People relate to their lives, their relationships, their feelings, their culture, and so on, as things, torn away from the process of their creation and from their creators. While such 'thingification' is a major factor in people's emotional and learning problems, therapists and educators vary widely in the extent to which they engage alienation in practice, and almost none speak about it theoretically or methodologically.

Performing sociality

If we are commodified and alienated individuals, then transformative social change needs to entail the de-commodification and de-alienation of 'human products' through a positive and constructive process of *producing sociality*. The synthesis of Vygotsky's cultural-historical contributions with postmodern psychology's challenge to the philosophical-psychological conceptions of self, truth, reality and identity yields a method to de-commodify and de-alienate, through a deconstruction–reconstruction of the ontology of modernist psychology in which human beings are understood to be only who we are. The performatory process ontology of the development community relates to human beings as both who we are and who we are becoming. And who we are becoming are creators of tools (-and-results) that can continuously transform mundane specific life practices (including those that produce alienation) into new forms of life. Creating these new kinds of tools is the *becoming activity* of creating/giving expression to our sociality.

For Newman, myself and the development community, the human capacity to perform – that is, to be both 'who we are' and 'who we are becoming/who we are not' at the very same time – is the source of development (Newman, 1996; Newman & Holzman, 1997). Performance is the activity by which human beings transform and continuously reshape the unity that is *us-and-our environment*. As Neimeyer has noted, there is great socio-political potential in this activity perspective on performance:

> The ironic but liberating insight that the basic 'reality' of human beings is that they are 'pretenders' lies at the heart of [the] performative approach to social therapy . . . This non-essentializing stance undermines the totalizing identification of self with any given role, and gives impetus to activity-based initiatives that prompt communities of persons to transcend the limiting scripts they are offered by dominant social institutions.
>
> *(Neimeyer, 2000: 195)*

This non-essentializing activity calls into question the subjectivist accountings of truth (many truths, all with a small 't') offered by some postmodernists. The social therapeutic methodology rejects truth (in both its upper- and lower-case forms) *in favour of activity*. The ontological shift to activity transforms discourse (in particular, therapeutic discourse) from an epistemological appeal to either an objective, outer Truth/Reality or subjective, inner truths and realities – to an activistic, self-reflexive engagement of the creating of the discourse itself (what is/is becoming). The shift involves relating to therapeutic discourse as performance, and to clients as an ensemble of performers who are, with the therapists' help, staging a new therapeutic conversation (a therapy play) each session. Performing therapy exposes the fictional nature of 'the truth' of our everyday language, our everyday psychology and our everyday stories, and allows people to experience themselves as the collective creators of their emotional growth (Holzman & Mendez, 2003; Newman, 1999).

In the current economic, political and cultural climate, human beings are socialized as commodified and alienated individuals. Mainstream psychology relates to them as such – that is, as *who we are*, not as simultaneously *who we are and who we are becoming*. Transforming the current economic, political and cultural climate involves de-commodifying and de-alienating its human 'products'. Neither negative nor destructive, it is the positive and constructive process of producing sociality by the continuous transformation of mundane specific life practices into new forms of life.

This postmodern understanding of activity dissolves the dualist gap between self and world, between thought and language, between who we are and who we are becoming, between theory and practice, in such a way that we can approach human beings as activists and activity-ists, as tool-makers, meaning-makers and culture-makers, rather than as knowers and perceivers. Further, it actualizes the postmodern critique of modernist psychology's isolated individual through a new ontology – group activity. As a process ontology, a social-relational ontology, group activity raises a new set of questions and challenges for postmodernists, activity theorists, critical psychologists and humanists. For the unit of study and transformation becomes the social unit creating itself.

This shift in focus from the individual to the relationship or group exposes a problematic assumption of psychology – namely, if it is individuals that perceive, read, problem-solve, experience emotional distress or disorder, and so on, then the instruction, learning, teaching, treatment or therapy must be individuated. While groupwork in general and group therapy in particular might at first appear to be challenges and counter examples, the group is typically understood to be a context for individuals to learn and/or get help. In contrast, the process ontology of group activity suggests that individuals need to be organized as social units in order to carry out the tasks of learning and developing, not unlike countless other human endeavours in which people become organized as social units to get a specific job done (Holzman & Newman, 2004).

We are faced with the question, 'What does all this look like in practice?' Some years ago, a group of scholars (Danish critical psychologists) published a review of three of Newman's and my books in which they commented that it might well be that one has to experience our work in order to understand it (Nissen, Axel & Jensen, 1999). I suspect that they meant that comment critically (i.e. negatively) and, yet, I think they make a critical (i.e. methodological) point – descriptions and maps are not identical to what they describe or map, but all too often, the two are confused. Technology has freed us, to some extent, of having to use words to describe what happens in a given situation or environment. I say 'to some extent' because it is even more seductive to mistake video images for 'what *actually* happened', despite the fact that the camera also represents and has a point of view. With that caveat, I invite you to view some videos of the ways the performance process ontology is manifest differently in the various projects of the development community. I also now provide a few words of description of two of the projects (with the same caveat).

Developing in social therapy

The Social Therapy Group (STG) is the New York City-based home of the clinical practice of social therapy. (It is a group practice in two ways – it is comprised of a group of therapists who practise a group approach.) Each week, approximately 200 adults, teens and children are in therapy in the Brooklyn and Manhattan centres. There are STG-affiliated centres and private practices in cities in the USA and Mexico, and hundreds of psychologists, social workers, mental health counsellors and psychiatrists worldwide whose practices have been influenced by their social therapy training. The STG is the practicum site for those who train at the East Side Institute. Observations of STGs are also a feature of the study and training programmes run by the East Side Institute, including its International Class – a 10-month programme in the Institute's approach to human development and community building.

Combining residencies in New York City with seminars, supervision and project development sessions conducted online, the programme is open to practitioners, social entrepreneurs and scholars across all disciplines. Since 2003, more than 100 people from 24 countries have graduated from the Class. They include grassroots educators and community organizers; practising psychologists, counsellors and social workers; and psychology, education and drama professors working to empower and develop the poor in their countries.

STGs conducted in centres for social therapy in the USA are comprised of 10–25 people, a mix of women and men of varying ages, ethnicities, sexual orientations, class backgrounds and economic status, professions and 'presenting problems'. Such heterogeneous groups are designed to challenge people's notion of a fixed identity (e.g. based on gender, ethnicity, diagnostic label, or 'That's the kind of person I am'). By virtue of this diversity, such groups have more varied 'material' with which the group can work. Those from other countries who have trained in social therapy have created practices in a structure and manner that is coherent with their specific cultural environments, different in varying ways from those in the USA.

Clients who come together to form an STG are given the task of creating their group as an environment in which they can get help. This *group activity* is a collective, practical challenge to the assumption that the way people get therapeutic help is to relate to themselves and be related to by others *as individuals*, complete with problems and inner selves. This is not to say that people don't come to social therapy individuated and wanting help to feel better or to change. They come to social therapy as they might to any therapy, relating to feelings as individuated and private. This way of relating contributes to people feeling isolated and alone with the 'possession' of their feelings. They look to the therapist for some advice, solution, interpretation or explanation. The social therapist works with the group to organize itself to create a method of relating to emotional talk relationally rather than individualistically, and as activistic rather than as representational (Newman & Gergen, 1999; Newman & Holzman, 1999).

The focus of the social therapeutic group process is, 'How can we talk so that our talking helps build the group?' Speaking as truth-telling, reality representing, inner thought and feeling revealing, are challenged as people attempt to converse in new ways and to create something new out of their initial individuated, problem-oriented presentations of self. In this process, people come to appreciate what (and that) they can create, and simultaneously to realize the limitations of trying to learn and grow individually. Group members, at different moments, realize that *growth comes from participating in the process of building the groups in which one functions* (Holzman, 2009; Holzman & Mendez, 2003; Holzman & Newman, 2004, 2012; LaCerva & Helm, 2011; LaCerva, 2016).

Developing in the All Stars Project

The All Stars Project, Inc. is a US-based non-profit organization whose mission is to transform the lives of youth and poor communities through programmes that are based in the developmental aspects of performance and play. Founded in 1982, the All Stars operates in six US cities, with several affiliated projects around the world.

In the programmes of the All Stars, young people (and, more recently, adults) who are typically from low-income, Black, Latino and immigrant families participate in performance activities, both on and off the theatrical stage. They are invited to develop through the activity of becoming and widening their choices. Two specific developmental issues are prioritized: (1) to help them become more worldly and cosmopolitan, i.e. to perform their way from the margins into the mainstream of American society; and (2) to have them experience, over and over again, their capacity to grow, i.e. to create an active understanding *that* they can create endless performances for navigating life's complex mix of scripted (institutional) and unscripted (non-institutional) situations. All Stars programmes are voluntary. Participants are reached through multiple methods of grassroots outreach – door-knocking in housing projects, posting and handing out flyers in neighbourhoods, subways and outside of schools, and making presentations at schools and churches. There is also significant neighbourhood word of mouth.

When young people come to an All Stars programme, they participate in creating ensemble performances in which they are taken seriously and given the opportunity to perform as community citizens (Newman & Fulani, 2011). They are helped to do so by the staff and middle-class and affluent adults, often business professionals and performing artists who are also volunteers, who perform 'a head taller' along with them. All Stars programmes intervene on the impact that these young people's life circumstances have on their capacity to see possibilities and to act on them. Growing up in poverty more often than not creates hopelessness, a narrow choice of identities and, not infrequently, anger – ways of being that in turn have negative consequences on so many aspects of people's lives. The work to re-initiate development as the capacity to see possibilities and to act on them is a new form of social activism based in a psychology of becoming (Holzman, 2009).

Whether rich or poor or in between, all people need to have the opportunity to participate in qualitatively transforming themselves – and the world. In my experience, performing – with and as 'other' – is the humanistic imperative of our day.

References

Anderson, H. (1997). *Conversation, Language and Possibilities: A postmodern approach to therapy.* New York: Basic Books.

Association of Black Psychologists. ABPSI History. goo.gl/nTGxzO. Accessed 5/10/13.

Association for the Psychological Study of Lesbian, Gay, Bisexual and Transgender Issues. About Division 44. www.apadivision44.org/about/. Accessed 5/10/13.

Association for Women in Psychology. Objectives. goo.gl/hPLszR. Accessed 5/10/13.

Bakhtin, M. M. (1981). *The Dialogic Imagination: Four essays.* Austin: University of Texas Press.

Bakhtin, M. M. (1986). *Speech Genres and Other Late Essays.* Austin: University of Texas Press.

Cole, M. (1996). *Cultural Psychology: A once and future discipline.* Cambridge, MA: Harvard University Press.

Cushman, P. (1996). *Constructing the Self, Constructing America: A cultural history of psychotherapy.* New York: De Capo Press.

Danziger, K. (1990). *Constructing the Subject: Historical origins of psychological research.* New York: Cambridge University Press.

Danziger, K. (1997). *Naming the Mind: How psychology found its language.* London: Sage.

Fox, D. & Prilleltensky, I. (1997). *Critical Psychology: An introduction.* London: Sage.

Fox, D., Prilleltensky, I., & Austin, S. (2009). *Critical Psychology: An introduction,* 2nd edn. London: Sage.

Friedman, D. (2013). Performance and development: Some reflections on the relationship between theatre, community and social change. *RIGS, 2:* 157–77. Available at https://portalseer.ufba.br/index.php/rigs/article/view/9728. Accessed 3/4/17.

Gadamer, H. G. (1976). *Philosophical Hermeneutics.* Berkeley, CA: University of California Press.

Gergen, K. J. (1994). *Realities and Relationships: Soundings in social construction.* Cambridge, MA: Harvard University Press.

Gergen, K. J. (2001). *Social Construction in Context.* London: Sage.

Gergen, K. J. (2006). *Therapeutic Realities: Collaboration, oppression and relational flow.* Chagrin Falls, OH: Taos Institute Publications.

Gergen, K. J. (2015). The neurobiological turn in therapeutic treatment: Salvation or devastation? In D. Loewenthal (Ed.), *Critical Psychotherapy, Psychoanalysis and Counseling: Implications for practice* (pp. 53–73). Basingstoke: Palgrave Macmillan.

Holzman, L. (1997). *Schools for Growth: Radical alternatives to current educational models*. Mahwah, NJ: Lawrence Erlbaum (Chinese edition, 2015).

Holzman, L. (Ed.) (1999). *Performing Psychology: A postmodern culture of the mind*. New York: Routledge.

Holzman, L. (2006). Activating postmodernism. *Theory and Psychology, 16*: 109–23.

Holzman, L. (2009). *Vygotsky at Work and Play*. Routledge: London & New York.

Holzman, L. & Mendez, R. (2003). *Psychological Investigations: A clinician's guide to social therapy*. New York: Brunner-Routledge.

Holzman, L. & Newman, F. (2012). Activity and performance (and their discourses) in social therapeutic practice. In A. Lock & T. Strong (Eds), *Discursive Perspectives in Therapeutic Practice* (pp. 184–95). Oxford: Oxford University Press.

Holzman, L. & Newman, F. with Strong, T. (2004). Power, authority and pointless activity: The developmental discourse of social therapy. In T. Strong & D. Paré (Eds), *Furthering Talk: Advances in discursive therapies* (pp. 73–86). New York: Kluwer Academic.

John-Steiner, V. (1997). *Notebooks of the Mind: Explorations of thinking* (rev. ed.). New York: Oxford University Press.

Kozulin, A. (2001). *Psychological Tools: A sociocultural approach to education*. Cambridge, MA: Harvard University Press.

LaCerva, C. (2016). Social therapy and family play. In P. Smagorinsky (Ed.), *Creativity and Community among Autism-spectrum Youth: Constructing positive social updrafts through play and performance* (pp. 79–103). New York: Palgrave Macmillan.

LaCerva, C. & Helm, C. (2011). Social therapy with children with special needs and their families. In C. Lobman & B. O'Neill (Eds), *Play and Performance: Play and culture studies*, Volume 11 (pp. 180–200). Lanham, MD: University Press of America.

Levinas, E. (1998). *Otherwise than Being*. Pittsburg, PA: Duquesne University Press.

Lock, A. & Strong, T. (2010*). Social Constructionism: Sources and stirring in theory and practice*. New York: Cambridge University Press.

Marx, K. (1967). Economic and philosophical manuscripts. In E. Fromm, *Marx's Concept of Man* (pp. 90–196). New York: Frederick Ungar Publishing Co.

Marx, K. (1974). Theses on Feuerbach. In K. Marx & F. Engels, *The German Ideology* (pp. 121–3). New York: International Publishers.

McLeod, J. (1997). *Narrative and Psychotherapy*. London: Sage.

McNamee, S. & Gergen, K. J. (Eds) (1992). *Therapy as Social Construction*. London: Sage.

McNamee, S. & Gergen, K. J. (1999). *Relational Responsibility: Resources for sustainable dialogue*. Thousand Oaks, CA: Sage.

Merleau-Ponty, M. (1962). *Phenomenology of Perception*. London: Routledge & Kegan Paul.

Monk, G., Winslade, J., Crocket, K., & Epston, D. (Eds) (1997). *Narrative Therapy in Practice: The archaeology of hope*. San Francisco, CA: Jossey-Bass.

Neimeyer, R. A. (2000). Performing psychotherapy: Reflections on postmodern practice. In L. Holzman & J. Morss (Eds), *Postmodern Psychologies, Societal Practice and Political Life* (pp. 100–201). New York: Routledge.

Newman, F. (1996). *Performance of a Lifetime: A practical-philosophical guide to the joyous life*. New York: Castillo International.

Newman, F. (1999). A therapeutic deconstruction of the illusion of self. In L. Holzman (Ed.), *Performing Psychology: A postmodern culture of the mind* (pp. 111–32). New York: Routledge.

Newman, F. & Fulani, L. (2011). *Let's pretend: Solving the education crisis in America, a special report*. New York: All Stars Project.

Newman, F. & Gergen, K. (1999). Diagnosis: The human cost of the rage to order. In L. Holzman (Ed.), *Performing Psychology: A postmodern culture of the mind* (pp. 73–86). New York: Routledge.

Newman, F. & Holzman, L. (1997). *The End of Knowing: A new developmental way of learning*. London: Routledge.

Newman, F. & Holzman, L. (1999). Beyond narrative to performed conversation ('In the beginning' comes much later). *Journal of Constructivist Psychology, 12*: 23–40.

Newman, F. & Holzman, L. (2003). All power to the developing! *Annual Review of Critical Psychology, 3*: 8–23.

Newman, F. & Holzman, L. (2006/1996). *Unscientific Psychology: A cultural-performatory approach to understanding human life*. Lincoln, NE: iUniverse Inc. (orig. publ. Westport, CT: Praeger).

Newman, F. & Holzman, L. (2013). *Lev Vygotsky: Revolutionary scientist* (Classic Edition). New York: Psychology Press (orig. publ. 1993, London: Routledge).

Nissen, M., Axel, E., & Jensen, T. B. (1999). The abstract zone of proximal conditions. *Theory and Psychology, 9*: 417–26.

Paré, D. A. & Larner, G. (Eds) (2004). *Collaborative Practice in Psychology and Therapy*. New York: Haworth Clinical Practice Press.

Prilleltensky, I. (1994). *The Morals and Politics of Psychology: Psychological discourse and the status quo*. Albany, NY: State University of New York Press.

Richardson, F. C., Fowers, B. J., & Guignon, C. B. (Eds) (1999). *Reenvisioning Psychology: Moral dimensions of theory and practice*. San Francisco, CA: Jossey-Bass.

Ricœur, P. (1996). *The Hermeneutics of Action*. London: Sage.

Rogoff, B. (2003). *The Cultural Nature of Human Development*. New York: Oxford University Press.

Rosen, H. & Kuehlwein, K. T. (Eds) (1996). *Constructing Realities: Meaning-making perspectives for psychotherapists*. San Francisco, CA: Jossey-Bass.

Sampson, E. E. (1993). *Celebrating the Other*. Hemel Hempstead: Harvester Wheatsheaf.

Sloan, T. (Ed.) (2000). *Critical Psychology: Voices for change*. London: Macmillan.

Strong, T. & Paré, D. A. (Eds) (2004). *Furthering Talk: Advances in discursive therapies*. New York: Kluwer Academic.

Vygotsky, L. S. (1978). *Mind in Society*. Cambridge, MA: Harvard University Press.

Vygotsky, L. S. (1987). *The Collected Works of L. S. Vygotsky, Volume 1*. New York: Plenum.

Vygotsky, L. S. (1993). *The Collected Works of L. S. Vygotsky, Volume 2*. New York: Plenum.

Vygotsky, L. S. (1994). The problem of the environment. In R. van der Veer & J. Valsiner (Eds), *The Vygotsky Reader* (pp. 338–54). Oxford: Blackwell.

Vygotsky, L. S. (1997). The historical meaning of the crisis in psychology: A methodological investigation. In *The Collected Works of L .S. Vygotsky, Volume 3* (pp. 233–343). New York: Plenum.

Wertsch, J. V. (1991). *Voices of the Mind: A sociocultural approach to mediated action*. Cambridge, MA: Harvard University Press.

White, M. & Epston, D. (1990). *Narrative Means to Therapeutic Ends*. New York: W. W. Norton.

7

THE FUTURE OF HUMANISM

Cultivating the humanities impulse in mental health culture

James T. Hansen

In this chapter I argue that the future of humanism is dependent upon the cultivation of the humanities impulse in mental health culture. Certain orientations to helping can be categorized as humanities approaches because their focus is on human meaning systems. The dominant medical model, in contrast, purposefully eschews human meaning systems. Unfortunately, humanities approaches are generally disconnected from each other, which weakens their ability to impact mental health culture. Humanism will have a bright future if it is conjoined with other humanities-based orientations. This would create a powerful, unified humanities response to the technical approaches that currently dominate the helping professions.

I am pleased and honoured to have been invited to share my thoughts on the future of Humanistic Psychology. I have given this topic a great deal of thought over the past couple of decades, so I appreciate the opportunity to consolidate my ideas into a succinct essay. In short, I believe that the future of humanism is dependent upon the ability of helping professionals to cultivate the humanities impulse in mental health culture. To understand what I mean by this, I provide a brief history of humanism below.

Brief history of humanism

The humanistic revolution in psychology echoed many of the themes present in Renaissance humanism, which emerged centuries before (Davidson, 2000).

Rather than understanding human beings as pawns of God or as scientific specimens, Renaissance humanists endeavored to appreciate people on their own terms (Tarnas, 1991). Analogously, the mid-20th-century psychological humanists revolted against the reductionist image of human beings proffered by psychoanalysis and behaviorism, which were the dominant treatment orientations at the time (deCarvalho, 1990). According to the psychological humanists, human experiences (e.g. love, anxiety, aesthetic awe) should not be reduced to psychic parts or stimulus–response contingencies, but could only be adequately understood holistically, as unique elements of the human condition (Matson, 1971).

There are potentially many ways to conceptualize the changes in mental health culture that the pioneering psychological humanists hoped to achieve. For various reasons (which I elaborate below), I prefer to think of Rogers (1957), Maslow (1968) and their colleagues as advocating for a mental health culture based on the humanities (Hansen, 2012). Indeed, the psychological humanists argued that the humanities (e.g. history, literature, philosophy), not science, should serve as the intellectual foundation for the helping professions (Fishman, 1999). This is a sensible proposition because the fundamental data of both the humanities and the helping professions are human meaning systems.

Naturally, as an outgrowth of their conceptual emphasis on unreduced human experience, the psychological humanists viewed the therapeutic relationship as the central area of concern in the helping encounter (Rogers, 1957). Rogers (1957), for instance, theorized that the establishment and maintenance of certain relational conditions is all that is needed for successful client outcomes. Indeed, decades of outcome research has consistently verified the humanistic premise that the therapeutic relationship, not specific techniques, is the most important variable in treatment outcomes (Wampold, 2001).

Why, then, given the tremendous amount of research that supports humanistic conceptualizations of the helping situation, has humanism been suppressed in contemporary mental health culture? To ask this question another way, why has the humanities emphasis in the helping professions, which is known to be the conceptual path to positive outcomes, been replaced by a supposedly scientific emphasis on techniques, which has been consistently shown to contribute little to treatment outcomes?

The answers to these questions are complex, and a full exploration of them is beyond the scope of this chapter. However, Elkins (2009), in his outstanding book, offered insightful opinions about the fall of humanism that are worth reviewing. Humanistic Psychology, Elkins argued, empowered clients, a move that threatened the established power base of mental health professionals. Humanism made helping client-centered instead of expert-centered. Mental health professionals, hoping to re-establish their power, reacted against this egalitarian view of the therapeutic relationship. As a result, the helping professions became increasingly scientific and medicalized, thereby fortifying the supposed expertise of practitioners and diminishing the power of clients. Contemporarily, the humanities vision of the founding humanists has been buried under a scientific, technical and medicalized view of the therapeutic encounter (Hansen, 2009).

Humanities impulse in contemporary mental health culture

The humanities impulse (which emphasizes human meaning systems over techniques) has been an omnipresent force throughout the history of mental health (Hansen,

2009, 2012). However, the manifestation of this impulse has varied, depending on the era in which it arose. During the mid-20th century, the humanities impulse gave rise to psychological humanism. Although humanism has been suppressed in modern times, the humanities impulse continues to be an important force in contemporary mental health culture. Arguably, this contemporary humanities impulse has taken the form of the postmodernist movement. In order to understand postmodernism, the basic assumptions of modernism must be reviewed.

Briefly, modernism presumes that: (a) there are singular truths that human beings can objectively apprehend; and (b) each person has a self, which is the center of their human agency (Hansen, 2004). Both of these modernist assumptions are present in traditional psychological humanism (Hansen, 2005b). That is, psychological humanism presumes that: (a) psychological truths about clients can be apprehended by an empathic therapist; and (b) clients have a true self, with mental health being equated with fidelity to one's congruent, actualized self (Hansen, 2005b). Postmodernists reject these modernist assumptions about truth and self (Gergen, 1999). For postmodernists, truth and self are human creations that shift and change as a function of the community in which one is currently participating (McNamee, 1996).

A number of innovative approaches to practice and research were formulated as a result of the introduction of postmodernist ideas to mental health culture. For example, solution-focused (de Shazer, 1985) and narrative therapies (e.g. White and Epston, 1990) have direct conceptual ties to postmodernism because these therapeutic systems emphasize the creation of new, adaptive meaning systems, rather than the discovery of fixed truths. Qualitative research, as another example of a movement informed by postmodernism, is a method of inquiry that does not presume universal laws, but attempts to understand people in their local environments (Berg, 2004).

The general emphasis of postmodernism, then, at least as it has been applied to the helping encounter, has been on the creation of human meaning systems (Hansen, 2006). New meanings are judged by their adaptive utility within the therapeutic relationship, not by their epistemological proximity to a supposed objective truth about clients (Hansen, 2007a). In contrast, psychological humanism, because it remains steeped in modernist assumptions, is epistemically aimed at the accurate, empathic discovery of truths about clients (Hansen, 2005b). Psychological humanism, therefore, is a mid-century manifestation of the humanities impulse that has generally not been philosophically updated to embrace contemporary ideas about truth and self. As I note below, these conceptual divisions among humanities orientations play a role in preventing the humanities impulse from rising as a strong, unified force in contemporary mental health culture.

Cultivating the humanities impulse

To review, I have argued that an emphasis on human meaning systems (which I have called the humanities impulse) regularly arises in mental health culture. This humanities impulse is also regularly suppressed by a technical, medicalized view of human nature. Indeed, mental health history can be read as a continual battle for dominance between humanities and technical views of the helping encounter (Hansen, 2009). Contemporarily, humanism is suppressed, and technical approaches are dominant (Elkins, 2009).

In this regard, there are strong conceptual advantages to defining psychological humanism as a particular instance of the humanities impulse in mental health culture, rather than as an isolated theoretical orientation. Specifically, by making this conceptual move, humanism can be conjoined with, and thereby fortified by, other humanities-based orientations, such as postmodernist approaches. Also, the humanities represent an established disciplinary category that has larger implications for the professional life of helping professionals than a single theoretical orientation, such as humanism. There are, therefore, wider professional implications of adopting a thoroughgoing humanities mindset than there are for simply endorsing humanism as a treatment orientation (Hansen, 2012).

From this conceptual vantage point, the future of humanism is dependent upon the ability of helping professionals to cultivate the humanities impulse in contemporary mental health culture. In order for humanism to re-emerge as a vital helping orientation, this cultivation must occur in several professional realms: (a) theoretical, (b) empirical, (c) practice and (d) professional culture.

Theoretically, as mentioned above, humanism continues to be steeped in modernist assumptions (Hansen, 2005b), a situation that keeps humanism theoretically sequestered from other humanities orientations. Arguably, humanism should be brought up to speed with postmodernism, so that movements that emphasize human meaning systems can become a unified humanities force in mental health culture (Hansen, 2005b). For instance, the consolidated self of humanism makes little sense in a postmodern world, wherein selves are continually bombarded by multifarious identity opportunities (Gergen, 1991). Diverse masks of self that adapt to various communal demands should arguably be the new standard for mental health, not the stubborn, unyielding consolidated self of traditional humanism (Gergen, 1995).

The humanistic ideal of therapists finding the truth about their clients also smacks of an outdated modernist view of the helping encounter. In this regard, I have suggested that the traditional humanistic ideal of 'accurate empathic understanding' (Rogers, 1957: 99) be replaced by the concept of 'emotional resonance' (Hansen, 2005b: 10), a phrase that conceptually subtracts the truth ideal inherent in the concept of accurate empathic understanding, yet retains the idea that therapists should intervene in ways that are experientially meaningful to clients. In turn, therapeutic systems based on postmodernist assumptions can be significantly enriched by the traditional humanistic focus on the therapeutic relationship (Hansen, 2005b). After all, meanings are not constructed in a vacuum; they require certain relational conditions (which were best articulated by the traditional humanists) to emerge and take hold. Humanism, then, needs to be theoretically updated so that it can join forces with other manifestations of the humanities impulse in mental health culture. There is strength in numbers. Humanism stands a much better chance of survival if it is theoretically brought into the fold with other humanities-based orientations.

Although there has been work done in this area (e.g. Hansen, 2005b), there is still much to do.

Of course, there are other, more practical actions that can be taken to strengthen the humanities impulse in contemporary mental health culture. Psychotherapy researchers, for instance, should abandon the failed empirically supported treatment movement, which was designed to discover optimal treatments for particular conditions (Elkins, 2009). The problems with this anti-humanistic movement are too numerous to detail in this chapter. Wampold (2001), however, provides some excellent suggestions for alternative research agendas, which, in my estimation, are congruent with a humanities-based conceptualization of the helping encounter.

Practitioners can cultivate the humanities impulse in mental health culture by carefully considering whether to participate in anti-humanities-based realms of practice. For instance, the medical model, with its emphasis on biological reductionism, disorders and techniques, is the antithesis of humanities ideals (Hansen, 2005a, 2007b). Of course, I am fully aware that the medical model is a reality of contemporary practice, and that practitioners might have difficulty making a living if they do not participate in it. Therefore, I am not advising practitioners to boycott the medical model, only to think critically about the ideological impact of participating in it.

Professionally, the structure of the helping professions has been founded upon a hierarchical model that is reminiscent of technical/scientific professional culture (Hansen, 2012). Research knowledge from on high is disseminated to the lowly practitioners below; licensure, approved continuing education credits, and mandated supervision are culturally entrenched components of professional life for helping professionals (at least in the United States). My humanities colleagues (e.g. English and history professors) operate in professional cultures that are far less hierarchical and rule bound. No one tells them how to think and practice, or the proper way to educate themselves after graduation. Cultivating the humanities impulse would mean bringing elements of the humanities' professional culture to the helping professions. Some ideas about reconfiguring professional life for helping professionals have been offered (e.g. Hansen, 2012; House, 2003), but there is still a good deal of work to be done in this area.

Conclusions

I have argued that the future of humanism depends upon the ability of helping professionals to cultivate the humanities impulse (i.e. emphasis on human meaning systems) in mental health culture. Conceptualizing humanism as a manifestation of a larger humanities impulse has at least two conceptual advantages over regarding humanism as an isolated theory: (a) humanism can be theoretically conjoined with other humanities-based orientations, thereby creating a powerful and united humanities response (rather than a weak, conceptually disjointed one) to the technical, medical ideologies that currently dominate mental health culture; and (b) the humanities, as an organizing construct, is richer and more theoretically inclusive than humanism. Therefore, ideas from the humanities can provide mental health professionals with greater guidance and direction than humanism alone, particularly with regard to professional culture (i.e. mental health professionals can consider adopting elements of long-established humanities' professional cultures). In my opinion, then, humanism has a bright future if theoreticians, researchers and practitioners focus their professional energies on human meaning systems instead of the technical aspects of the helping encounter.

Perhaps, though, there is a better, simpler reason to believe that humanism has a bright future than the ones I have offered. In this regard, I regularly invite my students and supervisees to engage in an introspective task. Specifically, I ask them to recall a time when they felt emotionally burdened, spoke to someone (e.g. a friend, family member, minister, counselor, etc.) about their troubles, and left the conversation feeling renewed. After providing a few minutes of silence, I ask them to tell me what the person to whom they spoke did to help them feel better (as part of the initial instruction, I deliberately tell them not to reveal the nature of their problem to me, just the type of responses that the helper provided). At this point, I would like to invite you, the reader, to take a break from reading, and engage in this introspective task for a few moments.

I suspect that your responses are very similar to the responses of my students and supervisees. Indeed, over the many years that I have conducted this experiment, there has been almost universal agreement that the helper listened intently with a non-judgmental attitude, tried to see the problem from the individual's point of view, validated the concerns of the individual, and, perhaps, through empathy, gently helped the person to see a side of the issue that she or he had not seen before. No one has ever said that the helper corrected irrational thoughts, told the person that she or he had a particular disorder, or made a list of goals for the person to accomplish with accompanying strategies and timelines. This, then, is the fundamental reason that humanism has a bright future: everyone knows that it works.

References

Berg, B. (2004) *Qualitative Research Methods for the Social Sciences*, 5th edn, Boston: Allyn & Bacon.
Davidson, L. (2000) 'Philosophical foundations of humanistic psychology', *The Humanistic Psychologist*, 28: 7–31; reprinted in *Self & Society: International Journal for Humanistic Psychology*, 40 (2), 2013, pp. 7–17.
DeCarvalho, R. (1990) 'A history of the "third force" in psychology', *Journal of Humanistic Psychology*, 30 (4): 22–44.
De Shazer, S. (1985) *Keys to Solution in Brief Therapy*, New York: W.W. Norton.
Elkins, D. (2009) *Humanistic Psychology: A Clinical Manifesto. A Critique of Clinical Psychology and the Need for Progressive Alternatives*, Colorado Springs, CO: University of the Rockies Press.
Fishman, D. (1999) *The Case for a Pragmatic Psychology*, New York: New York University Press.
Gergen, K. (1991) *The Saturated Self: Dilemmas of Identity in Contemporary Life*, New York: Basic Books.

Gergen, K. (1995) 'The healthy, happy human being wears many masks', in W. Anderson (ed.), *The Truth about the Truth: De-confusing and Re-constructing the Postmodern World* (pp. 136–50), New York: G.P. Putnam's Sons.

Gergen, K. (1999) *An Invitation to Social Construction*, Thousand Oaks, CA: Sage.

Hansen, J.T. (2004) 'Thoughts on knowing: epistemic implications of counseling practice', *Journal of Counseling and Development*, 82: 131–8.

Hansen, J.T. (2005a) 'The devaluation of inner subjective experiences by the counseling profession: a plea to reclaim the essence of the profession', *Journal of Counseling and Development*, 83: 406–15.

Hansen, J.T. (2005b) 'Postmodernism and humanism: a proposed integration of perspectives that value human meaning systems', *Journal of Humanistic Counseling, Education and Development*, 44: 3–15.

Hansen, J.T. (2006) 'Discovery and creation within the counseling process: reflections on the timeless nature of the helping encounter', *Journal of Mental Health Counseling*, 28: 289–308.

Hansen, J.T. (2007a) 'Counseling without truth: toward a neopragmatic foundation for counseling practice', *Journal of Counseling and Development*, 85: 423–30.

Hansen, J.T. (2007b) 'Should counseling be considered a health care profession? Critical thoughts on the transition to a health care ideology', *Journal of Counseling and Development*, 85: 286–93 (reprinted in the October 2007 edition of *Therapy Today*, British Association for Counselling and Psychotherapy).

Hansen, J.T. (2009) 'On displaced humanists: counselor education and the meaning-reduction pendulum', *Journal of Humanistic Counseling, Education and Development*, 48: 65–76.

Hansen, J.T. (2012) 'Extending the humanistic vision: toward a humanities foundation for the counselling profession', *Journal of Humanistic Counseling*, 51 (2): 131–44.

House, R. (2003) *Therapy beyond Modernity: Deconstructing and Transcending Profession-centred Therapy*, New York and London: Karnac Books.

Maslow, A. (1968) *Toward a Psychology of Being*, 2nd edn, New York: Van Nostrand Reinhold.

Matson, F. (1971) 'Humanistic theory: the third revolution in psychology', *The Humanist*, 12: 7–11.

McNamee, S. (1996) 'Psychotherapy as a social construction', in H. Rosen and K. Kuchlwein (eds), *Constructing Realities: Meaning-making Perspectives for Psychotherapists* (pp. 115–37), San Francisco, CA: Jossey-Bass.

Rogers, C.R. (1957) 'The necessary and sufficient conditions of therapeutic personality change', *Journal of Consulting Psychology*, 21: 95–103.

Tarnas, R. (1991) *The Passion of the Western Mind: Understanding the Ideas that Have Shaped Our World View*, New York: Harmony.

Wampold, B. (2001) *The Great Psychotherapy Debate: Models, Methods, and Findings*, Mahwah, NJ: Erlbaum.

White, M. and Epston, D. (1990) *Narrative Means to Therapeutic Ends*, New York: W.W. Norton.

8

CLIMATE DYNAMICS

A study in psycho-social analysis

David Wasdell

It was 22nd of July and the year was 1975. Dr Pierre Turquet, the Director of the Tavistock Institute of Human Relations had invited me to meet him in his office. (Or had I been summoned? I had no idea why I was there.) Eventually he came to the point: 'We would like you to lead a research project into the psycho–analysis of Schonian networks.' Donald Schon had recently written *Beyond the Stable State* (Schon, 1973) and the new research initiative represented a major innovation for the 'Tavi', breaking out beyond the usual structured frame of hierarchical systems into the realm of interconnected cellular networks. It opened up exploration of the psychodynamics of systems that eventually evolved into 'Chaos Theory', 'Complexity Science', social networks and beyond. It was to lay the foundations of 'Psycho-Social Analysis'.

To support the project Pierre assembled and introduced a team of four. He would himself be joined by Gordon Lawrence and Drs Daniels and Gosling. It was an awesome foursome and my appointment left me puzzled and bewildered. Only with over four decades of hindsight am I able to make sense of the selection of a partially dyslexic polymath, a conceptualizer of multi-dimensional patterns in highly complex contexts, with a tendency to 'think outside the box' and challenge the constraints and boundaries of any paradigm no matter how deeply embedded in institutional dynamics and defences it might be. At the time, however, I was naively unaware of the fraught dynamics at the very heart of the Tavistock Institute, or of the fact that the splits and opposition to Pierre's innovative thinking and creative leadership were focused right at the core of the new research project he had conceived. I never saw him again.

Five months later Pierre Turquet was dead. He died with his partner in a high-speed impact with the support structures of a bridge in his beloved France. Road conditions were good and no other vehicle was involved. Rumours of suicide circulated. The research group never reconvened.

In *Exploring Individual and Organizational Boundaries*, a book edited by Gordon Lawrence, published in 1979, and dedicated to the memory of Dr Turquet, Lawrence wrote:

> In the last two months or so of his life he was full of sadness at the human condition. He felt passionately that the Tavistock Clinic, with which he had been associated for just under half his life, had failed to move psycho-analysis from its essentially dyadic preoccupations to become a cultural tool, which he, along with others, had tried to do within the frame of group relations training. And he, at times would despair at the inability of men and women in contemporary society to question the authority structures and organisations of their institutions; to get behind the easily understood and taken-for-granted assumptions of group and institutional living.
>
> *(Lawrence, 1979: xvi)*

A little later in 1979 I wrote:

> At and after the time of his death I was forced to the conclusion that Pierre Turquet's last act was his most potent consultative word, an interpretative happening in partnership with Jean Wagstaff, his co-consultant, which acted out the despair, the constraint, and the regression which he experienced in his abortive attempt to break out of the controlling matrix of the Tavistock Model.
>
> *(Wasdell, 1979b)*

Pierre had hired his apprentice but had neither the cognitive paradigm nor the institutional support to sustain the research agenda. In the aftermath of his sudden and violent demise I inherited a legacy that laid the foundations for a lifetime of consultancy research.

Our immediate objective was to explore the dynamics, processes, defences and paradigm at the heart of the Tavistock Institute which had so effectively contained and neutered the initiative of its Director. Our initial conclusions were encapsulated in two papers delivered in dynamic seminar during the Consultancy Training Group of the Tavistock Leicester Conference in March 1979. First came the seminal presentation of '*Towards a Unified Field Theory of Human Behaviour*' (Wasdell, 1979a). It combined the prenatal world of foetal formation with the post-natal field of infant development, joined by the caesura of the trauma of birth. The primitive psychotic defences identified by Melanie Klein as 'innate/instinctive' (Klein *et al.*, 1952), grounded in Freud's delineation of the conflict between the life instinct and the death instinct and developed by Bion in his '*Experiences in Groups*' (Bion, 1961) lay unchallenged at the core of the Tavistock paradigm (Wasdell, 1997). The repeated assertion that 'life begins at birth' was clearly a myth whose function was to annihilate all trace of previous trans-marginal impingement. It established the whirling sword that rendered taboo any connection with time past. Once the continuum of experience across the boundary of parturition had been established, it became clear that while the primitive defences were indeed 'innate' they were not instinctive. They were learned on the journey between the worlds.

The matrix of defences against anxiety

While personal, object and part-object relations may be learned in the domain of the developing infant, environmental relations evolve in the watery cosmos of foetal experience. Connectivity to this living world requires no work. Nutrients and energy sustain exponential growth. Waste-products are removed from the system and absorbed elsewhere. Awareness of mother as protective container precedes the experience of mother as nurse.

Existentially, as full-term approaches, the holding environment shrinks. Overcrowding becomes the order of the day. Pollution embitters the amnion. Resource availability is diminished. Growth falters. The hormonal cocktail reflects rising anxiety in symbiotic resonance between mother and child. Environmental relations mutate imperceptibly from good to bad. Future sustainability is called into question. Survival demands transition.

Birth-time is an evolutionary compromise between enlarged cranial diameter and diminished pelvic elasticity, between the requirements of an expanding brain and the consequences of an upright posture. Species-specific prematurity optimises the chance of survival for both mother and child, but at a cost.

In *The Secret Life of the Unborn Child*, Thomas Verny, (the founder and initial president of the Pre and Perinatal Psychology Association of North America) wrote: 'Even in the best of circumstances, birth reverberates through the child's body like a seismic shock of earthquake proportions' (Verny, 1982: 86). Almost identical words were used to me in New York about the experience of 9/11, where 'anxiety went off the Richter scale' and Rich Picciotto, the 'Last Man Down', described his experience of being caught in the crushing collapse of the North Tower as 'being born again' (Picciotto, 2002: 91).

From the nuance of ambivalence to full-blown splitting, the tree-form of the placenta morphs from the tree of life to the carrier of the knowledge of good and evil, and its snake-like companion shifts symbolic association from cornucopia to harbinger of eviction. Waves of muscular contraction become more frequent and intense. The cushioning sack of amniotic fluid ruptures leaving the neonatal head to act as a gynaecological instrument. Hypoxia builds. Anxiety climaxes into terror and pain. Endorphins peak but cannot sedate foetal distress (mother can have some pain-relief but little of it will reach her child). As the remains of the known world implode from behind, the head is crushed, moulded and forced through an opening that is too small. Rage collapses into impotence and hope of deliverance dies in despair facing the threat of annihilation. Passivity and violent retaliation, self-destruction, guilt and the search for salvation, all have their origins in this matrix. The past might have had its problems, but in contrast to this hell it beckons in reversed time to a veritable heaven. Eventually, with one last push the trauma is over. This is an encounter with climate change in the context of world-loss.

All connection with the past is severed, and knotted at the belly. Never again will oxygen and nutrients flow from the placenta. Gaseous exchange and oral resources will be the means of survival. Comfort is provided. The moment is treated as the beginning of life. It is as if nothing traumatic has happened. Birth-days are celebrated lest resonant memories come flooding back into the conscious mind.

For significant numbers, the transition will not have been so benign. Hyper-stress may have occurred much earlier in the journey. Some will have survived near-miscarriage or attempted abortion. Stressors and crises in the maternal world are transmitted across the uterine container. Prematurity, pre-eclampsia, anoxia, cord-strangulation, in-utero surgery, blockage of the birth canal with associated ventuse, forcepting or rescue caesarean section, can all play their part in exacerbating primal trauma. Then for some males among us, many Americans and nearly all Jews, just as recovery is under way, there is the secondary impingement of post-natal male genital mutilation or circumcision. Perhaps it should not be so surprising that castration anxiety played such a dominant part in Freudian psycho-analytic formulation.

Another sub-group are delivered by a different doorway. Pre-labour, elective caesarean section might avoid the trauma of vaginal delivery, but lays down an imprint of unanticipated traumatic shock, blurred by the numbness of anaesthesia. The resultant anxieties, defences, body-language, dynamics and life-script are different but profound.

Anxiety defences and their role in social dynamics

My second contribution to the Consultancy Training Group in 1979 was entitled '*The Boundaries of Group Dynamics*' (Wasdell, 1979b). It was a devastating analytic critique in response to *Exploring Individual and Organizational Boundaries* (Lawrence, 1979), published earlier that year and edited by Gordon Lawrence. It exposed the unexaminable defences embedded at the heart of the Tavistock paradigm and constituting the core of the Tavistock Model used as the framework of its training conferences. The subsequent psychodrama ruptured the dynamics of the Consultancy Training Group and had implications for other sectors of the conference. As I was about to leave, one of the staff, who was professionally dependent on Melanie Klein's delineation of the primitive paranoid-schizoid defences, refused to treat my contribution as a working initiative. It was interpreted in Freudian terms as an attack on leadership, a working-out of the myth of the attempted murder of the father of the primal horde, an example of paranoid phantasy associated with castration anxiety. It was made abundantly clear that my continued work under the aegis of the Tavistock Institute was no longer welcome.

I was evicted, excommunicated, cast into outer darkness, where for a time there was a very real experience of 'weeping and wailing and gnashing of teeth'! Part of the role of anxiety defences in social and organizational dynamics is to protect the dominant paradigm from examination and potentially disruptive intervention. It was obvious that Turquet's research initiative could not be contained within the old wineskins of his institutional home. If his self-immolation closed the boundary at one end, then my eviction sealed it at the other. A few years later, Eric Miller, Turquet's successor as Director of the Tavistock Institute, confided that he agreed with my analysis, but could not see how to apply it!

In retrospect, exclusion from the Tavi was a passport to creative freedom. Within two years we had established the 'Unit for Research into Changing Institutions' as a registered educational research Trust. We published '*Foundations of Psycho-Social Analysis*' (Wasdell, 1983, 1985) and a whole series of papers, presentations and studies that would make a book in their own right. By 1987 I had been invited to the USSR to give the opening and closing plenaries to the inaugural global conference of 'The Manhattan Project of Behavioural Science', and was subsequently appointed its director, renaming it 'The Meridian Programme'. Over 50 behavioural research workshops were conducted around the world. Thousands of hours of analytic research were conducted with individuals, groups, organizations and wider social institutions. Just nine months after the destruction of the twin towers I delivered the prize-winning two-part treatment of '*The Psychodynamics of War and Religion*' (Wasdell, 2003a) in downtown Manhattan. In September 2003 we pulled together the emerging theoretical construct in the presentation: '*Roots of the Common Unconscious: Towards a New Paradigm of Psychosocial Analysis*' (Wasdell, 2003b) given to the 14th Scientific Meeting of the A.K. Rice Institute in M.I.T.

The early years of the 21st century threw into sharp relief the dysfunctional effect of social defences against anxiety in the dynamics of global behaviour. It is perhaps worth quoting a few points from the text of the '*Open Letter on World Dynamics*' distributed to world leaders in December 2002. The comments apply even more powerfully today.

- That leadership emerges in large groups and social systems when there is a match between the unconscious dynamics and defences of the leader and the unconscious needs and wishes of the led. This relationship between pathology and politics exposes the system to significant risk in times of transition or crisis.
- That the global context of the human species within its holding environment is raising increasing social anxiety about future viability. The result is an increasing state of collective paranoia coupled with despair and impotence in the face of the enormity of scale and difficulties encountered in mobilising effective international action.
- That another response to the global situation is the social retreat into passivity, dissociation, collective trance and anxiolytic behaviour. Energy is invested in attempts to sedate the presenting symptoms of anxiety rather than focused on the underlying problems that are causing it.
- That heightened social anxiety leads to the reinforcement of fundamentalist ideologies, whether philosophical, political, economic or religious. These constructs defend individuals and systems from anxiety while detaching them from reality. Extreme pressure for conformity and collusion is experienced within the groups concerned, while intense conflict is engendered at their boundaries.

My concluding paragraph is worth reproducing in full:

- Under certain conditions normal defences, used to contain the experience in unconscious repression, are weakened, precipitating an acting-out of birth trauma in collective behaviour. Current global conditions constitute precisely such a context on a massive scale. Living space is constricted, resources are seen as inadequate to sustain current or future patterns of growth, the pace of change is accelerating, increased pressure is universally experienced and issues of environmental pollution are significant. Collective identification of the species as a mega-humanoid foetus within its global uterine space, leads to the perception of reaching critical mass within its holding environment. Under these conditions the collective foetal assumption is that the titanic struggle of birth is imminent. Realistic anxiety about the actual condition of the species is massively inflated by re-stimulated anxiety released from the collective unconscious, the threatened acting-out of which on a global scale probably constitutes the most severe crisis ever encountered by our human species.

(Wasdell, 2002: 2–5)

Clarifying climate change

In May 2005, the 'severe crisis' was spelled out in the virally circulated '*Global Warning*' (Wasdell, 2005). It identified three issues: the collision between exponential consumerism and limited global resources; the environmental implosion threatened by accelerating global warming; and the predictable social disruption from the unleashed response of psychotic social defences against anxiety. Within just over a year I took up responsibility for 'The Manhattan Project of Climate Science', quickly re-named the 'Apollo-Gaia Project'. The research agenda was concentrated on the most critically important 'known unknown', namely the amount by which the complex feedback dynamics of the global climate system would amplify the impact of the increasing concentration of atmospheric carbon dioxide. The second, and 'absolutely scary', question concerned the boundary conditions of the potential condition of 'runaway climate change'. Robust answers were essential if effective responses were to be mobilized and the dysfunctional defences and reality-denying dynamics were to be deconstructed at a scale and in a time-frame determined by the rate of change in our holding environment (Wasdell, 2012).

The ensuing (and continuing) period has proved to be the most demanding, stressful and occasionally life-threatening few years I have ever known. It has pushed my boundaries psychologically, physically and intellectually. The story of the journey will have to be told elsewhere, but the multi-media output of the Apollo-Gaia Project together with its critical strategic implications for global problem-solving are widely accessible via the website; see for instance '*Climate Dynamics: Facing the Harsh Realities of Now*' (Wasdell, 2015).

Defence delineation

In the early days, exploration of the processes, behaviour and embedded paradigmatic dogma of religious, analytic and psycho-therapeutic organizations, together with the complex set of their inter-relationships, constituted the 'royal road' into the collective unconscious. Today, those dynamics are being acted out in public space for all to see, albeit with increasingly powerful repression of insight into their origins and functions.

Any reality-related context that raises anxiety becomes a canvas onto which the social defences against anxiety are projected. The task is to reduce (defend against) the anxiety. Tragically, one outcome of the process is to elide the anxiety-generating information. Reducing anxiety, rather than realistic problem-solving, becomes the order of the day. Knowledge-generating activity ('scientia') has to be attacked, contradicted, discredited, de-funded, institutionally closed down, refused publication, undermined and ignored in proportion to the intensity of anxiety generated by its implications. Potentially angst-generating conclusions can serve to repress research findings and distort methodology across the scientific community. This diversion of reality-related attention into the inner task of anxiety management lies at the very core of psychosis, whether individual or collective.

Anxiety enters the awareness of social systems from two discrete but linked sources. The first we can term reality-related anxiety. It stems from contextual information associated with real threats requiring appropriate response. That is a healthy survival mechanism. The second (and under certain conditions far more powerful) source emerges into consciousness from deeply buried trauma normally held at bay by the ubiquitous defences against anxiety. This we can categorise as neurotic or even psychotic anxiety. It is activated by strong association, re-stimulation or triggering set off by current context. As defences weaken and previously unconscious content floods social awareness, process from the precipitating matrix comes to dominate collective dynamics. Grounding the imprint in its causal experience is a prerequisite for defence deconstruction and recovery of greater reality-orientation.

So against what are the 'primitive defences against anxiety' in place? Access, as in all effective post-traumatic-stress recovery, is gained at a point in time before trans-marginality is encountered. Attempts to access the material from a post-trauma perspective risk re-traumatization as the system is flooded by response to peak impingement without any protective defences.

First indications that all is not well may emerge from encounter with limits to growth: overcrowding, pollution, constraints in nutrients and energy resources. Triggering in post-trauma context drives the paranoid dynamics of capitalism, the obsessive dependence on exponential growth in energy and economics, and the commitment to 'sustainable development' (Wasdell, 1992). The defensive task is to internalize resources by all means available, whether the source be the physical/biological environment, the wealth of vulnerable others, the assets of less competitive companies, or the trading imbalance of the global economy. Foetal assumptions become fatal assumptions when extrapolated to the global environment. Enough is never enough to sedate the rising stress of the needy parasite as it encounters the constraints of the finite world. Interesting that the response of the UK government to the 1972 publication of the Club of Rome (Meadows *et al.*, 1972) was to assemble a team of expert economists and computer modellers in an attempt to destroy its conclusions. They failed, but paid scant regard to the warning.

As the prenatal journey moves forward in time, stressors mount beyond the bearable. The same context evolves from its historic form of good-enough holding environment to its current experience of crushing collapse and unbearable pain. Here, splitting or idealization has its roots. In retrospect the schizoid process empties the past of all negativities, and cleanses the present from all vestiges of hope. The split between good and bad, us and them, in-group and out-group, friend and enemy, heaven and hell, originates here and is projected universally in the dynamics of the post-natal world.

As reactivity, rage, retaliation and revenge collapse in the overwhelming experience of terror, impotence and helplessness, so hope of deliverance yields to feelings of overwhelming despair. In our post-natal presentation we recognise the point of abdication. It is all too big to cope with; the best we can do is give up and die in paralysed passivity. Or perhaps we should wait for rescue from somewhere else (there is always hope of salvation) or just mobilize some acting-out of anarchic rage in a frenetic orgy of violent destruction that only makes the situation immeasurably worse.

Time comes to a dead-end. There is no exit through this hell. The journey reverses and in phantasy is directed backwards into some idealized pre-trauma position. Post-trauma presentation is of regression to some utopian state held out seductively as promised future bliss. Religious myth and ritual, political ideology, the power-seeking manipulation of the electorate, and the irresistible attraction of winning the war are all manifestations of this defence.

Birth is the archetype of bereavement. The loss is of the original holding environment and its accompanying placental and umbilical companions, but seen through the rear-view mirror of idealization. The regaining of paradise lost is a ubiquitous but futile cultural imperative. Grieving is cosmic, pitched past pitch of grief, but for ever unresolved. Repressed behind the imprint of trans-marginality, the only way out is marked 'NO EXIT'. It is as if the transition has not happened. If birth is existential death from which we live in regressed retreat, then the dominant myth of post-natal life is one of collective foetal phantasy perpetuated in frozen time. The terminal boundary of death is reframed as birth. The repetitive cycle leaves no room for tears.

Civilisation unconsciously reifies foetal assumptions in fractal patterns of uterine ecology. Against this backdrop of psycho-social defence, the intimation of climate change triggers the collective re-staging of the trauma of birth as threatened change with no survivable outcome. The projected spectre of future traumatic catastrophe, to be denied and avoided at all costs, sits as an impassable phantasy across the bows of reality-related collective action. Realistic hope lies in the recognition that the psychotic level of anxiety does not emanate from future environmental disruption (that is quite tough enough in its own right!) but from the long past boundary between the dependent world of uterine regression and the new beginnings of post-natal work and responsibility.

Perhaps the time is fast approaching for us to deconstruct the primal defences, to recover from collective foetal phantasy, to acknowledge birth as survivable transition, to weep with burning tears as we mourn the loss of the known world, and to get on with the realistic task of problem-solving on the surface of a changing planet. Within that overall context the process of Humanistic Psychology must be one of reflection leading to the deconstruction of any residual defences at the heart of its own collusional dynamics. Our collective future calls for a catalytic contribution to the renaissance of civilisation as we prepare to ride the stormy waves of complexity in an unpredictable and turbulent environment.

Note

As final proof of the book was being sent to print we received news that Chapter 8 has been accepted for review by the Intergovernmental Panel on Climate Change in the psychology/sociology section of the Special Report on achieving the 1.5°C target.

References

Bion, W. R. (1961) *Experiences in Groups and Other Papers*, London: Tavistock Publications.

Klein, M., Heimann, P., Isaacs, S., & Rivière, J. (1952) *Developments in Psycho-Analysis*, No. 43, International Psycho-Analytic Library, London :Hogarth Press & Institute of Psycho-Analysis.

Lawrence, G. (1979) *Exploring Individual and Organizational Boundaries*, Chichester: John Wiley & Sons.

Meadows, D. H., Meadows, D. L., Randers, J., & Behrens III, W. W. (1972) *The Limits to Growth*: a report for the Club of Rome's project on the predicament of mankind, New York: Universe Books.

Picciotto, R. (2002) *Last Man Down*, London: BCA.

Schon, D. (1973) *Beyond the Stable State*, New York: Norton.

Verny, T. (1982) *The Secret Life of the Unborn Child*, London: Sphere Books.

Wasdell, D. (1979a) *Towards a Unified Field Theory of Human Behaviour*, www.meridian.org.uk/_PDFs/TUFT.pdf (accessed 31 March 2017).

Wasdell, D. (1979b) *The Boundaries of Group Dynamics*, www.meridian.org.uk/_PDFs/Boundaries%20of%20Group%20Dynamics.pdf (accessed 31 March 2017).

Wasdell, D. (1983) *Foundations of Psycho-Social Analysis, Part I: Diagnosis*, www.meridian.org.uk/_PDFs/FoundationsI.pdf (accessed 31 March 2017).

Wasdell, D. (1985) *Foundations of Psycho-Social Analysis, Part II: Analysis*, www.meridian.org.uk/_PDFs/Foundations%20II.pdf (accessed 31 March 2017).

Wasdell, D. (1992) *The Pre and Perinatal Grounds of Capitalism and the Free-Market Economy*, www.meridian.org.uk/_PDFs/Capitalism.pdf (accessed 31 March 2017).

Wasdell, D. (1997) *Tavistock Review, Self and Society*, May 1997, www.meridian.org.uk/_PDFs/Tavistock%20Review.pdf (accessed 31 March 2017).

Wasdell, D. (2002) *Open Letter on World Dynamics*, www.meridian.org.uk/_PDFs/Open%20 Letter%20Article.pdf (accessed 31 March 2017).

Wasdell, D. (2003a) *The Psychodynamics of War and Religion*, www.meridian.org.uk/_PDFs/ W&R%202.pdf (accessed 31 March 2017).

Wasdell, D. (2003b) *Roots of the Common Unconscious: Towards a New Paradigm of Psychosocial Analysis*, www.meridian.org.uk/_PDFs/Boston.pdf (accessed 31 March 2017).

Wasdell, D. (2005) *Global Warning*, www.meridian.org.uk/_PDFs/GlobalWarning1.pdf (accessed 31 March 2017).

Wasdell, D. (2012) *Feedback Dynamics, Sensitivity and Runaway Conditions in the Global Climate System*, www.apollo-gaia.org/Climate Sensitivity.pdf (accessed 31 March 2017).

Wasdell, D. (2015) *Climate Dynamics: Facing the Harsh Realities of Now*, www.apollo-gaia.org/ harsh-realities-of-now.html (accessed 31 March 2017).

9

STEPS TO A POLITICS OF HEART

Nick Duffell

> Man's nature is not a set thing . . . it is ever emergent . . . it is an open system, not a closed system.
>
> Clare Graves[1]

Searching for a New Politics

Politics seems to have taken a turn for the worse. There is widespread mistrust of politicians; voting apathy paralyses the young. Political views within nations are acutely polarized, making electoral prediction impossible. In our uncertain world, rapid changes in technology, economic austerity, mounting inequality and the migration of the global poor assist the politics of fear to strike popular chords. Frighteningly, the main beneficiary is an isolationist far Right, while a lack of international cooperation means massive global problems still remain unsolved.

My own view is that we have yet to fully acknowledge that an entirely new era is upon us and there has been a consequent failure of democracy. Equally, the mainstream media, that bridge between citizens and politicians, have failed to identify the rising politics of blame and hatred or to condemn the emergence of divisive personalities riding on this wave. This is inflamed by a lack of psychological-mindedness in news anchors and political commentators and facilitated by an obsession with superficial time-limited debate that masquerades as 'balanced'. Perversely, we have never been more exposed to information: we can know more about what is going on, and about ourselves – especially about what makes us healthy and what makes us sick – than at any time in history.

In many parts of the world, however, the search is on for a new politics that has more wisdom, empathy and authenticity – more heart, we might say. Increasingly, I detect a shift in attitudes in psychotherapy practitioners. Many are now beginning to believe it is time for the powerful psychological knowledge we have been gathering to emerge from the rare confines of the consulting room in order to help our political life mature and create a better world. As a contribution to this trend, this chapter looks at problems and opportunities raised by attempting to consider current affairs through a nascent psychology of the heart. Such a somatic orientation is increasingly important, I believe, as the election of Donald Trump heralds the triumph of the gut-reaction to the postmodernist obsession with living in the head, leaving us with what Mark Lilla, Professor of Modern History at Columbia, calls 'The End of Identity Liberalism'.[2]

My title echoes the work of one of the founding giants of Humanistic Psychology, the British anthropologist and systems theorist Gregory Bateson (1904–1980), whom I wish to honour here. Despite his phenomenal mental output, Bateson's life was rooted in personal grief. His eldest brother was killed in the First World War in 1918 – a year after Gregory went to public school. The year after he left, his middle brother shot himself beneath the statue of Anteros (popularly mistaken for Eros) the god of selfless love, in Piccadilly Circus. Bateson's life reminds us that creative thinking that can inspire a generation can be founded in a heart awakened by deep emotion.

It is one thing to talk the talk about the heart, or of love, but it is quite another to 'walk' it, to apply such qualities. A Native American proverb, 'Don't tell me about your visions unless they grow corn', is an appropriate warning[3]: we have to approach with humility. For clues to what a politics of heart might look like, let us begin by seeing how we use the word 'heart' and how this organ actually functions.

Heart talk

The heart has long been associated with a deep interiority, centrality and spirituality, with wisdom, intuition, enthusiasm, and empathy. English has countless phrases with a multiplicity of prepositions, demonstrating the universality of the heart's power. 'My heart goes *out* to you' conveys deepest sympathy. To say what is *in* one's heart commends transparency; to speak *from* the heart implies steadfast truth. To listen *with* all one's heart suggests a deep personal commitment to understand another. Footballers are said to 'play with heart' when they show passion, commitment and work rate, making up for any lack of skill or experience. 'Follow your heart' recommends being true to one's self despite an uncertain path. In these sayings the heart is positioned as the locus of a profound kind of receptive understanding and value-based agency – ideal fundaments for a politics of heart.

Throughout all cultures the heart has been associative with love, whether neighbourly, familial, intimate or romantic. 'The child of my heart' suggests a mature tenderness; 'I give you my heart' is the ultimate pledge. 'You're forever in my heart' suggests a vision of endurance perceived in the ecstasy of falling in love. Being broken-hearted conveys the grief that can only arise having given one's heart to another. But it also suggests a sober response to the folly of human behaviour, as polarization and wars continue despite the pressing global problems that ought to be uniting us.

At the same time the heart also implies a certain vulnerability: 'Don't take it to heart', advises self-protection. 'My heart says this but my head something else' suggests fallibility or the misguided sentimentality of an emotional response; it implies that the heart is invariably prone to naivety, while the head is supplied with unfailing reason. Sometimes this naivety seems to be ripe for manipulation: in recent years, we have heard much on the news of the geopolitical ambitions of winning 'hearts and minds', in projects devised by invading powers rightly suspicious of their welcome.

Again, the heart is where our deepest and sometimes darkest truths are said to reside. 'Who knows what is in his heart?' we might say, thinking of someone who seems to retreat from transparency; hardness of the heart is another possibility. Gandhi said: 'It is better to be violent, if there is violence in our hearts, than to put on the cloak of non-violence to cover impotence.'[4] The choice to give our lives for another can only 'come from the heart'. For the heart is also where life can effect the profoundest transformation and spiritual inspiration to motivate change, as Nobel Peace Prize-winner Mairead Corrigan Maguire said in the context of Northern Ireland: 'As our hearts are disarmed by God of our inner violence, they become God's instruments for the disarmament of the world.'[5]

Heart functions

The heart is primary: the first organ to develop *in utero* and the last to fail at death. Its prime job is to pump plasma and blood-cells carrying oxygen, nutrients, heat and energy through the vascular system to every part of the body, and then to return the spent fluids. As the body's hub and distribution centre in a closed system with arteries, capillaries and veins circulating the blood, its function is one of connecting, relating, nourishing, replenishing and cleansing in a direct feedback loop with all tissue. Despite its centrality, the heart works in close partnership with the lungs, liver and brain. This direct connection in life-giving agency, systemic feedback and partnership is in itself a good foundation metaphor for a new politics. And there is more.

Along with its electrical 'wiring', the heart's rhythmic pumping produces an electro-magnetic field that is measurable up to two metres outside of the body and probably further. So far, our knowledge of this field is in its infancy, but it seems likely that it is involved in communication and composes the energetic substratum of loving relationships, empathy and intuition. The deeper and wider the relationship bond between mammalian hearts, regardless of sex and even sometimes species, the more intense the empathic connection can be – even over great distances. So when people say, 'My heart goes out to you in your time of need', this could well be realistic and it might prove to have healing capacity. Outpourings of national sympathy, such as when a child is missing or when Princess Diana was killed, for example, when our 'hearts are as one' do meet their target. In political discourse, genuine empathic connection can be as easily applied for the common good as it is when manipulation whips up fear and blame.

The heart's 'intelligence' is not just metaphorical, for it is also a cybernetic information-processing centre connected into the entire nervous system. With its neural tissue receiving perceptual data from the brain and sending messages back up to it via the large Vagus nerve the heart can be said to determine whether to fire either the Sympathetic (fight/flight) or Parasympathetic (rest/repair) responses of the Autonomic Nervous System (ANS). Here we appreciate the heart's central regulatory role for the whole organism.

The human body is a marvel of interlocking systems with discrete individual functions that relate with each other. The body's basic drivers are self-preservation and reproduction, but the operating mode of the systemic whole is *self-regulation* in response to environmental conditions. In this purpose, each cell and each organ cooperates and self-regulates. Aided by the lungs, the heart has a commanding role in how it influences response and behaviour through its ability to alter its beat rate and rhythm, release hormones to suppress internal organs or facilitate interpersonal connection, and, crucially, its control of the ANS.

Prioritizing at times of need, in service of the whole, is *autonomic*; that is to say it does not require *conscious* effort. But our understanding of how these processes work has lately been revolutionizing trauma therapy, because we can learn how to apply *intentional* self-regulation to our bodies. We can influence our heart rate, and thereby our central nervous system and overall wellbeing, by how we breathe, behave, and even by what we think. Conscious self-regulation is increasingly becoming the most important 'new' idea in mental-health care, chiefly because it works and puts patients back in charge of their own lives. Methods such as Mindfulness, Mentalization, the use of biofeedback devices and Cognitive Behaviour Therapy are being integrated into mainstream approaches not as self-development aids but as self-*management* tools. At a systemic level, self-regulation works better than insight therapy to counter conditioned trauma-inspired knee-jerk defensive responses that produce more adrenalin and cortisol than is good for us.

In biology, the ability to self-regulate is one of the concepts that define maturity in organisms. Regularly a challenge for adolescents, self-regulation is the key to self-driven behaviour change and becoming properly autonomous and accountable. Of all the functions of the heart that already holds lessons for us in empathy, connection and feedback, the regulatory one is perhaps the least appreciated. But here we may find perhaps *the most* important principle that has to underpin a new politics: it must embrace the need for conscious self-regulation if we are to survive and thrive. And this, in a globalized world, means we must increase regulatory governance through democratically enforced international cooperative legislation.[6]

Heart values

A politics of heart will evidently be rooted in values. Narratives of values already inform political movements, if frequently undermined by ideology. Neoliberalism, for example, seems to have entirely bypassed the values of fairness or inclusiveness.

Goldsmiths economist Will Davies argues that competitiveness has become an 'über-virtue', leaving societies unable 'to find value in things, other than their being "better" than something else'[7]. Politics gets consequently more polarized, for demonising 'the Other' is at the heart of the competitive ideal, and in times of crisis it tends to get worse rather than better.

Heart functioning is antipathetic to demonization, for it operates in cooperative mediation within the body's potentially polarized energetic centres, according to Dutch development psychologist Willem Poppeliers.[8] Besides, whether cooperation is a virtue, a value or a spiritual goal, it is an effective antidote to the destructive tit-for-tat competition between governments that is now viral, argues John Bunzl, who founded the International Simultaneous Policy Organisation.[9]

Equally, values can be employed divisively or erroneously: talk of 'British values', for example, assumes they can be owned. Neo-Platonic psychologies such as Psychosynthesis see this as a category error: understanding values as self-existent, we can only try to invoke or align with them. Besides, 'man's nature is not a set thing . . . values change from system to system as his total psychology emerges in new form with each quantum-like jump', as Professor Clare Graves reasoned.[10] Evolutionary theories based on Graves and Piaget's work, such as 'Spiral Dynamics', show how values are not fixed but differ and succeed each other in complexity as consciousness and worldviews evolve toward an increasingly global and inclusive perspective, which a politics rooted in human potential must take note of.[11]

Most humanistic practitioners recognise that values are context-dependent and closely tied to feelings. Values become important according to both the degree of emotional intelligence associated with mature or immature levels of self-awareness and the prevailing environmental conditions. Social justice can go out of the window when we feel under threat, when we are more likely to regress to being driven by survival impulses, as Maslow knew. Values influence choice, and the work of neuroscientists such as Antonio Damasio[12] has shown us the importance of emotions in good decision-making. I have argued elsewhere that the British political elite – mostly hyper-rationally attachment-deprived 'Wounded Leaders'[13] – are predictably likely to underperform here, however much they broadcast visions of one-nationism. Being made to attend boarding schools at a tender age will have atrophied their cortical feedback systems as a result of too much training in left-brain cognitive faculties at the expense of too little emotional literacy.

The heart in its emotional capacity can be a gauge. Popularly, we think of the heart not 'opening' or remaining 'closed', as it will when we are full of fear, being defensive, intolerant of difference. In these cases our emotional worlds are conditioned by what could be called 'lower' emotions or affects: anxiety, fear, anger, hatred, disgust. Then the world is not seen as safe enough to fire our rest and repair response. Instead we tend to fire fight/flight, or as Polyvagal expert Stephen Porges has shown in his work on the Social Engagement System, we resort to 'immobilization' and fail to send or receive the appropriate relational signals of safety.[14] This can become chronic: in a learned default system where the world is experienced as hostile,[15] dissociating or projecting out blame or scorn is logical.[16] This is precisely the kind of knowledge we must instruct our powerful news anchors in, so that political commentary starts to become *psychologically* intelligent.

Only deep feeling, such as grief, longing, empathy, compassion – even sometimes outrage – can 'open' the heart so it fires the parasympathetic response, pumping blood rhythmically, creating inner repose and influencing the out-going connecting electro-magnetic field. Now, with its relational transforming potential, the heart releases hormones that evoke kindness, empathy and bonding. As Elizabeth Kübler-Ross's work showed us many years ago, grieving regularly has a transformational potential and is particularly effective in countering the defensive emotionality of anger, denial, and bargaining with difficult realities. This is an important lesson for any politics faced with the fact that national sovereignty under globalization has become a myth however hard we still cling to it and however loudly the Right trumpets it.[17]

Applying the heart's resources

Birgitta Jonsdottir is a poet and the founder of the Icelandic Pirate Party, a fringe party that at the time of writing was likely to become part of the next government. Jonsdottir plans to visit every family in her admittedly small country to find out what their fears, wishes, visions and good ideas are.[18] This kind of relational encounter is likely to make people feel included, less likely to 'act out' and potentially to generate an enormous fund of ideas. I suggest that such a process is less about pluralism or 'getting everybody in the big tent', than an application of the politics of heart's toolkit: in this case as an *empathic consultative resource*. Pluralism is a mark of societal health, but as a policy goal risks becoming excessively conceptual, because it tends toward replication, or – according to the helpful distinction offered by Ken Wilber – it favours *translation* rather than *transformation*. Our language shows this: the heart seeks connection and wants effective transformation for the sake of the whole; the ego frequently wants to see itself as tolerant, plural or diverse – adjectives as opposed to substantive values.

Further creative approaches that combine vision and practicality are happening in other small Scandinavian countries. Denmark's *Alternativet* party already has ten elected parliamentarians. In July 2016, MPs Helle Engelbrectsen and Brian Fransden ran a workshop (to which I was invited) in the home of former Independent Mayor of Frome, Peter MacFadyen, author of *Flatpack Democracy*, to teach citizens and community activists their groundbreaking political methods.[19] Seeking to be value-based for the good of the whole, the Danish Alternative Party has identified six basic core values: courage, empathy, generosity, humour, transparency and humility. From these values they formulate rules and principles, which are applied to how they conduct their debates, even if some are – they admit – difficult to apply. Engelbrectsen adds: 'Some people laugh at me in Denmark, that's why we *need* humour!'[20] *Alternativet*'s debating principles include:

- empathise core values;
- be curious;

- listen more than you speak;
- argue openly and factually;
- openly discuss the advantages and disadvantages of your arguments;
- acknowledge when you don't know the answer.

I was impressed by how these MPs were able to include vulnerability within a robust and pragmatic approach to politics. Their principles seem to come directly from the heart, especially its receptive and connective aspects – a revolutionary policy in a world often dominated by hyper-masculine competitiveness. Other issues that arose in the interchange over these days were:

- What can citizens do? Do we just give up after polling day?
- Since everyone needs support to keep their hearts open, we should consider the need to train, coach and support our politicians, rather than universally criticising them.
- Listening is primary; it has to be trained. How do you listen when you are thinking about what you have to say?
- Feedback has to do with learning; the bridge is being inspired.
- We need to find a language that is accessible enough for citizens and sophisticated enough for the issues.
- The gap between citizens and politicians could be mediated by community politics.
- A local-to-global alliance might become more important than national ones in the future.

It is time now to consider some of the challenges for a politics of heart.

Questions and limitations

As I write, immigration has been the dominating factor in current affairs. Surveys indicate that the majority of the UK population oppose immigration and many blame immigrants for their economic and social problems. This is becoming a global phenomenon: the unexpected success of Donald Trump rests largely on such fears. How can we welcome strangers into our community when we are afraid of them? Our biology limits us in conceiving of empathy for the object of fear. Brains are designed to scan for safety and to mistrust strangers, our nervous system to respond to prevailing conditions ascertained. When fear is the dominant emotion, hearts will pump harder to avoid danger and shut off rest and repair.

Humanistic Psychology practitioners know that the best way to counteract this in clients is to first create safety in the consulting room, then to establish a sympathetic relationship within which to allow the client to speak about their anxieties. This way ANS self-regulation begins to calm both parties, as the parasympathetic system fires in both listener and receiver; once self-regulated, the client might be able to voice complex and disturbing thoughts and feelings. Exactly this has been missing in our political scene. Many of our citizens have not been heard about their fears of change, their fears of globalization, their fears of being swamped by foreigners. Unless people are listened to, when fear grips them, they can easily dissociate and project onto scapegoats. Our politicians and media have not been good at listening to ordinary people's fears, so when false information suggests foreigners are already taking their disappearing jobs people act their unheard fears out. For example, when, with almost no idea of the consequences, Britain voted for 'Brexit', some people imagined all foreigners would immediately go home. In reality, manufacturing has already been exported out of the West in pursuit of competitive advantage, while labour for service industries is only now catching up.

This raises profound questions for a politics of empathy:

- Whether in a democracy absolute respect for the number of views should prevail, or:
- Whether a deeper awareness has the right to challenge them even if risking charges of elitism?
- Understanding how fear gets displaced, should an unwelcome populist majority be subject to psychological explanation?
- What *is* empathy in such a case?

These are difficult issues, but if, preventively, we were to take *Alternativet*'s principle of 'Listen more than you speak' seriously, then listening, feedback, and receptivity are more than values of the political heart – they are cost-effective tools to be prioritized. The Left has been worse at this than the Right, who know perfectly well – from the 1930s – that fanning fears works to their electoral advantage. Sheer pragmatism could guide the use of heart resources to make empathic consultation much more effective.

A further more philosophic question is whether we get the politics we deserve? At a conference on the psychology of the 2016 presidential election in San Francisco, keynote speaker Andrew Samuels declared:

> Many of my American friends and colleagues have fulminated as never before about the 2016 electoral process, using emotive words like 'disgusting' to describe (for example) the distortions that the power of money brings. From an international perspective, this has surprised me. Don't they know there is a systemic problem always inherent in political life, and no reason to expect anything else?[21]

A politics of heart naturally favours a systemic approach, even though the power of money to dominate should not be underestimated. The heart begins in a system with the mother, in synch, dependent, but also autonomous and destined for increasing autonomy, within on-going relationships. The heart 'knows' the territory between dependence and independence – the *inter-dependence* that Humanistic therapists often remind their clients of. But this does not mean shying away from real power.

The pragmatic Scandinavians recommend increasing interaction between citizens, communities and politicians, so we do not just leave it to them. We need to train our politicians, to support and monitor them through supervision, in a way well known to the therapy community. But we also need to retrain ourselves: in his Berlin Ted-Talk, John Bunzl shared how citizens might *empower* themselves to vote for policies rather than parties, *driving* governments to implementation without fundamental changes to existing structures.[22]

Inner or outer?

John Lennon advised changing minds prior to revolution, and some humanistic practitioners believe that widespread spiritual transformation has to take place before any new political discourse has a chance. The only way is seen as rekindling spirituality inside. It is true that our politicians appear often to lag behind the times, as Michael Edwards writes in *Open Democracy*:

> New social and political parties like *Podemos* and *Nuit Debout* carry within them the seeds of personal-political change . . . though in most cases they have yet to be connected to the representative elements of democracy in any sustained or substantive fashion.[23]

Radical political theorist Mark Satin, whose 1976 book *New Age Politics* has recently been rereleased and updated, says political change must be inspired by a transformed consciousness: a new politics needs new leaders to emerge until some sort of tipping point is reached.[24] There will not be any breakthrough in politics, he suggests, without a shift *inside* those taking part, for which both therapy and meditation practices are essential disciplines. But he is also realistic and pragmatic: such shifts are far more likely to occur through new political institutions that encourage openness and collaboration rather than individual practice. So Satin has this advice: 'Inner before outer, but don't dawdle.'[25]

Given that the world's problems are dire and time is short, should we embrace visionary optimism or a determined resoluteness? Must we employ our lives to dedicated work whether inner or outer? Here is one view to conclude.

Work or child's play?

We have to be committed, but I think it important not to forget the danger of the work ethic, and how the West combined 17th-century Protestantism with 18th-century Enlightenment attitudes to come up with the present exploitative model that now needs correction. In *Wounded Leaders* I argued that turning away from the heart's wisdom left our colonial project founded on mass dissociation and projection. In the absence of heart-based empathy, what I called 'Enlightenment Pity' was exerted on those indigenous populations who seemed too fond of play and not serious enough about work. The conversion of the indigenous population to 'good citizens' was central to what I called the 'Rational Man Project', with boarding schools the means to break native children's will and community-solidarity in exchange for being taught English, Christianity and the work ethic.

Canadian parliamentary records show how a delegation was sent to visit the brutal Indian boarding schools in the US Mid-West in the 1880s. Deciding to make a better job of it, but also to do it on the cheap (how British!) they gave the job to the Church. You can imagine the abuse that occurred. The Native children's hair was cut short and their native tongue forbidden.[26] Right up to the 1920s one in six did not survive – some literally lost the will to live – according to the report of a six-year long inquiry into Indian Residential Schools commissioned by recent Canadian governments.[27] The full report out now tells the story, but fastening seat belts is advised. It was the success of survivors in retrospectively suing the Churches that galvanized the Canadian government over the last 20 years, while helping their communities re-coalesce. Prime Minister Harper had to hold the grief pipe between his teeth, to use an image from poet Robert Bly.[28] In 2008, he issued a formal apology to First Nation, Métis and Inuit peoples for the legacy of that schooling policy, calling it a 'sad chapter in our history'.[29]

We must 'grow corn', but the heart 'prefers' sober rather than sombre engagement, likes music and dancing more than emailing. *Alternativet*'s Engelbrectsen and Fransden are keen to stress humour, humility and playfulness alongside pragmatism and courage, as their video testifies. It is worth remembering that the heart favours both commitment and playfulness. A central concept to ecstatic Hinduism is that the universe is founded in play. The iconography of the Divine Absolute's play (*Leela* in Sanskrit) is the relationship between the cosmic male (*Purusha*)and female (*Prakriti*) at play, as they unfold creation through their heart–genital connection. Primal sexual play has a wider implication for an approach to life, as Alan Watts put it:

> The existence, the physical universe, is basically playful. There is no necessity for it whatsoever. It isn't going anywhere. That is to say it doesn't have some destination that it ought to arrive at. But it is best understood by analogy with music, because music, as an art form, is essentially playful: we say, 'you play the piano' – you don't 'work' the piano.[30]

The West had this once too: in the Middle Ages the Fool was an indispensable presence at court.[31] The wisdom of guarding innocence and not taking oneself too seriously was an indispensable – if not always heeded – component in medieval governance. I think humanistic practitioners have lots to offer here.

Notes

1 Graves, C.W. (1970) Levels of Existence: An Open System Theory of Values, *Journal of Humanistic Psychology, 10* (13): 133; http://jhp.sagepub.com, DOI: 10.1177/002216787001000205. Reprinted by permission of Sage Publications.
2 'The End of Identity Liberalism' by Mark Lilla in *The New York Times* Sunday Review Opinion, 18/11/16.

3 Attributed to the Native American teacher Sun Bear; see Crockett, T. (2003) *Stone Age Wisdom: The Healing Principles of Shamanism*, Gloucester, MA: Fair Winds, p. 93.

4 Gandhi's observation from Merton, T. (ed.) (1965) *Gandhi on Nonviolence: A Selection from the Writings of Mahatma Gandhi*, New York: New Directions, p. 54. This and the next reference are quoted in the much recommended McIntosh, A. (2010) *A Nonviolent Challenge to Conflict*, Houndmills: Palgrave Macmillan, pp. 44–64, to whom acknowledgement is given.

5 Corrigan Maguire, M. 'Gandhi and the Ancient Wisdom of Nonviolence', in Wink, W. (2000), (ed.) *Peace is the Way: Writings on Nonviolence from the Fellowship of Reconciliation*, Maryknoll: Orbis Books, pp. 159–62, quoted in McIntosh, A. (2010).

6 For the arguments why and how this might be achieved see Bunzl, J. & Duffell, N. (2017) *The Simpol Solution: Solving Global Problems Could Be Nearer Than We Think*, London: Peter Owen, p. 173.

7 http://evonomics.com/how-competitiveness-became-one-of-the-great-unquestioned-virtues/ (retrieved 1/9/16).

8 Poppeliers, W. & Royers, T. 'Beyond Shame', in Bormans, L. (ed.) (2013) *The World Book of Love*, Tielt, Belguim: Lannoo.

9 https://en.wikipedia.org/wiki/International_Simultaneous_Policy_Organization (retrieved 27/11/16).

10 Graves, C.W. (1974) 'Human nature prepares for a momentous Leap', in *The Futurist*, April 1974.

11 I use the term *Spiral Dynamics* broadly to refer to the work begun by Clare Graves and developed independently by Don Beck, Chris Cowan and Ken Wilber. For a summary of its application to New Politics and references please see Bunzl, J. & Duffell, N. (2017).

12 Damasio, A.R. (1994) *Descartes' Error: Emotion, Reason, and the Human Brain*, New York: Avon Books.

13 Duffell, N. (2014) *Wounded Leaders. British Elitism and the Entitlement Illusion: A Psychohistory*, London: Lone Arrow Press.

14 Porges, S.W. (2011) *The Polyvagal Theory: Neurophysiological Foundations of Emotions, Attachment, Communication, and Self-Regulation*, New York: Norton.

15 Duffell, N. (2014) p. 246.

16 Duffell, N. (2014) p. 86.

17 See Bunzl, J. & Duffell, N. (2017) pp. 58–9.

18 Personal conversation with Birgitta Jonsdottir at the June 2016 'Alter Ego' conference, a gathering of 80 'leaders' in the field of integrating spiritual and psychological tools into policy making, to which the author was invited. http://www.alterego.site

19 An interview with Helle Engelbrectsen and Brian Fransden can be seen on www.youtube.com/watch?v=0Jt3zx7QlW4 (accessed 27/11/16).

20 MacFadyen, P. (2014) *Flatpack Democracy: A DIY Guide to Creating Independent Politics*, Bath: Eco-logic Books.

21 Andrew Samuels, keynote speaker at 'Politics, Culture and Soul: A National Conference on the Psychology of the 2016 Presidential Election', San Francisco, 14–15 October 2016, in an address entitled: 'So What Did You Expect? Personal and Depth Psychological Issues in Elections', www.sfjung.org/public-programs-and-extended-education/politics-culture-and-soul-a-national-conference-on-the-psychology-of-the-2016-presidential-election/

22 www.youtube.com/watch?v=gWW5LPBmwdo (accessed 27/11/16).

23 www.opendemocracy.net/transformation/michael-edwards/is-there-any-hope-for-new-age-politics (retrieved 27/11/16).

24 www.huffingtonpost.com/rick-heller/the-new-age-40-years-late_b_9765486.html (retrieved 27/11/16).

25 Ibid.

26 See the story about a 97-year-old Native American boarding school survivor still busy with his childhood suffering, retrieved from www.indianz.com/News/2016/08/19/97 yearold-indian-boarding-school-survivo.asp (retrieved 27/11/16). See also http://woundedleaders.co.uk/unable-forget-native-americans-now-use-boarding-school-survivor-word/

27 www.trc.ca/websites/trcinstitution/File/2015/Honouring_the_Truth_Reconciling_for_the_Future_July_23_2015.pdf (retrieved 27/11/16).

28 Bly uses a metaphor that evokes the Native American peace pipe in 'Listening to Shahram Nazer' from Bly, R. (2005) *My Sentence Was a Thousand Years of Joy*, New York: Harper Perennial.

29 https://en.m.wikipedia.org/wiki/American_Indian_boarding_schools (retrieved 20/8/16).

30 Recorded discourse by Alan Watts, *Why Your Life is Not a Journey*, https://vimeo.com/176370337 (retrieved 20/8/16).

31 Thanks to Helena Løvendal for this reminder.

PART III

Current applications, tensions and possibilities

EDITORS' INTRODUCTION TO PART III

*Richard House, David Kalisch and
Jennifer Maidman*

In this section, our contributors examine current applications of Humanistic Psychology in practice, identifying areas of strength in the approach, areas of tension and potentially significant differences, and also areas – including potentials for overlap with other approaches – to explore and develop. Issues of how far Humanistic Psychology needs to adjust and accommodate to the 'powers that be' in the form of licensing, regulatory, insurance and funding authorities, and to what extent it needs to stay resistant to what can seem to some like an over-accommodation, are addressed and thought through, sometimes with strikingly different conclusions. These situational tensions, as well as the identification of strengths and potential, are explored in both UK and US contexts. The focus of humanistic approaches on relationship, the search and need for meaning, and the emphasis given to embodiment are seen as significant and abiding strengths.

Caroline Brazier, in Chapter 10, opens this section. She identifies how the growth of individualism and the assertion of personal rights have paradoxically strengthened bureaucratic proceduralism, creating standardization of services and diminished quality of relating. Using a Buddhist psychological model, Brazier describes how existential anxiety underlies many unhelpful human behaviours, and suggests how elements of Buddhist-informed psychotherapy can challenge some of our assumptions about human psychology. She offers a searching examination of the Mindfulness phenomenon, and reaffirms therapy as 'a quest for the unknown'.

In Chapter 11, Andy Rogers follows with a powerful and closely written chapter on how he sees the once liberatory discovery by Carl Rogers of the 'client-centred' approach in danger of paradoxically becoming rigidified in recent times into something of a conservative orthodoxy of its own. He cautions against a move too far away from the core values of the humanistic approach. Following this, in Chapter 12, Katherine McArthur and Mick Cooper, on the other hand, in an equally cogently presented chapter, argue precisely for just such an open-mindedness to other approaches and methodologies, and set forth an understanding based on self-determination theory, advocating 'more collaboration with other approaches (relatedness) and a greater commitment to research (competence), to balance the existing focus on the uniqueness of the humanistic approach (autonomy)'.

In Chapter 13, Harris L. Friedman, writing from the USA, considers the overlaps as well as the current and historic tensions between Humanistic and Positive Psychology, and considers how the divide between the two could be bridged for the betterment of both, concluding that '[a] better future for both humanistic and positive psychology could stem from their eventual reconciliation through valuing all research methodologies in a holistic way'.

Next there follow two chapters focusing on the current strengths of Humanistic Psychology in practice, especially in relation to what has become a key theme in the field: trauma. Again from the USA, Stanley Krippner and Daniel B. Pitchford, in Chapter 14, expertly survey the recent trauma literature, and point out the relatively unsung successes of the humanistic approach in this area, specifically highlighting the importance of repairing the meaning systems of people whose lives and sense of safety and belonging in the world have been shattered by trauma. Olivia Merriman-Khanna continues, in Chapter 15, with a scholarly overview of trauma: its history, developments, controversies and treatment approaches, emphasizing one of the abiding strengths of the humanistic approach: namely, its emphasis on the (therapy) relationship as the key healing component. Merriman argues that humanistic therapists are well placed to work with the complexity of responses to trauma, as well as attending to the growth potential of their clients. Both of these chapters also discuss the important areas of post-traumatic growth and the concept of resilience.

In the final chapter of this section, Alexandra Chalfont looks at some 'accidental affiliates' of Humanistic Psychology (as she calls them) – namely, artist Caspar David Friedrich, academic psychologist Jordan B. Peterson and writer Franz Kafka. Writing from a personal slant, she tracks developments in Humanistic Psychology over the decades, finding parallel motifs in her own life.

As these chapters reveal, there is clearly room for more than one perspective in Humanistic Psychology; and this diversity of opinions and philosophies, which has characterized the movement from its earliest days, sometimes turning into open conflict, is arguably one of Humanistic Psychology's greatest strengths – as long as it is able to contain these tensions and dynamics, and see the possibilities inherent in them. It is hardly surprising that Humanistic Psychology is not immune to the wider and deeper strains that are polarizing modern culture and our politics more generally, and that as a movement it finds itself embodying these splits and tensions while also being capable of the kind of reflection needed to help transcend them.

Underlying many of these differences of opinion and perspective are questions of how knowledge is presently constituted, especially in societies like our own that are organized democratically, but within a global neoliberal capitalist system that is manifesting multiple signs of systemic crisis. In such societies, how mental and emotional – as well as physical – health is defined, constructed, diagnosed and responded to is neither politically nor morally neutral. So while the wider socio-political context inevitably shapes, configures and constrains the psychological field, a politically and socio-culturally aware psychology – which, traditionally, Humanistic Psychology has always been – is well equipped to be able to reflect on, and respond to, these pressures, as the subsequent chapters in Part IV of the book demonstrate.

10

CREATING SPACE

A way forward for Humanistic Psychology

Caroline Brazier

The development of counselling and psychotherapy practice over the last fifty years has had a substantial effect, not only within the field of mental health, but also far more broadly in areas such as education, social provision, business and politics. With such wide-ranging impact, it is the duty of those engaged in the psychological professions to reflect on this influence, and on the implicit and explicit value systems that are being communicated. This chapter addresses questions raised by this expansion of interest, reflecting on the effects of recent changes within the psychological professions, on shifting power dynamics of the therapeutic field and, in particular, on the impact of Buddhist models, mindfulness teaching and the other-centred approach in this context.

The psychologization of society

Psychology has, arguably, been one of the major influences upon society in the 20th century and beyond (Furedi, 2004) and its reach has extended well beyond the consulting room and the treatment of mental and psychosomatic illness with which it started. It has impacted upon the fabric of modern life in all manner of ways, often far divorced from its clinical origins. In the growing subtlety of advertising and propaganda, for instance, to which we are exposed through the plethora of media available today, or in the widespread concern for the emotional and physical wellbeing of children in our education and welfare systems. In myriad ways, psychology has influenced us for better or worse. At one extreme, at worst, it has enabled oppressive regimes to create new methods of torture and manipulation, and to exert psychological as well as physical pressure on their populace. On the other hand, it has been employed in benign ways, such as in the fostering of sporting excellence, with athletes increasingly coached in mind as well as body, or in the training of astronauts to withstand the psychological impact of extended periods in the extraordinarily demanding conditions of space.

Psychological knowledge can aid social cohesion or help us to understand divisions between social groups. It might be used to solve crimes and understand causes of such behaviours in the psyche of the perpetrators. However, recourse to diagnoses can also result in a reliance on labels which set apart the supposedly 'bad' from the rest of the population, insulating the rest of us from an awareness of our own capacity to commit harm. Psychological theory can be used to protect the vulnerable and avoid some of the crass treatment of children in earlier ages, but it can also create a culture so anxious about repressing the young or exposing them to possible dangers that it fails to set boundaries, overlooks common-sense responses, and effectively imprisons young people in their own homes, passive in front of computers or televisions, rather than allowing them the freedom to actively explore and develop once associated with childhood.

Psychology, and its application through therapeutic and quasi-therapeutic interventions, has infiltrated our lives in both public and private spheres to such an extent that we have ceased to even question its impact. Whether in giving birth, entering marriage and parenting, or facing death and bereavement, people's experiences are interpreted through the medium of a therapeutic ethos. At every turn, guidance and counselling are now considered reasonable and even necessary if such events are to be negotiated without danger. This has its impact. According to Furedi, numerous studies have noted that, with the advent of a more therapeutically orientated culture, conventional moral meanings attached to concepts such as guilt and responsibility have lost their salience in circumstances where the therapeutic ethos is dominant (Furedi, 2004: 12). The language of pathology and diagnosis is habitually substituted for the more everyday interpretation of emotion and misdemeanour.

A culture of dependence

The impact of this changing culture of personal responsibility is also seen in our relationship to authority. The trend toward the psychologization of society has been amplified by a tendency over the second half of the 20th century toward increasing dependence on the 'expert' in certain key areas of human experience. Of course, it is nothing new for people to look to professionals for advice. In earlier times, the professions were highly respected, and people sought guidance from doctors, priests, bank managers or school teachers without question. Through the 1970s and 1980s, however, led by the consumer movement and fuelled by media attention to incidents of malpractice, a gradual distrust of this kind of authority arose. This challenge to the status quo, however, created its own authorities. It looked to television, to science, to new norms regarding 'expertise', and saw codified practices and regulations as reference points; and it transmitted these assumptions to the populace, sometimes under the guise of self-help.

The effect of this has been paradoxical and a movement that set out to empower ordinary people has arguably, it would seem, enslaved them in new ways. In the past, areas of life such as health, education or religion were unquestioningly conducted under the advice of professionals, but in most everyday matters people trusted their own judgement, based on behaviour learned from parents, grandparents and peers, as well as from direct personal observation. In the 21st century, young people trust sell-by dates on food products more than their own ability to distinguish what is safe to eat and what is not. They resort to the self-help book, the specialist website and to the therapist for advice on how to live their lives, and manage the lives of those for whom they have responsibility. This phenomenon is not new, for self-help manuals have been in circulation for centuries, but as Furedi points out (2004: 12), the phenomenon has escalated substantially in recent times.

In a climate where the role of the expert as advisor and guru has grown, the potential for social manipulation through the provision of advice and information increases. Just as, in the past, compliant groups succumbed to the propaganda of governments and religious leaders (one only has to think of the way in which women's working habits changed before, during and after the Second World War[1] for example), so too the potential influences of therapy culture are a factor for concern, both to the profession and to society at large.

Growth and austerity

Furedi wrote about the rise of 'therapy culture' in the early years of the current century and his observations are still relevant more than a decade on. The language of psychology still dominates in fields of education, social organization and public policy, and concern for the protection of the vulnerable, and the population at large, still underpins a culture of legislation and regulation which, though beneficial in reducing accidents and abuse, can also sometimes be restrictive and bureaucratic. At the same time, economic and social changes have shaped attitudes in mental health provision and in broader social contexts. Specifically, the de-centralization and privatization of health services has concentrated power in the hands of funders and commissioners, often more interested in balancing the accounts than in seeking excellence, especially when funding is under pressure. The hard-nosed pragmatism of 'austerity' has created a vogue for outcome-focused approaches and the focus on economics has given weight to therapies that are seen as demonstrably evidence-based and cost-effective. As a result, competitive tendering has introduced market values into fields that were once considered beyond the reach of productivity deals.

At the same time, in economies driven by market forces, the power of multi-nationals has increased, and this in turn is considered by some to have influenced policy in the mental health field, especially in the US (Whitaker, 2010), but in Britain too. Supported by the rising interest in neuroscience and the study of brain chemistry enabled by new developments in research and technologies, human psychology has increasingly come to be seen in terms of mechanical and chemical changes in the brain rather than as the product of experience and behaviour. As a consequence we have seen steady growth in the pharmaceutical industry, and the development and prescribing of a new generation of psychoactive drugs for psychological problems. As a relatively low-cost choice in mental health, this increasing use of pharmaceuticals has been accompanied by a corresponding growth in the range of potential diagnoses, evidenced by proliferating editions of the DSM.[2]

On the other hand, in recent years, perhaps prompted by soaring drugs budgets, some talking therapies are also enjoying a revival in the UK, courtesy of the IAPT programmes.[3] These newly introduced services, intended to improve access to therapy for those with common mental health problems such as depression and anxiety, have in practice also become target driven, and, one suspects, subject to economic pressures as well as therapeutic factors. These pressures are both resource based, being linked to minimising treatment costs, and outcome based, being linked to achieving savings in other budget areas of public life such as unemployment or sickness benefits. Certainly it seems that, in the public domain, therapeutic provision is linked to maintaining as great a section of the population in the workforce as possible. For example, there have recently been concerns among the professional bodies of the psychological world[4] at government plans to introduce counselling into job centres – plans that, while cloaked in benevolent language, could all too easily lead to coercion of the more vulnerable members of society.

Coming full circle

When we review the social processes that are impacting on therapeutic provision in recent decades, we can observe a number of ways that psychological thinking is influencing wider culture. For example, the influence of psychology and psychotherapy that Furedi described initially fostered a culture of individualism. We have seen a tendency to fragmentation in modern society, and, while other factors such as social mobility and changes in the workforce have played a part, an underlying preoccupation with individual rights and the pursuit of personal fulfilment have no doubt contributed considerably to this process. The growth of individualism is evidenced by an increase in single-person households, changes in patterns of family life and marriage, and the prevalence of the rhetoric of personal fulfilment in the popular media. While causality for such large-scale trends must remain a matter of speculation, it seems reasonable to hypothesize some link between these changes and the rise of personal-growth movements through the 1960s and 1970s, and beyond.

This concern for the individual has, among other things, led to a demand for protective measures and the assertion of individual rights. These responses seem often based on fear, and we have seen increasing regulation arising out of accidents and incidents that 'should never be allowed to happen again'. Counselling has become part of this safeguarding process, and has commonly been offered in the aftermath of incidents, so that victims of crime or disaster can be supported and mental wellbeing repaired as far as is possible. Besides the introduction of new regulations to ensure safety, we have also seen an increase in testing to maintain quality and achieve 'value for money' in a wide range of public fields such as health, education and social services. Although sometimes establishing important guidelines, many of these interventions are experienced by professionals as stifling creativity and taking time away from genuine person-to-person interaction. Thus processes that start out seeking to support individual human wellbeing may sometimes, paradoxically, come to dehumanize services. The growth of interest in personal fulfilment and empowerment brings with it genuine concerns for individual safety and rights, but this can also contribute to an increase in legislation and the externalization of the locus of control, to some extent defeating the original intent.

Other social trends that we have discussed have also influenced therapy provision, to some extent dictating the preferred type of therapy on offer. Whereas Furedi proposed an influence of therapy upon popular culture, social culture is now dictating to the profession. In particular, in the UK over the last couple of decades we have seen a move away from the predominance of humanistic counselling models in mainstream services, toward the increasing use of cognitive behaviour therapy (CBT). An interest in 'happiness', 'wellbeing' and the introduction of mindfulness also seem to suggest that there has been a re-framing of the current understanding of psychological health. The emphasis of state-delivered talking therapies has shifted from the exploration of problems and unconscious process toward a more function-focused, and arguably more mechanistic approach, in which mental process is adjusted through active intervention and the modification of thoughts and behaviours. Revolutions in understanding offered by recent research, complemented by a medical-model, diagnose-and-treat model, based in a scientific paradigm, are tending to favour evidence-based interventions, while, in parallel with these developments, economic forces continue to steer therapies toward short-term, results-focused approaches.

The rise of mindfulness

In the current professional climate, mindfulness-based approaches, and in particular mindfulness-based stress reduction (MBSR) and mindfulness-based cognitive therapy (MBCT), have gained considerable popularity. Developed by Jon Kabat-Zinn (Kabat-Zinn, 1990) these approaches have been adapted for public consumption in the UK, notably by Mark Williams and John Teasdale (e.g. Segal *et al.*, 2002). The meteoric rise of mindfulness as a therapeutic intervention has come about in large part because it seems to have caught the flavour of the times and, among other things, adapted to the popular 'spiritual but not religious' culture. Although derived from Buddhist roots, a deliberate process of secularization of these methods has taken place. In the government report, *Mindful Nation UK* (The Mindful Initiative, 2015), Jon Kabat-Zinn is credited with 'freeing [mindfulness methods] from any religious or dogmatic content' (ibid.: 14).

Mindfulness methods are evidently helpful, as extensive research has shown, and provide a welcome alternative response to a range of mental health problems. They offer people tools with which to take charge of aspects of their own mental health. They are positively orientated, non-stigmatizing and applicable in many different settings and circumstances. They have the potential to be empowering and to help people toward autonomy. It is, therefore, a welcome and refreshing development to see these body-based, spiritually grounded approaches being taken up so widely as an alternative to drug-based treatments.

There are, however, aspects of the large-scale introduction of mindfulness-based approaches that have given rise to concern in some quarters. First, mindfulness methods have been developed as therapeutic interventions and marketed based on their replicability, meeting the research agenda by producing a uniform delivery method via the eight-week course. This means that, along with other pre-determined programmes, the approach can become over-rigid and the training agenda can override real therapeutic depth. The approach has also been critiqued as being normative, encouraging participants in the programme to adjust dysfunctional thinking to the expectations of society.

> At times, it felt as if the facilitators' loyalty to their weekly teaching agenda restricted them somewhat and made them less open and, on the whole, uninterested in suspending judgment and staying with questions participants raised, hastening instead to soothe issues emerging from the class . . . I couldn't help feeling that the quality of self-discovery of an embodied meditation practice had been replaced with an emphasis on self-improvement and adjustment.
>
> *(Greenslade, 2014: 120)*

In addition, as with all therapies, the quality of the practitioner who delivers the training is paramount to its success. Based on meditation methods, mindfulness requires a solid and regular practice in order to be effective. Kabat-Zinn, despite his efforts to distance himself professionally from his religious roots, was a serious Buddhist practitioner, but many of his successors are not. Although latterly, in part responding to critiques from the Buddhist world, there has been more emphasis placed on regular meditation practice in the training of mindfulness facilitators, many of those delivering classes and workshops at the grassroots are not as well versed in the practice as one might wish and, consequently, are less able to deal with difficulties when they arise.

The current popularity of mindfulness as a therapeutic intervention is in some ways surprising, because meditation methods have been studied scientifically since the 1960s and have been found by many to be helpful, yet it has not been until relatively recently that they have entered mainstream mental health provision. There are probably a number of reasons why mindfulness has become popular now.

The mindfulness movement in the UK has been skilful in presenting a well packaged, relatively simple intervention, which is evidence-based and can be delivered by a variety of mental health professionals, trained to various levels of competence, to different client groups. The method is cost-effective as delivery of mindfulness training in groups over a limited period is a relatively low-cost intervention. With increasing levels of mental illness in the population at large causing concern, not least because of their economic impact, according to the *Mindful Nation* report (The Mindful Initiative, 2015), cost-saving is one factor driving the search for new approaches to mental health and the implementation of widespread mindfulness programmes. 'This burden of ill health is distressing . . . is also immensely costly as it affects people of working age' (ibid.: 5).

More than this, however, it could be that part of the approach's success is that it fits comfortably into the prevailing culture of pragmatism. In its measured approach to mental health, mindfulness meets the demands of the wellbeing agenda. It does not involve messy spillages of emotion and is as much at home in the corporate world or even in Parliament as it is in a therapeutic setting. Indeed, its primary focus, although body-based, is on learning the recognition and containment of anxiety, pain and emotion. Mindfulness-based approaches, as taught on the eight-week programme, generally encourage positivity and control, avoiding the darker aspects of the human psyche.

Roots of the Buddhist paradigm

Mindfulness as a practice is rooted in the Buddhist tradition. The presentation of mindfulness that is offered in the eight-week programme is based upon practices outlined in the Buddhist texts, and particularly the *Satipatthana Sutta*, on which Bhikkhu Analayo has written an excellent commentary (Analayo, 2004). The mindfulness of the eight-week programme is, however, relatively limited and, as I have discussed elsewhere (Brazier, 2014), the *Satipatthana* offers a much broader and deeper investigation into human experience. Here mindfulness is concerned with teaching the practitioner to relate to experience in a particular way, and has the purpose of moving the practitioner from an identified, self-invested position to a more dispassionate, objective observance of experiencing. The teaching is structured as a series of observations, which start from the immediate experience of the body while sitting, walking, standing and breathing, and include observations of the body's anatomy, activity, composition and demise. This study concludes with an investigation of the decomposition of a corpse – something rarely found in mindfulness classes.

Mindfulness practice of the *Satipatthana* also brings to awareness aspects of mental process. It explores patterns of reactivity that arise in relation to experience, and the mental states that arise dependent upon them. In its final section, the text includes observation based on many of the key Buddhist teachings. Throughout the text, there is a repeating refrain which, among other things, contextualizes each observation in terms of dependent arising and impermanence, the two central Buddhist concepts.

In the *Satipatthana*, we are provided with an outline of Buddhist psychology. The practice guides the practitioner toward the realization that everything, and especially the sense of a permanent identity, is constructed and impermanent. Mindfulness in its original form involves an encounter with our own mortality. Buddhism teaches that, as humans, our psychology is based on a flight from this recognition and from the inevitability of affliction and impermanence. In response to our fears of these existential truths, we create an illusion of permanence through our perceptual and behavioural habits. We seek to control experience, looking for familiarity amid the flow of life in order to build a sense of self. This sense of self is, however, constructed rather than being 'real' in any absolute sense. It depends upon conditions (dependently arising) and exists only in as much as those conditions remain in place.

The notion of the conditioned self is fundamental to the Buddhist understanding of the mind, which sees identity as contingent upon perceived objects. The world is viewed in ways that confirm the sense of self. We have prejudices and blind-spots, enthusiasms and passions. Each person surrounds him- or herself with a protective self-world of subjective relationships, all of which support the identity. This is like a psychological and perceptual bubble made up of bias and delusion. It forms a defence structure, warding off anxiety about the uncertainty of life and our existential position as mortal beings.

This model offers insight into the psychology of the individual, and also into that of the collective. For example, the rise of individualism which was referred to earlier, can be seen in the context of Buddhist psychology as a fear-based response, enacted at both individual and collective levels. In times of uncertainty, people tend to cling to a strong sense of identity and to views which support that identity. Groups also congregate around shared views and collective identities. In the craving for self-actualization and in the agendas of corporate identity and nationalism we can see manifestations of the defensive processes of clinging, and as global threats, whether conflict or climate change, become apparent, the process of craving narrows people's thinking, and they tend to increasingly cling to procedural habits and other behavioural rigidities.

The bubble that people create through conditioned responses is both a fortress and a cage. While it allows us to function, it also limits us. Breaking out of it, however, involves facing the darker side of life and unpleasant experiences. It also involves taking a leap in the dark and venturing away from the known into the unknown.

Humanistic therapies: in praise of not knowing

Humanistic psychotherapies were born out of a period of exploration and creativity. In the boom times of the post-war era, despite cold war anxieties, most of the population in the West were relatively well-off and comfortable compared with previous generations. In this relaxed milieu, it felt safe to question and explore beyond the bounds of ordinary expectations. A creative explosion broke open the certainties of the past and pushed back the boundaries of the known. Bubbles of social norms were broken, and there were openings for new innovative approaches, and explorations into areas of human experience that had previously been taboo.

One of the themes identified in this chapter has been the shift from this atmosphere of curiosity to one of regulation and control. Initially, the human potential movement fostered a period in which individuals quested for peak experiences and self-actualization, but this movement gradually became popularized, encouraging a widespread search for identity and psychological wellbeing. This, in turn, gradually formalized as professional associations came into being and began to introduce codes of practice. New methods emerged that were more commercially based. The world in general and the therapy world in particular gradually became more cautious, more procedural and more commodified. This shift has been marked by a reduction in tolerance for the 'unknown' among the mental health professions and those who fund them. Measurable outcomes and therapeutic protocols introduce a semblance of control and thus serve to reduce professional anxieties.

As Buddhist psychology suggests, however, this quest for certainty often runs counter to real therapeutic process. In a recent publication, *The Wisdom of Not Knowing* (Chisholm & Harrison, 2016) a number of authors explored the importance of 'not knowing' in therapeutic settings. As the editors write in the introduction, 'We often find the state of not-knowing can be a precursor to moments of rich discovery which possess a dynamic, transformative power that exceeds any prior expectation' (ibid.: 7). This valuing of the un-known, which is still, thankfully, alive and well in the Humanistic Psychology world, seems a long way from the quasi-certainties of IAPT and other mainstream approaches today.

Therapy in its truest form is a quest for and into the unknown. While therapist and client both arrive in the therapy room with certain resources – the client with his story and life experience, the therapist with her skills, gained through training and years of practice – neither can or should know where the shared journey will take them or even how to conduct it. Remaining open to the emerging process and trusting the client's innate wisdom about what needs to happen has always been a central tenet of humanistic approaches. 'It is the client who knows what hurts, what directions to go, what problems are crucial, what experiences have been deeply buried' (Rogers, 1961: 11).

In the modern mental health context, however, the balance of power within the therapeutic relationship is shifting in ways that are subtle and not so subtle. Although the government plan to regulate the psychotherapy professions under the control of the Health Professions Council, with its consequent implications to place counsellors and psychotherapists firmly within the medical domain, was rejected in 2009, reliance on a medical-model paradigm of diagnosis, treatment and evaluation still seems to have crept into professional practice. In public spheres, the emphasis on accountability, regulation and cost-effectiveness is driving a shift to short-term interventions that often involve advice giving, treatment plans and monitoring of efficacy rather than the therapies that we have known in the past. These goal-orientated approaches are often normative, measuring success through factors such as the client's return to work.

While it is possible to work in a short-term, outcome-directed way while still supporting the client's autonomy, the temptation toward coercive practices and more didactic or functional approaches is considerable when organizations are working on a payment by results basis. Modern approaches to mental health are, therefore, tending to drive a return to the position where the therapist working in public services is obliged to take on the position of expert and source of authority, operating within a system which itself exerts authority and control. Uncertainty comes to be seen as a sign of failure, and the space for 'not knowing' is eroded.

Other-centred therapy

In this context, I would like to take this opportunity to reflect on the therapy that I am involved in teaching. The other-centred approach is derived from Buddhist roots and, having its origins in the values and culture of that paradigm, presents a somewhat different worldview to that of many Western therapies. Other-centred therapy (Brazier, 2009) is so named because it investigates the relationship between a person and the 'others', human and non-human, who make up his personal world. Based on the understanding outlined above, that identity is formed in reaction to a constructed view of reality, the therapy invites a person to review and adjust their view of, and relationships with others, bringing to them an attitude of enquiry and uncertainty.

With its orientation toward perception and the relationship with an object-world, the other-centred approach tends to focus predominantly on an enquiry into how the client perceives his world, bringing into question the assumptions upon which the sense of identity rests. The methodology is concerned with exploring the distortions that perception inevitably introduces, reflecting personal patterns of worldview, and facilitating a clearer view of others and real connection with them. For this to happen, however, both client and therapist need to step into the unknown. The self, or identity, is reflected in the worldview that maintains it. In Buddhist theory, self-structures are associated with rigidity, and their relinquishment with increasing fluidity and clarity. Rather as with Carl Rogers' description of the fully functioning person (Rogers, 1961), the person inhabits the flow of their experience.

The other-centred approach is concerned with relationship. It helps the client to explore and develop empathy for the important others in their life, encouraging a shift from a self-orientated viewpoint to multiple perspectives, through techniques that invite the client to step into the shoes of those people who are significant in their lives. Whether through empathic reflection or role reversal, the client attempts to see the world, and even himself, through the eyes of the people to whom he is closest. In this way, they break up the client's sense of being a special case, and build the sense of relatedness. They question the self-story, and push the client to investigate the truth of their history, their impact on others and their current situation (Krech, 2001). They also tend to focus on relatedness and to appreciate connection with others, promoting values of social context and cohesion.

The other-centred approach also places the client in the context of an environment. The 'others' that create supports for the identity can be environmental as well as human. In fact, this model lends itself particularly well to environmentally based work (Brazier, 2011) and ecotherapy (Tariki Trust, 2013). While this sort of work can be done in human-centric ways, using the environment as ground for personal projection, with the other-centred framework the methodology is once again more concerned with direct encounter and relationship than with supporting the sense of identity. Where methods are projective, they involve exploring the limits of perception, its embeddedness in conditioned views, or the use of collective myth and story as a basis for creative work. Such work takes seriously the client's relationship to the planet, not just as a screen for personal growth, but as the inhabitant of an eco-system for which they have a shared responsibility.

Other-centred working rests upon the therapist–client relationship. This relationship is itself conceived as non-hierarchical and grounded in collaborative investigation; it is based on side-by-side accompaniment. The importance of direct reference to experience means that both therapist and client must be willing to deal in uncertainty. Together, their purpose is to question and reject formulae in favour of new discovery and to face the discomfort of not knowing.

Therapies can shape the way that individuals and groups view the world. They can collude with prevailing trends both of popular culture and of government policy, or they can challenge them. They themselves create cultures that might or might not be conducive to the good of individuals or society. A detailed exploration of what benefits and insights particular therapies bring is something beyond the scope of a short chapter.

So this is a starting point. By flagging up the possibilities and the pitfalls, I invite discussion of ways forward for the profession, not only in continuing its powerful influence into the 21st century, but also in taking responsibility and critically reviewing our practice. While pragmatism has its value, and we cannot but be influenced by the demands of the services for which we work, therapists need to stand against the flow of false certainties and share with our clients the courage to face discomfort and uncertainty.

Notes

1   The original film, *Rosie the Riveter* (Redd Evans and John Jacob Loeb, Paramount Music Corporation, 1942) recounts many real-life stories of women who helped the war effort but later returned to domestic duties as the men came back from war.
2   The *Diagnostic and Statistical Manual of Mental Disorders*, published by the American Psychiatric Association.
3   Improving Access to Psychological Therapies, www.england.nhs.uk/ mental-health/ adults/iapt/ (accessed 12 April 2017).
4   www.bacp.co.uk/media/ index.php?newsId=3906 (accessed 12 April 2017).

References

Analayo, B. (2004) *Satipatthana: The Direct Path to Realization*, Birmingham: Windhorse.
Brazier, C. (2009) *Other-Centred Therapy: Buddhist Psychology in Action*, Ropley: O-Books.
Brazier, C. (2011) *Acorns among the Grass: Adventures in Ecotherapy*, Ropley: Earth Books.
Brazier, C. (2014) 'Beyond mindfulness: an Other-centred paradigm', in M. Bazzano (ed.) *After Mindfulness: New Perspectives on Psychology and Meditation* (pp. 23–36), Basingstoke: Palgrave.
Chisholm, R. & Harrison, J. (2016) *The Wisdom of Not Knowing*, Axminster: Triarchy.
Furedi, F. (2004) *Therapy Culture*, London: Routledge.
Greenslade, R. (2014) 'Mindfulness and therapy: a skeptical approach', in M. Bazzano (ed.) *After Mindfulness: New Perspectives on Psychology and Meditation* (pp. 112–23), Basingstoke: Palgrave.

Kabat-Zinn, J. (1990) *Full Catastrophe Living: Using the Wisdom of Your Body and Mind to Face Stress, Pain, and Illness*, New York: Delacorte Press.

Krech, G. (2001) *Naikan: Gratitude, Grace, and the Japanese Art of Self-reflection*, Berkeley, CA: Stone Bridge Press.

The Mindful Initiative (October 2015) *Mindful Nation UK: Report by the Mindfulness All-Party Parliamentary Group.*

Rogers, C.R. (1961) 'A process conception of psychotherapy', in *On Becoming a Person* (pp. 125–62), London: Constable.

Segal, Z.V., Williams, J.M.G., & Teasdale, J.D. (2002) *Mindfulness-based Cognitive Therapy for Depression: A New Approach to Preventing Relapse*, New York: Guilford.

Tariki Trust (2013) Ten Directions course programme, http://buddhistpsychology.typepad.com/amida_france/ten-directions.html (accessed 12 April 2017).

Whitaker, R. (2010) *Anatomy of an Epidemic: Magic Bullets, Psychiatric Drugs, and the Astonishing Rise of Mental Illness in America*, New York, Crown Publishing House.

11

CARL ROGERS

Absence and presence in the contemporary therapy landscape

Andy Rogers

Carl Rogers is everywhere and nowhere. As founder of the Person-Centred Approach and a hugely influential figure in Humanistic Psychology, his work continues sending up shoots of insight for students of the therapeutic relationship but, as we survey the contemporary field of counselling and psychotherapy, the Person-Centred challenge to psychotherapeutic orthodoxy – and to the power structures beyond – is conspicuously dormant. What are we to make of this telling absence and presence? Did Rogers' own contribution to the expansion of therapy unwittingly encourage the very professional and cultural conditions that now thwart his once radical vision?

Back to the future

Picture this. It is the late 1930s and Carl Rogers, a young psychologist with the Society for the Prevention of Cruelty to Children in Rochester, New York, is trying to convince a mother that her son's difficulties lay in her early rejection of the child. But his apparent insight is having no effect: 'we got nowhere. Finally I gave up. I told her that it seemed we had both tried, but we had failed, and that we might as well give up our contacts' (Rogers, 1961: 11). Then, just as she is about to leave, the mother asks Rogers if he will see her for counselling. He agrees, so she returns to her seat and begins to 'pour out her despair . . . all very different from the sterile "case history" she had given before' (ibid.).

'Real therapy began then', (ibid.) Rogers observed later, attributing to the event considerable significance in the development of his approach to therapeutic relationships:

> [It] helped me to experience the fact – only fully realized later – that it is
> the client who knows what hurts, what directions to go, what problems

are crucial, what experiences have been deeply buried. It began to occur to me that unless I had a need to demonstrate my own cleverness and learning, I would do better to rely upon the client for the direction of movement in the process.

(ibid.: 11–12)

Note that Rogers' ideas emerge in response to his own relational experience, rather than through grappling with existing therapy theories. As his biographer tell us,

[Rogers] was always grateful that his thinking did not come from the teachings of one special mentor, nor out of the writings of one special person, nor out of endless philosophical debates on the merits of the various schools of therapy, or the nuances and changes in some 'master's' thinking over the years.

(Kirschenbaum, 2007: 80)

So what happened next? Leap forward to the present and we find a striking, if politically out-of-favour, structure in the professional landscape: a principled, well-researched and extensively articulated cluster of therapies, gathered under the banner of the Person-Centred Approach (PCA). The irony being that it is now Rogers who is the 'special mentor', the 'master' whose writing is 'endlessly debated' and whose 'nuances and changes' in thinking remain the reference point for contemporary divisions and alliances among his followers. Despite Rogers' caution about theory becoming a 'dogma of truth' (Rogers, 1959: 191), the PCA is arguably as dogmatic as any other tradition. Debates rage about what it means to be authentically 'person-centred', about whether certain ideas and actions fit with Rogers' own theory and practice at this or that point in his life, and there seems little to distinguish it from other therapies in this regard. When Rogers wrote of Freudian theory that, 'at the hands of insecure disciples . . . the gossamer threads became iron chains of dogma' (ibid.: 191), he might easily have been predicting the future of his own creation.

A fascinating paradox, then, that one of Rogers' key insights came from operating without allegiance to a specific model of psychological theory, as happened with the mother in Rochester. This was an idiosyncratic encounter located within a particular personal, professional, cultural and historical moment. The subsequent success of the approach theoretically and professionally says less about the potential meaning of that experience than it does about the relationship between Rogers' character and career, and the facilitative social conditions necessary for the flourishing of his ideas.

Clearly this context does not discredit anything Rogers said, wrote or did; it is the history of all 'big ideas' and the thinkers who have them. But it is important to distinguish between the growth of a movement and the potential meaning of its originator's eureka moments. The former does not own the latter and it might be that the movement – with all its books, organizations, trainings and so on – is not the only, or even the best, expression of the insights from which it was born. In the case of the PCA, the theory and other structures that evolved from the complex interaction of people, places and moments in Rogers' lifetime potentially obscure something vital about his meeting with the mother, which is that 'real therapy' began – and was 'ultimately . . . very successful' (Rogers, 1961: 11) – when Rogers gave up knowing all sorts of things that someone in his position would normally be expected to know.

Order and clarification

It is hard to picture Carl Rogers in this encounter, before Client-Centred Therapy or the PCA existed. Rather than being grounded in the presence of well-established principles, propositions and practices, here his approach is defined by absence: an absence of psychological theory and treatment protocols; an absence of specific goals and intentions; an absence, importantly, of professional therapeutic expertise, which makes way for something yet to be identified. Presumably Rogers does not realize suddenly that this new 'way of being' – as he would come to describe it (Rogers, 1980) – will function in a particular way with regard to the mother's personality dynamics. More likely there is just nowhere else to go. He is, in a sense, floundering. Professional psychological knowledge and skills have proven not up to the task, he does not know what to do, so he does nothing. Or rather, he does nothing that would have been expected of someone in the role of psychological therapist. He does not attempt to 'treat' the mother by implementing theory and technique to facilitate shifts in her cognition, affect or behaviour. Instead, Rogers meets her compassionately in her distress, knowing neither what is wrong, nor how to make it right.

The story is no doubt important to some scholars and practitioners because it heralds the arrival of an idea that would be central in the development of an influential school of therapy, as if its value derived from it being a catalyst for construction. But if theory for Rogers was 'an attempt to give order and clarification' (Thorne, 1992: 42) to the subjective experiences of client and therapist, then what is fascinating about the event is the fact that none of this imminent order or clarity existed at the time, nor proved necessary for therapy to occur. It is true that Rogers gets to the experiential moment itself by being trained and employed in psychology – he arrives there by being a more conventional therapist in the first place – but it is his letting go of all this that makes it uniquely interesting. Crucially, the thing Rogers suddenly found himself lacking at that pivotal point in his life and work was deference to external authority on the nature of distress and the meaning and purpose of therapy, a subordination previously internalized as professional psychotherapeutic expertise but which had now become redundant, opening the way for a shift in the source of authority to the client.

All of which begs an important question. What would it mean to meet a client in this way today? Perhaps there is no need, we might reply, because for us Person-Centred (or some other) therapy exists already and provides an ideal philosophical and theoretical framework to enable us to meet clients as persons, with the utmost respect for their unique subjectivities and right to self-determination. But this rationale did not exist for Rogers in the moment we have been discussing and in any case it seems a rather lazy response that highlights the conundrum under consideration here.

In the session, Rogers experiences first-hand the limits and flaws in both psychological theory and 'theory-mindedness' (House, 2008), so from exasperation more than intellectual rigour he subverts the conventional therapy dynamic by letting go his expertise and putting the client's reality first. We could describe this as an act of spontaneous experimental enquiry into human distress, personal relationships and therapy itself, one arrived at not through commitment to an existing system of psychotherapeutic thought but via the visceral experience of ordinary human compassion.

Following the event, however, Rogers tries to clarify and order his experiences back within the domain of psychological theory. Rogers himself acknowledged the personal and political drivers of theoretical work when he identified the twin motivations for writing his most comprehensive theory statement as, on the one hand, his own 'need for order' (Rogers, 1959: 188) and on the other, 'insistent pressure from my colleagues [in the American Psychological Association]' (ibid.: 185). So, Rogers' pursuit of order and clarity was a personal response to the internal and professional forces at work in his life at the time. It had little to do with the beginnings of 'real therapy' for the mother in Rochester. But the resulting theoretical system developed a life of its own. Supported by helpful social changes (Barrett-Lennard, 1998), the PCA gained traction in the field and growing popularity in the culture at large, the upside-down result being that for therapists following Rogers, his imposed order ended up functioning as an essential ('necessary and sufficient') touchstone for meeting others in their distress.

External authority and the politics of therapy

To put it another way, an unintended negative consequence of the success of the PCA was the creation of a new authority, or, in Rogers' own terms, 'external locus of evaluation', which the events of therapy must satisfy. It might have seemed a more palatably humane authority and been necessary at the time – as part of psychology's 'third force' challenge to the psychoanalytic and behaviourist strangleholds on the client's subjectivity – but it jars with the claim that Person-Centred Therapy is 'politically centred in the client' (Rogers, 1977: 14). Therapist deference to psychological theory is still internalized as professional expertise; it is just that this time the expertise is in offering certain relational qualities (the 'core conditions') that are hypothesized to have specific effects on the client's personality. By trying to clarify and order his own experience within a self-contained 'theory of therapy, personality, and interpersonal relationships' (Rogers, 1959), Rogers unwittingly reinforces the theory-centred instrumentalism of psychotherapeutic practice, the very freedom from which enabled him to meet the mother as a person, rather than as a 'case' or 'patient', and offered for a brief moment the glimpse of a more radical shift in our understanding of the therapy encounter.

I should say here that it is not my intention to denigrate Carl Rogers, the PCA or its many committed practitioners. Rogers' work had a profound and positive impact on the field of psychology and the fact that he was a person of his time, culture, personal history and interests, is in itself no grounds for criticism. Contemporary Person-Centred Therapy is certainly valued by many clients and is no doubt practised with degrees of artfulness and compassion by its adherents. It has never tired of critical reflection upon the intricacies of therapeutic work and the subtle ways in which power can become centred in the practitioner, and I know too that in their encounters with clients, Person-Centred therapists tend to be relatively unburdened by the weight of theory and the 'need to appear "clever"' (Mearns, 1994: 27), possibly because this aspect of the approach attracted them to Person-Centred work in the first place (ibid.). So it might seem unduly critical to be challenging the least obviously theory-centred of all therapies on the grounds that it is too bound by theory.

But we face a dilemma in the psychological therapies, and one that is particularly poignant for the PCA. Our once radical alternatives might have been briefly entertained but it is other therapies that have risen to prominence. Witness the growth of Cognitive Behaviour Therapy (CBT), which has achieved widespread dominance in the UK National Health Service (NHS) as the chosen evidence-based talking treatment in the Improving Access to Psychological Therapies (IAPT) scheme. This endorsement has powerfully boosted its popularity in the wider culture and brought economic rewards too: jobs in the NHS, research grants, funding for services and a booming business in training, not to mention the less tangible psychological benefits of enhanced status for CBT practitioners. The temptation for other therapies is to play catch up, to prove that they too are evidence-based, reliable, fast and efficient.

What, then, should the PCA – or any other relational, explorative, non-medicalized therapy – do? Should we chase what 'works', as if this were an unambiguously benign goal? Should we accept the shift away from dialogue and encounter and toward therapy as a drug-like treatment for psychological 'disorders' (Guy et al., 2011)? Should we pursue certainty via 'systematic outcome monitoring' and ever more diagnostic theory systems? Should we mimic the research strategies other therapies have used to gain acceptance, however philosophically and methodologically problematic they may be for our own values and practices? Should we do whatever it takes to sell our services to powerful social institutions and to appease the will of governments, ignoring their ideological agendas and destructive real-world impacts?

Some individuals and groupings within the relational approaches seem to advocate just such a strategy, apparently seeing therapy as an unquestionably virtuous endeavour. There is an ends-justify-means mentality here, in which as long as we spread the good works of counsellors and psychotherapists, then all shall be well. If that means using the research methods that powerful healthcare organizations deem legitimate, regardless of their many errors and distortions (Rogers et al., 2011;

Rogers, 2014), then so be it. If that means rebranding our practice as a manualized treatment for specific psychiatric diagnoses, even though we are opposed to the medical model upon which this diagnosis and treatment approach is based (Sanders, 2005), then so be it. If that means failing to challenge or even grasp the potential for oppressive coercion in UK government moves to have Jobcentre staff – operating in a system defined by the threat of sanctions – refer benefits claimants to psychological therapists located in the same building (MWF, 2016), then once again, so be it.

For many practitioners and campaigners, however, these 'pragmatic' – or politically expedient – strategies are deeply incongruent, if not downright unethical (MWF, 2016; Rogers & Atkinson, 2015; Rogers *et al.*, 2011). So do we take an 'at all costs' approach to expanding the worlds of counselling and psychotherapy, and in the process risk sacrificing the essence of our work by aligning with forces that are coercive, disempowering and anti-therapeutic? Or do we take a stand against the narrowing of what is deemed an appropriate response to – and understanding of – distress; a stand against the medicalization of experience and the self-defined authority of the 'evidence-based regime' (Rizq, 2013: 20)? Can we resist the siren call of the State and the promises of jobs and funding for those who collaborate with its aims? Dare we articulate therapy as uncertain, unpredictable and idiosyncratic, as the 'art of not knowing' (Schmid, 2001)? Can we generate new spaces for dialogue about an alternative future for our field?

Which way forward?

One difficulty, of course, is that efforts to do any of this are often hampered by our entanglement with forces that close down such spaces. This happens most obviously when professional self-interest converges with dominant discourses of mental health and the agendas of governments. Professional bodies want jobs for their members and for therapy to be as accessible as possible, while competing with each other for influence in the corridors of power. At the same time, mainstream society's take on the meaning of distress has seen a retreat from Humanistic views and instead embraced the idea of diagnosis, treatment and cure, thanks in part to celebrity-endorsed mental health campaigns around 'parity of esteem' and de-stigmatization, which have mobilized the medical model to subtly self-defeating effect (Watts, 2015). Governments, meanwhile, have become more interested in how the psychological therapies can help reduce the welfare budget by getting people off benefits and into work (Rogers & Atkinson, 2015). And all of this is occurring in a socio-economic system in which everything – including therapy, relationships and even the idea of happiness itself – can be commodified; everything can be bought and sold in order to turn a profit.

This has become a toxic mix, with each centre of power feeding off and feeding into the others. And it seeps into everything, from the policy decisions of governments, to the actions of large professional organizations, to the relational moment in an individual therapy encounter, to our own subjective experiences of distress.

It becomes hard to think outside of what appear to be uncontested truths: psychiatric diagnoses are legitimate; distress can and should be cured; the faster we cure it, the better; therapy is a healthcare profession that treats discrete psychological disorders with evidence-based expertise; competition is inevitable and desirable; work is good and so on.

But these versions of truth *are* contested, or at least should be, by Humanistic Psychologies such as the PCA. Yet we see the PCA chasing CBT's profile by trying to prove that it 'works' too (Cooper *et al.*, 2010) – and with some success. In the UK, the approach has found its way into National Institute for Health and Clinical Excellence (NICE) recommendations for NHS treatment under the guise of 'Counselling for Depression' (Murphy, 2013), rebranding itself as a manualized intervention for a specific psychiatric diagnosis when it could be challenging the 'regime of truth' (House, 2003) that encourages precisely this kind of manualization and medicalization. As a community of psy-practitioners who are simply trying to survive, or perhaps even actualize, amid the economic, ideological and cultural conditions of Western capitalism – or 'neo-liberalism' – it is no wonder such initiatives evolve. There is nothing inherently wrong with trying to promote our ideas and practices to powerful social institutions. But when the compromises involve a corrosion of our core values, then claims for the radicalism of the PCA ring rather hollow, or at least seem nostalgic rather than present- or future-oriented.

Person-Centred Therapy – certainly in its less diluted forms – might still have a good deal to say about our times but just because we keep calling something 'revolutionary' does not make it so. The field is changing in ways that cast doubt on the possibility that Person-Centred thinking and practice will alter the current course of our 'implausible professions' (House & Totton, 1997), let alone trigger a 'quiet revolution' in the world beyond the counselling room. For one thing, the PCA's radical focus on the centrality of the therapy relationship has now been absorbed – albeit in distorted form – into conventional psychotherapeutic wisdom. And the idea that any one approach has the answer and will ultimately win the day, while still a belief that fuels many an internecine conflict, is rapidly looking dated. Versions of 'pluralism' are gaining legitimacy (Cooper & McLeod, 2010; Samuels, 1997) and research regularly points to the irrelevance of the practitioner's theoretical school in determining what clients get out of therapy (Wampold, 2015). Even the seemingly intractable dominance of CBT is faltering (Johnsen & Friborg, 2015).

Elsewhere, in the philosophy of therapy, a 'paradigm war' wages between modernity and post-modernism, with the welcome articulation of 'post-professional', 'trans-modern' and 'post-existential' perspectives (House, 2010; Loewenthal, 2011), which again suggest a future for therapy beyond theoretical allegiance; while from within the PCA, an 'ethics-alone' approach has emerged, 'free from empirical claims, the vagaries of experimental research and the conceits of psychological theories' (Grant, 2004: 162). In any case, it has been argued, whatever wisdom our fallible theories do contain might be better expressed in more 'common sense' language (Purton, 2014).

We see this predicament in the politics of the professions too, with the dissolution of old conflicts and the formation of new alliances and fractures. In 2008, practitioners from a wide variety of approaches united against the State regulation of counselling and psychotherapy in the UK (Postle & House, 2009), successfully defeating the proposal in 2011. In the midst of all the ferocity around the issue – with Rogers' incendiary lament that 'there are as many certified charlatans and exploiters of people as there are uncertified' (Rogers, 1980: 244) hovering nearby throughout – it was telling that the issue did not escalate feuds between the traditional schools but revealed commonalities between them and simultaneously exposed fundamental divisions within the ranks of each approach. Since then, these politicized cross-modality alliances in the UK have gone on to new campaigns, working in coalition with service user and disability rights groups to challenge government policies around welfare and mental health (*Guardian* press letter, 2015; MWF, 2016).

The practice of freedom

Interesting, then, that some in the field see therapy as an apolitical, instrumental, evidence-based and expert-led psychological treatment, one that is able and willing to appease the demands of power, while others are travelling in a quite different direction, deconstructing the edifices that enclose thought and practice (Postle, 2013), challenging anti-therapeutic socio-economic conditions, and uncovering once more the principled humanity and humility of the encounter. Which brings us back to Carl Rogers' meeting with the mother in Rochester and how professional and cultural forces have overwhelmed some of the quiet meaning of that encounter.

The story draws our attention to the experience of being a therapist – with all the socially sanctioned authority the role now brings – yet meeting clients with a curious and deeply respectful *not knowing*; encountering the subjectivity of the other with an 'ordinary' (Lomas, 1999), non-instrumental compassion (Smail, 2005). This is therapy not as a tool to deliver outcomes but as an outcome in itself:

> The rampant instrumentalisation and bureaucratisation of society is such that we can hardly think straight about an activity being good in its own right. Everything, we imagine is a means to some other end, some other outcome. . . . Therapy can be something we greatly value . . . even though it 'goes' nowhere and 'delivers' no particular 'outcomes'. Life consists in more than solving problems and achieving outcomes.
>
> *(Howard, 2005: 230–231)*

As David Smail has argued of the Rogerian core conditions, '[t]hey should be, simply, ends in themselves' (Smail, 2005: 83).

What actually happens in this kind of genuinely explorative encounter – what is discussed, and how, and what it means to the participants – will depend on the people involved, the context in which they find themselves and the environments they inhabit beyond the therapy space. It will also be constantly in flux, amenable to all sorts of shifts in perception and external influence. Just as in the pivotal Rogers encounter, therapy becomes an act of research in itself (Mearns, 1994: 33), a 'cooperative enquiry' into the human condition (Postle, 2012); one rooted in a deep respect for each person's right to self-determination, with direction, inspiration and meaning emerging idiosyncratically within each moment, session and relationship.

Removed from expectations of change defined by a traditional psychotherapeutic framework, the combined gazes of client and therapist can also have a wider horizon than just intra- and inter-personal dynamics. The world and its power structures may come into view. This is not, therefore, an approach that would curry much favour with a rigid healthcare model of psychological treatment, nor would it have a great deal to offer the UK government's back-to-work agenda, other than ongoing critical analysis. But it is also against the direction of travel in our own field, which is precisely the dilemma facing the PCA. Can it express its radical potential in new ways and challenge the mainstream trajectory of counselling and psychotherapy? Or will it seek State endorsement as an 'effective intervention' for 'psychological disorders'? The danger being, of course, that in appeasing the demands of an increasingly medicalized and evidence-obsessed market in psychological treatment, it risks disconnecting irretrievably from the spirit of its inception, as embodied by Rogers' meeting with the mother in Rochester.

I guess we will never know how that session really went, or the sessions that followed, but the story is nonetheless a defiant allegory of all that is so beautiful and liberating, yet simple and humble, about the therapeutic encounter: 'the practice of freedom by free beings for free beings' (Grant, 2004: 163). In the embellishments I have given here, it is equally a tale of therapy's hubris. The further away from that moment in the late 1930s that Person-Centred and other therapies get, the further away they are from articulating what is so meaningful about our work.

As I said at the start, Carl Rogers is everywhere and nowhere. And it seems we have to find him and forget him all over again.

References

Barrett-Lennard, G. (1998) *Carl Rogers' Helping System: Journey & Substance*. London: Sage.

Cooper, M. & McLeod, J. (2010) *Pluralistic Counselling and Psychotherapy*. London: Sage.

Cooper, M., Watson, J., & Hölldampf, D. (eds) (2010) *Person-Centred and Experiential Therapies Work*. Ross-on-Wye: PCCS Books.

Grant, B. (2004) 'The imperative of ethical justification in psychotherapy: the special case of client-centred therapy', *Person-Centred & Experiential Psychotherapies, 3*(3): 152–165.

Guardian press letter (2015) 'Austerity and a malign benefits regime are profoundly damaging mental health', www.theguardian.com/society/2015/apr/17/austerity-and-a-malign-benefits-regime-are-profoundly-damaging-mental-health [retrieved 18/05/2016].

Guy, A., Thomas, R., Stephenson, S., & Loewenthal, D. (2011) NICE under scrutiny: the impact of the National Institute for Health and Clinical Excellence guidelines on the provision of psychotherapy in the UK. UKCP Research Unit.

House, R. (2003) *Therapy Beyond Modernity: Deconstructing and Transcending Profession-Centred Therapy*. London: Karnac.

House, R. (2008) 'Therapy's modernist "regime of truth": from scientistic "theory-mindedness" towards the subtle and the mysterious', *Philosophical Practice, 3*(3): 343–352.

House, R. (2010) *In, Against and Beyond Therapy: Critical Essays towards a Post-Professional Era.* Ross-on-Wye: PCCS Books.

House, R. & Totton, N. (eds) (1997) *Implausible Professions: Arguments for Pluralism & Autonomy in Psychotherapy and Counselling.* Ross-on-Wye: PCCS Books.

Howard, A. (2005) *Counselling and Identity: Self Realisation in a Therapy Culture.* Basingstoke: Palgrave MacMillan.

Johnsen, T. J. & Friborg, O. (2015) 'The effects of cognitive behavioral therapy as an anti-depressive treatment is falling: a meta-analysis', *Psychological Bulletin, 141*(4): 747–768.

Kirschenbaum, H. (2007) *The Life and Work of Carl Rogers.* Ross-on-Wye: PCCS Books.

Loewenthal, D. (2011) *Post-existentialism and the Psychological Therapies: Towards a Therapy without Foundations.* London: Karnac Books.

Lomas, P. (1999) *Doing Good? Psychotherapy Out of its Depth.* Oxford: Oxford University Press.

Mearns, D. (1994) *Developing Person-Centred Counselling.* London: Sage.

Murphy, D. (2013) 'Counselling for depression' https://personcentredpsych.wordpress.com/2013/06/14/counselling-for-depression/ [retrieved 24/03/2016].

MWF (Mental Wealth Foundation) (2016) Public statement on psycho-compulsion. https://allianceblogs.wordpress.com/2016/03/21/mwf_jobcentretherapy_letter/ [retrieved 22/03/2016].

Postle, D. (2012) *Therapy Futures: Obstacles and Opportunities.* WLR London: Lulu.com.

Postle, D. (2013) 'The richness of everyday relationships', *Therapy Today, 24*(3): 30–32. www.bacp.co.uk/docs/pdf/15326_therapy%20today%20april%202013.pdf [retrieved 03/04/2017].

Postle D. & House, R. (eds) (2009) Compliance? Ambivalence? Rejection? Nine papers challenging the Health Professions Council July 2009 proposals for the State regulation of the psychological therapies. WLR London: www.lulu.com/content/7709462.

Purton, C. (2014) *The Trouble with Psychotherapy: Counselling and Common Sense.* London: Palgrave Macmillan.

Rizq, R. (2013) 'The language of healthcare', *Therapy Today, 24*(2): 20–24.

Rogers, A. (2014) '"The master's tools will never dismantle the master's house": reflections from the PCCS Books anniversary conference: shared practice in non-medicalised mental health care', *Self & Society, 41*(2): 58–60.

Rogers, A. & Atkinson, P. (2015) 'Ethical dialogue', *Self & Society, 43*(4): 375–383.

Rogers, A., Maidman, J., & House, R. (2011) 'The bad faith of evidence-based practice: beyond counsels of despair', *Therapy Today, 22*(6): 26–29.

Rogers, C.R. (1959) 'A theory of therapy, personality, and interpersonal relationships as developed in the client-centred framework'. In S. Koch (ed.) *Psychology: A Study of Science, Vol. 3: Formulations of the Person and the Social Context* (pp. 184–256). New York: McGraw-Hill.

Rogers, C.R. (1961) *On Becoming a Person.* London: Constable.

Rogers, C.R. (1977) *Carl Rogers on Personal Power.* London: Constable.

Rogers, C.R. (1980) *A Way of Being.* Boston, MA: Houghton Mifflin.

Samuels, A. (1997) 'Pluralism and psychotherapy: what is a good training?' In R. House & N. Totton (eds) *Implausible Professions: Arguments for Pluralism & Autonomy in Psychotherapy and Counselling* (pp. 199–214). Ross-on-Wye: PCCS Books.

Sanders, P. (2005) 'Principled and strategic opposition to the medicalisation of distress and all of its apparatus'. In S. Joseph & R. Worsley (eds) *Person-Centred Psychopathology: A Positive Psychology of Mental Health* (pp. 21–42). Ross-on-Wye: PCCS Books.

Schmid, P.F. (2001) 'Comprehension: the art of not knowing. Dialogical and ethical perspectives on empathy as dialogue in personal and person-centered relationships'. In S. Haugh & T. Merry (eds) *Rogers' Therapeutic Conditions: Evolution, Theory and Practice, Volume 2: Empathy* (pp. 53–71). Ross-on-Wye: PCCS Books. And http://web.utanet.at/schmidpp/paper-compr.pdf [retrieved 16/01/2013].

Smail, D. (2005) *Power, Interest and Psychology: Elements of a Social Materialist Understanding of Distress.* Ross-on-Wye: PCCS Books.

Thorne, B. (1992) *Carl Rogers.* London: Sage.

Wampold, B.E. (2015) *The Great Psychotherapy Debate.* Second edition. London: Routledge.

Watts, J. (2015) 'Is mental suffering really "just like any other illness"?' www.huffingtonpost.co.uk/dr-jay-watts/mental-healthillness_b_8460340.html [retrieved 23/03/2016].

12

THE FUTURE OF HUMANISTIC PSYCHOLOGY

Autonomy, relatedness and competence

Katherine McArthur and Mick Cooper

The world has changed dramatically since the 1940s when Carl Rogers developed the client-centred approach to therapy: a key moment in the development of Humanistic Psychology. Psychologists, psychotherapists and counsellors are working within multiple worldwide crises across economic, ecological and psychological spheres. Hawkins and Shohet (2012: 9), quoting Gilding's (2011) book title, refer to this as the 'great disruption' to life as we know it. For Humanistic Psychology and, indeed, any helping profession, to meet the challenges of the modern world it must evolve and adapt, continually improving its theory and practice. In this chapter, we will discuss the ways in which Humanistic Psychology can grow and adapt through actualizing its potential in three key areas: autonomy, relatedness and competence. These are three fundamental human needs highlighted by self-determination theory (Ryan & Deci, 2000), which is itself a key theoretical development in Humanistic Psychology. By thinking about these as three areas for growth in the humanistic approach itself, we explore potential directions for the future of the approach.

Establishing autonomy in the humanistic approach

Humanistic Psychology is unique in its emphasis on the therapeutic relationship as a force for healing, and in its view of human beings as autonomous, inter-related and essentially motivated toward growth. As the 'third force' in psychology, it can be tempting for humanistic psychologists to define the approach by its differences from what went before: a counter-cultural phenomenon rejecting both the reductionism of the behaviourist tradition, and the determinism of the psychodynamic approach. Emerging as a reaction against more traditional psychological approaches, many see the humanistic approach as a more egalitarian and more ethical way for the helping professions to encounter those in distress. In this sense, the approach has established its autonomy by focusing on its uniqueness, and its departure from more traditional approaches to psychology. But is this still the most relevant, or the most adaptive way of viewing the humanistic approach? If the integrity of the approach is best served by balancing the three interwoven needs highlighted in self-determination theory, then development of relatedness and competence is also necessary.

Toward a pluralistic-humanistic approach

With the autonomy of the humanistic approach well-established, its identity can be seen as secure. From that position, it has the potential for its relationship to other approaches to become more collegial and less reactive. The dodo bird verdict, whereby research shows little difference in effectiveness between therapeutic approaches (Wampold & Imel, 2015), suggests that no particular psychological approach is of more value than another. In addition, clients have reported little interest in the theoretical orientation of therapists (Binder, Holgersen & Nielsen, 2009). These findings do not negate the philosophical differences between approaches, which are keenly felt by many therapists. However, philosophical differences can be over-emphasized, usually in tandem with practitioners' assumptions that their own approach is best. It is likely that in-group bias explains at least some of these feelings (see social identity theory, Tajfel & Turner, 1979). By contrast, a pluralistic approach to therapy might be more likely to meet the needs of a diversity of clients (Cooper & McLeod, 2011; Cooper & Dryden, 2016). This pluralistic standpoint involves an openness to a range of different approaches and a facilitation of dialogue between therapist and client about what is preferred. It is a way of working that maintains the humanistic emphasis on the therapeutic relationship, and the humanistic view of the person who is actively engaged in the relationship as autonomous, inter-related and motivated toward growth. For a humanistic therapist to take a pluralistic approach does not mean becoming a jack of all trades, but being open to the influences of other approaches while working congruently within their own personal value system and training. In this sense, pluralistic practice is highly consistent with humanistic thinking, and could allow the approach to develop while maintaining its autonomy.

This need not be contradictory when we consider that the three fundamental needs of autonomy, relatedness and competence are interlinked and positively reinforce each other when adequately supported in the social environment. Ryan and Deci (2000) propose that the three needs 'must be satisfied across the life span for an individual to experience an ongoing sense of integrity and wellbeing' (pp. 74–75).

Growth in relatedness

In relation to the content of humanistic therapy, many contemporary theorists have argued for a greater focus on relatedness to balance the existing focus on auto-nomy. For example, Rogers' actualizing tendency is seen as a positive force working opposed to the usually negative impact of the social environment. Mearns and Thorne (2013) have reframed this as the 'actualizing process', whereby the growth of human beings depends on a balance between individual freedom and social responsibility. The emphasis on social responsibility is a growing edge within humanistic psychological theory and could be taken further, with more attention given to social justice. Given the close association between social inequality and distress, psychologists have a responsibility to work against tendencies to ignore or distort the realities of life in the 21st century. Already, humanistic psychologists make important contributions on a social level. For instance, the American Psychological Association's Society for Humanistic Psychology issued a statement of opposition in response to DSM-5 (the most recent version of the *Diagnostic and Statistical Manual of Mental Disorders*), and humanistic psychologists are involved in critiquing the increasing medicalization of distress. In this sense, humanistic therapy has moved its focus on the autonomy of human beings toward a balance between autonomy and relatedness. In a similar way, the second fundamental need for relatedness could be taken into account in the development of the approach itself. In other words, relatedness between Humanistic Psychology and other theoretical orientations could enhance the integrity and wellbeing of the approach.

One way of achieving this sense of relatedness would be collaboration with other approaches in training therapists. Trainers from different theoretical orientations could give trainee therapists a broader view of how distress is conceptualized, and highlight the similarities between approaches as well as the differences. Providing trainee therapists with the ability to speak the language of other therapeutic approaches would allow them to more fully understand their own practice and different therapists' ways of working. More importantly, for clients who might prefer a range of approaches, a level of understanding about the theory and practice of other therapies would enhance humanistic therapists' abilities to meet their needs.

Actualizing competence

Given the nature of the three fundamental needs as intertwined and mutually supportive, the third need, competence, can be actualized in parallel with autonomy and relatedness. A key move toward actualizing the competence of the approach would be a commitment among humanistic practitioners to research and evaluation of their practice. However, despite movements toward encouraging interest in research among practitioners of Humanistic Psychology, there remains a gap whereby a large number of counsellors working in the humanistic tradition are indifferent to the idea of conducting research (Daniel & McLeod, 2006).

Part of the reason for this reluctance among humanistic therapists to engage in research and evaluation is the sense of the approach existing outside of traditional psychology and its research methods. In other words, the aforementioned imbalance between the autonomy and relatedness of the approach within the broader field affects humanistic practitioners' relationship with research, and by extension, competence. Demonstrating competence in humanistic practice can be seen by therapists as an externally imposed demand, tied up with the research methods of incompatible ways of thinking. It can be argued that Humanistic Psychology, by virtue of its counter-cultural identity, thrives on occupying an alternative position, and can never truly integrate with the mainstream of research and practice in psychology lest the values underpinning it are compromised to a point that it is no longer an authentic reflection of humanistic thinking. But if the approach moves toward more relatedness with other therapeutic approaches, could humanistic therapists also become more open to a range of research methods? Could greater integration between research and practice actually enhance the approach in terms of autonomy, relatedness and competence?

Some have argued (see Guy et al., 2012) that research on humanistic therapies is better suited to methods that are rooted in similar philosophical and ethical traditions, i.e. qualitative methods. Unfortunately, these methods are considered inadequate by policy makers and funders to provide evidence of the value of a therapeutic practice. The gap between empirical research and humanistic therapy has contributed to the approach being somewhat sidelined. Compared to the behaviourist tradition's developmental trajectory through Cognitive Behavioural Therapy (CBT), Humanistic Psychology remains under-researched and therefore under-valued. CBT is often erroneously considered to be the most effective approach to therapy, due to the wealth of evidence provided by its long-standing commitment to research through randomized controlled trials (RCTs). Since the humanistic approach has not traditionally sought to prove itself through scientific research methods like this, the lack of evidence for its effectiveness can be misinterpreted as a lack of effectiveness per se.

Empirical research and the humanistic approach

Having been involved in research on humanistic counselling in UK schools, including pilot RCTs (Cooper et al., 2010; McArthur, Cooper & Berdondini, 2013; Pybis et al., 2015), we have argued that quantitative methods including RCTs are an acceptable and ethical option for researchers within the humanistic tradition, and one option for addressing the demand for evidence-based practice (Cooper, 2011; McArthur, 2011). However, others have argued that research methods associated with a reductionist view (and especially RCTs) are inappropriate for studying humanistic approaches, such that this course of action constitutes bad faith (Rogers, Maidman & House, 2011). But if humanistic psychologists refuse to engage with research methods outside of their own theoretical orientation, humanistic practice could remain in its sidelined position. This means that potential clients in distress, regardless of their preferences for therapy, might not have access to humanistic approaches. Through engagement with empirical research in school-based humanistic counselling, researchers from the humanistic tradition have been able to demonstrate clearly the effectiveness of humanistic therapy for distressed young people. Positive results in these studies have contributed to increased access to school-based humanistic counselling in the UK, and to ESRC funding for a fully powered trial: the ETHOS study.

This pragmatic approach to research could be viewed as too great a compromise for the humanistic approach to maintain its autonomy. Effectiveness demonstrated through RCTs does not necessarily reflect the true human value of humanistic therapy. But this does not mean that positive results through RCT research are meaningless. For one thing, humanistic therapists can modify how effectiveness is measured in order to reflect humanistic theory. The outcome measures used in RCTs of school-based humanistic counselling have included standardized measures of distress, but also an individualized measure of personal goal attainment developed by CORC, the Goal-Based Outcome (G-BO) measure (Law & Jacob, 2015). This tool allows practitioner-researchers to establish what an individual wants to achieve in therapy, in their own words, and to measure how well humanistic therapy has facilitated that. In relation to self-determination theory (Ryan & Deci, 2000), this could be described as a way of promoting and supporting intrinsic motivations as opposed to external goals. The measure has shown promising results in research on school-based humanistic counselling so far. The findings of the three pilot RCTs conducted so far indicate that, second to reducing psychological distress (as measured by the YP-CORE), increases in scores on the G-BO are the most common outcome of school-based humanistic counselling (Cooper, 2013). In other words, humanistic counselling in schools appears to help young clients to grow in their own self-determined, idiosyncratic ways. This suggests that researchers from the humanistic approach can feasibly meet demands for empirical evidence while promoting the unique values of the approach.

Young clients' experiences of humanistic therapy: an example from qualitative research

Additionally, conducting RCTs does not have to mean excluding other types of research. As an example, some of the qualitative data we collected during one pilot RCT study of school-based humanistic counselling (McArthur et al., 2013) has now been analyzed using a grounded theory approach to identify the change processes that young people experienced (McArthur, Cooper & Berdondini, 2015). Interviews conducted with 14 young people who had counselling as part of the RCT showed five distinct pathways of change, with each young person reporting multiple, over-lapping change processes. These change processes provide potential maps of what can happen for young clients in humanistic therapy, and have some implications for practice which feed back into the three interdependent needs of autonomy, relatedness and competence.

The first process, relief, reflected the finding that most young people in the study reported a simple process of catharsis, whereby talking about their experiences to the counsellor in itself led to feeling better (McArthur et al., 2013). The more interactive process of increasing self-worth was described by young people who developed a therapeutic relationship with the counsellor in which they experienced understanding and acceptance and gradually moved toward greater self-awareness and self-acceptance. Developing insight was the label given to the process of young people reflecting on and understanding aspects of their experience through having counselling. Improving relational skills was reported by young people who were able to use the counselling sessions as a way of practising healthier ways of relating to others, and then translate this skill into their own lives. Finally, enhancing coping strategies was reported by some of the young people as taking advice from the counsellor and learning to change their behaviour.

The differences between these overlapping processes are interesting since the counsellors in the study were all demonstrably using a humanistic approach in their practice. But while the clients' experiences of therapy included processes in line with this approach, there was also one process evidently outside of it, and these were not mutually exclusive. The process of enhancing coping strategies is more readily associated with CBT, while each of the others fits more neatly into the humanistic approach. This is striking because the counsellors and researchers involved all had a bias toward the humanistic approach, and did not conceptualize their practice as advice-giving. However, it is also in line with previous findings in school counselling research whereby young clients report wanting more advice from the counsellor (Griffiths, 2013), a result that was replicated in this study (McArthur *et al.*, 2015). It might be that young clients tend to have a different understanding of what constitutes advice in therapy, and that the same would not apply for adult clients. Whether or not this phenomenon is unique to humanistic therapy with young people, it suggests that what clients need and want from counselling, and how different clients experience humanistic counselling, do not necessarily fit neatly into one theoretical approach. In order to develop humanistic practice in a way that is responsive to what clients tell us about their experiences, it is important not to dismiss findings like this one which contradict our theoretical concepts. The challenge for humanistic practitioners is to be open to conflicting information from clients and researchers and thereby be willing to adapt our assumptions about what is good practice.

Conclusion

The danger for Humanistic Psychology in the modern world is that it remains, or becomes increasingly, sidelined in culture despite its great potential for contributing to a more psychologically healthy society. Self-determination theory is a relatively new development in humanistic thinking, and using this as a way of thinking about the approach itself can illuminate potential ways of enhancing, protecting and promoting humanistic practice. Balancing the already well-developed autonomy of the humanistic approach with equally important and interdependent needs, relatedness and competence, can contribute to the integrity and wellbeing of the approach. Greater integration with other approaches, more openness to alternative theories and practices, and a stronger emphasis on research are key to the future of the humanistic approach.

References

Binder, P-E., Holgersen, H. & Nielsen, G.H.S. (2009). Why did I change when I went to therapy? A qualitative analysis of former patients' conceptions of successful psychotherapy. *Counselling and Psychotherapy Research: Linking Research with Practice*, 9(4), 250–256.

Cooper, M. (2011). Meeting the demand for evidence-based practice. *Therapy Today*, 22(4), 10–16.

Cooper, M. (2013). School-based counselling in UK secondary schools: A review and critical evaluation. Glasgow: University of Strathclyde.

Cooper, M. & Dryden, W. (Eds) (2016). *Handbook of Pluralistic Counselling and Psychotherapy*. London: Sage.

Cooper, M. & McLeod, J. (2011). *Pluralistic Counselling and Psychotherapy*. Sage: London.

Cooper, M., Rowland, N., McArthur, K., Pattison, S., Cromarty, K. & Richards, K. (2010). Randomised controlled trial of school-based humanistic counselling for emotional distress in young people: Feasibility study and preliminary indications of efficacy. *Child and Adolescent Psychiatry and Mental Health*, 4(12).

Daniel, T. & McLeod, J. (2006). Weighing up the evidence: A qualitative analysis of how person-centred counsellors evaluate the effectiveness of their practice. *Counselling and Psychotherapy Research*, 6(4), 244–249.

Gilding, B. (2011). *The Great Disruption: How the Climate Crisis will Transform Society*. London: Bloomsbury.

Griffiths, G. (2013). *Helpful and Unhelpful Factors in School-based Counselling: Clients' Perspectives*. Lutterworth: BACP/Counselling MindEd.

Guy, A., Loewenthal, D., Thomas, R. & Stephenson, S. (2012). Scrutinising NICE: The impact of the National Institute for Health and Clinical Excellence Guidelines on the provision of counselling and psychotherapy in primary care in the UK. *Psychodynamic Practice*, 18(1), 25–50.

Hawkins, P. & Shohet, R. (2012). *Supervision in the Helping Professions* (4th edition). Maidenhead: McGraw Hill Open University Press.

Law, D. & Jacob, J. (2015). *Goals and Goal-Based Outcomes (GBOs): Some Useful Information*. CAMHS Press: London.

McArthur, K. (2011). RCTs: A personal experience. *Therapy Today*, 22(7), 24–25.

McArthur, K., Cooper, M. & Berdondini, L. (2013). School-based humanistic counselling for psychological distress in young people: Pilot randomized controlled trial. *Psychotherapy Research*, 23(3), 355–365.

McArthur, K., Cooper, M. & Berdondini, L. (2015). Change processes in school-based humanistic counselling. *Counselling and Psychotherapy Research*, 16(2), 88–99.

Mearns, D. & Thorne, B. (2013). *Person-Centred Counselling in Action* (4th edition). Sage: London.

Pybis, J., Cooper, M., Hill, A., Cromarty, K., Levesley, R., Murdoch, J. & Turner, N. (2015). Pilot randomised controlled trial of school-based humanistic counselling for psychological distress in young people: Outcomes and methodological reflections. *Counselling and Psychotherapy Research*, 15, 241–250.

Rogers, A., Maidman, J. & House, R. (2011). The bad faith of evidence-based practice: Beyond counsels of despair. *Therapy Today*, 22(6), 26–29.

Ryan, R.M. & Deci, E.L. (2000). Self-determination theory and the facilitation of intrinsic motivation, social development, and well-being. *American Psychologist*, 55, 68–78.

Tajfel, H. & Turner, J.C. (1979). An integrative theory of intergroup conflict. In S. Worchel & W.G. Austin (Eds), *The Social Psychology of Intergroup Relations* (pp. 33–47). Monterey, CA: Brooks/Cole.

Wampold, B.E. & Imel, Z.E. (2015). *The Great Psychotherapy Debate: The Evidence for What Makes Psychotherapy Work* (2nd edition). New York: Routledge.

13

RECONCILING HUMANISTIC AND POSITIVE PSYCHOLOGY

Further bridging the cultural rift[1]

Harris L. Friedman

Humanistic Psychology is often mis-portrayed as dying or dead, a claim that is especially egregious when made by positive psychologists who minimize their debt to, as well as co-opt a narrow version of, Humanistic Psychology. This rift rests on a cultural divide that cuts broadly across many sectors of modern life. Despite a denigration of, and a distancing from, Humanistic Psychology, Positive Psychology has derived considerable benefits from Humanistic Psychology. Positive Psychology claims to bring more rigorous science to areas long considered by humanistic psychologists; however, recent claims that Positive Psychology is more dedicated than Humanistic Psychology to rigorous science have been shown to be questionable through a series of critical articles debunking a number of prominent Positive Psychology research findings, while other claims, such as the incommensurability of the two fields, have been shown to be unsupported (Friedman, 2014).

Dilthey's (1989) collection of essays, written prior to his death in 1911, distinguished between natural and human sciences, with the former focused on material explanations and the latter focused on understanding humans and their unique lives within socio-historical contexts. Later, Snow (1959) bifurcated intellectual culture into two conflicting camps, the sciences and the humanities, a split that many others have since attempted to mend (e.g., Gould, 2003). What Snow identified as disparate cultures (i.e., the sciences seeking universal objective truths vs. the humanities seeking particularistic subjective understandings) has resulted in what some have referred to as 'the paradigm wars'. Opinion seems divided as to whether these wars continue or have ended (e.g., Oakley, 1999).

Within psychology, Kimble (1984) applied this cultural delineation, bifurcating research and clinical psychology into scientific and humanistic cultures, respectively. This approach to understanding rifts within psychology has been revisited a number of times (e.g., Nunez, Poole, & Memon, 2003), including recently in relationship to divides within Positive Psychology (Bacon, 2005). Although some speculate that cultural reconciliation has finally percolated into psychology, which has been the last social science to resist acceptance of qualitative methods, the jury is still out (Willig & Stainton-Rogers, 2008).

For example, the American Psychological Association is working hard to advance psychology as a science-technology-engineering-mathematics (STEM) discipline, which might bring enhanced benefits (e.g., status and money) for psychology departments (Kurtzman, 2012). Likewise, many psychology departments are even going to the extreme of renaming themselves to more closely identify with these STEM disciplines. These include the following major U.S. universities: Dartmouth and Indiana (both now called the Departments of Psychological and Brain Sciences); Northern Kentucky, Ball State, and Missouri (all three now called the Departments of Psychological Science); Duke (now called the Department of Psychology and Neuroscience); and Brown (now called the Department of Cognitive, Linguistic and Psychological Sciences) (Jaffe, 2011). Evidently much of psychology is attempting to disavow its humanistic aspects in an effort to be seen as a hard science.

One area in which this culture war manifests is in the rift between Humanistic and Positive Psychology. Such cultural divides are not always peaceful, and that is why they are referred to as wars. Seligman (2009), one of the co-founders of Positive Psychology, has frequently denigrated Humanistic Psychology for supposedly lacking 'mainstream, cumulative, and replicable scientific method' (p. xvii), which he claims to be foundational to Positive Psychology. Seligman does, however, admit that both Humanistic and Positive Psychology share a common interest in what is positive (e.g., goodness and health) in contrast to the prevailing mainstream focus in psychology on the negative (e.g., evil and pathology). Positive Psychology has often asserted itself as being a unique approach from its predecessor, Humanistic Psychology, by virtue of its embracing of quantitative research, while evaluating Humanistic Psychology as unscientific for its frequent reliance on qualitative methods (Friedman, 2008).

In addition to this methodological divide, another major delineation between Humanistic and Positive Psychology rests on the former's emphasis on holism, including the negative, while the latter tends to exclude the negative, creating an imbalance. Recently I illustrated this problem using the example of the largest applied psychology research study ever conducted, which trained every U.S. soldier in resiliency (Friedman & Robbins, 2012). In this paper, I argued that such emphasis only on the positive, while ignoring its potentially complementary shadow, could have a very negative backlash, for example resulting in resilient warfighters who could simultaneously be less likely to suffer from post-traumatic stress but more likely to commit atrocities. In a more general way, I argue that to be humanistic involves recognizing the holistic relationship between both positive and negative, and including both. In many other areas of psychology, this is becoming increasingly recognized, such as in the growing recognition of the importance of the understudied emotion of disgust, which is now being seen not just as a negative emotion to be avoided but, rather, one to be embraced as adaptive (Curtis, 2011). Likewise, I am increasingly interested in complex emotions central to humanistic thought, such as awe, which involves a rich intermixture of positive and negative affect (Bonner & Friedman, 2011).

Mruk (2008) provided a good way to delineate the complex rift characterizing the cultural divide separating Humanistic from Positive Psychology. Specifically, he delineated between what he called 'positivistic positive psychology' and 'humanistic positive psychology'. He outlined their commonalities and differences, while denying that they constitute separate fields. With the increasing cultural ascendency of Positive Psychology, claiming superiority over Humanistic Psychology by supposedly restoring hard science approaches to positive phenomena constitutes both a threat and an opportunity for Humanistic Psychology. Although Humanistic Psychology usually identifies more with the humanities and the 'softer' areas of the sciences (in contrast to the tide of STEM disciplines on which Positive Psychology is rising), it has no inherent need to exclude any approach to understanding human experience and behavior, and can include both positive and negative. Humanistic Psychology thus has a strategic advantage over Positive Psychology, as it can include and potentially transcend its rival.

To understand this rift, it needs to be appreciated as having developed from two complementary prejudices, paralleling Snow's (1959) two cultures. Positive Psychology seems to have become overly rigid, ignoring its shadow side (Friedman & Robbins, 2012), as well as becoming stuck in a naive positivistic view of research favoring quantitative approaches while hardly acknowledging the usefulness of the qualitative (Friedman, 2008). But Humanistic Psychology is also complicit here, in having veered in the opposite direction, often denigrating quantitative approaches while favoring the qualitative (Friedman, 2008). Reframing these opposites as complementary, I think they can perhaps be usefully viewed as cultural traps (see Bohanon, 1995; Friedman, 2009), which mirror the larger struggles of the culture wars. In regard to Humanistic Psychology, its rebellion against the established forces within the 1960s psychology of behaviorism and psychoanalysis led to an initially adaptive so-called third force but, in accord with how cultural traps work, this stance became increasingly maladaptive. And, this led to a lacuna in which the opposite emerged, namely a Positive Psychology movement that disavows its connection with its humanistic progenitor. Such is the nature of revolutions, in the sense that they often revolve back to their starting points, spurring counter-revolutions *ad nauseum*.

Lately, I have been addressing efforts to reconcile the split between Humanistic and Positive Psychology through emphasizing the importance of using mixed methods, which would not privilege any singular approach (Friedman, 2008). To privilege either qualitative over quantitative or vice versa exemplifies *methodolotry*, the elevation of a method to an object of worship (Friedman, 2002a), and I have noted in past work why it is important to not privilege any singular methodology (Friedman, 2003). Basically, I argue that there are two traps to avoid: the elevation of the qualitative, as prevalent in many areas of Humanistic Psychology constitutes an error of *romanticism*, and the elevation of the quantitative approaches, as prevalent in Positive Psychology, constitutes an error of *scientism* (Friedman, 2002b, 2005). Quantitative and qualitative methods can be conceptualized and delineated in various ways (e.g., abstract/grounded, hard/soft, hypothesis testing/speculative, fixed/flexible, objective/subjective, survey/case study, and value-free/political; Silverman, 2001), but I conclude they cannot be valued as good or bad in any absolutist way. However, this contention can be debated (see Franco, Friedman, & Arons, 2008).

That Humanistic Psychology is often depicted as dying or even dead ignores its continuing importance to psychology, science, and even humanity (Friedman, 2011). This misperception of its demise has arguably been promoted by Positive Psychology. Through this strategy, Positive Psychology has gained considerable benefits through attracting scholars and students under its banner, and has achieved many successes (e.g., through funding, media coverage, and publications) (Friedman, 2008).

Brent Robbins and I explored these dynamics within two special issues of *The Humanistic Psychologist* (Friedman & Robbins, 2008; Robbins & Friedman, 2009). We also responded to this need by chairing the Positive Psychology interest group of the American Psychological Association Division 32 (Society for Humanistic Psychology), as well as offering a symposium seeking rapprochement between leaders of both movements at a recent annual convention of the American Psychological Association. Essentially, I consider it of paramount importance that Humanistic and Positive Psychology become reunited, otherwise each will siphon off energy from the other to the detriment of both. Thus the *future* of Humanistic Psychology hinges on its ability to reclaim those elements that Positive Psychology has co-opted, as well as to recover what it has itself abandoned by over-emphasizing one methodological stance to the detriment of others. The optimal path forward which I advocate is for Humanistic Psychology to explicitly espouse epistemological and methodological pluralism, thus countering any accusations of being antiscientific, while building bridges with Positive Psychology, including advising that it no longer ignore the negative in pursuit of the positive. It is important to realize that, if Humanistic Psychology were to remain primarily wedded to only one method (i.e., qualitative), it would short shrift its potential to make many important contributions. Humanistic Psychology also needs to actively showcase its numerous successes in having influenced many areas within psychology, including in its seminal relatedness to Positive Psychology. That it has been relatively ignored or even denigrated by many key forums within contemporary psychology (e.g., in undergraduate textbooks) requires overt challenge against its being further marginalized. For example, one area of science that could benefit from a more humanistic perspective is neurobiology, which unfortunately is often approached in solely reductionist ways (e.g., equating mind with brain) which minimizes the role of the human as a whole, including experience. Humanistic psychologists can demonstrate the importance of understanding consciousness from holistic perspectives that go beyond hard science neurobiological reductionism, an area I have recently been pursuing (e.g., Krippner & Friedman, 2010). It is also important that Humanistic Psychology demonstrate its broader impact on science in general, as well as on how it benefits humanity and many of its social institutions. In these regards, Humanistic Psychology has a great future, but only if past cultural traps are circumvented, starting with resisting its co-option by, and working toward reconciling with, Positive Psychology.

Recently I have been disputing claims from leaders of Positive Psychology that assert its distinctiveness from Humanistic Psychology, such as a claim that Humanistic and Positive Psychology are philosophically incommensurate (see Friedman, 2015) and another claim in which a proponent of Positive Psychology reduced complex phenomena into simplistic clichés (see Friedman, 2015). In addition, one of the main bases for Positive Psychology's claim to differ from Humanistic Psychology is that, comparatively, it has greater scientific rigor. However, in a series of critical papers published in major scientific journals, I and my colleagues have shown systematic scientific errors by one of the leading positive psychologists (see Brown et al., 2014; Brown, Sokal, & Friedman, 2013, 2014a; Heathers et al., 2015). These papers debunk widely publicized and over-reaching claims in this prominent Positive Psychology research in a way that clearly demonstrates that delineating Humanistic from Positive Psychology based on scientific rigor is an untenable assertion. If Humanistic Psychology can rightly be accused of being overly romantic, then Positive Psychology can also be accused of 'romantic scientism' (Brown, Sokal, & Friedman, 2014b), namely through obfuscating its romanticism under the guise of what *appears* to be rigorous research but actually exhibits many scientific flaws.

In conclusion, I believe a better future for Humanistic Psychology requires the making of an explicit effort to be more holistic, through the valuing of all methodologies and the inclusion of both positive and negative phenomena within its purview. The same can be argued for Positive Psychology. Thus both disciplines might reclaim largely dormant aspects of their own approaches, perhaps facilitating an eventual reconciliation between Humanistic and Positive Psychology.

Note

1   This chapter is an updated revision of the following: Friedman, H. (2013). Reconciling humanistic and positive psychology: Bridging the cultural rift. In R. House, D. Kalisch, & J. Maidman (Eds) *The Future of Humanistic Psychology* (pp. 17–22). Ross-on-Wye, UK: PCCS Books. Before that, an earlier version was previously published as the following: Friedman, H. (2013). The cultural rift dividing humanistic and positive psychology: The future possibilities of reconciliation. *Self & Society, 40*(2), 21–25.

References

Bacon, S. (2005). Positive psychology's two cultures. *Review of General Psychology, 9*(2), 81–192.

Bohanon, P. (1995). *How Culture Works*. New York: Free Press.

Bonner, E., & Friedman, H. (2011). A conceptual clarification of the experience of awe: An interpretative phenomenological analysis. *The Humanistic Psychologist, 39*, 222–235.

Brown, N., Sokal, A., & Friedman, H. (2013). The complex dynamics of wishful thinking: The critical positivity ratio. *American Psychologist, 68*(9), 801–813.

Brown, N., Sokal, A., & Friedman, H. (2014a). The persistence of wishful thinking. *American Psychologist, 69*(6), 629–632.

Brown, N., Sokal, A., & Friedman, H. (2014b). Positive psychology and romantic scientism. *American Psychologist, 69*(6), 636–637.

Brown, N., MacDonald, D., Samanta, M., Friedman, H., & Coyne, J. (2014). A critical reanalysis of genomics and well-being. *Proceedings of the National Academy of Sciences.* 10.1073/pnas.1407057111.

Curtis, V. (2011). Why disgust matters. *Philosophical Transactions of the Royal Society: Biological Sciences, 366*(1583), 3478–3490.

Dilthey, W. (1989). *Selected Works, Vol. 1: Introduction to the Human Sciences.* R.A. Makkreel and F. Rodi (Eds). Princeton, NJ: Princeton University Press.

Franco, Z., Friedman, H., & Arons, M. (2008). Are qualitative methods always best for humanistic psychology research? A conversation on the epistemological divide between humanistic and positive psychology. *The Humanistic Psychologist, 36*, 159–203.

Friedman, H. (2002a). Psychological nescience in a post-modern context. *American Psychologist, 57*, 462–463.

Friedman, H. (2002b). Transpersonal psychology as a scientific field. *International Journal of Transpersonal Studies, 21*, 175–187.

Friedman, H. (2003). Methodolotry and graphicacy. *American Psychologist, 58*, 817–818.

Friedman, H. (2005). Problems of romanticism in transpersonal psychology: A case study of Aikido. *The Humanistic Psychologist, 33*, 3–24.

Friedman, H. (2008). Humanistic and positive psychology: The methodological and epistemological divide. *The Humanistic Psychologist, 36*, 113–126.

Friedman, H. (2009). Xenophilia as a cultural trap: Bridging the gap between transpersonal psychology and religious/spiritual traditions. *International Journal of Transpersonal Studies, 28*, 107–111.

Friedman, H. (2011). It's premature to write the obituary for humanistic psychology. *Journal of Humanistic Psychology, 51*(4), 424–427.

Friedman, H. (2014). Are humanistic and positive psychology really incommensurate? Response to Waterman. *American Psychologist, 69*(1), 89–90.

Friedman, H. (2015). The need for a more nuanced conclusion than life is pretty meaningful. *American Psychologist, 70*(6), 570–571.

Friedman, H., & Robbins, B. (Eds) (2008). Special issue on positive psychology. *The Humanistic Psychologist, 36*(2).

Friedman, H., & Robbins, B. (2012). The negative shadow cast by positive psychology: Contrasting views and implications of humanistic and positive psychology on resiliency. *The Humanistic Psychologist, 40*(1), 87–102.

Gould, S. (2003). *The Hedgehog, the Fox, and the Magister's Pox: Mending the Gap between Science and the Humanities.* New York: Harmony.

Heathers, J., Brown, N., Coyne, J., & Friedman, H. (2015). The elusory upward spiral: Comment on Kok et al. (2013). *Psychological Science, 26*(7), 1140–1143.

Jaffe, E. (2011). Identity shift: US psychology departments change their names to reflect the field. The new labels spell out what psychological scientists actually do. *Observer, 24*(7). Retrieved April 20, 2017 from www.psychologicalscience.org/index.php/publications/observer/2011/september-11/identity-shift.html

Kimble, G. (1984). The scientific review of mental health practice. *American Psychologist, 39*(8), 833–839.

Krippner, S., & Friedman, H. (Eds) (2010). *Mysterious Minds: The Neurobiology of Psychics, Mediums, and Other Extraordinary People.* Santa Barbara, CA: Praeger.

Kurtzman, H. (2012). A year of progress: APA works to advance psychology as a STEM discipline: Initiatives in 2011 encompass federal advocacy, public education, multi-disciplinary training, treatment guidelines and K-12 education. Retrieved April 20, 2017 from www.apa.org/science/about/psa/2011/12/stem-discipline.aspx

Mruk, C. (2008). Self-esteem, humanistic positive psychology and positivistic positive psychology. *The Humanistic Psychologist, 36*(2), 143–158.

Nunez, N., Poole, D., & Memon, A. (2003). Psychology's two cultures revisited: Implications for the integration of science with practice. *Scientific Review of Mental Health Practice, 2*(1), 8–19.

Oakley, A. (1999). Paradigm wars: Some thoughts on a personal and public trajectory. *International Journal of Social Research Methodology, 2*(3), 247–254.

Robbins, B., & Friedman, H. (Eds) (2009). Special issue on methodological pluralism. *The Humanistic Psychologist, 37*(1).

Seligman, M. (2009). Foreword. In S. Lopez (Ed.), *The Encyclopedia of Positive Psychology* (pp. xviii–xix). Malden, MA: Wiley-Blackwell.

Silverman, D. (2001). *Interpreting Qualitative Data: Methods for Analyzing Talk, Text, and Interaction* (2nd edition). London: Sage Publications.

Snow, C.P. (1959). *The Two Cultures.* London: Cambridge University Press.

Willig, C., & Stainton-Rogers, W. (Eds) (2008) *The Sage Handbook of Qualitative Research in Psychology.* London: Sage.

14

HUMANISTIC AND EXISTENTIAL APPROACHES IN THE TREATMENT OF PTSD

Stanley Krippner and Daniel B. Pitchford

It is common for men and women to undergo *potentially traumatizing events*; however, some of these become *traumatizing events* that lead to *traumatic experiences*. Post-traumatic stress disorder (PTSD) results not from events but from experiences, the way someone constructs meaning from an event. This attribution of meaning is a core concept of the humanistic and existential psychologies and psychotherapies, which are undervalued resources in the treatment of PTSD. Humanistic and existential perspectives on dealing with PTSD can be practised on their own or as a supplement to *cognitive-behavior therapy*, *implosive therapy*, *group therapy*, or any of the other mainstream approaches to alleviating suffering and helping clients turn *post-traumatic stress* into *post-traumatic strengths*. For example, *narrative implosive therapy* includes written narration, visualization, and artistic renditions to supplement a client's verbal account of the trauma.

The field of psychology is making an impact in contemporary society. Psychologists write blogs and books. Psychologists are interviewed in the media, and many of these interviews are transformed into videos made widely available by advances in technology. Humanistic and existential psychologists, who have unique insights to offer, need to make the most of these opportunities, especially in dealing with such human problems as PTSD.

One of the areas in which humanistic psychologists can make an impact is *bioethics*, where they can provide responses to such questions as: 'What role can psychologists play in alerting people to the factors that have put the planet and its inhabitants at risk?', 'What are the motives that compel some individuals to commit murder in school settings, and to kill civilians while serving overseas on military duty?', and 'How can psychologists help traumatized people who are coping with the aftermath of an event that not only was life-threatening, but radically challenged their prevailing worldview, leading to what Greening and Vallejos (2013) have termed an "existential shattering"?'

In focusing on this last question, one must acknowledge that there are numerous ways to treat PTSD (see Krippner, Pitchford, & Davies, 2012). Many of these treatments interweave and overlap with one another, and many have had high success rates in reducing or extinguishing stress-related symptoms. Sometimes a combination of treatment approaches produces especially positive results, where 'meaning and connectedness to lived experiences can emerge' (Pitchford, 2009, p. 441). One size does not fit all (Greening, 1997; Steinkamp & Liz, 2014). Since each case of PTSD is different, an integrated approach will often provide something of value for those who experience it.

Humanistic and existential psychotherapists typically take a *whole-person approach* to their clients, a perspective reflected by Frewen and Lanius (2015), who have used electrophysiological monitoring to discern four elements of *trauma-related states of consciousness*, namely, time, thought, body, and emotion. The therapist's goal is to bring clients back to a *normal waking consciousness*, which can be done by using such humanistic procedures as reducing negative self-judgmental thoughts and feelings, restoring self-value, and establishing a client–therapist relationship that is safe, secure, and hopeful.

From our perspective, successful PTSD therapy embraces all four of these elements to induce changes in the client's brain, belief system, and behaviors. All four are reflected in PTSD nightmares, which the brain processes differently from ordinary nightmares. Hence, a whole-person approach needs to include one of several useful therapies for transforming PTSD nightmares into ordinary dreams and nightmares, complete with the metaphors and symbols typically missing from the repetitive PTSD varieties (Lewis & Krippner, 2016).

People express social, cultural, and individual 'reflections that capture the most personal of experiences' (Pitchford, 2009, p. 445). However, individually, human beings do not adapt easily to trauma. Further, the factors that make a potentially traumatizing event a traumatic experience differ from person to person. A significant change mechanism necessary for trauma to take form, then, is the brokenness of the psyche – encountered through its shattering from a loss of meaning, purpose, and identity (Greening & Vallejos, 2013), and from its loss of safety due to the disruption of one's world experiences and belief system.

As a current example of social, cultural, and individual expressions of not easily adapting to times of stress that might lead to trauma, we can pull from the wake of the political changes in the West, in particular, the aftermath of the United States' 2016 pre- and post-presidential election.

Now, we want to be clear this is not a political piece, and this is not representing either of our political views; rather, we are accessing this context to demonstrate a real-world example that can show very specific behaviors that have led to thousands of people to have high emotional and behavioral reactions to the actions and, ultimately, the final result of the 2016 presidential election. In this case, we discuss Donald Trump. Trump's behaviors during the campaign (e.g., misogyny, and ethnic bigotry, prejudice, and discrimination), and his subsequent success have ignited and perpetuated feelings and beliefs characterized by fear of and hostility toward particular groups, and major shifts in beliefs and perspectives that reveal potentially significant challenges people could face as a result of the disruption of a particular worldview (e.g., Galam, 2016; Hall, Goldstein, & Ingram, 2016; Larsen, 2016; Major, Blodorn, & Blascovich, 2016; Western, 2016).

Specifically, the demonstrated threats to human rights and civil liberties have raised disturbing challenges for many American citizens and undocumented immigrants in the form of deep concern at being led and governed by an individual who does not promote public safety, equality, and human dignity in language and behavior (Goldstein, 2016; Hier, 2016; Johnson, 2016). This, combined with the shock (for some) of the result, can lead to a 'shattering' of one's role in this world, especially for those not expecting the result and who were vehemently against it as an option; the once perceived sense of safety and meaning felt by being part of a Western nation founded and usually functioning on liberal values can seem to be weakened, thereby leading to feelings of disempowerment and disenfranchisement.

There are several outcomes in support of this possible position as a potentially traumatizing impact, but again, it depends on the individual's experience and relationship to the events (both from these outcomes and leading up to their occurrence): (a) Post-election protests (seen as both reactivity to trauma and as post-stress growth as well as depending on whether the protests are peaceful or violent [for example, as seen in Los Angeles, California, and Portland, Oregon]); e.g., Solis & Miller, 2016; (b) a climate of fear about safety for one's self, family, and community (e.g., many have taken to social media sharing stories of horror about the results, what they have been witnessing, difficulties feeling safe now, and even wanting to move out of the country; e.g., Hatch, 2016); and violence and hate crimes being enacted; e.g., Dearden, 2016; Yan, Sgueglia, & Walker, 2016.

Medication is often helpful in the short term, but it cannot address the deep existential issues of PTSD; furthermore, its side effects often alter brain functioning in a manner counter to the positive effects of effective psychotherapy. Van der Kolk (2014) has pointed out that the U.S. Departments of Defense and Veterans Affairs, in one decade, spent over 4.5 billion dollars on anti-depressants, anti-psychotics, and anti-anxiety medications, reflecting a medical model that encourages passivity rather than active self-healing. Trauma changes the brain in several ways: the threat perception system is enhanced, the brain's filtering system is damaged, and the brain's sense of self is blunted. Medication does not provide long-term repair for any of these issues and, when it is given for *traumatic brain injuries*, additional damage can occur (Billings, 2016).

Contrary to popular stereotype, early human beings rarely engaged in long-term warfare or other forms of deadly assault. As a result, a number of biological defenses that could have fostered *rapid recovery* did not have an opportunity to develop. Early humans might have been attacked by wild animals or beset by natural disasters, but these dangers were rarely accompanied by guilt, shame, or other emotions. Such feelings elicit withdrawal, suspicion, and suicide among today's combat veterans and survivors of rape and bullying. Urbanization, globalization, and the Internet have had their advantages, but they have been accompanied by unpredictability, terrorism, and cyber-attacks.

Systematic programs have been designed to eliminate or reduce the problematic symptoms and unpleasant experiences associated with a person's or a group's post-traumatic stress. Usually, a qualified person administers these programs to an individual or a group, but some programs are self-administered. All of these treatments are *therapeutic*, because they have been designed to promote healing and recovery.

Most of the treatment approaches for PTSD fall under the category of *psychological therapy* or *psychotherapy*. The goals of such programs include increasing self-understanding and self-acceptance, reducing problematic symptoms, and learning how to change behaviors and beliefs that are harmful because they block the PTSD survivor's enjoyment of life. The humanistic and existential psychotherapies are unique in that they purposefully help clients encounter fundamental issues such as guilt (e.g., survivor's guilt), emotional pain (e.g., feelings of shame), and personal loss (e.g., the end of a relationship) through the confrontation and development of purpose and meaning. This is not an easy journey; moreover, it requires a mature, willing, courageous therapist to travel alongside the suffering individual. Clients may become vulnerable through the nakedness of viewing the core areas of self as changed by trauma, often bringing them to separate themselves from inadequate ways of relating to their self-identity. The courage to act also rests upon the trauma survivor, as the *will* to make a choice might not appear so freely available and can often seem risky to face, given that the outcome is uncertain.

This is a paradoxical point that might be the most liberating moment from PTSD's binding chains upon the psyche. It can be freeing, because, in facing the anxieties and horrors of the trauma, moments are created for 'new opportunities to occur and provide tools for engaging life and future encounters' (Pitchford, 2009, p. 446). Such parts of the journey require time for rituals of 'goodbye', but with openness to the re-emergence of the 'new' person. This is often a spiritual process wherein the metaphorical demon that suffocates the individual's soul via the trauma(s) is vanquished, and the person, through his or her courage to face the unknown, is thereby freed.

This liberation, however, often occurs beyond mainstream psychotherapy's understandings of healing. At the same time, individuals are often accommodated by therapeutic programs that are not steeped in conventional psychological principles. These treatments range from acupuncture and hypnosis to art and dance, from MDMA (commonly known as *Ecstasy*) and music therapy to massage and *mindfulness meditation*, from *energy medicine* and *virtual reality therapy* to pet therapy and sports.

Some people with PTSD have a religious crisis, because a trusted pastor or priest took sexual advantage of them. Some people have spiritual crises, because they are plagued with guilt after a good friend is killed in a highway accident when they were driving the car. Others have existential crises, because their very being-in-the-world has lost meaning due to the inadvertent killing of civilians during a combat operation. For many trauma survivors, sexual dysfunction prevents them from the full development of intimacy with a prospective partner. Despite how the trauma might affect specific individuals, the overarching therapeutic 'goal' is to support them in reconnecting to self and psyche, and in unveiling the choices over which they have control. This goal is meant to empower clients in demonstrating how they might decide 'to act on those choices and potentially transform their lives' (Pitchford, 2009, p. 446).

An epidemic of trauma

The future of Humanistic Psychology is becoming linked to the epidemic of traumatic stress reactions. The U.S. military has invested millions of dollars in *comprehensive soldier fitness* and suicide prevention programs only to see morale deteriorate and the suicide rate increase year after year. Far more U.S. combat veterans take their own lives than their civilian peers of the same age. At least 15% of the men and women returning from duty in Iraq and Afghanistan develop PTSD; half of them never seek help, and half of those who do drop out after the first one or two sessions (Paulson & Krippner, 2010). Relatively few are directed to a humanistic or existential psychotherapist, one who would do more than prescribe medication and focus on symptom reduction. By virtue of their training and orientation, humanistic psychologists attempt to help veterans face their existential crises and focus on developing post-traumatic talents and skills.

When a tsunami hit Asia, the media interviewed local members of the Christian and Muslim clergy. When people were asked why God or Allah allowed such a tragedy to occur, the typical response was, 'We do not know the reason, but we must trust the Divine, who is all-powerful.' Some survivors found consolation in this response, but others did not. Nor, on other occasions, were family members satisfied with similar palliatives when their children were killed in the wars overwhelming Iraq, Afghanistan, and Pakistan. Immigrants flooding Western Europe bring belief systems with them that might not serve them well in their new environment.

From the point of view of humanistic and existential psychologists, the 'disorder' in PTSD describes not only the survivor but the society. A social order that sends its youth into unnecessary combat, does not protect ethnic or sexual minorities against discrimination and ridicule, and fails to provide a safety net when people are struck by natural or human disasters is, indeed, disordered. All too often, conventional religion and conventional psychotherapy ignore the trauma survivors who question the notion of a compassionate God, a benevolent government, and a benign universe. Yet these are exactly the questions that humanistic and existential psychotherapists are equipped to confront. They are also prepared to foster positive *personal myths*, which might serve as a means for deeper discovery of self and reality, providing opportunities to view one's hidden internal capabilities not otherwise known and shape the present moment, meaning, and understanding of the world.

When it comes to what Feinstein and Krippner (2008) refer to as *mythic conflicts*, humanistic and existential therapists rely on a legacy that has incorporated insights from the humanities into treatment. Feinstein and Krippner have proposed a five-step program to deal with dysfunctional personal myths:

1. Identify the underlying conflict between a prevailing myth (e.g., a benign universe) and an emerging challenge (e.g., a universe without meaning).
2. Understand both sides of the conflict (e.g., 'If the universe takes care of us, why did my best friend die in a car crash?' vs. 'The universe might not be benevolent but might still have an underlying purpose').
3. Conceive a new myth that integrates the most vital aspects of the prevailing myth and the challenging myth (e.g., 'The universe might or might not be purposeful, but there is no way to tell; however, I will infuse meaning into my life because I cannot function without purpose').
4. Refine the new myth and make a commitment to live by it (e.g., 'I cannot bring my friend back to life, but I can do something that will honor her').
5. Begin to live from this new myth (e.g., 'I will do volunteer work at a hospice one day each month in honor of my friend').

A trauma survivor can always fall back upon such personal myths such as 'Everything happens for a reason,' or 'It is not for us to question God's actions.' Unfortunately, not only are those beliefs superficial, but they preclude an approach to life that is both rational and emotional, both contemplative and action-oriented.

Historically, there has been some reluctance for therapists to discuss their clients' religious and spiritual issues. This reluctance has changed, thanks, in part, to humanistic and existential psychology, which has never shied away from discussing these issues. As an example of this change, the American Psychological Association has published excellent books on the topic, including *Spiritually Oriented Psychotherapy for Trauma* (Walker, Courtois, & Aten, 2015). This book provides several examples of how mythic conflicts can be resolved; for one, it is possible to deepen one's faith in God while simultaneously losing one's ties to a religious congregation. Rethinking one's concept of God is often an important part of recovery from trauma; that is, the refining and rethinking of one's personal spiritual and religious convictions often play a major role. This is especially pertinent when one has been abused by a member of the clergy or traumatized by domestic abuse in a household supposedly dedicated to honoring the Divine. These issues can arise when a therapist is treating members of ethnic minorities, where the questioning of traditional values is especially problematic.

In contemporary society, trauma is everywhere. Civilian deaths in recent wars have outnumbered those of combatants. Girls and women are mutilated or killed for alleged religious transgressions. Ethnic and tribal rivalries trigger random murders, and innocent people are caught in the cross-fire of interminable drug wars or territorial disputes. It is naive to think that an infusion of Humanistic Psychology could stop the escalation of trauma, but at least this goal of violence reduction could be put on the agenda of humanistic and existential psychologists and the groups with which they have influence.

Developing post-traumatic strengths

Psychotherapy has addressed the sequelae of trauma since its beginning. For decades, research studies had failed to demonstrate its effectiveness appropriately. However, more recent data not only support the proposal that psychotherapy works; a comparison of half a dozen interventions for U.S. combat veterans with PTSD found that each *bona fide treatment* alleviated suffering, and in comparable proportion. Furthermore, medication without therapy was less effective than therapy without medication. When an anti-depressant was used without therapy, its effect upon patients varied little from that upon those given only a placebo (Benish, Imel, & Wampold, 2008).

Humanistic and existential psychotherapies were not among the treatments evaluated for a very simple reason: not enough data were available for comparisons to be made. As a result, these psychotherapies are out of the loop when funding is available to study treatments for PTSD. Sadly, humanistic psychotherapy is not the only intervention that has failed to receive attention from funding agencies; so, too, have rational emotive behavior therapy, expressive arts therapy, and hypnotically facilitated psychotherapy, not to mention such self-regulation regimens as biofeedback, neurofeedback, and Yoga. Because several of these treatments have amassed supportive data, Bohart (2005) has introduced the term *evidence-informed treatment* to describe a range of procedures, especially those in which the client serves as an active self-healer. Another useful term, *trauma-informed therapy*, focuses on treatments that pay special attention to PTSD and related problems (Elmore & Patterson, 2012).

The proactive stance fostered by most of these treatments not only helps trauma survivors to recover, but enables them to take advantage of new opportunities produced by the trauma for their further growth and development (Southwick & Charney, 2012). Rodin (2014) has used the term *resilience dividend* to describe a traumatized person's ability not only to return to pre-trauma functioning, but to surpass it in some ways. Considerable research indicates that how people conceptualize stress has an effect on the way that the stress affects their health, happiness, and work performance. Some people find ways to put stress to positive use rather than pathologize it. McGonigal (2015) has listed three characteristics of this group:

1. They find ways to engage in meaningful activities even if they cannot control the source of their stress.
2. They see stress as a catalyst for strengthening relationships and building communities of support.
3. They look back at past adversities to see what learning can be applied to the current stressful situation.

From an evolutionary point of view, early humans would not have survived had they not found ways to cope with stressful situations. Those who did not have these coping mechanisms succumbed to adverse circumstances and their genes dropped out of the gene pool. As a result, contemporary humans have biological, psychological, and social capacities for transforming stressful circumstances into positive actions, using adversity to foster growth (Joseph & Linley, 2006).

These positive attitudes are reflected in data from a 2015 study concerning veterans. More of them vote in local elections than non-veterans, more volunteer for community projects, and more are gainfully employed. This number includes PTSD survivors. Both groups have benefitted from training that makes them uniquely qualified to participate in *community engagement* and tackle the special challenges of the 21st century. Combat veterans can recall instances of courage and leadership, as well as instant 'intuitive' decisions that saved lives. Even following the divisive Vietnam War, 70% of returning veterans referred to their military experience as positive. Those who were imprisoned for years in the infamous 'Hanoi Hilton' experienced positive growth when they returned, with a PTSD rate far lower than that recorded for Vietnam veterans in general. The camaraderie of the prisoners appeared to be a critical factor in their resilience (Krippner et al., 2012, pp. 137–142).

The humanistic and existential psychotherapies are an overlooked asset in restoration, rebounding, and healing. These treatment approaches can help traumatized clients discover what is most meaningful in their lives, even though they might involve a departure from conditioned, conventional beliefs and behaviors. Former beliefs and values might no longer make sense after experiencing a trauma falling outside of their customary expectations of normality, fairness, and justice. Tedeschi and Calhoun (1996) have developed an inventory to help therapists identify what they call *post-traumatic growth*. Some of the areas explored in this inventory are perceived changes in self-concept, appreciation for life, relationships with others, spirituality, and personal philosophy.

In a study of thirty aviators who were imprisoned during the Vietnam War, the inventory revealed greater post-traumatic growth among those who were imprisoned the longest. These data revealed that women were more likely than men to experience post-traumatic growth, possibly because they were more likely to rely on spiritual or religious resources (Tedeschi & McNally, 2011). Tedeschi and Calhoun (1996) have created a model of post-traumatic growth based on the data obtained from their inventory. Several factors have the potential to increase positive outcomes:

1. The trauma survivor's ability to think through the trauma and confront the issues it brings up.
2. The survivor's ability to disclose one's concerns surrounding traumatic experiences and observe other people's reactions to this self-disclosure.
3. The survivor's attempts to process, disclose, and resolve the trauma, given the social and cultural context in which the trauma occurred.
4. The personal dispositions of the survivor and the degree to which he or she is resilient.
5. The degree to which specific traumatic experiences foster or repress these processes.

We take the position that resilience and post-traumatic growth are not the same. Highly resilient people are sometimes less likely to experience post-traumatic growth than less resilient people. Resiliency reflects one's capacity to 'bounce back,' but the 'bounce' is less profound among those who are already resilient than among their peers who have to put forth more effort to recover.

Rendon (2015), a journalist, followed up on the Tedeschi and Calhoun data by reading related literature and conducting his own interviews. He was especially impressed by Viktor Frankl's experiences in a Nazi concentration camp and how they led to his development of *logotherapy*, a type of existential psychotherapy. He also recalled a fictional 1936 story about a young boy who saw his parents murdered and vowed to fight crime, becoming 'Batman' in the process. Rendon found that about half of the trauma survivors he read about or interviewed reported positive change as a result of their experience, assisted by social support, faith, and creativity – talking or writing about the experience. However, hope is often preceded by despair, optimism by depression. A woman who fell in front of a train (as a result of an overenthusiastic hug) left her life of meaningless jobs to become a counselor for low-income clients in South London. Her former life of partying ended, because she had to wear a colostomy bag at all times.

In this regard, families and friends can play a pivotal role in reintegrating veterans into civilian life. More than two million U.S. children have parents in the military, many of whom are dealing with multiple deployments, war injuries, and PTSD (Elmore & Patterson, 2012). Sports, pets, cookouts, and other family activities can be therapeutic. The National Child Traumatic Stress Network is attempting to facilitate such pastimes. Honoring the Path of the Warrior is a non-profit group that sponsors group retreats for veterans and their supporters. Humanistic Psychology has pioneered many innovations in both family therapy and the use of support groups to assist personal development and to prevent substance abuse and other self-destructive behavior (Billings, 2016; Satir, 1983).

Howard Wasdin, a member of the U.S. Navy's elite Sea, Air, and Land (SEAL) team, survived combat with three bullets in his leg, chronic pain, and PTSD. His wife urged him to write about his experiences and, much to his surprise, the process diminished his symptoms. Wasdin recalled the training he had received and the quick decisions he had to make. After he began to visit a firing range, he found that he enjoyed recreational target practice. His muscles recalled his previous training, despite his wounds (Wasdin & Templin, 2011). Needless to say, this type of writing is not a panacea, and one must choose the correct time and place to avoid becoming retraumatized in the process.

Potentially traumatizing events occur frequently. Genetics and early life experiences predispose some people to experience certain events as traumatizing. For others, a single traumatic experience itself can lead to PTSD. Whether one or several traumas trigger PTSD, those persons' worldviews and sense of self are assaulted. Their personal myths are shattered, leaving a residue of *moral and ethical wounds*. These injuries result when people feel extreme guilt or shame for something they did or witnessed that goes against their values. Not all people with moral or ethical wounding have PTSD; nonetheless, an adroit psychotherapist will recognize the condition and attempt to treat it.

Recurring nightmares and flashbacks try to replay the traumatic experience (or experiences) until they make sense, but these attempts fail. Hyper-arousal tries to protect PTSD survivors against further assault, while emotional numbing and dissociation attempt to buffer the feelings of guilt, shame, fear, depression, and anxiety. Social activities are avoided, work opportunities are ignored; dissociation and impaired concentration prevent mindful, joyous living. A survivor who is barely surviving has not completed the journey to wholeness. For most trauma survivors, there is a need to discern whether their personal myths are hampering or fostering the continuation of their life paths.

Sarah's story

Sarah came from a small American town, one in which good deeds and honest relationships were not only valued, but were everyday events. Filled with excitement and anticipation, she entered a university in a neighboring state. Eager to learn, she spent long hours in the library. One night, walking home, she was intercepted by a bulky figure who put a knife to her throat and warned her not to struggle. When the rape ended and the figure disappeared, Sarah was left helpless in a timeless space of pain, revulsion, and fear. She felt that the wound had penetrated the depths of her soul, for she could not cry, nor summon up a voice appropriate enough to tell others of the horror.

Sarah's grades plummeted, she lost interest in her friends, and she cancelled a trip back home. She would not venture outside at night, and, when she was able to sleep, the husky figure assaulted her over and over again in her dreams. Sarah's inherent mythology was that the world was a safe place, the university was a protective abode, and people were basically good at heart. Once these myths were blown apart, there was nothing to take their place. Eventually, she summoned the courage to talk to a university chaplain and a physician. Both listened sympathetically. The chaplain told her to pray, and the doctor put her on medication.

Both of these measures gave palliative relief, but did not strike at the core of Sarah's existential and spiritual struggles. Fortunately, her university had a long-standing women's support group and Sarah became a regular member. It was in this group that she felt listened to, respected, understood, and supported. Other women shared similar stories, and Sarah slowly began to put her life back together. When she shared her new personal mythology with her family, they found it somewhat cynical. But Sarah had substituted realism for naivety, spirituality for religion, and practical action for repetitive rumination. She had several counseling sessions with a social worker who was an advisor to the women's group, and found ways to reduce her nightmares through keeping a journal and illustrating it with images of the traumatic experience. She had found post-traumatic strengths that produced positive meaning from the trauma, imbuing her with empathy, resilience, and courage that she never realized she possessed.

In today's ruptured world, there are many Sarahs. Humanistic and existential psychotherapies offer countless methods of transformation, including establishing support groups, model communities, and psychotherapeutic services that will help those who are alienated, marginalized, and disempowered by trauma to search beyond the trauma for new sources of resilience (Rodin, 2014). This union of the personal and the transpersonal, the introspective and the communal, and the acknowledgment of chaos accompanied by the determination to create meaning, have the potential to actualize the vision that the humanistic and existential psychologies can share with Earth and its inhabitants.

Acknowledgment

Preparation of this chapter was supported by the Saybrook University Chair for the Study of Consciousness.

References

Benish, S., Imel, Z., & Wampold, B. (2008). The relative efficacy of bona fide psychotherapies for treating post-traumatic stress disorders: A meta-analysis of direct comparisons. *Clinical Psychology Review, 28*, 746–758.

Billings, B.P. (2016). *Invisible scars: How to beat combat stress and PTSD without medication.* Tampa, FL: Paradies/Inspire.

Bohart, A. (2005). Evidence-based psychotherapy means evidence-informed, not evidence-driven. *Journal of Contemporary Psychotherapy, 35*, 39–53.

Dearden, L. (2016). Donald Trump's victory followed by wave of hate crime attacks against minorities across US – led by his supporters. *Independent.* Retrieved November 2016 from www.independent.co.uk/news/world/americas/us-elections/donald-trump-president-supporters-attack-muslims-hijab-hispanics-lgbt-hate-crime-wave-us-election-a7410166.html

Elmore, D. & Patterson, T. (2012, May). Helping veterans and their families. *Monitor on Psychology*, p. 14.

Feinstein, D. & Krippner, S. (2008). *Personal mythology* (3rd ed.). Santa Rosa, CA: Energy Medicine Press/Elite Books.

Frewen, P. & Lanius, R. (2015). *Healing the traumatized self: Consciousness, neuroscience, treatment.* New York, NY: W. W. Norton.

Galam, S. (2016). The Trump phenomenon, an explanation from sociophysics, 1–24. arXiv:1609.03933 [physics.soc-ph]

Goldstein, D. M. (2016). Some thoughts on the critical anthropology of security. *Ethnofoor, 28*(1), 147–152.

Greening, T. (1997). Posttraumatic stress disorder: An existential-humanistic perspective. In S. Krippner & S. M. Powers (Eds.), *Broken images, broken selves: Dissociative narratives in clinical practice* (pp. 125–135). Washington, DC: Brunner/Mazel.

Greening, T. & Vallejos, L. (2013). *Existential shattering.* Unpublished paper presented at APA Division 32 conference in Santa Barbara, CA.

Hall, K., Goldstein, D. M., & Ingram, M. B. (2016). The hands of Donald Trump: Entertainment, gesture, spectacle. *Journal of Ethnographic Theory, 6*(2), 71–100.

Hatch, J. (2016). It's not 'melodramatic' to fear for our safety after this election. *Huffington Post.* Retrieved November 2016 from www.huffingtonpost.com/entry/its-not-melodramatic-to-fear-for-our-safety-after-this-election_us_5823831ce4b0d9ce6fc08f1c

Hier, S. (2016). Good moral panics? Normative ambivalence, social reaction, and coexisting responsibilities in everyday life. *Current Sociology.* doi:10.1177/0011392116655463

Johnson, D. (2016). Politics, civilisation, and the survival of the West. *Quadrant, 60*(11), 24–29.

Joseph, S. & Linley, P. A. (2006). Growth following adversity: Theoretical perspectives and implications for clinical practice. *Clinical Psychology Review, 26*, 1041–1053.

Krippner, S., Pitchford, D. B., & Davies, J. (2012). *Posttraumatic stress disorder.* Santa Barbara, CA: ABC-CLIO.

Larsen, H. G. (2016). The antecedent of fear in the public discourse: From Donald Trump's nativism to transgender bathroom access. *International Journal of School and Cognitive Psychology, 3*(2), 1–4.

Lewis, J. & Krippner, S. (Eds.) (2016). *14 ways of working with dreams and PTSD nightmares.* Santa Barbara, CA: ABC-CLIO.

Major, B., Blodorn, A., & Blascovich, G. M. (2016). The threat of increasing diversity: Why many White Americans support Trump in the 2016 presidential election. *Group Processes & Intergroup Relations*, 1–10.

McGonigal, K. (2015, August/September). The upside of stress. *The Commonwealth*, p. 45.

Paulson, D. S. & Krippner, S. (2010). *Haunted by combat: Understanding PTSD in war veterans.* New York, NY: Rowman & Littlefield.

Pitchford, D. B. (2009). The existentialism of Rollo May: An influence on trauma treatment. *Journal of Humanistic Psychology, 49*(4), 441–461.

Rendon, H. (2015). *Upside: The new science of post-traumatic growth.* New York, NY: Touchstone.

Rodin, J. (2014). *The resilience dividend: Being strong in a world where things go wrong.* New York, NY: Public Affairs.

Satir, V. (1983). *Conjoint family therapy.* Palo Alto, CA: Science and Behavior Books.

Solis, S. & Miller, R. (2016, November 13). Anti-Trump protest in Portland, Oregon, devolves into riot. *USA Today Network.* Retrieved November 2016 from www.usatoday. com/story/news/nation-now/2016/11/13/anti-trump-protest-portland-devolves-into-riot/93760244/

Southwick, S. M. & Charney, D. C. (2012). *Resilience: The science of mastering life's greatest challenges.* Cambridge, UK: Cambridge University Press.

Steinkamp, M. M. & Liz, B. T. (2014). One size fits all approach to PTSD in the VA not supported by the evidence. *American Psychologist, 89*, 706–707.

Tedeschi, R. G. & Calhoun, L. G. (1996). The Post-Traumatic Growth Inventory: Measuring the positive legacy of trauma. *Journal of Traumatic Stress, 9*, 455–471.

Tedeschi, R. G. & McNally, J. (2011). Can we facilitate post-traumatic growth in combat veterans? *American Psychologist, 55*, 19–44.

Van der Kolk, B. A. (2014). *The body keeps the score: Brain, mind, and body in the healing of trauma.* New York, NY: Viking.

Walker, D. F., Courtois, C. A., & Aten, J. D. (Eds.) (2015). *Spiritually oriented psychotherapy for trauma.* Washington, DC: American Psychological Association.

Wasdin, H. E. & Templin, S. (2011). *SEAL Team Six: Memoirs of an elite Navy SEAL sniper.* New York, NY: St. Martin's Press.

Western, S. (2016). Political correctness and political incorrectness: A psychoanalytic study of new authoritarians. *Organisational and Social Dynamics, 16*(1), 68–84.

Yan, H., Sgueglia, K., & Walker, K. (2016). 'Make America White again': Hate speech and crimes post-election. *CNN.* Retrieved December 2016 from www.cnn.com/2016/11/10/us/post-election-hate-crimes-and-fears-trnd/

15

HUMANISTIC PSYCHOLOGY, TRAUMA STUDIES AND POST-TRAUMATIC GROWTH

Olivia Merriman-Khanna

The word 'trauma' is of ancient Greek origin, literally meaning to wound, damage or defeat (Cachia, 2010). Prior to the nineteenth century, the word signified a bodily wound usually received during war; however with the development of empirical approaches to the mind, trauma was 'psychologized' (Fierke, 2007, p. 125). This chapter explores how contemporary understandings of trauma have developed, including the current conceptual debates in the field of trauma, and then discusses how trauma might best be conceptualized from a humanistic stance. Research findings on approaches to working with trauma are then examined and a selection of the literature discussing the therapist's use of self in trauma work is considered. Finally, future directions in humanistic therapy with trauma are discussed.

Toward an intersubjective understanding of trauma

The diagnosis most closely associated with trauma – post-traumatic stress disorder (PTSD) – was incorporated into the *Diagnostic and Statistical Manual of Mental Disorders* by the American Psychiatric Association in 1980. Micale and Lerner (2001) state that this was partially as a result of lobbying on behalf of veterans of Vietnam, allowing their suffering to be recognized. According to Herman (2001), our current conceptualization of trauma is based on these three areas: hysteria, shell shock, and sexual and domestic violence, and each of these areas of trauma has been associated with a political movement. Indeed, as defined by the *DSM-V* (American Psychiatric Association, 2013), PTSD is held to result from exposure to a traumatic event involving actual or threatened death, serious injury or sexual violence to self or others and symptoms of re-experiencing, avoidance, negative cognitions/mood, and hyperarousal.

Notably, there is a debate within the field of trauma about the value of making a distinction between 'simple' and 'complex' trauma (Herman, 2001). While simple trauma is conceptualized as a one-off traumatic event, complex trauma is the experience of repeated, cumulative trauma, as might be experienced by a prisoner of war, or in domestic violence (Schottenbauer et al., 2008). In proposals for ICD-11 a distinction is made between PTSD, a fear-based response to trauma with resulting avoidance and hypervigilance, and Complex PTSD, which involves PTSD symptoms as well as difficulties with emotional regulation, interpersonal relationships and self-concept, and is linked with multiple and chronic traumas (Briere & Rickards, 2007). A number of studies demonstrate this distinction between PTSD and Complex PTSD (e.g. Cloitre et al., 2013; Elklit, Hyland, & Shevlin, 2014; Knefel & Lueger-Schuster, 2013) and provide support for the proposed distinction in ICD-11. In addition, it appears that where there are numerous different traumatic experiences, these are associated with a number of different symptoms – especially where there is a background of chronic childhood trauma (Briere, Kaltman, & Green, 2008; Cloitre et al., 2009; van der Kolk et al., 2005).

However, it is questionable whether a list of symptoms and disorders can capture the entirety of the impact of psychological trauma on a person, in that trauma can result in significant ruptures in the meanings we hold about our lives and can lead to feelings and internal changes that diagnoses do not encompass (Briere and Scott, 2006). Micale and Lerner (2001) argue that since there is such a variety of events that are considered traumatic and, further, such a range of different responses to events considered traumatic, it is not possible to use objective criteria to define trauma. Bracken (2001, 2002) argues that traumatic responses have been mistakenly viewed to be universally valid with consistent symptoms, irrespective of historical or cultural period and that the characteristics of shell shock, such as spasms, blindness and muteness, do not in fact concur with symptoms of PTSD. In *The Harmony of Illusions* (1995), Young reaches a similar conclusion, arguing that while the pain and suffering that people experience following horrific events is real, the facts now associated with PTSD/psychological trauma are not 'true' or timeless as such, but are constructed through prevailing scientific (and cultural) discourses (p. 10). Summerfield (1999) argues that the concept of PTSD is a reflection of the wider trend within Western cultures to medicalize emotional pain, the result of which is a distraction from a social understanding of trauma in terms of human lives and a move toward a pathologizing medical perspective. These strong critiques of modernist notions of trauma highlight the importance of recognizing the cultural and historical specificity of responses to horrifying events and the dangers of uncritically treating such responses as a psychiatric illness.

Nevertheless, some events such as combat and violent crime are more likely to lead to psychological distress, and for some events there is a positive relationship between the magnitude of the event and severity of symptoms, which provides support for the notion of being able to class some incidents as potentially more 'traumatic' than others (O'Brien, 1998). Further, particular characteristics of traumatic events have been shown to have an impact on the post-traumatic response, including intentional violence, sexual violence and the presence of life threat, among other factors (Briere and Scott, 2006). In addition, the roles of the individual's personal characteristics and their social environment have been found to play a part in the response to potentially traumatic events: so-called 'victim-variables' include less functional coping styles, having a previous history of trauma, and being from a social group more frequently exposed to emotionally disturbing events, including those from an economically deprived background, ethnic minority groups and women (Briere & Scott, 2006). In terms of social support, research indicates that the way in which *people around the victim* respond to their traumatic experience is one of the most influential factors in terms of the response to the trauma (ibid.). This also indicates the importance of relational support to recovery from trauma, and thus the centrality of the therapeutic relationship in therapy for trauma. Thus, research evidence highlights the inextricably social and contextual nature of trauma – and while the characteristics of the event are important, so is the relational context, including both social support and the demographic status of the individual. This emphasizes the impossibility of fixing a definitive, objective conceptualization of what constitutes 'trauma'.

Writers such as Herman (2001) and De Zulueta (2006) are of the view that what has come about is the *recognition* of the psychological impact of trauma. These authors critique the historical lack of recognition of people's traumatic experiences, stating that psychiatry has alternated from being fascinated by trauma to resolutely ignoring their patients' biographical experiences in the contexts of their distress. Thus, while it might be problematic to state that we can objectively define 'trauma', there are strong arguments for the importance of the concept of trauma to allow for the social recognition of the psychological implications of violence and oppression. From a humanistic perspective, there is considerable value in what might be termed an *intersubjective* understanding of trauma. On this view, trauma is not defined by the event itself, but rather, what is traumatic is how a distressing experience is meaningful within a particular relational and socio-cultural context. Thus, trauma refers to the way in which an event is meaningful within an individual's intersubjective context (this includes both the individual's family and friends, as well as the wider social context) and previous traumatic or abusive experiences.

Therapy with trauma: key research findings

Seven meta-analytic studies indicate that trauma-focused interventions, namely eye movement desensitization and reprocessing (EMDR) and trauma-focused CBT, are effective in reducing PTSD symptoms (Ehlers et al., 2010). This is understood to be because recovery from traumatic experiences requires exposure to, and processing of, traumatic memories, as well as consideration of the individual meanings of the traumatic event(s) (Briere & Scott, 2006). Some support has also been found for psychodynamic psychotherapy in reducing PTSD symptoms (Brom, Kleber, & Defares, 1989; Sherman, 1998), and American Psychological Association guidelines note that '[m]any clinicians currently believe that psychodynamic psychotherapy is better able to address the complications of complex trauma, especially with regard to interpersonal functioning, than cognitive and behavioural treatments' (Schottenbauer et al., 2008, p. 15). However, Ehlers et al. (2010) note that psychodynamic therapy and humanistic therapy for PTSD have been insufficiently studied to reach conclusions about their efficacy.

When interpreting research evidence, a number of theorists have argued that rather than fitting neatly into one diagnostic category, clients seen by therapists in the community are complex with varied responses to trauma, and so they argue that research trials can be unrepresentative (e.g. Chetoff, 1998; Schottenbauer et al., 2006). Indeed, the results of a meta-analysis on studies of PTSD indicate that because of participant drop-out rates, sample screening and other factors, randomized clinical trials offer less guidance to practitioners than one would expect (Bradley et al., 2005). Schottenbauer et al. (2008) state that there are high non-response and drop-out rates for CBT and EMDR for PTSD in published studies, and that this might be because not all areas of distress are addressed by these approaches (particularly as regards 'complex trauma').

In their review of outcome research, Solomon and Johnson (2002) highlight the importance of non-specific factors to effective therapy with trauma, including establishing and maintaining trust and a good therapeutic relationship. In addition, research indicates that recovery from trauma can be an opportunity for growth that might include 'new levels of psychological resilience, greater self-knowledge and appreciation and increased empathy' (Briere & Scott, 2006, p. 68). This is an important perspective to hold when working with clients, in terms of valuing the human capacity for growth and development (Joseph, 2005). Further, some evidence indicates that the therapeutic alliance might be of even more importance to the therapeutic outcome in human-induced trauma (e.g. Cloitre et al., 2004). Certainly, for clients who have experienced extreme distress within a relationship, a different relational experience is considered to be highly valuable (Briere & Scott, 2006).

However, while viewed as being central to therapeutic work, van der Kolk, McFarlance and Weisaeth (1996) state that the therapeutic relationship with trauma can be highly complex in terms of potentially replaying aspects of damaging interpersonal dynamics and involving intense, previously avoided emotions that might be almost intolerable for both client and therapist (p. xvi). This highlights the potential challenge to the therapists' 'use of self' in therapy with trauma, but also indicates the significant value of humanistic approaches in therapeutic work with trauma, given the emphasis on the therapist's use of self in the training and continuing professional development of humanistic therapists.

The therapeutic use of self

Gelso and Hayes (2007) state that there has been an increasing focus on the therapist's subjectivity as a trans-theoretical concept. From a theoretical perspective, the Rogerian notion that in order to enter another's world without presupposition '[i]n some sense . . . means that you lay aside your self' (Rogers, 1980, p. 143), draws on the practice of phenomenology rooted in the philosophy of Edmund Husserl.

This involves the attempt to bracket one's natural attitude in order to study phenomena in terms of their essence. However, the validity of this transcendental phenomenology has been questioned; as we establish meaning by interacting with objects from the historical position we occupy, we are not transcendental subjects (Matthews, 2006). Indeed, later in his career, Rogers emphasized the value of therapists involving themselves in the relationship, while simultaneously maintaining an empathic stance (Gelso & Hayes, 2007). The recognition that the therapist's subjectivity is an inevitable component in the therapeutic process has led to a number of developments within humanistic approaches (Rowan & Jacobs, 2002; Wosket, 1999).

The intersubjective perspective focuses on the therapist's mindfulness of the mutually influencing process of therapy where the therapist's responses both shape and are shaped by the therapeutic process. Central to therapeutic work from an intersubjective stance, is the client's experience of attunement, allowing previously unacknowledged emotional pain to find a 'relational home' (Stolorow, 2007). Creating a narrative for oneself and one's traumatic experiences is linked with increased 'reflective self-functioning' (the ability to reflect on our own states of mind and those of others), and also holds the possibility of building a greater sense of coherence, self-integration and resilience (Holmes, 1993).

Working with trauma is considered to place personal and existential demands on the therapist; Mearns and Cooper (2005) state that working relationally and 'meeting' the client within their traumatic experience will be highly distressing, and will have a long-lasting effect on the therapist. In staying alongside the client, the therapist will need to be able to reflect on their own experiences of loss, and be able to draw upon this in their work (Du Plock, 2010).

Further, Herman (2001) attests that working in the field of trauma is inherently political because it highlights the situations of those people in our society who are oppressed. Thus from Herman's perspective, one must first name and conceptualize as crimes various forms of violence in order to address them. De Zulueta (2006) takes a similar position, arguing that not only must violence be acknowledged by the victims but also by witnesses, especially because frequently perpetrators do not see their actions as violent or abusive. Herman (2001) also focuses on the importance of examining the meaning of the experience, not only for the client but also for the client's significant others (based on the understanding of the importance of the client's social context in their recovery and on-going well-being). Herman states that this involves exploring issues of guilt and responsibility in terms of the traumatic experience. This is in order to generate a new understanding of morality and meaning to illuminate the client's experience and repair their sense of self-esteem, even in the midst of the undermining views of other people. In this task the moral position of the therapist is vitally important. For Herman, a non-judgemental stance is insufficient; rather the therapist must engage deeply and personally with these questions of meaning, not by giving answers, but by standing in 'moral solidarity' with the client (p. 178).

Challenges and growth in therapeutic work with trauma

The challenges for therapists working with trauma are well documented in the empirical literature. Research has highlighted the potentially negative impact of working with clients who have experienced trauma with the concepts of compassion fatigue (CF), which is also known as secondary traumatic stress (STS), and vicarious trauma (VT). VT is believed to develop from exposure to traumatic material, empathic attunement with clients and feelings of responsibility for their well-being, and results in cognitive, affective and relational changes (Pearlman & MacIan, 1995). CF is held to be the result of hearing about the trauma experienced by others, and empathizing with those who experience pain and suffering, leading to lessened capacity and motivation to empathize with clients (Adams, Boscarino, & Figley, 2006). Burnout has also been associated with trauma work (Sabin-Farrell & Turpin, 2003) and is characterized by a sense of emotional exhaustion, loss of idealism and feelings of reduced self-efficacy in relation to one's work (Sprang, Clark, & Whitt-Woosley, 2007).

However, more recently, positive findings about therapists' responses to trauma work have led to the creation of concepts such as 'vicarious post-traumatic growth' and 'compassion satisfaction', with some researchers (e.g. Arnold et al., 2005) arguing that these positive aspects need greater recognition within the therapeutic literature. Compassion satisfaction (CS) is characterized by experiencing therapeutic work as an energizing experience as well as having a strong sense of self-efficacy (Sprang et al., 2007).

In Steed and Downing's (1998) qualitative study on VT, all participants reported that their work with trauma survivors had led to the experience of some positive personal outcomes. Many of the therapists interviewed described positive changes in their sense of identity and in their beliefs about themselves and others. In Arnold et al.'s (2005) interviews with psychotherapists about the personal impact of trauma work, all 21 described positive consequences of the work such as increased insight, tolerance, sensitivity, empathy and compassion, as well as a greater appreciation of human resilience (and for 16 participants, this was their first response to an open question about trauma work). Descriptions of positive aspects of trauma work included positive changes in self-perception, interpersonal relationships and philosophy of life – all three major categories of post-traumatic growth outcomes identified by Tedeschi and Calhoun (1995). Arnold and colleagues (2005) conclude that the potential benefits of trauma work could be much more significant than the existing literature indicates.

Humanistic and existential literature clearly articulates the potential opportunity for growth that is provided through traumatic experience (Joseph, 2005; Mearns & Cooper, 2005; Tedeschi & Calhoun, 1995). Joseph and Linley (2006) highlight that growth can be conceptualized as a component of the trauma response that can coexist with distress. Joseph (2005) notes that it is through facing and working through difficulties that people might discover a sense of meaning and purpose in their lives, and then disasters and tragedies are viewed as the catalyst in creating a more satisfying and meaningful life. Tedeschi and Calhoun (1995) argue that it is vital that therapists have an appreciation of the value and importance of this way of viewing trauma; further, Joseph and Linley (2006) caution that therapists who are not aware of this, or who do not work from this perspective, are in danger of 'thwarting the growth potential of their clients' (p. 1048).

Finally, an area of increasing interest in humanistic-existential literature is the concept of working directly with the body in therapy with trauma. Ogden, Minton and Pain (2006) argue that by focusing on the body directly as they advocate in their 'sensorimotor psychotherapy' for trauma, it is possible to work with habituated trauma responses that are pre-reflexive and non-voluntary. The same authors state that while psychological therapists are trained to attend to the client's body, working *directly* with the somatic experience is not a focal point of traditional therapies. This, they argue, leads to serious therapeutic limitations. Further, the implications of 'embodied intersubjectivity' and therapists' physical responsiveness to traumatic material are complex and the work of Babette Rothschild (2006) discusses practical, physical strategies for therapists to 'unhook' from unconsciously mirroring their clients' physical postures. Rothschild states that the process of 'body empathy' is not well understood. This is an area worthy of further consideration in the research literature as the field moves forwards.

Conclusion

This chapter has argued for the value of an intersubjective conceptualization of trauma, where trauma is viewed within its particular relational and socio-cultural context. Research into therapy with trauma indicates the efficacy of trauma-focused interventions, namely EMDR and trauma-focused CBT, in allowing distressing memories to be processed. Research also indicates that the therapeutic alliance might be of even more importance to therapeutic outcome following interpersonal trauma, highlighting the value of a deeply respectful and committed therapeutic relationship. Trauma painfully exposes what lies at the heart of our humanity: our physical and psychological vulnerability. Humanistic therapists are particularly well placed to work with the complexity of our human responses to trauma, the challenges to the therapeutic use of self in therapy with trauma, as well as attending to the growth potential of their clients and themselves.

References

Adams, R. E., Boscarino, J. A., & Figley, C. R. (2006). Compassion fatigue and psychological distress among social workers: A validation study. *American Journal of Orthopsychiatry*, 76(1), 103–108.

American Psychiatric Association. (2013). *Diagnostic and statistical manual of mental disorders* (5th ed.). Washington, DC: American Psychiatric Association.

Arnold, D., Calhoun, L. G., Tedeschi, R., & Cann, A. (2005). Vicarious posttraumatic growth in psychotherapy. *Journal of Humanistic Psychology*, 45(2), 239–263.

Bracken, P. (2001). Post-modernity and post-traumatic stress disorder. *Social Science & Medicine*, 53, 733–743.

Bracken, P. (2002). *Trauma: Culture, meaning and philosophy*. London: Whurr.

Bradley, R., Greene, J., Russ, E., Dutra, L., & Westen, D. (2005). A multidimensional meta-analysis of psychotherapy for PTSD. *American Journal of Psychiatry*, 162(2), 214–227.

Briere, J. & Rickards, S. (2007). Self-awareness, affect regulation, and relatedness: Differential sequels of childhood versus adult victimization experiences. *Journal of Nervous and Mental Disease*, 195, 497–503.

Briere, J. & Scott, C. (2006). *Principles of trauma therapy: A guide to symptoms, evaluation and treatment*. London: Sage.

Briere, J., Kaltman, S., & Green, B. L. (2008). Accumulated childhood trauma and symptom complexity. *Journal of Traumatic Stress*, 21, 223–226.

Brom, D., Kleber, R. J., & Defares, P. B. (1989). Brief psychotherapy for posttraumatic stress disorders. *Journal of Consulting and Clinical Psychology*, 57(5), 607–612.

Cachia, P. (2010). The impact of psychic trauma on love relationships: Implications for the practice of couple counselling. *Counselling Psychology Review*, 25(2), 34–41.

Chetoff, J. (1998). Psychodynamic assessment and treatment of traumatized patients. *Journal of Psychotherapy Practice and Research*, 7, 35–45.

Cloitre, M., Stovall-McClough, K. C., Mirandad, R., & Chemtob, C. M. (2004). Therapeutic alliance, negative mood regulation, and treatment outcome in child abuse-related posttraumatic stress disorder. *Journal of Consulting and Clinical Psychology*, 72(3), 411–416.

Cloitre, M., Garvert, D. W., Brewin, C. R., Bryant, R. A., & Maercker, A. (2013). Evidence for proposed ICD-11 PTSD and complex PTSD: A latent profile analysis. *European Journal of Psychotraumatology*, 4, 20706, doi: http://dx.doi.org/10.3402/ejpt.v4i0.20706.

Cloitre, M., Stolbach, B. C., Herman, J. L., van der Kolk, B., Pynoos, R., & Wang, J. (2009). A developmental approach to complex PTSD: Childhood and adult cumulative trauma as predictors of symptom complexity. *Journal of Traumatic Stress*, 22, 399–408.

De Zulueta, F. (2006). *From pain to violence: The traumatic roots of destructiveness* (2nd ed.). Sussex: Whurr.

Du Plock, S. (2010, April). *Trauma in the relational world: An existential-phenomenological perspective*. Keynote paper presented at the Division of Counselling Psychology Approaching Trauma Conference. London, UK.

Ehlers, A., Bisson, J., Clark, D. M., Creamer, M., Pilling, A., Richards, D., et al. (2010). Do all psychological treatments really work the same in posttraumatic stress disorder? *Clinical Psychology Review*, 30(2), 269–276.

Elklit, A., Hyland, P., & Shevlin, M. (2014). Evidence of symptom profiles consistent with posttraumatic stress disorder and complex posttraumatic stress disorder in different trauma samples. *European Journal of Psychotraumatology*, 5, 24221, doi: http://dx.doi.org/10.3402/ejpt.v5.24221.

Fierke, K. M. (2007). *Critical approaches to international security*. Cambridge: Polity Press.

Gelso, C. J. & Hayes, J. A. (2007). *Countertransference and the therapist's inner experience: Perils and possibilities*. London: Lawrence Erlbaum Associates.

Herman, J. L. (2001). *Trauma and recovery: From domestic abuse to political terror*. London: Pandora.

Holmes, J. (1993). *John Bowlby and attachment theory*. London: Routledge.

Joseph, S. (2005). Understanding post-traumatic stress from the person-centred perspective. In S. Joseph & R. Worsley (Eds), *Person-centred psychopathology: A positive psychology of mental health* (pp. 190–202). Herefordshire: PCCS Books.

Joseph, S. & Linley, P. A. (2006). Growth following adversity: Theoretical perspectives and implications for clinical practice. *Clinical Psychology Review*, 26, 1041–1053.

Knefel, M. & Lueger-Schuster, B. (2013). An evaluation of ICD-11 PTSD and complex PTSD criteria in a sample of adult survivors of childhood institutional abuse. *European Journal of Psychotraumatology*, 4, 22608, doi: http://dx.doi.org/10.3402/ejpt. v4i0.22608.

Matthews, E. (2006). *Merleau-Ponty: A guide for the perplexed*. London: Continuum.

Mearns, D. & Cooper, M. (2005). *Working at relational depth in counselling and psychotherapy*. London: Sage.

Micale, M. S. & Lerner, P. (Eds) (2001). *Traumatic pasts: History, psychiatry, and trauma in the modern age, 1870–1930*. Cambridge: Cambridge University Press.

O'Brien, S. L. (1998). *Traumatic events and mental health*. Cambridge: Cambridge University Press.

Ogden, P., Minton, K., & Pain, C. (2006). *Trauma and the body: A sensorimotor approach to psychotherapy*. London: Norton & Company.

Pearlman, L. A. & MacIan, P. S. (1995). Vicarious traumatization: An empirical study of the effects of trauma work on trauma therapists. *Professional Psychology, Research and Practice*, 26(6), 538–565.

Rogers, C. R. (1980). *A way of being*. Boston, MA: Houghton Mifflin.

Rothschild, B. (2006). *Help for the helper: The psychophysiology of compassion fatigue and vicarious trauma*. New York: W.W. Norton and Company.

Rowan, J. & Jacobs, M. (2002). *The therapist's use of self*. Buckingham: Open University Press.

Sabin-Farrell, R. & Turpin, G. (2003). Vicarious traumatisation: Implications for the mental health of health workers? *Clinical Psychology Review*, 23, 449–480.

Schottenbauer, M. A., Arnkoff, D. B., Glass, C. R., & Gray, S. H. (2006). Psychotherapists in the community: Reported prototypical psychodynamic treatments of trauma. *Journal of the American Psychoanalytic Association*, 54, 1347–1353.

Schottenbauer, M. A., Arnkoff, D. B., Glass, C. R., & Gray, S. H. (2008). Contributions of psychodynamic approaches to treatment of PTSD and trauma: A review of empirical treatment and psychopathology literature. *Psychiatry*, 71(1), 13–34.

Sherman, J. J. (1998). Effects of psychotherapeutic treatments for PTSD: A meta-analysis of controlled clinical trials. *Journal of Traumatic Stress*, 11(3), 413–435.

Solomon, S. D. & Johnson, D. M. (2002). Psychosocial treatment of posttraumatic stress disorder: A practice-friendly review of outcome research. *Psychotherapy in Practice*, 58(8), 947–959.

Sprang, G., Clark, J. J., & Whitt-Woosley, A. (2007). Compassion fatigue, compassion satisfaction, and burnout: Factors impacting a professional's quality of life. *Journal of Loss and Trauma*, 12, 259–280.

Steed, L. G. & Downing, R. (1998). A phenomenological study of vicarious traumatization amongst psychologists and professional counsellors working in the field of sexual abuse/ assault. *The Australasian Journal of Disaster and Trauma Studies*. Retrieved October 14, 2010, from www.massey.ac.nz/~trauma/issues/1998-2/steed.htm

Stolorow, R. D. (2007). *Trauma and human existence: Autobiographical, psychoanalytic, and philosophical reflections*. Sussex: The Analytic Press.

Summerfield, D. (1999). A critique of seven assumptions behind psychological trauma programmes in war-affected areas. *Social Science & Medicine*, 48, 1449–1462.

Tedeschi, R. G. & Calhoun, L. G. (1995). *Trauma and transformation: Growth in the aftermath of suffering*. Thousand Oaks, CA: Sage.

van der Kolk, B. A., McFarlance, A. C., & Weisaeth, L. (Eds) (1996). *Traumatic stress: The effects of overwhelming experience on mind, body and society*. London: The Guilford Press.

van der Kolk, B. A., Roth, S., Pelcovitz, D., Sunday, S., & Spinazzola, J. (2005). Disorders of extreme stress: The empirical foundation of a complex adaptation to trauma. *Journal of Traumatic Stress*, 18, 389–399.

Wosket, V. (1999). *The therapeutic use of self: Counselling practice, research and supervision.* London: Routledge.

Young, A. (1995). *The harmony of illusions: Inventing post traumatic stress disorder.* West Sussex: Princeton University Press.

16

AN ACCIDENTAL AFFILIATION

Alexandra Chalfont

In 1965 the brochure for the seminar programme at Esalen in California laid out what is perhaps the fundamental question posed by Humanistic Psychology: 'What are the limits of human ability, the boundaries of human experience? What does it mean to be a human being?' (Anderson, 2004).

In that year, as a teenager living in England, I was confronting that very question when trying to understand the East–West situation in Europe. A number of school students had won places in an essay-writing competition on aspects of international understanding, and the prize was a trip to Berlin to learn about the city and its situation, to be guests of the Mayor, and to visit East Berlin. This visit was one of the markers of my life, and the experience of going through Checkpoint Charlie at the height of the Cold War was one I would not forget. One effect of this moment was to viscerally anchor what I knew of the appalling, and very different experiences of both my Polish parents, survivors of the excesses of the Second World War. I only realized decades later how much this little trip influenced what had become key refrains in my life – an individual and personal study of, and search for, deeper intercultural understanding, and the potential for a more peaceful being-together in the world.

Meanwhile in California, according to Walter Anderson, Esalen adopted the phrase 'human potential movement' around this time. People like Alexander Lowen and Joseph Campbell came in. Fritz Perls was energetically developing Gestalt, and Ida Rolf and Will Schutz were installed at Esalen.

Schutz recognized that society was in need of 'openness and honesty, a willingness to take personal risks and accept responsibility for one's acts, a deeper capacity for feeling and expressing emotions and greater freedom from false morality' (Anderson, 2004: 157). By 1968 Esalen had become a centre for the resolution of racial conflict in America. It was also a year of 'giddiness' for the American Association for Humanistic Psychology's annual meeting in the USA, where one saw such people as Abraham Maslow, Herbert Marcuse and Thomas Szasz, and which included Rankians, Adlerians, Jungians and neo-Freudians (ibid.: 184).

In Europe, I found myself in Paris, in the throes of the student revolution. As I read about the growth and development of Esalen, I noticed small resonances with my own life and interests, and recognized names of people appearing at Esalen that I had only known from my reading at the time. Ronnie Laing was, according to Walter Anderson, enjoying a bawdy life there, and I had read *The Divided Self* as a 15 year old. I found great solace (as well as disquiet) in noticing that, while I was not schizophrenic in the pathological sense, there were others who were experiencing similar things to me. At the same time I was reading Huxley's *The Doors of Perception* and *Heaven and Hell*, and was surprised that other people needed drugs to experience what my brain seemed to do of its own accord from time to time!

In the mid-1970s, teaching English literature in Germany, I enjoyed Maxwell Maltz's book *Psycho-Cybernetics* (1969), and now I read that Werner Erhard, the founder of 'est' and another Esalen visitor, was particularly moved by this book. At the same time I was teaching Shakespeare's *Macbeth*, and took Berne's *Games People Play* (1968) as one particular lens to study the human interactions in the play, together with my students. Little did I know then that Eric Berne would be known as the father of Transactional Analysis, one of the three main streams to form and inform Humanistic Psychology, along with Gestalt and the Person-centred Approach. I could go on, tracking developments in Humanistic Psychology and finding parallels in my own life. I think, though, that I have listed enough to make the point: that I have found myself, like so many contemporaries, to be an 'accidental affiliate' of Humanistic Psychology throughout my life.

A while ago I was thinking of a particular artist I used to like in the 1980s, but his name refused to come to mind. A few days later I found myself leafing through a book I had not looked at for years – Piero Ferrucci's *What We May Be* (1982) – and my eyes were drawn to an exercise called 'Inner Beauty', which invites us first to think of a trait, a capacity or an attitude in ourselves that we consider beautiful, whether it be fully manifest or just the seed of an attitude. I thought of my love of art. The second step is to acknowledge and enjoy this element, and let an image appear in our mind's eye that symbolizes what we have chosen. The image that came up for me was the memory of a landscape painting, and with a flash of recognition the name that had escaped me now danced before my eyes: Caspar David Friedrich.

Friedrich was known as a significant artist and exponent of Romanticism in the 'Age of Goethe', at the beginning of the nineteenth century. His moody landscapes have been at times assigned to kitsch art, have been appropriated for albums of Goth music, and, I learned more recently, have been the subject of attention in psychoanalysis.

For me, these paintings simultaneously express both the transpersonal dimension and the subjective experience of an inner landscape; perspective seems to shift unexpectedly, and a dark foreground shadows against a clear and luminous distance. This art seems thus to hold an inversion of the present and the past, and a sense of our vulnerability in the face of an immaterial nature that we believe to be both a given, and something commonly known to us in our everyday experience of living. Although his depiction of nature is based on empirical observation, Friedrich himself says that an artist shows not 'what he sees before him, but what he sees within him'. It is thus not only the case that nature imposes boundaries on us, but also that we impose limitations on ourselves – through our internal understandings of the world outside – just as much as we are limited by conditions beyond our skin.

The ultimate and inevitable existential boundary is imposed on us by death. George Berguno, Professor of Psychology at the American University in London, discusses in the journal *Existential Analysis* (Berguno, 2008) the two kinds of boundary situations that humans are confronted with, which he considers relevant for 'existentialist thought for our times and the possibility of a new existentialism' (p. 246). As noted above, these are those boundaries that are imposed upon us, as well as those that are brought about by our own actions. Berguno claims that self-imposed boundary situations such as conflict, guilt, historicity or fidelity are 'more expressive of the paradoxical nature of our human condition' (p. 248). To survive such boundary situations, organisms need to develop an ability to adapt to life's challenges. We, as organisms, need to adapt to what the situation asks of us, and in the process we move toward becoming fully functioning.

Barrett-Lennard, in a wonderful book on person-centred therapy (Barrett-Lennard, 1998), cites attributes of the fully functioning person as follows: an 'openness to experience'; 'Living in an existential fashion . . . fluid motion, unpredictability and an ongoing quality of becoming and transcendence' (p. 129). A person who lives thus will experience their 'Self becoming emergent from experience . . . would find his organism a trustworthy means of arriving at the most satisfying behaviour in each existential situation' (Anderson, 2004: 184). Working out 'the most satisfying behaviour' presupposes that we are able to identify the challenge in the situation. We need to be able to recognize whether our senses are telling us 'the truth'.

Jordan B. Peterson, Professor of Psychology at Toronto University, asks us in *Maps of Meaning: The Architecture of Belief* (1999a) to presuppose that all experience, the objective as well as the emotional and subjective, is real. He goes on to wonder whether human beings are 'adapted to the significance of things, rather than to "things" themselves' (1999b: 3, para. 6). Peterson traces back the preoccupations of our human mythologies, finding that even in going back to the most ancient mythologies that we know, these narratives have common denominators. The stories tell of challenges in living, and there seem to be two fundamental domains to which human beings need to adapt, if we are to survive and live successfully: the known and the unknown.

Our brains seem to have one mode of operation when faced with known and predictable 'familiar territory', and another mode when confronted with the unknown and the unexplored. Faced with a challenge, we try to ascertain what it is. However, it is not enough to work out what it is; we need also to work out what it means, what it signifies. Is it something that belongs to the order we have learned through our cultural conditioning to expect, or is it chaos, something unexpected, unmet and out of our experience? As soon as something unknown appears or happens, we attribute meaning by analogy. If it seems like a snake, a dragon, we know to fear it and to have a fear response that will trigger fight or flight. We use our creative imagination to mediate between the known and the unknown, between order and chaos, in order to be able to deal with the unexpected. This is exemplified in the language of metaphor, and has always been our human way of making sense of the world. Jordan Peterson points out that the 'objective world is something that has been conjured up for us recently' (1999b: 1, para. 1) through the process of science. This implies that the environment of humans can be regarded as spiritual as well as material.

One of my favourite authors is Franz Kafka. In his 'Aphorisms' he writes: 'There is nothing other than a spiritual world; what we call a sensory world is the Evil in the Spiritual, and what we call evil is simply the necessity of a single moment in our eternal development' (cited in Friedländer, 2012: 228, my translation). The connection I want to make between Friedrich, Berguno, Peterson and Kafka is that they could all be regarded, like me, as 'accidental affiliates' of Humanistic Psychology; and I could think of many others.

My most recent accidental affiliation was more direct, and took place about 16 years ago. After a couple of decades abroad, involved in adult personal development, philology, translation and cross-cultural understanding, I had returned to England and trained in various modalities of psychotherapy. One of the additional activities I took on was as managing editor of *Self & Society*, the house journal of our Association for Humanistic Psychology in Britain (AHPB). After six years it was time to leave, and I needed to acknowledge a frustration and disappointment with what I felt was sometimes a shadow side of Humanistic Psychology associations. The notion that process is more important than product seemed to sit deep in some people's psyche. I felt that discussions tended to stretch into the ether, and simple decisions seemed sometimes impossible to make, let alone to carry out. Along with this, there seemed to come an occasional belief for some that commerce is inherently a very bad thing, and that words such as 'profit', 'outcome', 'efficiency' and 'technology' were unacceptable concepts, the application of which would imply an adoption of these concepts as values in themselves, rather than useful tools.

A while later, in 2009, I received a phone call from the editor of *Self & Society*. The Association was to be closed, there was no money – *Self & Society* was to disappear. A small group was gathering to try to save the AHP. Would I be involved? Loving *Self & Society* as I did, I said 'yes', for its sake alone. People in the group came and went, and through hefty cost-cutting and support from good friends, the Association gained an even keel by the autumn of 2010.

At the Annual General Meeting, the co-chairs stepped down to resume their earlier lives. We needed new co-chairs; John Rowan, our stalwart guardian and early adopter of Humanistic Psychology in Britain, offered to take on one role, and somehow I found myself in the other. From being a person of accidental affiliation, I was now in the thick of it.

With a dearth of volunteers, and coffers that emptied as soon as a penny was tossed in, trustees of the Association acted simultaneously as members of the Board as well as Management Committee and odd-job people. Some of us felt that what we needed was to envisage a clearer initial direction, and resolved to explore emergent possibilities. Our aim was to eventually reach beyond a core membership, as various groupings had developed directions which they felt were autonomous and markedly different in some way. Thus, although we still consisted of a strong number of gestaltists, existentialists, transactional analysts, transpersonal practitioners and person-centred people, some had wandered away from the community to concentrate on their more specialized direction. One consequence was that many newer colleagues in the counselling and psychotherapy world had never heard of the AHP or *Self & Society*. Did the term 'Humanistic Psychology' still hold currency for the future? This question still needs to find its answer, I feel. It might go some way to doing this if it creates some new spaces where practitioners of broadly similar philosophy and practice – including those whose affinity with Humanistic Psychology might be more accidental than deliberate – can explore their common factors, as well as recognizing potential for common growth, collaboration and development.

Self & Society is now published by Routledge in association with the AHP, with potential to reach a far larger constituency. It remains to be seen to what extent it can reflect and encourage the further evolution of a humanistic attitude in therapy, education, medicine and other domains of relational being.

The inherent beauty of this humanistic approach lies for me in its acceptance of the wholeness of living beings and life. If Humanistic Psychology can consign its stereotypical 'hippie' public image to its formative phase as a beginning movement; if it can loosen its attachment to individualism in favour of an individuality that pays equal attention to exploring and accepting the collective nature of being human; if it can relax its sometimes wholesale antipathy to scientific method and accept science as one essential way of learning among many; and if it can allow itself to continue becoming a vital, bold and experimental undertaking, then why would it not grow and develop?

As humanistically versed practitioners, we can continue to engage fully with the personal, political, social and spiritual in an inclusive and differentiated way. As transpersonal beings, as individuals as well as collectives, some of us have been able to tap into a consciousness beyond the dual, in deepening awareness of non-duality and a vast nothingness beyond time and space, beyond matter and non-matter.

But we can also choose to keep returning, as material organisms ourselves, to the level of all the various manifestations of matter in the world, in order to live toward and beyond whatever might be our present understanding of our human potential. As humans we are still only at the beginning of being, of doing and of learning. History keeps repeating this lesson. I suspect many of us would agree with Berguno when he says, 'the debt that history imposes on us in the form of the past can be transformed through our responsible actions into a creative commitment to the future' (2008: 249).

Particularly now, as the challenge of worldwide migrations and ageing societies spawn an atmosphere of fear and scarcity, and herald an impending global conflict between cultures and generations, humanistic values of understanding, empathy and integration could, despite all contrary currents, encourage us to move toward integrity and wholeness.

References

Anderson, W. T. (2004). *The Upstart Spring: Esalen and the Human Potential Movement: The First Twenty Years*. Bloomington, IN: iUniverse.

Barrett-Lennard, G. T. (1998). *Carl Rogers' Helping System: Journey and Substance*. London: Sage.

Berguno, G. (2008). Towards a new conception of the human condition. *Existential Analysis, 19*: 246–53.

Berne, E. (1968). *Games People Play: The Psychology of Human Relationships*. Harmondsworth: Penguin.

Ferrucci, P. (1982). *What We May Be: The Vision and Techniques of Psychosynthesis*. Harmondsworth: Penguin.

Friedländer, S. (2012). *Franz Kafka*. Munich: C. H. Beck.

Maltz, M. (1969). *Psycho-Cybernetics*. New York: Simon and Schuster.

Peterson, J. B. (1999a). *Maps of Meaning: The Architecture of Belief*. London: Routledge.

Peterson, J. B. (1999b). *Maps of Meaning: The Architecture of Belief*, précis. Retrieved 24 May 2002 from goo.gl/H1AiFW (no longer available as of 11 December 2016).

PART IV

Future prospects – existential, transpersonal, postmodern

EDITORS' INTRODUCTION TO PART IV

Richard House, David Kalisch and Jennifer Maidman

And so to the final section of the book, in which you will have an opportunity to consider a diverse range of views on the crucial matter of what the future might hold for the humanistic field as a whole, and for some of the principles it espouses.

In Chapter 17, we hear again from Dina Glouberman, who started off this book (with John Rowan) back in Chapter 1. In an optimistic piece, Glouberman explores some of the many approaches to human potential work which have evolved over the years – approaches which, while perhaps not always *explicitly* calling themselves 'humanistic', do implicitly draw upon humanistic ideas. A bright future then, perhaps – at least for humanistic values and principles, as the philosophical underpinning of a diverse range of practices.

In Chapter 18, however, Kirk J. Schneider pulls no punches in grounding that possible future in the many challenges our field faces right now, such as ideologically radicalized young people, a machine-mediated, consumerist ethos, and the challenges posed directly to humanistic practitioners by demands for short-term, behaviourally focused outcomes. On this analysis, the humanistic 'tribe' has an important message for the wider psychology field, about real, deep and embodied change – but is anyone willing to listen?

In Chapter 19, senior elder of British Humanistic Psychology, John Rowan, unpacks some prescient humanistic-relevant ideas he has been exploring, in particular the theory of the 'Dialogical Self', which he sees as taking the place of the Unconscious. As ever with John's work, there is much here to inspire and stimulate our thinking, as we consider concepts that are at the very leading edge of humanistic theory. Keith Tudor, in Chapter 20, also takes us on a journey, as he characterizes it, 'from humanism to Humanistic Psychology and back again', challenging one of the great humanistic 'articles of faith' head on – as he critiques the assumption that Humanistic Psychology represents a 'Third Force'. In fact, Keith argues, this constitutes a 'philosophical category error' which ultimately might fail to serve the broader principles that underpin our approach.

Moving on to Chapter 21, in a very forward-looking and thought-provoking cameo, Robin Shohet considers four possible foci for the future of Humanistic Psychology, all of which see the approach as having a major contribution to make in a world beset by the psychology of 'revenge', by shock and trauma, by global warming and other ecological issues, and by an 'I' concept that tends to use 'attack' as a strategy for self-protection.

In Chapter 22, we hear from one of the giants of the therapy field, Windy Dryden, originally a person-centred counsellor, and a longtime advocate of key humanistic ideas such as the Core Conditions. Applying his characteristically forensic, critical but highly constructive thinking to the question of 'where are we and where do we go from here?' Dryden comes up with some very practical ideas as to how the humanistic field might 'get its act together'.

In Chapter 23, Gaie Houston, another major voice in the humanistic world, explores, through a personal narrative, some of the ways in which Gestalt has evolved, and shows how these ideas still have much to offer in the future, not just as a therapy, but also as a useful prophylactic approach in the wider society.

And so to Chapter 24, where Peter Hawkins sees the need for a 'necessary revolution in Humanistic Psychology'. Yes, he argues, Humanistic Psychology has brought much to the world, but it is now imperative we also look deeper. There is a way forward for our field, and for our planet in the twenty-first century, but only if we can begin to look with greater clarity at the 'shadow side' of humanistic culture, and 'own' how our humanistic approach has contributed to some of the very cultural crises we are now experiencing.

In Chapter 25, one of the key figures in the history and development of Humanistic Psychology in Britain, John Heron, looks deeply into what Humanistic Psychology would look like if it were an expression of what he characterizes as 'fourth wave humanism'. For John, it would firmly put spirituality back where it belongs, 'in an enhanced, more rounded and grounded form at the very core of the human realm', thus manifesting as collegiality, and 'a collaborative regeneration of what it is to be a human being'. In such a realm, people 'co-operate to explore meaning, build relationship and manifest creativity through collaborative action inquiry into the integration and consummation of many areas of human development'. John goes on to outline a number of distinguishing features of such collegially applied spirituality, which he sees as 'encourag[ing] us to inquire together, imaginatively and creatively, about how to act together in a spirited way to flourish on and with our planet'.

Finally, in the book's final chapter, the wonderful Jill Hall asks some 'big questions' about where Humanistic Psychology fits into, arguably, the 'biggest picture' of them all – the evolution and ongoing unfolding of consciousness itself. Isn't Humanistic Psychology ultimately about *connection*, Jill suggests, about *feeling* our affinity with each other, and also with something much greater than ourselves? Is it not imperative that we avoid slipping into a reductionist mind-set that would sacrifice the long-term, big picture, for short-term professional advantage?

We editors will be back with some of our own reflections and conclusions following Part IV. We hope you enjoy it.

17

HUMANISTIC PSYCHOLOGY

How it was and how it may be

Dina Glouberman

Humanistic Psychology was a wonderful thing when I was coming up in the psycho-therapy/personal development world in the late 1960s and early 70s. I was attending Brandeis University where Maslow was teaching, and partly as a consequence I was profoundly influenced by the writings of Erich Fromm, Carl Rogers, Fritz Perls, Rollo May, Jacob Moreno, and all the Humanistic Psychology pioneers.

How it was

Humanistic Psychology at that time represented everything that was young, progressive, open to change and politically on the side of the angels. It encouraged us to begin a lifetime of development and expansion without ever having to label ourselves as 'ill' or lacking.

Some of the things I am talking about here might not be associated in everyone's mind with Humanistic Psychology, so perhaps this is a broad picture of a movement and a way of thinking that characterized that time and which I associate with Humanistic Psychology. But I want to give a feel of what it was like for us at that time, and then to explore a few possibilities of what the way forward might be today. I also want to express my immense gratitude for the ways in which Humanistic Psychology inspired me to become what I am, both personally and professionally.

My work on imagery, or Imagework as I call it (Glouberman, 2010, 2014), the focus that has significantly defined my approach, my writing, and my life, had its roots in Humanistic Psychology. I can still picture the first time I was in a workshop and someone introduced Fritz Perls' method of becoming the image in a dream and speaking as that image. It was an astounding moment, one in which a new window on life opened for me.

And I remember too the moment my friend Robin who was in a humanistic personal development group with me, told me she was working on her 'stuff' at home. What? It's not just in a group? The idea of self-help Imagework, indeed of giving away the secrets of psychotherapy to be used by anyone anywhere, probably had its seed thought there.

My commitment to group work also came from that background. My father, who was a genuine seeker way ahead of his time, introduced me to humanistic group work at a group work conference in New York in the late sixties. In fact, he was partly responsible for my being at Brandeis University, because he loved Maslow.

At the time of the conference, I had been trying to work on my feelings about my mother's death a year or so before in my psychoanalytic therapy with not much success. I found myself attending a workshop called The Psychodrama of Death, with the wonderful psycho-dramatist, Hannah Weiner.

I talked about the way my mother's presence was haunting me, and Hannah stood on a table, becoming my mother. She asked me what I wanted. I told her I just wanted her to be alive somewhere, even if I could never see her. Hannah, as my mother replied, 'I can't do that for you'. I heard myself saying, 'Well if you can't be alive, then I want you to be dead!'

At her suggestion, I pushed Hannah/mother out of the room. I must have done it with incredible force because it seemed easy, and yet Hannah was a very big woman and she told me later that she was doing her best to resist.

Then I slammed the door, three times, to the cheers of the group. Could you really push your dead mother out the door and be cheered for it? At that moment, I let go of her ghost, and could honour my love for her.

My analyst, Joe Sandler, got it when he saw me in London afterwards and I told him what had happened. He said, 'You must be very disappointed in our work together.'

Fritz Perls actually invited me to participate in his first training course in California. I did not go. Instead I chose to come to the Henderson Hospital in Sutton and work as a lowly social therapist, the equivalent of an assistant nurse, in the therapeutic community set up by founder Maxwell Jones, who was, however, no longer there. At the same time I turned down a chance to be a Clinical Psychologist working with Maxwell Jones himself in Dingleton Hospital in Scotland.

Why did I make such an odd choice? My reasoning was that I wanted to learn the most I possibly could, and being totally innocent of normal social considerations, I thought that the best idea was to go to a new country (more difference), and be lower status and therefore closer to the patients (more connection). I was in search of truth, and I felt I could not know the truth if I was blinded by my culture and my assumptions.

In some ways it was a rather mad choice, knowing what I know now, and there were certainly moments when I regretted it. But perhaps unconsciously I was not only ignorant about the uses of status, but was also avoiding the charismatic leaders in order to forge my own path. This path led to Skyros,[1] Imagework, and, for that matter, to burnout and then *The Joy of Burnout* (Glouberman, 2007). This probably would not have happened if I had followed the leaders.

Perhaps that was part of the legacy of Humanistic Psychology, to attract those of us who were seekers and initiators and not simply followers.

How it may be

To be sure, the future of Humanistic Psychology cannot mimic the past, because by its nature it was a new phenomenon responding to what was around. It expanded our limits, broke open our normal ways of thinking. If we try to hold onto what we have, which is an attitude you find in so many institutions and schools, we end up with an ossified way of thinking.

I am reminded of my stay at the Henderson Hospital. It had been created by Maxwell Jones in 1958 as a revolutionary community environment in the setting of an NHS hospital, where each person no matter their rank had one vote. As such, it had had a big international impact (Rapoport et al., 1979). But by the time I worked there for six months in 1968, not only was he absent, but the new and revolutionary were no longer welcome.

I discovered through bitter experience that to get anything changed you had to either get a psychiatrist to agree with you, since they were highest in the supposedly non-existent pecking order, or you had to say it five times until they thought it was familiar and not new. One of the nurses literally said, 'If it was good enough for Maxwell Jones, it's good enough for me'.

I would not want that for Humanistic Psychology.

And yet though we cannot mimic the past, the underlying approach of expanding limits and challenging limiting categories must guide us, and the basic foundations of Humanistic Psychology do need to be honoured. My utopian vision would be of a whole-person psychology based on seeing how we can be at our best, with a central core of meaning and value in the driving seat, with a many faceted interior world that represents many different ways of seeing and being, and a connected empowered and creative relationship to the world around. As Merleau-Ponty (2002) said, our consciousness is not in our head but in our relationship to the world. That world includes the social, emotional, mental and spiritual worlds as well as the physical world.

When we were starting Skyros in Greece, I became excited about the ancient Greek idea of health, which was a Western form of holism. It spoke not only of health as based on mind, body and spirit being in harmony with each other, but also, and this was more surprising, with the natural environment, and with the social environment. To be healthy, you needed good politics and good ecology. Indeed according to Hippocrates (e.g. Hippocrates, 1983), the way the wind is blowing needed to be factored into a diagnosis. This kind of holistic notion of health is what Humanistic Psychology has always espoused; we are keeping good company with Hippocrates.

Much of what we are known for in Humanistic Psychology has now seemingly been accepted in the mainstream. This is our success as visionaries and also our challenge. But if we look closely at some of the areas where we have been pioneers, we will see that the ideas might have been adopted, but the application has narrowed so that they no longer represent the original vision.

Here are a few of the many areas in which we could be said to be pioneers, and where we could take up the baton again and run with it. I choose these because these are the ones I am most familiar with through my own work. There are so many others, for example in the fields of political psychology and of eco-psychology, which are crucial. Some of this is already being worked with and written about in *Self & Society* and other Humanistic Psychology forums, but maybe we need to toot our own horn more.

Coaching: The success of coaching is based at least in part on the fact that it implies that you are a go-getting person with nothing wrong with you except that you could use some visioning and hand-holding to do your job and life better. This idea that we can be normal healthy people who want to expand is what Humanistic Psychology pioneered, except that this has become rather aligned with the business and personal success world. My own response to this has been to offer 'Mind, Heart and Soul Coaching'. Humanistic Psychology can more generally pioneer the kind of coaching that develops the whole person, in the context of spirit, society and nature. This means that we include psycho-spiritual, creative, ecological and social transformation development among the aspects we want to get coaching in, not just traditional success.

Mindfulness: Like coaching, mindfulness has exploded as a panacea, and has been taken up most obviously by the CBT people for healing depression and other problems, often with excellent results Yet my own first memory of an experience of mindfulness was in the early 60s, reading the seminal book *Gestalt Therapy: excitement and growth in the human personality* by Fritz Perls, R. F. Hefferline and Paul Goodman (1951). The first exercise in the book was simply to say sentences that began 'Right now I am aware of . . .' again and again. I can still remember the altered state I moved into as I really saw my kitchen for the very first time. The purpose was to bring us into the present moment and expand our consciousness, rather than to fix us. I have also followed the Vietnamese Buddhist Thich Nhat Hanh who was one of the major figures who introduced mindfulness in the West as part of a spiritual discipline (e.g. Thich Nhat Hanh, 1991). I have been surprised to find that he is hardly mentioned in traditional psychology mindfulness circles. A new Humanistic Psychology take on mindfulness that preserves a wider and deeper vision could be remarkable.

Imagery: My own introduction to imagery was, as I said above, via Fritz Perls and Gestalt Therapy. I was also inspired by Jung's active imagination (1997), by David Spangler's *Laws of Manifestation* (2008), by the imagery precision of Grinder and Bandler's NLP (1989), and by many similar broad and deep approaches. Imagery has a wonderful function as a way of understanding and guiding the whole person within a multilevel environment. One image can have a meaning on a physical, mental, emotional, social, spiritual and ecological level. Amazingly, you can often find images travelling from one person to another in a group because on a deep level there is no real boundary between us; in one of my groups, nine people sitting near each other had images of trees, and no one else in the room did. We also use each image as a perspective, to see ourselves and the world from as many perspectives as there are images, i.e. infinite. I could go on and on. But as in coaching and mindfulness, the original breadth of approach has been narrowed down either to a kind of spiritual materialism, as in some of the creative visualization, law of attraction and NLP approaches, or to heal psychological problems, as in CBT and again NLP. Could Humanistic Psychology now pioneer a broader approach to the humanistic uses of imagery?

Community: Humanistic Psychology always included within it the importance of the environment and the community and the idea that we need to create worlds that heal, not just good therapy. This was certainly my intention in creating Skyros holidays, which represented all my own yearnings to be part of a larger whole. The first principle of Skyros was community, not a traditional community, where we get care, belonging, connectedness and approval in exchange for social control, but rather a step forward into a new kind of community where we can celebrate individuality as well as connectedness. Caring and belonging and connectedness need to be predicated on honouring each other for what we are and are becoming, not how we fit in. And we need to give each member a voice in determining how the community will be. Again, revisioning community is a ripe field for Humanistic Psychology.

Holistic approaches applied to particular psychological issues

Burnout has been one such subject for me. Out of my own experience of burnout, I discovered that it is not about working too hard, but about our heart going out of what we are doing, and driving ourselves to do it anyway, because our identity is tied up in the old path. It is our ability to find the meaning in what we are doing that carries us through. When that stops, we are truly unable to continue. The therapy here is, basically, stepping back and considering how to become wholehearted again (Glouberman, 2007).

In my research on fear of the future, I discovered that our very worst fear is not of what we think it is, poverty or illness or loss, but of losing ourselves. Unless we can find that in us that will be there when all else fails, we will be frightened (Glouberman, n.d.).

Again, we are talking of the whole person, not the problem. In how many such fields can we create a unique and specifically humanistic approach?

The inspiration and the challenge

More generally, for me, the future of Humanistic Psychology is to peep through everything we do and create an inspiration for a different approach to life. It includes so many wonderful windows to see the world as one in which we are each in our own process of personal development throughout our lifetime, and that rather than be ashamed that we need it, we can wear this as our badge of courage. It reminds us that the personal, the spiritual, and the political are all part of the same human yearning to move beyond the status quo to new understandings and new realities.

It tells us that we will never ever succeed if we simply box ourselves up in old categories and old diagnoses, nor will we be able to help others if we do not give them a chance to define themselves rather than telling them who they are and what they need.

And above all, it reminds us always to challenge our own limits, to go beyond what we think is true, to that which we do not yet know. The pioneers of Humanistic Psychology did that for us. We must do this for the generation that follows.

Note

1   Skyros Holistic Holidays, founded in 1975 by Dr Dina Glouberman and Dr Yannis Andricopoulos, www.skyros.com

References

Glouberman, D. (2007) *The Joy of Burnout: How the End of the World Can Be a New Beginning*, London: Skyros Books.

Glouberman, D. (2010) *Life Choices, Life Changes: Develop your Personal Vision with Imagework*, London: Skyros Books; (see also www.dinaglouberman.com/ approach/imagework/)

Glouberman, D. (2014) *You Are What You Imagine: 3 Steps to a New Beginning Using Imagework*, London: Watkins.

Glouberman, D. (n.d.) *Future Fear*. Available at www.dinaglouberman.com/approach/future-fear/

Grinder, J. and Bandler, R. (1989) *The Structure of Magic, I and II*, Palo Alto, CA: Science and Behavior Books.

Hippocrates (1983) *Hippocratic Writing* (trans. J. Chadwick and others), London: Penguin Classics.

Jung, C.G. (1997) *Jung on Active Imagination* (ed. Joan Chodorow) (Series: 'Encountering Jung'), Princeton, NJ: Princeton University Press.

Merleau-Ponty, M. (2002) *Phenomenology of Perception: An Introduction*, New York: Routledge Classics.

Perls, F.S., Hefferline, R., & Goodman, P. (1951) *Gestalt Therapy: Excitement and Growth in the Human Personality*, New York: Gestalt Journal Press.

Rapoport, R., Rapoport, R., & Rosow, I. (1979) *Community as Doctor*, London: Ayer Co. Pub.

Spangler, D. (2008) *Laws of Manifestation: A Consciousness Classic*, Newburyport, MA: Weiser Books.

Thich Nhat Hanh (1991) *The Miracle of Mindfulness*, London: Rider Books.

18

HUMANISTIC PSYCHOLOGY'S CHIEF TASK

To reset psychology on its rightful existential-humanistic base[1]

Kirk J. Schneider

The dangers of 'business as usual' in psychology could not be more pronounced in these challenging times. For example, the profession of psychology recently came through one of the most trying periods of its history – such as the American Psychological Association's (APA) involvement with national security interrogations during the Iraq war and the resultant backlash from that involvement, which raised serious questions about the APA's ethical and professional credibility; the alarming rates of depression, suicide, and addiction – despite broadening support for mental health services among industrialized nations; the harrowing increase in rampage killing by disaffected and ideologically radicalized youth, despite ostensible 'treatment' for many of those young people; and the disturbing trend toward machine-mediated, consumerist, and efficiency-oriented models of the ideal lifestyle among growing numbers of mental health professionals, not merely the lay populations they serve.

In the face of this onslaught, the question must be posed, how well is conventional psychology (and psychiatry) doing its job? The thornier question is how *can* conventional psychology and psychiatry optimally do their job if the emphasis of their services is on short-term, behavioural change, and not the fuller, deeper change promoted by existential-humanistic principles of living – the reconnection with a 'whole-bodied' experience of living? This is the challenge I pose to psychology and policy-makers in this chapter as we enter the next phase of our evolution.

While some in the field continue to believe that psychology proceeds purely on the basis of positivistic science (e.g. Baker et al., 2008), I contend that this is patently naive. Psychology was, and probably always will be, a philosophically based discipline. In this light, the field of psychology has actually been 'reset' many times over its relatively brief century-long history, and this resetting has had as much to do with philosophical fashion as it has had to do with empirical evidence (see Kuhn, 1962). The first time the field was reset was at the point where its standing as an explicit philosophy was replaced by its 'formalization' as an explicit laboratory science. This was the time when Wilhelm Wundt and his colleagues began basing psychology on the experimental method (or the philosophical approach of natural science) to evaluate laboratory findings. The second major time when psychology was reset was when psychoanalysis replaced laboratory science as the leading philosophical paradigm. This was a period, roughly the 1920s, when Freud and his colleagues emphasized the primacy of the so-called 'drive model' of human functioning over the conscious activities of laboratory investigation. The third major period of philosophical resetting was the usurpation of the psychoanalytic model by the behavioural model, where only overt and measurable human actions were considered the domain of legitimacy. The fourth major period of resetting was spearheaded by cognitive science, and the shift in emphasis from outward behavioural actions to inward informational processing. Now we are in a period where the pre-dominant paradigm is quickly moving from cognitive science to neuroscience, from intellective processes to behaviour–brain correlates.

So where does that bring us to at the present day? How should psychology be reset in the emerging era – and what role does that leave for Humanistic Psychology?

I believe that psychology should now be reset on its rightful base in existence. It is high time that psychology recognized what the great poets and thinkers the world over have recognized for centuries – that the main problem of the human being is the paradoxical problem: that we are both angels and food for worms; that we are suspended between constrictive and expansive worlds; and that we are both exhilarated and stupefied by this tension. The role this leaves for Humanistic Psychology is the role that William James so deftly set for it back in 1902. That was the year James wrote his book *The Varieties of Religious Experience*, calling for a radically empirical, experientially informed inquiry into the human being's engagement with the world (Taylor, 2010).

I also believe that Humanistic Psychology's role today is commensurate with the existential-phenomenological-spiritual tradition of successors to William James (see Mendelowitz & Kim, 2010), exemplified by Paul Tillich (1952), Martin Buber (1970), Rollo May (1981), R. D. Laing (1969), Ernest Becker (1973), and many others who called for a new 'whole-bodied' experience of inquiry and life. This whole-bodied psychology does not preclude other strands along its bandwidth, but it incorporates them as part of its awesome tableau. (Interestingly, this view was recently upheld in a special issue of the mainstream US *Journal of Psychotherapy Integration*, in which the impact of existential-humanistic principles of practice were touted as 'heartening' and 'formidable' for the field of 'empirical/academic psychology'; as a whole – Shahar & Schiller, 2016: 2).

In a nutshell, then: the chief task for Humanistic Psychology going forward is to reset psychology on its rightful existential-humanistic base. By 'rightful', I mean that if mainstream psychology is to become the field that Nietzsche once dubbed the 'queen of the sciences', if it is to maximally apprehend lives and the transformation of lives, then it will need to show how mainstream psychology's present bases – cognitive, behavioural and neuro-physiological – are wanting. It will need to show

how one's relation to information processing, overt and measurable actions, and physio-chemical structures are but part-processes of an infinitely unfolding venture, a venture that comprises those part-processes, to be sure, but that also far exceeds them both in scope and consequence.

Consider, for example, how we have corrupted the term 'substrate' today. Substrate simply means underlying process or 'base on which an organism lives' (Webster's, 2003: 1246); and yet we have usurped the literal meaning of this term by reducing it to neurology. We have confused the physical base of organisms, e.g. 'neural substrates', with the phenomenological base of organisms – which is mystery. That is, the substrates of human behaviour are not merely traceable to a cell or a molecule or even an atom, but to an enigma that underlies all these overtly measurable processes – the groundlessness of existence. The groundlessness of existence is the *experiential* substrate of human behaviour/consciousness (see Schneider, 2013). The groundlessness of existence is the experiential base on which all things revolve, and we (that is, our mainstream culture, our profession) hardly ever speak of this problem, let alone acknowledge that it exists. Yet the substrates underlying neural substrates, the substrates that cause us the most problems and open us to the greatest possibilities – the 800 pound gorilla in our 'room' – is the groundlessness of existence.

I propose the following hypotheses. First: *Most of our troubles as human beings can be traced to one overarching problem – our suspension in the groundlessness of existence.* Second and a corollary to the first – *Most of our joys, breakthroughs and liberations can also be traced to our suspension in the groundlessness of existence.*

What is the rationale for these postulates? Just consider what we normally call 'psychopathology'. Consider what we experience following a great loss, or an illness, or a disruption. Consider the kinds of words we use to describe these upheavals: we feel that the 'bottom has dropped out', that we have slipped into a 'black hole', that we are in 'free fall'. We feel 'crushed', 'sunk', or – in a word – 'groundless'. Further, consider how virtually all of these feelings drive us into 'disorders' characterized by our psychiatric manuals – e.g. depression, anxiety, mania and narcissism.

At the same time, consider what we experience when we can *confront* abysses of living – when we can sit with them, allow them to evolve, and potentially, incrementally, even become intrigued by them. How differently we can then experience the world; how fully we can then experience choice, possibility and poignancy, at every moment afforded to us.

That which I call 'awe-based' psychology is one possible inroad into the venture about which I speak (Schneider, 2004, 2009, 2013). By awe-based psychology, I mean a psychology that is grounded in the humility and wonder – adventure of living; and I mean a psychology that can radically enrich both *what* we discover, and *how we live* what we discover. Through awe-based psychology, we can impact every major sector of our lives, from child-rearing to education to the work setting to the governmental setting, and we can roundly enhance our science. Does this sound like a long sought-after cross-road?

Consider the following:

Mystery is a place where religion and science meet.
Dogma is a place where they part.
Awe-based psychology is a place where they can evolve and reunite.

Coda

We can talk until we are blue in the face about pat formulae and programmatic treatments. We can cite chemical imbalances in the brain, for example, or the lack of ability to regulate emotions, or the irrationality of conditioned thoughts as the bases for our disorders. However, until psychologists get down to the fundamental problem that fuels all these secondary conditions – our precariousness as creatures – they will be operating at a very restrictive level (and the results, I am afraid, are all too evident in our society). The question needs to be continually raised – is helping a person to change behaviour patterns and recondition their thoughts sufficient? Or do we owe it to that person to make available to him or her a deeper dimension of self-exploration? Do we owe it to that person to enable him or her to discover what really matters about his or her life, wherever that may lead? Do we owe it to his or her *society*? I believe so, and that the time for psychology to 'reset' is now.

Note

1   This chapter is adapted from the Special Section: The 50th anniversary of the *Journal of Humanistic Psychology*, 'Reflections on the state of the field'. See *Journal of Humanistic Psychology*, 51(4): 436–8. Copyright 2011 from Sage Publishing Co.

References

Baker, T. B., McFall, R. M., & Shoham, V. (2008). Current status and future prospects of clinical psychology: toward a scientifically principled approach to mental and behavioral healthcare. *Psychological Science in the Public Interest*, 9(2): 67–103.

Becker, E. (1973). *Denial of Death*. New York: Free Press.

Buber, M. (1970). *I and Thou* (transl. W. Kaufmann). New York: Scribner's.

Kuhn, T. (1962). *The Structure of Scientific Revolutions*. Chicago: University of Chicago Press.

Laing, R. D. (1969). *The Divided Self: An Existential Study in Sanity and Madness*. Harmondsworth: Penguin.

May, R. (1981). *Freedom and Destiny*. New York: Norton.

Mendelowitz, E. & Kim, C. Y. (2010). William James and the spirit of complexity. *Journal of Humanistic Psychology*, 50: 459–70.

Schneider, K. J. (2004). *Rediscovery of Awe: Splendor, Mystery, and the Fluid Center of Life*. St Paul, MN: Paragon House.

Schneider, K. J. (2009). *Awakening to Awe: Personal Stories of Profound Transformation*. Lanham, MD: Jason Aronson.

Schneider, K. J. (2013). *The Polarized Mind: Why It's Killing Us and What We Can Do about It*. Colorado Springs, CO: University Professors Press.

Shahar, G. & Schiller, M. (2016). A conqueror by stealth: introduction to the special issue on humanism, existentialism, and psychotherapy integration. *Journal of Psychotherapy Integration*, 26: 1–4.

Taylor, E. (2010). William James and the humanistic implications of the neuroscience revolution: an outrageous hypothesis. *Journal of Humanistic Psychology*, 50: 410–29.

Tillich, P. (1952). *The Courage to Be*. New Haven, CT: Yale University Press.

Webster's. (2003). *New World Dictionary*. New York: Simon & Schuster.

19

DIRECTIONS FOR HUMANISTIC PSYCHOLOGY

John Rowan

I have been involved in Humanistic Psychology since 1970, have been to conferences in the USA and elsewhere, have met some of the leading figures, and been to groups led by these people. I have also been writing about Humanistic Psychology since 1975. There have been some changes along the way. The great reliance on expressing feelings, so prevalent in the 1970s, has diminished. The emphasis on the individual, such a key issue in those days, has shifted. We are all relational now.

One of the most interesting changes has been the increased interest in the transpersonal. Humanistic and Transpersonal Psychology have always been close – after all, Abraham Maslow founded both of them – but in recent years, in the USA there have been some organizational moves that have brought the two into closer proximity. In Europe, too, there has been a huge growth in EUROTAS (the European transpersonal umbrella), which now has about 30 national organizational members. The EUROTAS conferences look and feel very much like humanistic conferences. In England, the United Kingdom Council for Psychotherapy (UKCP) has recently formed a sub-section devoted to Transpersonal Psychology.

At the same time there has been an increased interest in the relationship between the humanistic and the existential. The current editor of the *Journal of Humanistic Psychology* is the author of several books bringing together humanistic and existential ideas in the field of psychotherapy. James Bugental had the unique honour of being admitted to the editorial boards of both the *Journal of Humanistic Psychology* and the *Journal of Existential Analysis*. Rollo May is another important writer with a foot in both camps. In this country Mick Cooper is someone who has contributed to person-centred, experiential and existential writings, and to research too (e.g. Cooper, 2003, 2008). And the current editor of the *Journal of Humanistic Psychology*, Kirk J. Schneider, has written and spoken out many times about the connection between Humanistic Psychology and existentialism.

One of my own contributions has been the chapter in *The Handbook of Humanistic Psychology* (Rowan, 2002), where I outlined some of the similarities and differences between the humanistic and the existential, and in the next chapter Ernesto Spinelli (2002) presented some arguments with a different position in the same area. To me it seems obvious that the humanistic and the existential share an outlook which Ken Wilber calls the Centaur (e.g. 2001) – a belief in bodymind unity, an appreciation of authenticity, a way of thinking that is essentially dialectical. This is what Maslow (1994) called self-actualization.

It is interesting that in a recent book describing the newer tendencies in psychoanalysis, the writer says: 'Self-actualization, a term developed by humanistic psychologists, is one way to characterize the broadest aim of most psychoanalytic psychotherapists' (Curtis & Hirsch, 2011: 82). It is amazing to realize how many different schools of psychotherapy are now adopting a relational approach. Even the behavioural schools are starting to do this, as for example with ACT (acceptance and commitment therapy), which has aspirations to be the humanistic face of CBT and its relatives. I am giving a paucity of academic references here, because this is not a technical matter, but rather a human matter.

But we are under threat today. The problem is that most of us do not believe that randomized controlled trials (RCTs) are the right way to research psychotherapy. Such approaches are good for measuring the efficacy of techniques of treatment. But the techniques of treatment only account for a small percentage – about 15 per cent in most findings – of the efficacy of therapy. Why get involved in the very expensive trappings of the RCT, if that way of working in research is not going to measure anything that is worth measuring? Mick Cooper, who is a good friend and someone I respect, seems to have fallen for the blandishments of the RCT, but I do not really understand how.

There is now a serious attempt in motion to complain to the UK Health Service's National Institute for Health and Care Excellence (or NICE), who idolize the RCT, that this is not the way to go. It is to be hoped that this movement succeeds (and there are signs that it will) – otherwise, we are all going to be deprived of government funding and acknowledgement. There are serious signs that the humanistic therapies are being downgraded in many areas – for example, a recent compendium of therapies, the previous editions of which had chapters on Gestalt and on transactional analysis, has dropped these chapters from its current edition.

I became so worried about this that I wrote around to the chairs of all the humanistic organizations in the UKCP, asking them if they wanted to get together to fight this tendency. I even sent them a copy of my *A Guide to Humanistic Psychology* (2005) to remind them of what that speciality contained. I only got one reply. Whether this is apathy or adherence to a different approach, I do not know. What I do know is that I am a bit disappointed, and even disgusted, by such a low level of response. Who cares about this question?

So do we just concentrate on the transpersonal approach, and let the humanistic organizations stew in their own juice? One of the difficulties of the transpersonal approach is that in academia, it is even less known and even less welcomed than is

Humanistic Psychology. Part of the reason for this is that it is about spirituality, and there is no consensus as to what spirituality is, nor how it is to be treated. We thought in the 1970s that everyone accepted the perennial philosophy: there was really only one spiritual journey, even if people used different names to describe it. But in recent times this has been challenged, particularly by Jorge Ferrer of the California Institute of Integral Psychology (e.g. Ferrer, 2001). He has brought up huge academic batteries of argument to prove that the perennial philosophy is wrong. I have in fact engaged in wordy battles with him in the British Psychological Society's *Transpersonal Psychology Review* on this very point. But this is a contested area, and the final shape of the understanding of spirituality is still to come.

Recent work that is relevant to all this includes the Wiley-Blackwell *Handbook of Transpersonal Psychology* (ed. Friedman & Hartelius, 2013), a striking compendium of research and comment; the *Handbook of Dialogical Self Theory* (Hermans & Gieser, 2012), which has a chapter from me; my own book *Personification: Using the Dialogical Self in Counselling and Psychotherapy* (Rowan, 2010) which completely updates and critiques the notion of subpersonalities; and my chapter on Primal Integration in *The Beginner's Guide to Counselling and Psychotherapy* (Palmer, 2015). The rapprochement between Humanistic and Transpersonal Psychology, it seems to me, goes on apace, and I for one welcome this very much.

In view of all this, how can we regain our optimism? I do not have the answer. But I do have the question, and perhaps questions are more important than answers. Certainly, they are more stimulating and more full of the divine dissatisfaction that can lead to new ideas and, as we say, new vistas.

Recently I have been working on a new development of Humanistic Psychology, where we throw open our arms and embrace the existential, the authentic, the relational and the transpersonal. This is now fully written up in the third edition of my book *The Reality Game* (Rowan, 2016). In writing the index I was struck by how many references there are to different aspects of the self, and it came home to me that Humanistic Psychology is the only discipline that has much to say about the self. Such concepts as self-actualization, the real self, the false self, the self-image, the higher self and so forth are meat and drink to us, but apparently not of much interest to anyone else. This is, in my view, quite remarkable, because what is closer to us than our own selves? And of course there is a good deal in the book about my more recent discovery of the dialogical self, which seems to me one of the great leaps forward of the last twenty years. Of course it is quite close to the earlier idea of subpersonalities, but it is much better researched, and in many countries. And it can cope much better with the transpersonal, as I have explained in my 2010 book (Rowan, 2010). All in all, I think these are exciting times for Humanistic Psychology, which shows no signs of lying down and being absorbed by the mainstream. We are different, and we acclaim the difference.

References

Cooper, M. (2003) *Existential Therapies*, London: Sage.

Cooper, M. (2008) *Essential Research Findings in Counselling and Psychotherapy: The Facts are Friendly*, London: Sage.

Curtis, R.C. & Hirsch, I. (2011) 'Relational psychoanalytic psychotherapy', in S.B. Messer & A.S. Jurman (eds), *Essential Psychotherapies: Theory and Practice*, 3rd edn (pp. 72–104), New York: Guilford Press.

Ferrer, J.N. (2001) *Revisioning Transpersonal Theory: A Participatory Vision of Human Spirituality*, Albany, NY: State University of New York Press.

Friedman, H.L. & Hartelius, G. (eds) (2013) *The Wiley-Blackwell Handbook of Transpersonal Psychology*, Chichester: Wiley Blackwell.

Hermans, H.J.M. & Gieser, T. (eds) (2012) *Handbook of Dialogical Self Theory*, Cambridge: Cambridge University Press.

Maslow, A. (1994) 'Self-actualizing and beyond', in *The Farther Reaches of Human Nature* (pp. 40–54), New York: Arkana/Penguin.

Palmer, S. (ed.) (2015) *The Beginner's Guide to Counselling and Psychotherapy*, 2nd edn, London: Sage.

Rowan, J. (2002) 'Existential analysis and humanistic psychotherapy', in K.J. Schneider, J.F.T. Bugental, & J.F. Pierson (eds), *The Handbook of Humanistic Psychology: Leading Edges in Theory, Research, and Practice* (pp. 447–64), Thousand Oaks, CA: Sage.

Rowan, J. (2005) *A Guide to Humanistic Psychology*, 3rd edn, London: Association for Humanistic Psychology in Britain.

Rowan, J. (2010) *Personification: Using the Dialogical Self in Psychotherapy and Counselling*, Hove: Routledge.

Rowan, J (2016) *The Reality Game: A Guide to Humanistic Counselling and Psychotherapy*, 3rd edn, Abingdon: Routledge.

Spinelli, E. (2002) 'A reply to John Rowan', in K.J. Schneider, J.F.T. Bugental, & J.F. Pierson (eds), *The Handbook of Humanistic Psychology: Leading Edges in Theory, Research, and Practice* (pp. 465–71), Thousand Oaks, CA: Sage.

Wilber, K. (2001) *No Boundary: Eastern and Western Approaches to Personal Growth*, Boston, MA: Shambhala.

20

FROM HUMANISM TO HUMANISTIC PSYCHOLOGY AND BACK AGAIN

Keith Tudor

Introduction

This chapter reviews the origins of 'Humanistic Psychology' and critiques the view that it represents a 'third force' in psychology as, in philosophical terms, a 'category error'. The chapter argues that it is clearer and more congruent for practitioners who identify as 'humanistic' to return to principles and theories of humanism which underpin diverse psychological and therapeutic practice that might encompass working with unconscious as well as conscious material, the dynamics of the psyche, and working both cognitively and behaviourally. In doing so, the chapter contributes to the philosophical discourse of the book, and aims to appeal also to practitioners who might practise other approaches, such as psychodynamic therapy, but who regard themselves as humanists.

Personal background

Sometime in the early 1980s, I remember discussing with a fellow political activist our different experiences of therapy and our mutual interest to train in psychotherapy. As someone who had enjoyed a liberal upbringing and education, and was then actively involved in libertarian socialist politics, I was drawn to gestalt and to transactional analysis (TA) which, I then understood, were forms of therapy in the humanistic 'school' or tradition. Interestingly, my friend, who was involved in a Trotskyist socialist group which was more focused on the political party than class or movement, went on to train as a psychoanalyst – and, gradually and unfortunately, we parted company.

Although much of my training was framed as 'humanistic', it clearly drew on a number of ideas, concepts and practices from psychoanalysis which, historically, is viewed as the 'first force' of psychology (Freud's first paper on psychoanalysis was published in 1896), and behaviourism, the 'second force' (Watson's article 'Psychology as the behaviorist views it', which has been referred to as the behaviourist manifesto, was published in 1913). (Sutich (1968) has 'positivistic or behavioristic theory' as the first force, and 'classical psychoanalytical theory' as the second force.) This sense that humanistic therapies drew on, came from and, indeed, represented aspects of other traditions or forces was epitomized for me when, some years later (in 1999), when I was applying for full membership of the UK Association of Humanistic Psychology Practitioners (AHPP) as a Group Psychotherapist (an accreditation I maintained for some ten years), I met at my interview John Rowan, whose first question to me was, 'How come you think TA is a humanistic psychotherapy?' I responded robustly, and my successful interview and application was the beginning of a happy association and identification with the AHPP.

Organization, argument and terms

For many years, the three forces of psychology have been a major organizing principle, and while, these days, the term 'force' is rarely used in this context, these traditions or approaches have informed both the literature in the field of psychology, psychotherapy, counselling and counselling psychology and the organization of the profession, e.g. the United Kingdom Council for Psychotherapy (UKCP) and its Colleges (formerly Sections). They have, however, also led to 'turf wars' based on theoretical orientation or modality whereby, for instance, practitioners from one particular theoretical orientation have been excluded from placements and employment by practitioners from another. As I have trained, worked, reflected, read and written, I have become increasingly sceptical that the three 'forces' are so clearly differentiated as such (see Hinshelwood, in Rowan & Hinshelwood, 1987) or, more fundamentally, that they are, or represent, the same category of things.

Following some brief comments on the history of Humanistic Psychology, and on differences and similarities, I put forward the argument that viewing Humanistic Psychology as a third force is, in philosophical terms, a category error, and that therapists – and clients – would benefit from those 'humanistic' practitioners who identify as such being clearer about the philosophy or philosophies, including humanism, that underpin and inform their practice – which may be psychodynamic (if not psychoanalytic) and/or behavioural.

As a field and a discipline, 'psychology' is, of course, wider than its clinical or therapeutic applications. In this chapter, as I am predominantly concerned with humanistic counselling, psychotherapy, and counselling psychology, I use the term 'humanistic therapies' to encompass these therapeutic fields and activities; and reserve the term 'Humanistic Psychology' to when I refer to the history and background to my present concerns or to other authors' use of the term. The same logic, of course, also applies to therapies rooted in the other forces; thus it is more accurate to refer to 'psychoanalytic therapies' (from psychoanalysis) and 'behavioural therapies' (from behaviourism).

A brief history

Humanistic Psychology has commonly been referred to as 'third force' psychology. This phrase goes back to the early 1960s when the (then) American Association for Humanistic Psychology (AAHP) reported what it sought to represent:

> Humanistic Psychology may be defined as the third branch of the general field of psychology (the two already in existence being the psychoanalytic and the behaviorist) and as such, is primarily concerned with those human capacities and potentialities that have little or no systematic place, either in positivist or behaviorist theory or in classical psychoanalytic theory.
>
> *(Sutich, 1962)*

The background to the foundation of the AHPP was the fact that in the 1950s, a number of psychologists, most notably Abraham Maslow, were finding it difficult to get published, due to the dominance in psychology of behaviourism. In response to this, Maslow began to contact other like-minded psychologists and, in 1954, compiled a mailing list of about 125 people with a view to exchanging papers. In the early 1960s the individuals on this list became the first subscribers to the *Journal of Humanistic Psychology* (see DeCarvalho, 1990; and, for the history of Humanistic Psychology in Britain, see Rowan, 2013). Maslow called the list 'the Eupsychian Network' because, as he later reflected (Maslow, 1968: 237):

> All these groups, organizations and journals are interested in helping the individual grow toward fuller humanness, the society grow toward synergy and health, and all societies and all peoples move toward becoming one world and one species. This list can be called a network because the memberships overlap and because these organizations and individuals more or less share the humanistic and transhumanistic outlook on life.

DeCarvalho (1990) has dated the emergence of Humanistic Psychology as a 'third force' in American psychology to November 1964, when a conference was held in a small country inn in Old Saybrook, Connecticut, attended by George Allport, Jacques Barzun, James Bugental, Charlotte Bühler, George Kelly, Robert Knapp (chair), Abraham Maslow, Rollo May, Carl Moustakas, Gardner Murphy, Henry Murray, Carl Rogers, and others.

Third-force psychology has a rich and complex history (see DeCarvalho, 1990, 1991; Moss, 1999; Schneider, Bugental & Pierson, 2001; Cain, 2001), not least as Humanistic Psychology in America and in Britain draws on different views of philosophical traditions and, specifically, existentialism, and thus has different flavours. One aspect of the history of Humanistic Psychology which is particularly significant for this present discussion is that it began as a 'discontent', especially with behaviourism, and as an alternative, both to psychoanalysis and to behaviourism. As DeCarvalho (1990) has noted, 'At first . . . the AHPP was little more than a protest group. Its early organizational meetings were colored by a deep dissatisfaction with and rebellion against behaviourism' (p. 28).

The fact that, in the early days of this association, there was a distinct group that wanted and tended to define Humanistic Psychology in terms of what it did not stand for has left us, well, 'third'! One example of this was published in the first number of the (American) Association of Humanistic Psychology (AHP)'s *Newsletter*:

> If you are dissatisfied with a psychology that views man as a composite of part functions, a psychology whose model of science is taken over from physics, and whose model of a practitioner is taken from medicine – and you want to do something to change this state of affairs, fill out this application.
>
> *(AHP, 1963: 3)*

Despite the fact that, over the years, humanistic therapies have presented themselves more positively, I think this early sense of identity in opposition has left a certain legacy and, if you like, an organizational psychology of opposition and, to a certain extent, marginality. One still current example of this is that, despite outcome research in therapy which demonstrates parity between approaches, for instance, cognitive behavioural and person-centred approaches, such evidence has little or no impact on state funding of therapy which tends to favour and privilege cognitive behaviour therapy.

Claims and territory, roots and branches

As Humanistic Psychology became more confident, it began to claim its distinctiveness. Thus, Sutich (1962) suggested that Humanistic Psychology was humanistic because it derived from values and ideas such as:

> love, creativity, self, growth, organism, basic need-gratification, self-actualization, higher values, being, becoming, spontaneity, play, humor, affection, naturalness, warmth, ego-transcendence, objectivity, autonomy, responsibility, meaning, fair play, transcendental experience, psychological health, and related concepts.

Some 30 years later, the AHPP suggested that humanist practitioners share certain fundamental core beliefs about:

- The theory of human nature and of self – that the individual is unique, truth-seeking, an integrated and self-regulating whole, with a right to autonomy with responsibility.
- The aims of therapy and of growth – which is self-awareness and actualization, which, in turn, includes: wholeness and completion, authenticity, emotional competence, the furtherance of creativity, respect for difference, and integrity and autonomy while acknowledging interdependence.

- The nature of the therapeutic relationship – as the primary agent of change, and founded on the therapist's genuineness, empathy, openness, honesty, and non-judgemental acceptance of the client (see AHPP, 2009 [1998]).

While I do not disagree with this 'core', I am always struck by how often authors and practitioners who are secular, and even atheist, use the word 'belief' to describe fundamental principles or values.

In a more detailed contribution, Cain (2001) identified a number of characteristics which, he asserted, define humanistic psychotherapies. With regard to views of the person, these are:

- That she or he is self-aware, free to choose, and responsible.
- That she or he is holistic – 'The person is viewed *holistically*, as an indivisible, interrelated organism who cannot be reduced to the sum of his or her parts' (ibid.: 5) – and as embodied, and contextual beings.
- That she or he needs to make sense and find meaning, and to construe her or his realities.
- That she or he has a capacity for creativity.
- That, as primarily social beings, we have a powerful need to belong.

Cain also discussed the importance in humanistic psychotherapies of: the actualizing tendency, a relational emphasis, phenomenology, empathy, the concept of 'the self' (which, in my view, is often unthinkingly and uncritically reified as 'the Self'), and anxiety.

Such claims and lists, however, imply that neither psychoanalysis nor behaviourism (nor psychoanalysts or behaviourists) hold these beliefs and views – which, simply, is not true. In his correspondence with John Rowan, Hinshelwood (Rowan & Hinshelwood, 1987: 143) wrote that 'I am not sure that you are altogether correct in implying such a radical division between psychoanalysis and humanistic psychotherapy', adding that: 'The act of appropriating the term "humanistic" for one sector of psychotherapy is itself a little provocative'. I have some sympathy with Hinshelwood's objection as, similarly, I object to the kind of territorialism that is implied by 'cognitive behaviour therapy', as if no other therapies are cognitive or behavioural – for a critique of which and a response to which, see Tudor (2008a).

Such claims and divisions also ignore history. John Rowan's question to me about TA was, in part, probably based on his understanding of the centrality in TA of ego state theory, which derives from Federn's ego psychology, which, in turn, has its roots in psychoanalysis. Not many people would see any link between contemporary person-centred approaches and classical psychoanalysis, and yet Carl Rogers, who was influenced by Otto Rank (see Kramer, 1995), is only two degrees of separation from Sigmund Freud; and, while Rogers' (1942) 'newer psychotherapy' is a long way from Freud's psychoanalysis, there are elements of psychodynamic thinking in Rogers' theory, especially his concepts of defences, i.e. denial and distortion. While I agree with Rowan (in Rowan & Hinshelwood, 1987; Rowan, 2001) that there are roots of humanistic and certainly transpersonal psychotherapy that are independent of psychoanalysis, when humanistic psychotherapists are tracing their therapeutic lineage, both theoretically and personally (in terms of the influence of their therapists and supervisors and *their* therapists and supervisors, and so on), thereby acknowledging what Traue (1990/2001) has referred to as 'ancestors of the mind', most of us would be only a few handshakes away from the Viennese Doctor. (I myself am personally only three handshakes away from Sigmund Freud, via my Godmother, Margaret Proctor, who met Anna Freud; and, professionally, four degrees away, via Natalie Rogers, from Carl Rogers and Otto Rank.)

It is worth noting that Maslow (1962), who coined the phrase 'third force' psychology, described Humanistic Psychology as 'epi-behavioural' and 'epi-Freudian' (*epi* meaning 'building upon'). Bugental (1964) also did not see Humanistic Psychology as a competitor to the other two 'forces': 'Humanistic psychology generally does not see itself as competitive with the other two orientations; rather, it attempts to supplement their observations and to introduce further perspectives and insights' (p. 22). Similarly, Bühler (1965), an early feminist and one of the largely unacknowledged founders of Humanistic Psychology, wrote: 'Humanistic psychology . . . does not necessarily deny that many accomplishments and creations may be the by-product of procedures meant ultimately to satisfy an ambitious ego and indirectly a pleasure-seeking id' (p. 54).

As Hinshelwood (in Rowan & Hinshelwood, 1987) has observed, the criticism of psychoanalysis in the United States of America by American humanists is somewhat misplaced when translated to Britain – and, for that matter, to other countries in the world. As he put it:

> The character of the British schools of psychoanalysis (like many of the Continental ones) is deeply humanistic and is concerned with the struggling human being, and has left behind all the mechanistic trappings that Freud's nineteenth-century background encumbered him with. . . . The opposition between psychoanalysis and humanistic psychology has so much less relevance over here.
>
> *(p. 144)*

While there are some obvious differences between aspects of psychoanalytic, behavioural and humanistic theories, there are, I would argue, more and significant similarities, especially between 'humanistic' and 'psychoanalytic' traditions (see Tudor, 2010) – and there are certainly differences between and within different humanistic theories, therapies and therapists (on which see, for instance, Mearns and Thorne, 2000). Rowan (in Rowan & Hinshelwood, 1987) identified that the overlap between psychoanalysis and humanistic psychotherapy would include: projection, the importance of countertransference, the emphasis on the therapeutic alliance, and the use of therapy for the therapist. In her excellent article on this theme, Gomez (2004), who describes herself as a humanistic and psychoanalytic psychotherapist, reviewed the respective flag statements of the Analytic Psychology,

Psychoanalytic & Psychodynamic (APPP), and the Humanistic & Integrative (HIP) Sections of the UKCP, and found little to which practitioners from either Section would object. Finally (on this point), there are theoreticians and practitioners who have been very much identified with psychoanalysis, who are writing, as it were, across the divide (see, notably, McWilliams, 2005; Orange, 2010).

The old first, second and third force categorization is simply too general, and too generalized, to be relevant or useful in contemporary debates about psychotherapy and its practice.

Categories

Traditionally, there are five branches of philosophy: metaphysics, which deals with fundamental questions of reality; epistemology, which deals with concepts of knowledge (how we know things); logic, which studies the rules of valid reasoning and argument; ethics or moral philosophy, which is concerned with human values; and aesthetics, which deals with the notion of beauty and the philosophy of art. In logic, there are various rules by which reasoning is said to be valid, or not, and argument judged to be sound, or not. The term 'category mistake' or 'category error' is a mistake or error about ontology (the essence of things) or about semantics (meaning). For example, to claim that most readers of this book are humanists might or might not be true; it is not a category error since it could be contingently the case. On the other hand, to claim that most apples are humanists would be to make a category error since apples belong to a category of things that cannot be said to have beliefs or values. Although there are debates within philosophy about the enterprise of categorization and the approach to establishing a category error, here I use the concept of category to raise the question: is 'Humanistic Psychology' of the same nature of things as 'psychoanalysis' and/or 'behaviourism' – and, by implication, whether the first two 'forces' are the same category?

The first category error is, then, that the three 'categories', psychoanalysis, behaviourism and Humanistic Psychology (which is generally how the three forces have been named), are not the same order of things. Psychoanalysis, literally the analysis of the psyche, is, fundamentally, a *method* of psychological investigation (through free association and interpretation). The term, however, also refers to a therapeutic technique, which has gone through a series of modifications by Freud himself and others since; and to a body of facts and theories. Behaviourism is an approach to psychology that combines elements of philosophy, methodology and theory. Humanistic Psychology is also an approach to psychology that defines its description of and relation to psychology with reference to humanism, which encompasses a group of philosophies and ethical perspectives that emphasize certain values and the agency of human beings. Earlier, I acknowledged that psychology as a field and a discipline is wider than its clinical or therapeutic applications; this also applies to psychoanalysis and humanism, and these probably more so than behaviourism. If we are referring to three (four, or more) forces of psychology, then this category error is resolved by renaming the forces: psychoanalytic psychology, behavioural psychology, and Humanistic Psychology – with their respective therapies.

In the previous section I quoted Bühler (1965); she continued: 'But humanistic psychology conceives of the human being differently. It conceives of man as living with intentionality, which means as living with purpose' (pp. 54–5) – and, indeed, Bühler herself had advanced a theory of four basic tendencies (Bühler, 1959). My point here is that if 'Humanist Psychology' is different from other forms of psychology by virtue of its conception of human beings, then that is a difference about human nature (see DeCarvalho, 1990) and, more fundamentally, about ontology or the essence of things – differences that are more accurately and better described as *philosophical*, and not *psychological*.

In their work on paradigm analysis, Burrell and Morgan (1979) provided a way of understanding such differences. They identified four assumptions in social science and placed them on a subjective–objective continuum (see Table 20.1). I have added 'method' and changed the order of the terms so that it reads from the bottom (the more fundamental, underlying assumptions) to the top.

Drawing on this work, it seems to me more useful to name differences between practitioners and practice, theories and models as differences of ontology, human nature, etc., than of 'force'.

One reviewer of an earlier draft of this chapter suggested that the commonly held view of the distinctions between the three forces was that

> psychoanalytic psychology is based on a view of the essence of the person as 'basically destructive'; behavioural psychology is based on the view of the essence of the person as 'basically tabula rasa'; and humanistic [psychology] is based on the view of the essence of the person as 'basically intrinsically directional to maintain/enhance itself'.
>
> *(Anon.)*

I think that this is a good summary of what are broad and commonly held differences and, as such, are ontological differences. The problem is that they are too broad and 'common': there are psychoanalytic and behavioural psychologists

TABLE 20.1 The nature of social science (roughly based on Burrell & Morgan, 1979)

The subjectivist approach to social science	Assumptions	The objectivist approach to social science
Qualitative	Method	Quantitative
Ideographic	Methodology	Nomothetic
Anti-positivism	Epistemology	Positivism
Voluntarism	Human nature	Determinism
Nominalism	Ontology	Realism

and therapists who are humanistic in their outlook; there are behavioural psychologists who are very analytic; and there are certainly 'humanist' psychologists and therapists who do not value or support that view that people tend to actualize. The second category error, then, is an error of category: practitioners identify – and are too readily identified – with, in effect, a (one) category, rather than being specific about differences which are ontological, epistemological, methodological and practical. I suggest that this is due, in part, to the fact that training in therapy is still primarily organized with regard to theoretical orientations or modalities and thus engenders a certain conformity and loyalty to the 'brand'; and, in part, due to the paucity of philosophical input in therapy education and training.

To give a theoretical example: the person-centred approach is known for being 'non-directive' and, though there are differences within the approach about this (see Levitt, 2005), this principle and its practice are based on a theory of knowledge that the client 'knows' her or his own direction; as such it is a view that represents an anti-positivist epistemology. Theory and practice that privilege what the practitioner knows and, in effect, tell the client what to do are based on positivist epistemology. Thus, when a person-centred therapist tells a client what to do or how to think, they are committing a category error.

To give a practical and professional example: when I was active in the then Humanistic and Integrative Section (HIPS) of the UKCP, and also as a member of the Institute of Transactional Analysis, I remember great debates about the terms and conditions of personal therapy for training psychotherapists. Due to the fact that some trainees had presented for their qualifying examination without having done sufficient personal therapy, and the realization that some trainers were not taking the existing requirements seriously and, perhaps, more importantly, holding the principles and spirit of the existing requirements with integrity, there was much discussion about the necessity (or otherwise) of further requirements. In the end, the HIPS asserted its position by clarifying its further condition of 40 hours of personal therapy per year (see UKCP HIPS Training Standards Committee, 2003; for further commentary about which, see Tudor, 2008b, 2008c). The HIPS' decision was one clearly based on, in Burrell and Morgan's (1979) terms, a nomothetic or legal methodology. My own view was – and is – that personal therapy is too important to have as a requirement of training, a principle that was embodied in the training philosophy and standards of Temenos, Sheffield (www.temenos.ac.uk), which was, for some years a member organization of the UKCP and its HIP Section/College, and, as such, represents the ideographic end of what might be viewed as a methodological dimension.

If humanistic therapies are claiming, as their fundamental difference with and from the other two forces, that they are based on different philosophical assumptions about various aspects of human nature and our psychology, then it seems more straightforward and honest to claim these as such: as differences of philosophy and not 'force', 'tradition', 'approach', 'school' or 'modality'. By using and claiming the title of a 'force', Humanistic Psychology has – and, more specifically, the humanistic therapies that sit under this umbrella term have, especially with regard to psychoanalysis –

confused *philosophy* (as in humanism and, specifically, with regard to ontology and human nature) with *method* (as in psychoanalysis). In other words, the three 'forces' are not the same category of things, and to present them as such is to commit what, in philosophical terms, is a 'category error'. Rather than assuming a vague humanism about our colleagues' or practitioners' practice – and personally, I have found more humanism in certain psychoanalytic colleagues than in some nomothetic, regulatory members of HIPS – we should be asking the question, 'What is "humanistic" about "Humanistic" Psychology?'

Asking this question, I suggest, leads us to be able to resolve the second error of category by analysing or understanding both genuine differences and genuine similarities between different therapies across all forces, traditions, etc., as a result of which we might draw different conclusions. Gomez, for example, regards (or, at least, in 2004, regarded) herself as a 'humanistic and psychodynamic' practitioner, and I have some sympathy and association with that, in that one can hold broadly humanistic values and work with a psychodynamic or a psychodynamically informed understanding of therapy. Others might be clearer that humanism is fundamentally antithetical to the philosophical traditions on which psychoanalysis and, differently, behaviourism sit. Either way, this clarification, using the kind of paradigm analysis outlined by Burrell and Morgan (1979) (see, for example, Tudor, 1996), and the resulting philosophical congruence between values, theory and practice (see Tudor & Worrall, 2006), is only possible when we are clear about categories (what goes with what) and category errors (i.e. what does not). As Rogers (1957) put it, interestingly in an article he wrote as a comment on a previous article by Walker (1956), comparing Freud's view of the nature of man with his own:

> One cannot engage in psychotherapy without giving operational evidence of an underlying value orientation and view of human nature. It is definitely preferable, in my estimation, that such underlying views be open and explicit, rather than covert and implicit.

> *(p. 199)*

In this sense, it might be helpful for 'humanistic' practitioners or those who identify with this force or tradition of psychology to return to a broader and deeper understanding of humanism. As Heron (2013) put it: 'I think it is more fundamental and fruitfully radical to reconstruct the meaning of "humanism", and thus, by its extension, the meaning of "humanistic".'

Humanism

Humanism has a long history, dating back some seven centuries to Ancient Greece when, according to Cicero, Socrates 'called down Philosophy from heaven to earth' (Enfield, 1837, p. 92). The second of three waves of humanism (identified by Heron, 2013) derives from the umanisti of the late fifteenth century, based especially in Italy, a movement that 'affirmed the dignity and worth of human achievement'

(Heron, 2013, p. 156), and took various forms: Renaissance, secular, religious, inclusive, and even naturalistic, a term and tradition that addresses the criticism that humanism is overly anthropocentric. The third wave, which began with the European Enlightenment of the eighteenth century, represented a more rational, scientific, and secular humanism. To this history, Heron has argued that a fourth wave of humanism is represented by Humanistic Psychology and its developments.

By now, of course, there are many kinds of humanism, which may be defined by category, (literary humanism, Christian humanism, etc.) or by the different people who make different kinds of humanist, e.g., a Christian who is a humanist, an existentialist who is a humanist – as was Jean-Paul Sartre (see Sartre, 1948). While there is no absolute agreement about what humanism is, there are certain values and virtues that are associated with humanism:

- *Openness*: Rogers (1967b [1954]) described openness to experience (or extensionality) as being aware of this existential moment as it is, as one of three significant 'inner conditions' of creativity – and the opposite of psychological defensiveness. In other words, being open is who we are. In terms of the proposed shift from Humanistic Psychology to humanism, I am arguing in support of what some have referred to as 'ontological turn', i.e., a return to matters of and concerns about being and the nature of things. Interestingly, in his fourth wave account of Humanistic Psychology, Heron (2013) described it as being distinguished by a number of characteristics, including that of being 'ontologically holistic' (p. 166). In his book on humanism Blackham (1968) referred to 'the political philosophy of humanism' as being encapsulated in the concept of the 'open society' (see also Popper, 1945). For Blackham, 'The open society is not a womb .... It is not a family .... It is not a barracks .... *It is a grown-up bargaining affair*; interdependence is not dependence' (p. 63; my emphasis). Later, in discussing humanist virtues and values, Blackham argued that 'open' is a key word: 'to the open mind and the open society might well be added the open heart and the open hand' (p. 80).
- *Contextual*: In humanistic literature the word 'person' often appears in a particular plural form, i.e., 'persons', a convention that acknowledges the plural and contextual nature of the person. As Heron (2013) has put it: 'The "personal" ... always refers to a person in their local and wider eco-system, including all other forms of life' (p. 159). As advocates of humanity, humanists tend to be interested in others, and, historically, have articulated this in thinking about what it is to be human, and what constitute human rights, which as Heron has argued 'is rooted in an extended doctrine of rights with regard to social and ecological liberation' (p. 167).
- *Personal*: Humanism emphasizes that our reality is personal, not impersonal, a perspective that is well represented by Rogers' (1967a [1953]) famous assertion that 'What is most personal is most general' (p. 26). This reflects an emphasis on the authority of experience and on subjective knowledge – to which, in the spirit of being plural and relational, I would add intersubjective knowledge.

Reclaiming personal and interpersonal knowledge and the value of reflecting on and researching that knowledge is especially important as humanism and humanistic forms of research are under attack from postmodernism and other 'post' perspectives (poststructuralism, postfeminism, postcolonialiam, etc.) (see Adams St. Pierre, 2014).

- *Critical*: The origins of humanism, and of each wave of humanism, were based on and in some critique of the existing order, and, historically, usually the supernatural or superordinate order. Elsewhere (Tudor, 2015), I have written about Humanistic Psychology representing a critical counter culture with regard to the dominant theoretical cultures in psychology. As a methodology and method, I view critique as a product of what Blackham (1968) described as 'the open mind', i.e., 'a dedication to a disinterested search for truth' (p. 27). Indeed, Blackham viewed humanism itself as 'a practical personal inquiry into ways of being human' (p. 83). Thinking about this in terms of research, in the face of the dominant empirical (and pseudo empirical) paradigm in psychological and other fields, it is clear that we need a strong articulation of humanism to inform future research methodology and method (see Elkins, 2009).

I suggest that these values and virtues or perspectives represent, respectively, the ontology of humanism, the humanistic perspective on human nature, the epistemology of humanism, and the methodology of humanism, on which rests a variety of methods or practice in psychology as well as in other disciplines.

Conclusion

Clearly, Humanistic Psychology is an important part of our history, and I am proud to be associated with it and, not least, as an Associate Editor of the journal *Self & Society: International Journal of Humanistic Psychology*. Clearly, Humanistic Psychology as a third force has, and humanistic therapies have had, a crucial role in broadly humanizing psychology and psychotherapy, akin perhaps to an extra parliamentary political party: it has challenged the first two forces of psychology, especially with regard to their (implicit) values and the underlying assumptions of their theories and practices. It has been hugely successful in a number of ways:

- It is a recognized 'force' or tradition with a number of 'schools', 'modalities' or 'approaches', including: arts therapies; bioenergetics and other forms of body psychotherapy; co-counselling; creative and expressive therapies; encounter; experiential therapy; feminist therapy; gestalt therapy; the person-centred approach; primal integration; psychodrama; psychosynthesis and other trans-personal approaches; transactional analysis; and many others – and, of course, some of these would also identify with, or with aspects of, the other two forces.
- It has well-established training courses and programmes, from the first one established in 1966 in the Psychology Department of Sonoma State College, to others at West Georgia College and the Humanistic Psychology Institute,

San Francisco, and many others since (see DeCarvalho, 1990); and, of course, other training courses and programmes in the modalities noted above.

- It has been the subject of a number of publications with regard to Humanistic Psychology and its therapies (see, for example, May et al., 1986; DeCarvalho, 1991; Moss, 1999; Rowan, 2001; Cain and Seeman, 2001; Schneider et al., 2001; Whitton, 2003), as well as of numerous publications about its various modalities; and has given birth to three professional journals: in the USA, the *Journal of Humanistic Psychology* (from 1961) and *The Humanistic Psychologist* (from 1973), and in Britain, *Self & Society* (also from 1973).
- It has a presence in organizations, including, significantly, as a Division (32) in the American Psychology Association, and as a College of the UKCP.

We can – and should – take enormous confidence from this. Eight years ago, I and my family emigrated from the UK to Aotearoa New Zealand. As part of settling into our new professional home, both I and my wife, Louise Embleton Tudor, presented papers to colleagues (Tudor, 2010; Embleton Tudor, 2010). Having heard both talks, one colleague came up to me and said: 'You know, one thing that strikes me about you and Louise is that neither of you are apologetic for not being Freudian.' I thought this was an interesting comment, not only about us and, no doubt, him, but also about the dominance, or perceived dominance, of psychoanalytic thinking. My colleague is correct in that I am not apologetic for not being Freudian, although, following Maslow, I would claim to be epi-Freudian!

In so far as Humanistic Psychology arose as a 'third force' in some way to act, one might say (somewhat mischievously) as a corrective organizational or philosophical experience to its two older 'brothers', it has made its presence felt: 'Humanistic Psychology' or, perhaps, more accurately and robustly, humanistic therapies are here to stay; it is, in many respects, mainstream and institutional, if not institutionalized (see DeCarvalho, 1990). Perhaps now it is established and confident enough to regard itself not simply or merely as a 'third', but as representing, at best, a philosophy (humanism) in clinical practice (see Tudor and Worrall, 2006). In this sense, it is time that Humanistic Psychology looked forward. Whether we like it or not, too often we are associated with the 1960s and our language and ideas viewed as dated; at the same time, some of our ideas, such as those about the primacy of the relationship, have been appropriated. To some extent I think we need to refute these projections, and (re)claim our history, but, equally, we need to engage in contemporary psychological discourse, and to reach wider and newer audiences. This chapter is part of this project, arguing that we need to go back in order to go forward. Thus, I would argue that as a third force, 'Humanistic Psychology' is dead; long live humanism!

References

Adams St. Pierre, E. (2014) *Journal of Curriculum Theorizing*, 30(2): 2–19.
Association of Humanistic Psychology (1963) *Newsletter, No. 1.*
Association of Humanistic Psychology Practitioners (2009) *UKAHPP core beliefs statement*; document available online at: www.ahpp.org.uk/core-beliefs (accessed 12 April 2017) (original work published in 1998).

Blackham. H.J. (1968) *Humanism*, London: Penguin.

Bugental, J.F.T. (1964) 'The third force in psychology', *Journal of Humanistic Psychology*, 4(1): 19–26.

Bühler, C. (1959) 'Theoretical observations about life's basic tendencies', *American Journal of Psychotherapy*, 13(3): 501–81.

Bühler, C. (1965) 'Some observations on the psychology of the third force', *Journal of Humanistic Psychology*, 5: 54–5.

Burrell, G. & Morgan, G. (1979) *Sociological Paradigms and Organisational Analysis*, London: Heinemann.

Cain, D.J. (2001) 'Defining characteristics, history, and evolution of humanistic psychotherapies', in D.J. Cain & J. Seeman (eds), *Humanistic Psychotherapies: Handbook of Research and Practice* (pp. 3–54), Washington, DC: American Psychological Association.

Cain, D.J. & Seeman, J. (eds) (2001) *Humanistic Psychotherapies: Handbook of Research and Practice*, Washington, DC: American Psychological Association.

DeCarvalho, R.J. (1990) 'A history of the "third force" in psychology', *Journal of Humanistic Psychology*, 30: 22–44.

DeCarvalho, R.J. (1991) *The Founders of Humanistic Psychology*, New York: Praeger.

Elkins, D. (2009) *Humanistic Psychology: A Clinical Manifesto. A Critique of Clinical Psychology and the Need for Progressive Alternatives*, Colorado Springs, CO: Universities of the Rockies Press.

Embleton Tudor, L. (2010) 'Dissociation: a fragile process', talk given to the New Zealand Association of Psychotherapists (Northern Branch) meeting, Auckland, Aotearoa New Zealand, 9 September.

Enfield, W. (1837) *The History of Philosophy*, London: Tegg & Son.

Freud, S. (1962) 'The aetiology of hysteria', in *The Standard Edition of the Complete Psychological Works of Sigmund Freud* (Vol. 3, pp. 191–221; J. Strachey, ed. & trans.), London: Hogarth. (original work published in 1896).

Gomez, L. (2004) 'Humanistic or psychodynamic: what is the difference and do we have to make a choice?', *Self & Society*, 31(6): 5–19.

Heron, J. (2013). 'Humanism: The fourth wave', in R. House, D. Kalisch, & J. Maidman (eds), *The Future of Humanistic Psychology* (pp. 156–68). Ross-on-Wye: PCCS Books.

Kramer, R. (1995) 'The birth of client-centered therapy: Carl Rogers, Otto Rank, and "The Beyond"', *Journal of Humanistic Psychology*, 35(4): 54–110.

Levitt, B.E. (2005) *Embracing Non-Directivity: Reassessing Person-Centered Theory and Practice in the 21st Century*, Ross-on-Wye: PCCS Books.

McWilliams, N. (2005) 'Preserving our humanity as therapists', *Psychotherapy: Theory, Research, Practice, Training*, 42(2): 139–51.

Maslow, A.H. (1962) *Toward a Psychology of Being*, New York: Van Nostrand.

Maslow, A.H. (1968) *Toward a Psychology of Being*, 2nd edn, New York: Van Nostrand Reinhold.

May, A.H., Rogers, C.R., Maslow, A.H., et al. (1986) *Politics and Innocence: A Humanistic Debate*, Dallas, TX: Saybrook Publishers.

Mearns, D. & Thorne, B. (2000) *Person-Centred Therapy Today: New Frontiers in Theory and Practice*, London: Sage.

Moss, D. (1999) *Humanistic and Transpersonal Psychology: A Historical and Biographical Sourcebook*, Westport, CT: Greenwood Press.

Orange, D.M. (2010) *Thinking for Clinicians: Philosophical Resources for Contemporary Psychoanalysis and the Humanistic Psychotherapies*, New York: Routledge.

Popper, K. (1945). *The Open Society and its Enemies* (2 volumes). London: Routledge.

Rogers, C.R. (1942) *Counseling and Psychotherapy: Newer Concepts in Practice*, Boston, MA: Houghton Mifflin.

Rogers, C.R. (1957) 'A note on "The nature of man"', *Journal of Counseling Psychology*, 4(3): 199–203.

Rogers, C.R. (1967a) 'This is me', in *On Becoming a Person* (pp. 3–27), London: Constable (original work published 1953).

Rogers, C.R. (1967b) 'Toward a theory of creativity', in *On Becoming a Person* (pp. 347–59), London: Constable (original work published 1954).

Rowan, J. (2001) *Ordinary Ecstasy: The Dialectics of Humanistic Psychology*, 3rd edn, London: Routledge.

Rowan, J. (2013) 'Early days in humanistic and transpersonal psychology', *Self & Society: International Journal for Humanistic Psychology*, 40(2): 47–57.

Rowan, J. & Hinshelwood, B. (1987) 'Is psychoanalysis humanistic? A correspondence between John Rowan and Bob Hinshelwood', *British Journal of Psychotherapy*, 4(2): 14–27.

Sartre, J.-P. (1948) *Existentialism and Humanism* (P. Mairet, trans.), London: Methuen.

Schneider, K.J., Bugental, J.F.T., & Pierson, J.F. (2001) *The Handbook of Humanistic Psychology: Leading Edges in Theory, Research and Practice*, Thousand Oaks, CA: Sage.

Sutich, A.J. (1962) *American Association of Humanistic Psychology: Progress Report*, Palo Alto, CA: AAHP, 1 November.

Sutich, A.J. (1968) 'Transpersonal psychology: an emerging force', *Journal of Humanistic Psychology*, 8: 77–8.

Traue, J.E. (2001) 'Ancestors of the mind: a pakeha whakapapa', in R. Brown (ed.), *The Great New Zealand Argument: Ideas about Ourselves* (pp. 137–47), Auckland, Aotearoa New Zealand: Activity Press (original work published in 1990).

Tudor, K. (1996) 'Transactional analysis intragration: a metatheoretical analysis for practice', *Transactional Analysis Journal*, 26: 329–40.

Tudor, K. (2008a) 'Person-centred therapy, a cognitive behavioural therapy', in R. House & D. Loewenthal (eds), *Against and For CBT: Towards a Constructive Dialogue?* (pp. 118–36), Ross-on-Wye: PCCS Books.

Tudor, K. (2008b) 'To be or not to be in personal therapy, that is the question. Part I', *ITA News*, 35(1): 3–8.

Tudor, K. (2008c) 'To be or not to be in personal therapy, that is the question. Part II', *ITA News*, 36(1): 3–7.

Tudor, K. (2010) 'Building bridges across troubled waters: regarding humanistic and psychodynamic psychotherapies', *Forum* [The Journal of the New Zealand Association of Psychotherapists], 15: 8–25.

Tudor, K. (2015) 'Humanistic psychology: a critical counter culture', in I. Parker (ed.), *Handbook of Critical Psychology* (pp. 127–36), London: Routledge.

Tudor, K. & Worrall, M. (2006) *Person-Centred Therapy: A Clinical Philosophy*, London: Routledge.

United Kingdom Council for Psychotherapy Humanistic and Integrative Psychotherapy Section Training Standards Committee (2003, May) Personal Therapy Requirements [document]. London: UKCP.

Walker, D.E. (1956) 'Carl Rogers and the nature of man', *Journal of Counseling Psychology*, 3(1): 89–92.

Watson, J.B. (1913) 'Psychology as the behaviorist views it', *Psychological Review*, 20: 158–77.

Whitton, E. (2003) *Humanistic Approach to Psychotherapy*, London: Whurr.

21

ON THE FUTURE OF HUMANISTIC PSYCHOLOGY

Possible avenues for exploration

Robin Shohet

In this brief chapter I am describing my four current interests in psychology/ spirituality. These are forgiveness, the effects of shock, the future of the planet, and non-duality, or questioning the existence of a separate 'I'. Obviously these are huge topics and I do no more than touch on them, but I think each can have a place in the future of Humanistic Psychology.

Having been associated with Humanistic Psychology for 35 years, I was delighted to be asked to write something on this theme. The topic of the 'Future of Humanistic Psychology' is quite a daunting one. I barely know my own future for the coming months, so I have decided to describe some of my interests and hypothesize why they might be relevant.

The first is forgiveness. I ran a forgiveness conference at Findhorn in 1999, and another in 2013. As part of my research I came across a short article in which the author described how the future of humanity depended on forgiveness. This was not just his or her opinion – computer programmes had been run which said that the biggest danger to humanity was, in fact, the cycles of revenge that seemed to have been going since 'the year dot', but now the weaponry was so powerful that the danger was not localized.

The second topic that I think bears study is shock. I am in the middle of a book called *We Are All in Shock* by Stephanie Mines (2003). The title speaks for itself. My belief is that an inability to forgive reflects an inability to let go. What makes it so difficult to let go is partly shock. The whole body/mind system has contracted, and before it can loosen itself, the need for safety is paramount. And the world in many ways is less safe (although we should not exaggerate this – if we think of illness, mortality rates, world wars even as little as 60 years ago); what I think has happened is that our expectations have increased, so that the world feels less safe. Humanistic Psychology with a focus on bodywork would seem to play an important part in helping the release of shock. And this will open up the possibility of forgiveness.

The third area relates to the future of the planet. It would appear that we are fast running out of resources – well I do not need to go into detail. About 20 years ago I wrote an article called 'How green is your mind?' In it I asked the reader to imagine that they were a car and that their mind was the exhaust. Every time they had a negative thought, any negative thought, they would be polluting the planet. In other words, I put the responsibility for pollution not on to managing resources or global warming, but on the way our minds work, on the way we do not recognize our interdependence, how we create separation, and in doing so increase fear, which stresses our adrenals, making us more likely both to be shocked and to stay shocked. The Upanishads have a saying: 'Where there is another there is fear.' What I think they mean is that if I see you as separate, then you are potentially a threat. If I come from seeing you as connected, then even if it does not appear like it, we are on the same side, and just holding that possibility makes it more likely to happen. You cannot be green and have vengeful thoughts. And so connecting back to Humanistic Psychology, mindfulness, the work of such people as Eckhart Tolle seems very relevant.

My final strand is the field of non-duality, there being no separate 'I'. This is commonly associated with Buddhism, but I came across it through the Hindu path of Advaita Vedanta. In truth the non-dual approach transcends all approaches and paths. Teachers in this field include the great Indian sage Ramana Maharshi, and more recently Jeff Foster, Byron Katie, Roger Linden, Jac O'Keeffe (these can all be found by googling Conscious TV). Ramana Maharshi used to describe this approach as using a thorn to get out another thorn – using mind to go beyond mind. And this idea is quite radical for the future of Humanistic Psychology – using it to go beyond it, to question the existence of the separate 'I' is to question the need for a psychology of it. This is a huge topic, one worthy of a book in its own right, I think.

As I finished writing this chapter I was teaching a module on a supervision course, and I revisited John Rowan's *The Reality Game*, written in 1983. John was very instrumental in helping to spread Humanistic Psychology in Britain, and the book has a timeless simplicity in explaining some of the core concepts. I strongly recommend it. It is good to see that even though Humanistic Psychology might have grown and changed and will continue to do so, the foundations seem as sound to me now as they did all those years ago.

References

Mines, S. (2003) *We Are All in Shock: How Overwhelming Experiences Shatter You . . . And What You Can Do About It*, Pompton Plains, NJ: New Page Books.

Rowan, J. (1983) *The Reality Game: A Guide to Humanistic Counselling and Therapy*, London: Routledge & Kegan Paul (2nd edn, 1998).

22

HUMANISTIC PSYCHOLOGY

Possible ways forward

Windy Dryden

Introduction

In this chapter I outline and discuss four tasks with which I would like to see this therapeutic tradition engage, the purpose of which would be the strengthening of Humanistic Psychology: (a) carry out an inventory of strengths and weaknesses; (b) publish up-to-date texts on Humanistic Psychology; (c) consider whether or not to align with pluralistic developments in the field; and (d) engage with reality.

I am perhaps known as a practitioner within the Cognitive Behaviour Therapy (CBT) tradition and, thus, it might seem strange at first glance to find me writing about the future of Humanistic Psychology. Actually, it is not that strange. I have quite an affinity with humanistic therapy dating back to 1975 when I did the one-year full-time Diploma in Counselling in Educational Settings course at Aston University, the core theoretical model of which was client-centred therapy.[1] In retrospect, I was far more drawn to client-centred theory than I was to client-centred practice, which I found quite restricting and with which I did not resonate as a person. So I embarked upon an exploration of other approaches, and settled on what is now known as Rational Emotive Behaviour Therapy (REBT), which enabled me to be more active as a practitioner, but which was also rooted in a humanistic approach that encourages unconditional acceptance of self, others and the world (Ellis, 1973).

Having established my credentials, let me modify the task I have been given before I engage with it. I was originally invited to speculate on the future of Humanistic Psychology. My reaction to doing this was the same as my reaction to doing something similar for my recently published book on different CBT approaches (Dryden, 2012).[2] In the preface of that book I said the following:

> I was tempted to write a concluding chapter in the current volume speculating on the likely future direction of CBT. I have resisted this

temptation for one major reason. There was no way Bill Golden and I could have foreseen the developments that have taken place in CBT in Britain and in the world over the 25 years since the original book was published. Should I be around to edit this book again in 25 years' time (I will be 86 then!), then my guess is that CBT, as it exists then, will be as unrecognisable to me now as CBT now would have been to Bill and I back then.

(Dryden, 2012: xiii)

As I write (November 2016), Donald J. Trump has just won the vote to be the next President of the United States of America. Who could have predicted that even a year ago? This brings home to me the futility of trying to predict the future.

So rather than speculating on the future of Humanistic Psychology, let me outline a number of tasks with which I would like to see this therapeutic tradition engage – with the purpose of such engagement being the strengthening of Humanistic Psychology. Actually, a lot of what I have to say has been said by Nick Totton in his excellent book entitled *The Problem with the Humanistic Therapies* (Totton, 2010).

Carry out an inventory of strengths and weaknesses

In order to move forward, it would be useful if there were broad consistency about the strengths and weaknesses of Humanistic Psychology. Although not himself a humanistic practitioner, Totton (2010) outlined his view of the strengths and weakness of this therapeutic tradition. These are outlined in Table 22.1. This list might be a good place to begin the dialogue among practitioners of Humanistic Psychology, although as can be seen, each strength can be viewed as a weakness and vice versa, depending on one's point of view.

TABLE 22.1 Strengths and weaknesses of Humanistic Psychology (adapted from Totton 2010)

Strengths	*Weaknesses*
Takes a positive view of human nature	Demonstrates a Pollyanna complex
Focuses on growth, not cure	Tends to deny pathology
Empowers clients	Gives undue responsibility to clients
Adopts a style which is closer to ordinary communicating	Misses transferential issues
Adopts a contactful way of relating	Has boundary problems
Is spontaneous and improvising	Glorifies impulsiveness
Demonstrates a positive attitude to embodiment, to emotions	Has a negative attitude to rationality and theory
Demonstrates a positive attitude to spirituality	Is prone to mysticism and 'uplift'
Offers an inherent social critique	Is out of the mainstream
Favours an experiential paradigm of practice and research	Is weak on research

It might be that humanistic therapists may come up with a different set of strengths and weaknesses, and might well regard what Totton sees as weaknesses as misconceptions about the humanistic tradition. That is not the point. Developing an agreed list of strengths and weaknesses will lead the humanistic field to capitalize on the former, and mobilize its resources to deal in an orchestrated way with the latter.

Publish up-to-date texts on Humanistic Psychology

While preparing the original draft of this chapter, I asked for reading suggestions from the book's co-editor Richard House, and looked for up-to-date texts on Humanistic Psychology written by British authors.[3] Apart from the book by Totton (2010), which is a critique of the humanistic therapies rather than a text outlining its principles and practice, the most recent example of the latter I could find was written by Eric Whitton (2003), and this was published by a publisher that is now defunct. The two most recent editions of major texts written by the indefatigable John Rowan are well over ten years old: *The Reality Game: A Guide to Humanistic Counselling and Therapy*, 2nd edition (Rowan, 1998)[4] and *Ordinary Ecstasy: The Dialectics of Humanistic Psychology*, 3rd edition (Rowan, 2001). While there is a comprehensive edited text entitled *The Handbook of Humanistic Psychology: Leading Edges in Theory, Research, and Practice* (Schneider, Bugental & Pierson, 2002), this is written largely for those already committed to the field, and is quite expensive.

If Humanistic Psychology is going to get its message across to professionals from other therapeutic traditions, and particularly if it is going to appeal to prospective practitioners, then it is very important, in my view, for up-to-date accessible texts to be available and consistently updated so that Humanistic Psychology has a current 'feel' to it. If you compare this state of affairs with the plethora of up-to-date books on CBT available, then the size of the problem becomes stark.

I mentioned Totton's (2010) book earlier. This book is an excellent example of someone who is enthusiastic and knowledgeable about the field of Humanistic Psychology, but who does not align himself with it. He writes sensibly, critically and above all empathically about the field. Totton's book was originally published in book form by Karnac Books, for a time was only available as a PDF download from Open Mind Books, and now is not even available from that source. This development probably means that Totton's manuscript will not get the wide readership that it deserves, both within the field of Humanistic Psychology and without.

As Totton (2010) argued, Humanistic Psychology is a broad and diverse church, and yet it is difficult to get a current sense of the field's breadth and depth. I edit a book series entitled 'CBT: Distinctive Features'.[5] This series is designed to show the distinctive theoretical and practical features of a number of approaches within the CBT tradition. It is written for people who might be interested in CBT as well as for CBT therapists from a specific approach who want to learn about the distinctive features of other CBT approaches. Each book has the same structure to facilitate comparison.

I had planned to co-edit a similar series on Humanistic Psychology with John Rowan, but our plans did not materialize. I still think, however, that such a series would help to revitalize Humanistic Psychology, both from within and without, and I would encourage interested parties to pick up the publishing mantle here. Failing that, I would like to see one edited text that outlines the main humanistic approaches in Britain. I have edited such a book on CBT (Dryden, 2012), and again authors of each CBT approach have written to a set chapter structure to facilitate comparison. In summary, perhaps the field of Humanistic Psychology needs a Windy Dryden to coordinate these latter efforts!

Pluralism: to align with or not?

In my view, one of the most exciting trends to emerge recently in the field of counselling and psychotherapy has been that of pluralism (Cooper & McLeod, 2011; Cooper & Dryden, 2016; House & Totton, 2011; Samuels, 1993). There are three core principles of pluralistic counselling and therapy. These are:

1. There are different pathways to therapeutic change; it follows from this that there is no one best therapeutic orientation/method; and different clients are likely to have different therapeutic needs at different points in time.
2. If therapists want to know what is likely to be most helpful for individual clients, they should start by exploring it with them.
3. Pluralistic therapists demonstrate understanding of the views of practitioners from other therapeutic orientations, and respect for and acceptance of these practitioners, even when they disagree with some of their views.

The question for the field of Humanistic Psychology is whether, and to what extent, it should align itself with pluralism. This development has recently been spearheaded by Cooper and McLeod (2011), who are most closely connected with the humanistic-existential therapeutic tradition. This means that Humanistic Psychology would have less difficulty 'hitching its wheels' to the pluralistic 'wagon' than the psychodynamic and CBT traditions, particularly with respect to the second core principle listed above. In addition, humanistic therapists should be best placed to adhere to the third core principle, at least in theory. Whether they do so in practice is another matter (cf. Loewenthal & House, 2010). Perhaps, it is with the first principle that humanistic practitioners would have the most difficulty. For example, Totton (2010) noted that such practitioners tend to downplay unconscious and rational factors in the change process.

Assuming that obstacles to pluralism can be successfully addressed, the question remains as to whether or not Humanistic Psychology should align itself with the pluralistic movement. Whatever happens, I believe that it should seriously debate this issue. My view is that it should align itself with the pluralistic movement as long as it promotes simultaneously its distinctive features in a jargon-free way to the rest of the therapeutic world.

Engaging with reality

One of the challenges for those therapy approaches not represented in the Increasing Access to Psychological Therapies (IAPT) initiative is how to respond to this programme. Do they criticize CBT that largely comprises the initiative, do they petition the Government, play politics, or carry out the kind of research that is acceptable to the National Institute of Health and Clinical Excellence (NICE) so that it can become a part of the therapeutic establishment as conceived by the Government? My point here is that whatever stance or combination of stances the Humanistic Psychology movement decides to take, it would be best if it demonstrates the core conditions of empathy, acceptance and congruence in doing so. Thus, it is possible to mount a cogent critical response to CBT that is based on an understanding of CBT from its internal frame of reference, and accept and show respect to CBT therapists while criticizing aspects of CBT theory and practice to which one objects. In my view, these attitudes were not demonstrated by the majority of contributors to Loewenthal and House's (2010) edited book entitled *Critically Engaging CBT*, which should serve as a model of how *not* to engage CBT practitioners in a meaningful dialogue.

In summary, the future of Humanistic Psychology is largely within the hands of its adherents – i.e. no doubt including many readers of this book. If you practise what you preach while engaging with other approaches with which you agree, if you capitalize on the strengths of Humanistic Psychology and are honest about its weaknesses and address these in a concerted manner, then the future of Humanistic Psychology will be rosy. If not . . . well let's not go there! (as President Trump might say).

Notes

1 Now known as person-centred therapy.
2 This book, entitled *Cognitive Behaviour Therapies* (Dryden, 2012), is a British-based update of a book that I edited with Bill Golden called *Cognitive-behavioural Approaches to Psychotherapy*, that had British and North American contributors (Dryden & Golden, 1986).
3 I am referring here to the broad field of Humanistic Psychology. I am well aware that there have been published more recent texts on specific humanistic approaches.
4 The third edition of this text was published this year (Rowan, 2016).
5 There are currently 15 books in the series, with more in the pipeline.

References

Cooper, M. & Dryden, W. (Eds) (2016). *The Handbook of Pluralistic Counselling and Psychotherapy*. London: Sage.

Cooper, M. & McLeod, J. (2011). *Pluralistic Counselling and Psychotherapy*. London: Sage.

Dryden, W. (Ed.) (2012). *Cognitive Behaviour Therapies*. London: Sage.

Dryden, W. & Golden, W. L. (Eds) (1986). *Cognitive-behavioural Approaches to Psychotherapy*. London: Harper & Row.

Ellis, A. (1973). *Humanistic Psychotherapy: The Rational-emotive Approach*. New York: McGraw-Hill.

House, R. & Totton, N. (Eds) (2011). *Implausible Professions: Arguments for Pluralism and Autonomy in Psychotherapy and Counselling*, 2nd edn. Ross-on-Wye: PCCS Books.

Loewenthal, D. & House, R. (Eds) (2010). *Critically Engaging CBT*. Maidenhead: Open University Press.

Rowan, J. (1998). *The Reality Game: A Guide to Humanistic Counselling and Therapy*, 2nd edn. London: Routledge.

Rowan, J. (2001). *Ordinary Ecstasy: The Dialectics of Humanistic Psychology*, 3rd edn. Hove, East Sussex: Routledge.

Rowan, J. (2016). *The Reality Game: A Guide to Humanistic Counselling and Therapy*, 2nd edn. Abingdon, Oxon: Routledge.

Samuels, A. (1993). *The Plural Psyche: Personality, Morality and the Father*. London: Routledge.

Schneider, K.J., Bugental, J.F.T., & Pierson, J.F. (Eds) (2002). *The Handbook of Humanistic Psychology: Leading Edges in Theory, Research, and Practice*. Thousand Oaks, CA: Sage Publications.

Totton, N. (2010). *The Problem with the Humanistic Therapies*. London: Karnac Books; reissued as an e-book download by Open Mind Books under the title *The Problems of the Humanistic Therapies,* but no longer available from that source, as of 11 December 2016.

Whitton, E. (2003). *Humanistic Approach to Psychotherapy*. London: Whurr.

23

GESTALT IN A CHANGING WORLD

Gaie Houston

For – Jay Levin: www.jaylevin.net

My first degree was in English literature at Oxford, where I was always more interested in the characters I read about, than in finding smart answers to what critics had said. After that I wrote radio plays for the BBC, and for a time was on the management board of a vast psychiatric hospital, just before such places disappeared. It seems to me that all these events were part of my blind lurch toward Gestalt Therapy.

In the late 1960s I trained with National Training Laboratories in the United States, and got a diploma in applied behavioural science back in London. Someone at NTL said I was a natural as a T–Group trainer, and would be a better one if I went to the Tavistock Institute's training too. So I did, as well as hoovering up many humanistic weekend events in England. Stay with me. This is all part of the path gestaltwards.

Now comes the awkward bit, because it is true, but difficult to describe, and so far in my life, apparently difficult for listeners either to take on board or value. Right.

I was on a residential encounter group weekend involving long hours in the group, and dancing, and generally getting tired and over-stimulated. I woke in the middle of the night and experienced something that probably only lasted about three or four seconds. It was an experience without or perhaps before words, and I only have words to try to convey it. It seemed as if everything I had ever known, back through my own life, back through race history, was surely and inexorably rising and turning, like some kind of black dough. What emerged at the top was the next I Want. It was a clear image, and in this weird experience what came up was the need to write down something I suddenly felt I understood about improving educational methodology. So I wrote, and next morning at breakfast told people about what had happened and they gave that kind of smile which I read to mean I was slightly boring and incomprehensible, so I did not persist.

Some weeks later someone lent me PHG (Perls, Hefferline & Goodman, 1951) and I was jolted, excited, to find that what I had experienced was described there as Gestalt formation. I had somehow been allowed to peer at the stages before awareness. That meant that I had a different take on Field Theory from Perls and Lewin, but that has never worried me.

In the States John Weir from UCLA was a major influence in my training, before my Damascene bizarreness. He was a crypto-gestaltist, always aware of the context in which all figures are inextricably involved. He used to say that he was more interested in seeing how far he could go, than in sitting down writing about it. Among many of his enlightening therapeutic innovations, he invented a form of language he called Responsibility Language, which was highly supportive of Gestalt Therapy, and which I later wrote up.

After reading all of Perls' work that I could lay my hands on, I began going to whatever workshops had the word Gestalt in their title. Among others, Ischa Bloomberg taught me a very great deal in what became his Gestalt Centre in London. Then in 1974 I was invited to work on a Counselling Course, where I chose to teach Gestalt. The course was largely student-led, and it became embarrassing that my workshops were consistently full, while some other lecturers had no students. Gestalt caught everyone's imagination. Such was the enthusiasm for this approach, I set up evening workshops, on a drop-in basis, which I considered to be in the spirit of spontaneity. We sat on cushions and hell-raked our psyches, in the manner of the times, and had week-long residentials, largely therapeutic rather than about professional training.

But many students complained of what they considered the laborious language of PHG, so I set to it and wrote a small primer, *The Red Book of Gestalt*. It was full of training exercises as well as theory, and my students tried out everything and helped me modify, before each chapter passed muster. I knew I wanted the book to be accessible both intellectually and financially, so I was horrified at the price my academic publishers proposed asking for it.

Just at that time I was with my husband visiting many factories run by disabled people, for which he was the managing director. We went to a brand-new one set up as a print works, whose only difficulty was that it had no loading. I gave them my camera-ready manuscript and ordered three thousand copies. It sounded the sort of order one might give. The books duly arrived and sat in boxes and students bought a few copies. It never crossed my mind to ask for it to be reviewed. But a British humanistic journal, *Self & Society*, brought out the whole work in two successive issues. It must have saved them a lot of effort!

Maybe that is what publicized this slender volume. Or, Buddhism has the concept of The Whispered Transmission, and this is the way I tend to account for the continuing quite large sales of this book until some years ago, when I did not re-print, as I was sick of being a publisher. Now Amazon still shifts secondhand copies at outrageous prices.

I followed that book two years later with *The Red Book of Groups*, in the same format. This dealt with group and organizational theory both as I saw it affecting counsellor training, and as necessary knowledge for counsellors. It was not intended particularly as a Gestalt book, but I was by now linked in people's minds with that topic, and I suspect many students linked the book in the same way.

Idiosyncratic development

Looking back now, I would like to think that in one way and another, I have helped widen application and understanding of group theories in Gestalt. The Groups book was a beginning. Then through The Gestalt Centre, London, I have been enabled to introduce small, large and intergroup theory to students, and over the years see a synthesis or integration of insights from systems theory, from the Tavistock and humanistic sources, into mainstream Gestalt Therapy theory. There is much to learn, for example, from setting aside at times the useful Gestalt managed group technique I find in countries round the world, of starting proceedings with a go-round. There is much to commend it; but it is also a bit programmatic.

Awareness, contact and response-ability were to me the key concepts to impart in training or therapy groups. When people write and talk about Relational Gestalt, almost as a twenty-first-century discovery or invention, I am surprised. I never found the notion of a contact boundary a very illuminating metaphor. But much of the matter of groups I work in is about the subtle or unsubtle approaches, sidesteps, feints, embraces, withdrawals, whatever, happening from moment to moment between person and person. Whatever is described as contact boundary stuff cannot but be relational. Without someone or something to contact, the boundary is not operant, for goodness sake.

My early training did not include phenomenological dialogue as a named topic, though there was always emphasis on some of its components. Using I-statements, expressing the feelings or sensations behind a statement, making statements rather than asking questions, being accurate, avoiding value-judgements, and more, were drummed into us.

Now I bring myself often to enunciate the difficult syllables of phenomeno-logical dialogue, as I do my best to show students the simplicity, authority and efficacy of this kind of dialogue in therapy. For me, its use harks back to my three-second Aha experience, of trusting that the best response I am capable of is ready to emerge into awareness if I can just let be, rather than sit computing and agitating and blurting suggestions and speculations that come too heavily from the pre-frontal cortex, from worry.

Another development I have come to, rather than have started off with, is to want to know what any client wants from therapy. Clinical supervision takes much of my working time now, and whenever a supervisee professes him or herself a bit lost or uncertain, I am likely to ask what their client wants from seeing them. Time and again, they cannot remember, or they tell me what they call the presenting problem. A problem is not what you want. Well they want to not have the problem. So what

DO they want? Wanting to be without the problem is a not-want. They might then protest that they asked their client that very question, but he did not know.

Perls was very clear about what he called the endgain. He said you had to know what the endgain was, so all the means-whereby of the therapy were in its service. Otherwise, he did not say but implied, you could all go hang, because you were chasing round the neurotic bushes wearing blindfolds. Reaching an agreed fantasy of the endgain is to me the beginning of the work, and may take time. Besides discounting not-wants, I encourage students to talk through any statement by the client such as wanting to have a partner as the outcome of the therapy. Therapy is not a dating agency. But it can be used to raise awareness of what within them gets in the way of finding or keeping partners, and what facilitates that exciting process.

In 2013 I was asked to write *The Nutshell Book of Gestalt Therapy*, as part of a series. It was not as easy as I had supposed even to describe any aspects of the theory or method, as absolute and universal among the practitioners I had come across in different institutes and countries. I came back to Perls' dictum, that all are right, but some are righteous. I make that comment here, in case my enthusiasm for how I do Gestalt seems to suggest that I am proposing an orthodoxy, or being righteous.

To me one absolute criterion in therapy is to find the dance-step that answers the client's. The therapist's best powers, rather than adherence to any orthodoxy, I have come to value more and more. My belief is that good Gestalt work lets in the insights of Freud, of Klein, Adler or the wise postman down the road. And that can be done within the reality of recognizing that the client is in charge, and by means of dialogue and experiment rather than theorizing, or suggesting or persuading.

Gender

I have spent a long time on the heading of my style of therapy and its development. About whether it is important that I am a woman, I have little to say. It is part of the given, and must provoke projections that a man would not provoke; and vice-versa. Most of my career has been reactive rather than proactive; but even that is not necessarily a feminine characteristic. Enough.

What I think I am good at

What sort of people can I best help? Whoever is willing. My strengths as a therapist are probably clarity, and a wish to keep in awareness the distress that certainly underlies whatever shenanigans a client might present. Much of my work now is clinical supervision, and I find that my guesses about what is going on between therapist and client, and the client at home, are very often accurate. I do not know to what extent this comes from such a long career of directly observing people in interaction, or from the myriad, often sad life stories that are told to me by supervisees.

Being part of a very fluent family is another advantage I have. Journalism and writing books are around me. Often I find that I can help supervisees hone their language to be more economical and accessible. Messy talking worries me to the point that I sometimes run workshops called Plain Speaking, which are about all this, and also about being direct and challenging as therapists.

Community

I do feel that I am supported and educated every day by supervisees, as well as by a supervisor who uses Gestalt, but has a strongly psychoanalytic perspective. Being part of The Gestalt Centre, London, since 1982, has always been very important. I have colleagues there whom I love as well as respect, so I have the sense of a cooperative family beside or behind me, whatever country I am working in.

Work preference

It is hard to say what work I prefer. I do little therapy now, as it is not compatible with visiting overseas to do training, which I enjoy enormously. Supervision is easier to interrupt sometimes, or reduce to Skype or telephone on occasion, without much harm. It is another kind of work I find extremely rewarding, as long as the supervisee wants to learn.

After I am gone

The professional trend now is to integrate therapies, while the political or economic trend, at least in the UK, is rather the opposite, of funding manualized, apparently measurable approaches such as CBT. When I was asked a few years ago to write the book *Brief Gestalt Therapy*, I was tempted to write a manual that would pass muster with the bean-counters, and yet be free enough that users could get on as before, but with funding. That might have been politically adroit. But there is little evidence of political adroitness on an inter-disciplinary scale being something at which Gestaltists excel, and I did not buck the trend.

My guess about the future is that the interrupted care patterns that so many children experience now will reinforce the need for one to one and group therapy, for several more generations, if the planet holds up.

Tribal loyalty attracts me to wanting the philosophy and much of the method of Gestalt Therapy to emerge into much wider recognition than it has now. My guess is that Gestalt is more likely to be subsumed into the integrative tendency I have referred to. What is most important to me if I look wide, is that counselling and therapy evolve toward excellence, which means we ever more effectively raise awareness, and so restore function and love and excitement to people's lives. The brand name is secondary and the method is secondary.

That is part of what I expect of the future. What I hope, and have said on other occasions, is that as a profession we shall put more and more emphasis on education rather than therapy, so people know how not to fall over the edge of the cliff. Therapy is more like being the ambulance that helps them recover after they have fallen down. Groups in school using Gestalt methods have worked very well wherever I have seen them. Parenting classes instead of trigonometry seem to me an appropriate response to the social field in many parts of the present world. Understanding about the powerful feelings evoked by group membership needs to be in the educational syllabus, as experiential learning.

Anarchy is too sophisticated a concept for this or several generations to come, I suspect. But raising awareness of cooperation, of community, rather than competition and individualism, are paths toward Goodman's dream that I hope we shall take.

References

Houston, G. (1990) *The Red Book of Groups*. London: Rochester Foundation

Houston, G. (1995) *The New Red Book of Gestalt*. London: Rochester Foundation

Houston, G. (2003) *Brief Gestalt Therapy*. London: Sage

Houston, G. (2012) *Gestalt Counselling in a Nutshell*. London: Sage

Perls, F., Hefferline, Ralph H., & Goodman, P. (1951) *Gestalt Therapy: Excitement and Growth in the Human Personality*. London: Souvenir Press

24

THE NECESSARY REVOLUTION IN HUMANISTIC PSYCHOLOGY[1]

Peter Hawkins

> It was the best of times, it was the worst of times.
> *(Charles Dickens* Tale of Two Cities *(opening line))*

> So fair and foul a day I have not seen.
> *(William Shakespeare's* Macbeth, *Act One, Scene Two (Macbeth's first line))*

In his very powerful encyclical on the environment 'Laudato Si', Pope Francis (2015) writes about the destruction of our environment and the challenges now facing our collective world:

> These situations have caused sister earth, along with all the abandoned of our world, to cry out, pleading that we take another course. Never have we so hurt and mistreated our common home as we have in the last two hundred years. The problem is that we still lack the culture needed to confront this crisis. We lack leadership capable of striking out on new paths and meeting the needs of the present with concern for all and without prejudice towards coming generations.

This chapter will focus on the history of Humanistic Psychology, the great gifts it has given us, but also on how Humanistic Psychology has been part of the culture that has created the world's challenges we and sister earth now face. It will then look at how we address these shadow aspects of the humanistic culture in order to contribute to creating a new humanism that can address the challenges of the twenty-first century.

History of Humanistic Psychology

Humanistic Psychology had its roots in the early part of the twentieth century, but came into prominence in the three decades after the Second World War. In the war of 1939–1945, the world had witnessed the 'horrors of Mordor', such as: the extermination camps of Auschwitz and Belsen; the Blitz bombing of Coventry and Dresden; and the nuclear destruction of Hiroshima and Nagasaki. Much of the human species had descended into hell, and was now in search of redemption, healing, and a new hope and trust in the positive capacity of human beings.

The founding fathers (and they were mainly men), included Jacob Moreno, Carl Rogers, Abraham Maslow, Wilhelm Reich and Fritz Perls. Four of these were Jews, and three of them had fled from Nazi Germany and Austria. All of them opened up new perspectives on understanding the possibilities for human beings and ways of developing each person's potential.

The great gifts of Humanistic Psychology

I want to start by sharing what I see as some of the great positive contributions of Humanistic Psychology in my lifetime. Dina Glouberman (2013: 125) the founder of the Skyros Growth Centre writes:

> Humanistic Psychology was a wonderful thing when I was growing up – at that time it meant everything that was young and progressive, open to change and politically on the side of the angels. It encouraged us to begin a lifetime of development and expansion without ever having to label ourselves as ill or lacking.

For those of us in the UK, who grew up in the after-shadow of the Second World War, it is now hard to recall how grey, conformist and narrow life was before it burst into riotous technicolour in the late 1960s. Along with the Beatles, Carnaby Street, Hippies, LSD, women's liberation movement, anti-psychiatry, dialectics of liberation and Ronnie Laing, CND and anti-Vietnam marches, came Humanistic Psychology. We read Erich Fromm, Fritz Perls, Jacob Moreno, Carl Rogers, Wilhelm Reich and others. More importantly, we learnt to cry, to love, to shout our feelings, find our voice, throw off the shackles of our inherited beliefs and go for freedom. We believed that we could change the world. The trouble is, we did!

Humanistic Psychology was, and is, a broad church, with many different approaches and schools, but all are involved in experientially exploring the further reaches and the fullness of what it means in being human. The current website of the Association for Humanistic Psychology in Britain reads thus:

> The first thing to say is that Humanistic Psychology is many things. It is broader than just a psychological discipline, and A HUMANISTIC

PSYCHOLOGY is not just an organisation for psychologists, psychotherapists and counsellors; we are open to anyone who is interested in how to be human. It was founded by a broad band of people from many disciplines, such as history, poetry, philosophy and spirituality.

Humanistic Psychology is not in itself a psychotherapeutic discipline; rather it is an umbrella term for a number of disciplines which put the person at the centre of their ways of working and strongly believe that the realisation of our own potential is crucial to creating a better world.

(AHP in Britain, 2015)

What links the many different approaches that can be classed under the broad umbrella of Humanistic Psychology is that they share some important key concepts and values. Each of these core values has brought great benefits not only to the field of psychology, but to the wider society, and each has contributed to the cultural revolution of the late twentieth century. I believe the most important of these values are:

- *Emotionally expressive*: Humanistic Psychology focuses not just on the right brain neo-cortex, but also on the intuitive, imaginal and spontaneous capacities of the left brain. It focuses not just on the neo-cortex brain, but also on the emotions of the heart and gut brains. Without Humanistic Psychology we might never have had the growth in emotional intelligence (EQ) work, from Daniel Goleman (1996) and others.
- *Embodied*: Prior to Humanistic Psychology, many of us treated our bodies as necessary vehicles for transporting around our brain. Humanistic Psychology and the pioneers such as Wilhelm Reich, Kurt Lewin and Gerda Boyeson taught us not only to listen to our bodies but to fully inhabit them. This has had an impact on greater body awareness, attention to our own bodily health and Mindfulness training.
- *Relational*: Humanistic psychotherapies have always focused on authentic 'I–thou' relating (Buber, 1970) between the psychotherapist and the client, as opposed to the methodological fidelity of the behaviourist and the blank-screen approach of traditional psychoanalysis. Research has increasingly shown that the quality of the relationship is the most significant factor in the efficacy of psychotherapy, and other psychotherapeutic approaches have become more relational, leading to such developments as relational approaches in object relations and the development of inter-subjective psychotherapy (Stolorow and Attwood, 1992). Relational approaches have also impacted beyond therapy as the focus on EQ developed into (SQ) social intelligence, and then to RSI (relational systems intelligence; Rod and Fridjhon, 2015). It has also impacted on religion and theology, most notably in Raimon Panikkar's work where he writes: 'God is neither within you nor among you, but between you. Everything in the world is interrelated and beings themselves are nothing but relations' (Panikkar 1995).

- *Human potential*: Humanistic Psychology views the individual as naturally self-healing, and evolving to higher forms of maturity and self-functioning. It moves away from a focus on symptoms and pathology to a focus on positive features of the individual, and how they can best realize their latent potential. This has had enormous impact on education and the development of Positive Psychology (see Chapter 13, this volume), and many approaches to business and life coaching. Jacob Moreno, who was the originator of Psychodrama and sociodrama, a contemporary of Freud's, and who can be considered the grandfather of Humanistic Psychology, when he met Freud is reputed to have said to him: 'You analyse men's dreams; I give them the courage to dream again.'
- *Authenticity and self-responsibility*: Humanistic Psychology encouraged us to find our own truth and have the courage to express it, rather than be bound by the mores, beliefs or assumptions we have inherited and absorbed from our family and society, but in the words of Joseph Campbell to: 'follow your bliss. Find where it is, and don't be afraid to follow it' (Campbell, 1991: 120 and 149).
- *Experiential*: Focused on direct experience. My own Psychodrama teacher Marcia Karp would constantly use the phrase she had learnt from Jacob Moreno – 'Don't tell me, show me'. The humanistic psychologies all favour experimenting, learning through experience and phenomenological inquiry, rather than through theory and intellectual thinking. Carl Rogers (1961: 23–4) wrote:

> It is to experience that I must return again and again; to discover a closer approximation to truth as it is the process of becoming in me. Neither the Bible nor the prophets – neither Freud nor research – neither the revelations of God nor man – can take precedence over my own direct experience.

Humanistic Psychology's experiential focus has influenced many fields beyond the therapy room. Its experiential approaches have informed coaching and team coaching, collaborative and action research, and education.

Seven traps of Humanistic Psychology

The author, Tom McCarthy (BBC Four, 'Birth of the Novel', 15 February 2011) spoke about how every novel ought to contain within it, its own negation, an embedded anti-novel, which, like the grit in the oyster, creates the pearl of lasting quality. We too have to examine how the liberation movement of the post-war generation contributed to the more hidden horrors of our own generation. These include: the neo-liberal selfish consumerism of Thatcher and Reagan, the oppressive international wars of Blair and Bush, late-stage capitalism, tolerated and hidden sexual abuse and massive ecological destruction. The seven traps that I outline below have emerged in part as a consequence of humanistic belief systems, and have contributed to creating dangerous limiting mind-sets which, if unaddressed, will make it impossible to meet the challenges of our times, which I will outline in the next section.

Growth

The work of the early pioneers led to the development of the so-called 'growth movement' and of growth centres such as Esalen in California, and Quaestor and Community in London. 'Growth' was about realizing our potential, self-actualizing (a term coined by Abraham Maslow (1943), one of the founding fathers of Humanistic Psychology). We were the first generation not to have military service, but instead were blessed with greater access to higher education, international travel and sexual freedom. Those of us who went to growth and encounter groups were eager to find the fastest escalator up the Maslow pyramid (Maslow, 1943).

But James Hillman (1975), the archetypal psychologist and ex director of the Jung Institute, pointed out that we have made an idol of one part of the natural cycle: growth is healthy in spring, childhood and adolescence, but he asks us to consider the question 'What is growth in late middle age?' Hillman suggests that it is over-consumption, obesity and cancer!

I was brought up on the Protestant work ethic rhyme: 'Good better best, never let it rest, till your good is better, and your better best.' The Protestant work ethic in the late twentieth century became: 'Perpetual performance improvement, company quarter on quarter growth in profits, exponential growth in GDP (Gross National Product), and the worship of MORE'!

There is a parallel between Humanistic Psychology's focus on growth and the capitalist economies built on exponential growth dependent on an increasing consumerist society that advertising ensures is focused on constant new fashionable acquisitions, bringing in its wake the 'throwaway society'. This materialist growth culture is then psychologically paralleled and we, growth-addicted Westerners, go in search for the better and best: training workshop, charismatic teacher, bigger catharsis, better 'aha' moments of enlightenment and greater breakthrough experiences.

Individualism

The individualistic nature of Humanistic Psychology is probably best captured in Fritz Perl's Gestalt Prayer:

> I do my thing and you do your thing.
> I am not in this world to live up to your expectations,
> And you are not in this world to live up to mine.
> You are you, and I am I,
> and if by chance we find each other, it's beautiful.
> If not, it can't be helped.
>
> *(Perls, 1969: 75)*

Gestalt psychotherapy, in the late-stage Perlsian variety, along with much of the Humanistic Psychology movement of that time, was rampantly self-centred. It was part of the 'me generation'. In the words of Britain's Prime Minister Harold Macmillan, we 'had never had it so good', and we were going to make the most of it.

Caroline Brazier (2013: 94) suggests that:

> The growth of individualism is evidenced in an increase of single-person households, changes in patterns of family life and marriage, and more emphasis on personal fulfilment in the rhetoric of popular media . . . it seems reasonable to imagine a link between these changes and a rise of personal-growth movements through the 1960s and 1970s, and beyond.

Individualism is integrally entwined with Liberalism, Free Market Trading and Late-Stage Capitalism (Harari, 2014) as products of late twentieth- and early twenty-first-century Western hegemony.

In its wake, individualism has brought celebrityism and the idolizing of famous individuals, often followed by subsequent demonization, of individual heroic leaders. I have argued elsewhere that the 'Heroic CEO is dead – long live the team'; that no individual leader of any major organization can manage the myriad complexities, inter-relatedness and challenges of our time, and we need collective team leadership with a new ethic of collaboration (Hawkins, 2011/2014, 2012, 2014). We need to discover how leadership teams in government, companies, voluntary organizations and professional associations can be more than the sum of their parts, and one of the main barriers to this is the individualistic personal development that the team members have been schooled within.

A focus on the wrong unit of flourishing

As Gregory Bateson (1972), the great systems thinker of the twentieth century, wrote:

> In accordance with the general climate of thinking in mid nineteenth century England, Darwin proposed a theory of natural selection and evolution, in which the unit of survival was either the family line or species of sub-species or something of that sort. But today it is quite obvious that this is not the unit of survival in the real biological world. The unit of survival is organism plus environment. We are learning by bitter experience that the organism that destroys its environment destroys itself.
>
> *(Bateson, 1972: 491)*

As Bateson indicates, we need to recognize that both the unit of survival, and therefore by implication the unit of flourishing, is never the individual, the family, the team, the organization, the nation, the species. Narrowly focusing on, or competitively succeeding within, your own niche will at best lead to sub-optimizing your part of the system and, at worst, to contributing to destroying the environment that sustains it. Flourishing is always relational, so the individual, team, organization or species only flourishes in co-creative relationship with its environment, its ecological niche and its systemic context.

Self-actualization is a destructive myth and a mirage. So is species actualization. Replacing GDP with Gross National Happiness is still Gross and unhealthy. As Yuval Noah Harari (2014) argues, we might or might not have created a more beneficial world for *Homo sapiens* since 1945, but we have done so at the cost of thousands of other living beings.

Human centrism

In the very title, Humanistic Psychology, is rooted in its human-centricity. It puts the human being at the centre of everything. Grof (2004) and Heron (2011) show how both Maslow and Rogers turned more to the spiritual dimension later in their lives, and in the last 25 years there has been an increasingly close relationship between the humanistic and the transpersonal psychotherapies such as Psychosynthesis and the Buddhist- and Sufi-inspired psychotherapies. However, these transpersonal psychologies can also be very human-centric – privileging the focus on human beings developing *their (sic)* 'higher self'. As the Buddhist philosopher Maurice Ash has written:

> For those who have continued the search for the metaphysical Self, they are left with nothing but their needs. And need itself is the greatest of these needs. It is the defining characteristic of contemporary society. Man is one who needs. I need therefore I am.
>
> *(Ash, 1995: 12)*

While focusing on our personal and spiritual development, so many of us have been blind to the abusive destruction of the 'more-than-human world' that contains and sustains us. We talk about nature and the environment as if they are something outside of us; some non-systemic ecologists even talk with heroic hubris about 'saving the environment'. The biggest challenge of our time is to realize that the more-than-human world is desperately trying to tell the human species that we need to listen, learn and change, in order to align to the healthy co-evolution of the biosphere; but we humans neither want to listen, learn nor change.

Activism: purpose

Humanistic psychologies have also favoured an activist, purposive approach to improving the human condition. 'Take charge of your life', 'have the courage to dream again', 'be positive', and 'make your own future'. James Hillman (1975) once again can waken us to the shadow of this stance, when he points out that the Christian tradition can only bear Good Friday if Easter Sunday is already guaranteed; but the reality is that on Good Friday there is no Easter Sunday. Sometimes we need to stay with grief and despair, embrace descent, enter the dark night of the soul and avoid the rush to hope.

Counter-cultural

House, Kalisch and Maidman (2013: 170–1) argue that: 'an intrinsically indissoluble aspect of Humanistic Psychology is precisely that it is counter-cultural', with Richard Mowbray (1995, quoted in ibid.) arguing that Humanistic Psychology 'must stay on the margin and not be absorbed, not be tempted by the carrots of recognition, respectability and financial security in reverting to the mainstream, but rather remain on the fringe'.

This is what I refer to as 'the academic disease' – which I describe as wanting to stay as a spectator and critic in the stand, rather than get on the pitch and play. I remember talking to a number of Labour politicians who, when Labour finally got into power in 1997, talked of the shock of having to step into responsibility for making things better; several talked about having to wake up to the fact that 'Them' is now 'Us'. Humanistic Psychology has always focused on the importance of the individual taking responsibility for their own life and their own choices, but finds it much harder to step up to taking collective social responsibility.

The brave initiative by Judy Ryde and Andrew Samuels to start Psychotherapists and Counsellors for Social Responsibility soon led to the temptation to engage in strident criticism of society, blaming 'them', the others, which can soon drown out the space for critical self-reflection of ourselves and our own assumptions, and the time to explore, how we, who have had the privilege of a great deal of education, training and freedom, might use that to make a greater positive difference for others. In some humanistic circles one can witness the dictatorship of the impassioned protestors and the enactment of the Karpman drama triangle (Karpman, 1968) with: society as 'persecutors', clients as 'victims', and we humanistic psychologists, as heroic 'rescuers'. This, as so often happens with this systemic pattern, turns full circle, with the rescuers themselves becoming persecutors, often of each other – and then the humanistic movement starts to resemble the political in-fighting so characteristic of far-left political splinter parties of past generations.

Dualism

Humanistic Psychologies have worked long and hard to overcome the Cartesian mind–body split with emotional, imaginal, somatic and action-based approaches but, like nearly all Western-based humanism, have remained deeply embedded in dualistic thinking. Our English language and grammar are fundamentally dualistic, with an emphasis on subject nouns, doing something (verb), to object nouns. Many of our ways of thinking are based on thinking in opposites; night and day, me and you, good and bad, past and future, rather on the relational and inter-dependence of all being.

In Fritz Perl's Gestalt prayer that I quoted above we hear the dualistic splitting of self and other. The even bigger dualistic splitting, that I have mentioned above, is in splitting the human from the more-than-human world, in which we are inextricably nested; the failure to recognize that the whole human economy is a wholly owned subsidiary of the ecology, which has the power to shut down the subsidiary (Hawken, 2010).

Since the human species became first agrarian and then industrialized, it has moved further and further away from participative consciousness, feeling and sensing its deep participation in the wider flow of creation.

The challenges of our time

We need to recognize that in the last 40 years the world has radically changed. In the growth of Humanistic Psychology in the UK in the 1970s, we lived in a Western world that believed that perpetual economic growth was possible, and that with it would come constantly increasing resources, and improved quality of life for all. Although some wise and courageous writers with great foresight were already warning of the looming ecological crisis (such as Rachel Carson (1962) in *Silent Spring*, Bateson (1972) and the Club of Rome report on Limits to Growth), we could still pretend that it was a long way off, and hopefully human ingenuity and science would find ways of avoiding it.

In the second decade of the twenty-first century, this denial is no longer sustainable. Tim Smit, the founder of the Eden project, wrote that the next 30 years are one of the most exciting times to be alive in the whole of human history, for in that time we will either discover whether 'Homo is truly sapiens' or we will join the fossil records! Thomas Friedman wrote in the *New York Times* in the midst of the economic crisis on 7 March 2009:

> What if the crisis of 2008 represents something much more fundamental than a deep recession? What if it is telling us that the whole growth model we created over the last 50 years is simply unsustainable economically and ecologically and that 2008 was when we hit the wall – when Mother Nature and the market both said: 'No more.'

The economist Kenneth Boulding (quoted in Gilding, 2011: 64) went further and wrote: 'Anyone who believes exponential growth can go on forever in a finite world is either a madman or an economist.'

We cannot blame economists, bankers, governments or regulators for either the economic or the ecological crisis. We all created it with our addiction to, and reliance upon, growth, and we will all be living with the entwined ecological and economic crises for the foreseeable future until we make the necessary enormous changes to our expectations, our lives and our approach to living.

So what does this mean for Humanistic Psychology? There are four key incontrovertible forces that are shaping, and will continue to shape, the context for decades to come.

1. *Greater demand*: The world's population is still exponentially growing. When I was born in 1950 the global population was only 2.4 billion. It has now raced to over 7.3 billion, and the United Nations predict that population growth will continue at 0.7 per cent a year, which will lead to a world population of 9 billion

in 2050. So I have seen the global population treble in my own lifetime – an experience that has not happened since the dawn of *Homo sapiens*.

Some people say that the birth rate has been falling in developing countries; but in these countries the exponential rise in life expectancy is still fuelling the growth, as well as more infants surviving long enough to have their own children. Migration, despite political rhetoric, will continue to increase exponentially. The poorest in the world can increasingly discover the disparity between their living standards and those of the rich world, and the ecological crisis disproportionately creates severe hardship in the poorest parts of the world. Now we are seeing hundreds of refugees die while attempting to come to Europe, how will we respond when this number is thousands or tens of thousands?

2. *Higher expectations of quality of service*: Not only are there many more people to help, but the expectations of all human beings are increasing exponentially. Thomas Friedman (2008) wrote that the world was not only getting 'Hot' and 'Crowded', but also 'Flat' – by which he meant that we all know what each other are getting. The rest want what the best already have. The number of internet-connecting devices in the world reached 7 billion even before the world population reached that figure, and is now estimated at over 21 billion. Even the economically poorest parts of the world have internet access by mobile telephony, so we are all interconnected in new ways.

Propriety knowledge of the professions is now democratized and liberated so that clients can become better informed than the professionals in many areas, and can know what others are receiving in different parts of the country or in different parts of the world. Increasingly we are all demanding the best, and when caring services get it wrong the media and internet can ensure that everyone knows about it.

Five years after writing *Hot, Flat and Crowded*, Thomas Friedman (2012) demonstrated how we now live in a world of hyper-change:

> When I said the world is flat, Facebook didn't exist. Or for most people it didn't exist. Twitter was a sound. The Cloud was in the sky. 4G was a parking place. LinkedIn was a prison. Applications were something you sent to college. And for most people, Skype was a typo. That all happened in the last seven years. And what it has done is taken the world from connected to hyper-connected. And that's been a huge opportunity and a huge challenge.

3. *Fewer resources*: Many people still believe that the current economic down-turn is a temporary set-back in the inevitable rise in prosperity and continued economic growth. Yet the weight of scientific evidence shows us that this is a form of dangerous collective denial. Scientists show how it would take more than 1.5 worlds to sustain human life as it currently operates. That means we are annually using 150 per cent of the world's available resources, or in other words eroding the fundamental resources year on year in a way that cannot be sustained. Economic forecasts on population growth and world consumption predict that by 2050 we will have a world that will annually run at 500–700 per cent of capacity (Gilding, 2011: 51).

Our wealth and prosperity fundamentally come from the ecological world we live in, and we are massively over-drawn and eroding the base capital.

Combined with this we are seeing a large-scale move in economic power, with European and North American economies declining, and rapid growth in both the BRIC economies (Brazil, Russia, India and China) and the N11 (the next eleven that all have the potential to overtake the current G7 leading economies in this century). Economic growth is moving south and east.

In the over-spent first-developed countries, fewer resources in relation to the growing demand is an inevitability. We need to learn to adjust to living within our means and what the earth can sustain.

4. *The Great Disruption*: *The Great Disruption* is the title of Paul Gilding's book (Gilding, 2011) in which he presents an overwhelming body of evidence that the world is facing an unprecedented time of challenge on all fronts. Climate change is no longer a threat but a reality, and moving faster than the maligned ecologists of the last century were warning. Global warming is happening and leading to climate volatility, including: increased floods, droughts, heat waves and intense cold. Different regions will be differently and sometimes unpredictably impacted. Economic volatility is inevitable with our global interdependent economy at a time when we hit the limits to growth. We will see the price of basic food, energy and raw materials such as wood, fibre, concrete and minerals continue to rise more quickly than incomes. Political challenges will increasingly be beyond the capacity of nation-states to resolve, and we lack the global governance structures that can address them. We only need to look at the failure of the global eco-summits, the euro crisis, or the Israel–Palestinian conflict to realize the extent of this.

All this means that there is an inevitable increase in human disruption, disturbance, distress and dis-ease; and where will the human consequences of this be most felt? It will turn up daily in our schools, hospitals, prisons, care homes, on the streets and in our work-places. The helping professions will be at the front-line of addressing the human consequences, while they will also have to adjust to fewer resources and greater demand.

How can we respond?

In Hawkins and Shohet (2012: 9–10) I wrote:

> A few years ago I spoke to a conference of teachers from across the developed world. They were all complaining about more being demanded of them – larger classes, year on year improvements in the exam performance of their pupils, children and parents demanding more and giving less automatic respect, and yet no increase in resources. The more they complained the more powerless they became. I decided to challenge the disempowering consensual collusion and presented a few demographic, economic and scientific projections. I concluded by saying: 'It seems inevitable that you will year on

year be asked to do more at higher quality with less resources in a more disrupted and disturbed world. The question is what can we do together to step up to this challenge?'

I do not believe that our choices in response to the global challenges are either denial or powerlessness. Neither do I believe that heroically doing more, trying harder under greater pressure, will be sustainable. The challenges are beyond individual leadership or individual coping mechanisms. We need to work on this together and that means far greater levels of collaboration and combining than ever before.

I used to ask individual coaching clients what they wanted from coaching, and teams what they required from their team coach. Now I ask them: 'What is the world you operate in requiring you to step up to, and what are the areas in which you struggle to respond?' When I work with teams, I ask them, 'What is the world you operate in asking you as a team to collectively step up to, to which you, collectively, have not yet found a way to respond?' Contracting needs to move from starting with the individual's needs and the problems of last week, to being more focused on addressing the needs of the wider system and the future, with questions that are 'outside-in' and 'future-back'.

The world is requiring the human species to evolve and change. What is needed is major transformation in human consciousness, ways of thinking, behaving and relating, both to each other and 'the more-than-human world' (Abrams, 2007). Psychotherapists, counsellors, coaches, psychologists, teachers, nurses, doctors, social workers – all need to play their part. Helping professionals will need to be constantly increasing their individual and collective capacities to respond, and we all need to develop greater human capacity to address the increased demands of tomorrow. In his new book Malcolm Parlett (2015) passionately articulates the need for the development of whole intelligence and the capacities of being embodied, relational, responding, inter-relating and experimenting.

The necessary revolution in Humanistic Psychology

Let us now return to the seven limiting mind-sets that Humanistic Psychology has inadvertently brought in its wake, discussed earlier. For each of these, let us look at what the possible antidote might be.

The great Sufi poet Mevlana Jalal-adin Rumi said: 'Leadership is a Poison unless you have the antidote in your heart' (in Rumi, 2007). Let me suggest that excess of Humanistic Psychology is also a poison, unless we have the antidotes in our hearts.

From growth to 'enoughism'

The focus in global economics needs to move from national competition for greater GDP, to finding collaborative sustainable ways of improving the living ecologies of all of the human family.

Businesses need to move from focusing on exponential growth in quarterly profits, to discovering how to create sustainable value for all their stakeholders, including future generations and our collective grandchildren.

Individuals need to move from our focusing on growing our self and our own happiness to being of service to the larger ecologies that support and sustain us all.

We need to move from a focus on Growth and More, to 'enoughism' and learning to embrace the beauty of less.

From individualism to collaboration

Humanistic Psychology has helped us move from IQ to EQ, but now we urgently need to move from IQ and EQ to 'We Q' – a new ethic of collaboration; one that recognizes that we are all indigenous earthlings but also orphans, migrants on the 'Road from Damascus', and that we are one Human Family.

From the focus on the wrong unit of flourishing to co-evolution

Self-actualization is a destructive myth and a mirage. We need to replace it with each of us contributing to co-evolution, actualizing the next stage in the development of ourselves in dynamic co-creation with our ecological niche. This niche includes the human communities with which we inter-relate, the many beings with whom we share the planet, the air we breathe, the waters and earth that sustain us.

A Native American teacher said that to take true leadership is to pause before making any decision and consider the seven generations that have preceded you, the seven generations that will follow you, and all beings that share this moment with you.

From ego-centric to eco-centric

The biggest challenge of our time is to realize that the more-than-human world is desperately trying to tell the human species that we need to listen, learn and change in order to align to the healthy co-evolution of the biosphere, but as already argued, we humans neither want to listen, learn nor change.

John Heron (2011) talks about combining the trinity of the intra, with the inter, with the beyond, but I prefer Satish Kumar's trinity which is about reconnecting soul, society and soil. We need to not only move from IQ to We Q, but to the 'More than We Q'. We must become more open to the 'more-than-human world' and recognize that we are indigenous earthlings (Peter Reason (2015), personal communication).

From activism and purpose to bearing witness

Sometimes we need to stay with grief and despair, embrace descent, enter the dark night of the soul and avoid the rush to hope. Simone Weil (1952) responded to the horrors of the Second World War with a different sensibility to the (mainly male) humanistic psychotherapists. Hers was a path of staying with, bearing witness and fully accepting the bitterness:

> To accept what is bitter. The acceptance must not be reflected back onto the bitterness so as to diminish it, otherwise the acceptance will be proportionately diminished in force and purity, for the thing to be accepted is that which is bitter in so far as it is bitter; it is that and nothing else. We have to say like Ivan Karamozov that nothing can make up for a single tear from a child, and yet to accept all tears and the nameless horrors which are beyond tears. We have to accept these things, not in so far as they bring compensations with them, but in themselves. We have to accept the fact that they exist simply because they do exist.
>
> I think, a profound form of engagement, a way of entering into, participating in, the affliction of others that refuses the dubious comforts of distance or of resolutions. It is a form of accompaniment.
>
> *(Weil, 1952: 62–4)*

Elias Amidon (2012) and Rabia Roberts have long practised and taught the practice of 'bearing witness', which they have done in many of the world's places of conflict, not taking sides, not judging, just being with. A practice also carried out in Bristol by the dedicated psychotherapists working for Trauma Foundation South-West (www.tfsw.co.uk), with refugees who have been victims of horrific traumata in their own countries, and then the traumata of getting to and surviving in the UK. From Elias, I have also learnt the spiritual practice of 'Doing Nothing', to spend 24 hours having a complete holiday from the use of will-power and only doing what emerges as being necessary.

From 'counter-cultural' to taking leadership

As I have argued earlier, we have been part of creating the culture of the late twentieth and early twenty-first centuries, but many of us are reluctant to own what we have contributed to this creation. We need to step up to taking responsibility and leadership.

In 2005 I defined leadership as more an attitude than a role, an attitude that begins when we stop blaming others or making excuses (Hawkins, 2005).

Another difficulty with Humanistic Psychology being a movement of protest and oppositionalism is that you are only as strong as that which you are protesting about. Keith Tudor (2013: 139) eloquently writes about how 'this early sense of identity in opposition has left a certain legacy and . . . an organizational psychology of opposition, and to a certain extent, marginality'.

Much of what Humanistic Psychology initiated and fought for has entered the mainstream, and, as I have indicated earlier, the challenges of our time call for a new rhetoric of participation and co-responsibility.

From dualism to non-duality

As already discussed, the Humanistic Psychologies have worked assiduously to overcome the Cartesian mind–body split with a whole variety of approaches, but have still remained deeply embedded in dualistic thinking. In Fritz Perl's Gestalt prayer that I quoted earlier, we hear the dualism of the splitting of self and other. Bert Hellinger (1998) learnt one of the important antidotes from native Africans the principles of Ubuntu, the deep interdependency that transcends this separation – 'I am because you are'.

The bigger dualistic splitting that I have mentioned above is in splitting the human from the more-than-human world, in which we are inextricably nested: 'we and our environment, like a subject and an object, are actually inseparable' (Ash, 1995: 7). We have to move from just fighting for saving this or that species, to working with the preservation and development of living ecologies; from thinking of the environment as a thing, to seeing that it is a complex web of inter-connections; from seeing it as 'other' to experiencing it as part of us; from seeing it as resources to be exploited to realizing it is the source that sustains and flows through us.

There is no self apart from nature. Our nature-self is always part of the unfolding of creation in the dynamic dance of living nested ecologies.

The revolution into the Seventh Wave Humanism

John Heron (2011), a long-term colleague and one of the best British thinkers in Humanistic Psychology, has written about four waves of humanism in a very illuminative essay (see also Chapter 25, this volume). The first is that of Athens in the fifth century BC, the second in the Italian Renaissance of the fifteenth century. Heron locates the rise of Humanistic Psychology in the third wave which began with the eighteenth-century Enlightenment, before going on to argue that we are at the birth of a fourth wave.

I would suggest that Heron's general thesis is correct, but his history is limited and rather Euro-centric. I would posit that the first wave must include all the great thinkers of the axial age, not just the Greeks but also thinkers such as Buddha, Lao-Tsu, Zoroaster and many others. Then before we jump to the Italian Renaissance, we must include the humanism brought by Jesus and the early desert fathers of the fourth century, and the Islamic renaissance of the eleventh to fourteenth centuries, with philosophers such as Averoes, Avicenna, Ibn Arabi, and great poets such as Sanai, Mevlana Jalaladin Rumi, Hafiz, as well as the great Islamic architects, scientists and mathematicians, without whom the European Renaissance would not have been possible.

I would also separate out the eighteenth- and early nineteenth-century Enlightenment humanism from the modernist late nineteenth- and twentieth-century humanism which I believe is directly influenced by Darwin, Marx and Freud and the growth of secularism. I would join John Heron, however, in arguing that we are at the birth of a necessary new humanism, and my own Seventh Wave

Humanism is one that is based not just on systemic thinking, but systemic *being* (Hawkins, 2014). A humanism that is no longer rooted in human-centric, person-centred individualism, but an enlarged humanism that collaboratively inquires into finding a new compact and relationship with 'the more-than-human world'. A humanism where the needs of the group take precedence over the needs of the individual, the needs of the community over the needs of the group, the needs of the whole human family over the needs of nations, and the needs of the biosphere over the needs of the human species.

Let me end with a delightful story taken from the wisdom teacher Cynthia Bourgeault (2008):

> **Acornology**
> Once upon a time, in a not-so-faraway land, there was a kingdom of acorns, nestled at the foot of a grand old oak tree.
>
> Since the citizens of this kingdom were modern, fully Westernized acorns, they went about their business with purposeful energy; and since they were mid-life, baby-boomer acorns, they engaged in a lot of self-help courses. There were seminars called: 'Getting all you can out of your shell.' There were woundedness and recovery groups for acorns who had been bruised in their original fall from the tree. There were spas for oiling and polishing those shells, and various acornopathic therapies to enhance longevity and well-being.
>
> One day, in the midst of this kingdom, there suddenly appeared a knotty little stranger, apparently dropped 'out of the blue' by a passing bird. He was capless and dirty, making an immediately negative impression on his fellow acorns. And crouched beneath the oak tree, he stammered out a wild tale. Pointing upwards at the tree, he said, 'We . . . are . . . that!'.
>
> Delusional thinking, obviously, the other acorns concluded, but one of them continued to engage him in conversation: 'So, tell us, how would we become that tree?'
>
> 'Well', said he, pointing downwards, 'it has something to do with going into the ground . . . and cracking open the shell.'
>
> 'Insane', they responded. 'Totally morbid! Why, then, we wouldn't be acorns *any more.*'

Acknowledgements

A big thank you to all the many people who attended the Marianne Fry 2015 Lecture in Bristol, and for sharing the special time we had together; and a bow of thanks to the greater world of life and creation that sustains all of us.

Note

1 This chapter was first delivered as the Marianne Fry Memorial Lecture in Bristol, UK, September 2015.

References

Abrams, D. (2007). *The Spell of the Sensuous*. New York: Random House (orig. 1996).

AHP (Britain) (2015). http://ahpb.org/index.php/humanistic-psychology/what-is-humanistic-psychology/ (goo.gl/pbq3h8) (accessed 1 December 2016).

Amidon, E. (2012). *The Open Path: Recognising Non-Dual Awareness*. Boulder, CO: Sentient Publications.

Ash, M. (1995). *Beyond the Age of Metaphysics and the Restoration of Local Life*. Hartland, Devon: Resurgence Books.

Bateson, G. (1972). *Steps to an Ecology of Mind*. New York: Ballantine Books.

Bourgeault, C. (2008). *The Wisdom Jesus: Transforming Heart and Mind – A New Perspective on Christ and His Message*. Boston, MA: Shambhala.

Brazier, C. (2013). Creating space: the future of Humanistic Psychology. In R. House, D. Kalisch & J. Maidman (Eds), *The Future of Humanistic Psychology* (pp. 93–7). Ross-on-Wye: PCCS Books.

Buber, M. (1970). *I and Thou* (trans. W. A. Kaufmann). New York: Scribner.

Campbell, J. (1991). *The Power of Myth*. New York: Anchor Books.

Carson, R. (1962) *Silent Spring*. Boston, MA: Houghton Mifflin.

Friedman, T. (2008). *Hot, Flat and Crowded*. London: Allen Lane.

Friedman, T. (2009). The inflection is near? *New York Times*, 7 March. Available at goo.gl/URpFcc (accessed 12 December 2016).

Friedman, T. (2012). On connected to hyper-connected. *Huffington Post*, 28 September; www.huffingtonpost.com/2012/09/12/thomas-friedman-connected-to-hyperconnected-_n_1878605.html (accessed 30 March 2017).

Gilding, B. (2011). *The Great Disruption: How the Climate Crisis Will Transform Society*. London: Bloomsbury.

Glouberman, D. (2013). Humanistic Psychology: how it was and how it may be. In R. House, D. Kalisch & J. Maidman (Eds), *The Future of Humanistic Psychology* (pp. 125–30). Ross-on-Wye: PCCS Books.

Goleman, D. (1996). *Emotional Intelligence*. London: Bloomsbury.

Grof, S. (2004). A brief history of transpersonal psychology. Available at www.stanislavgrof.com/wp-content/uploads/pdf/A_Brief_History_of_Transpersonal_Psychology_Grof.pdf (accessed 27 March 2017).

Harari, Y. N. (2014). *Sapiens: A Brief History of Mankind*. London: Vintage Books.

Hawken, P. (2010). *The Ecology of Commerce*. New York: Harper Business.

Hawkins, P. (2005). *The Wise Fool's Guide to Leadership*. London: O Books.

Hawkins, P. (2011). *Leadership Team Coaching: Developing Collective Transformational Leadership*. London: Kogan Page (2nd edn, 2014).

Hawkins, P. (2012). *Creating a Coaching Culture*. Maidenhead: Open University Press/McGraw Hill.

Hawkins, P. (Ed.) (2014). *Leadership Team Coaching in Practice*. London: Kogan Page.

Hawkins, P. & Shohet, R. (2012). *Supervision in the Helping Professions*, 4th edn. Maidenhead: Open University Press/McGraw Hill.

Hellinger, B. (1998). *Love's Hidden Symmetry*. Phoenix, AZ: Zeig, Tucker & Co.

Heron, J. (2011). Humanism: the fourth wave. In R. House, D. Kalisch & J. Maidman (Eds), *The Future of Humanistic Psychology* (pp. 156–68). Ross-on-Wye: PCCS Books.

Hillman, J. (1975). *Loose Ends: Primary Papers on Archetypal Psychology*. Zurich: Spring Publications.

House, R., Kalisch, D., & Maidman, J. (Eds) (2013). *The Future of Humanistic Psychology*. Ross-on-Wye: PCCS Books.

Karpman, S. (1968). Fairy tales and script drama analysis (selected articles). *Transactional Analysis Bulletin*, 7(26): 39–43.

Maslow, A. H. (1943). A theory of human motivation. *Psychological Review*, 50: 370–96.

Mowbray, R. (1995). *The Case against Psychotherapy Registration: A Conservation Issue for the Human Potential Movement*. London: Trans Marginal Press; downloadable as a pdf file free of charge at: www.transmarginalpress.co.uk (accessed 30 March 2017).

Panikkar, R. (1995). *Invisible Harmony: Essays on Contemplation and Responsibility*. Augsburg Fortress, MN: Fortress Press.

Parlett, M. (2015). *Future Sense: Five Explorations of Whole Intelligence for a World That Is Waking Up*. Kibworth Beauchamp, Leicestershire, UK: Matador.

Perls, F. (1969). *Gestalt Therapy Verbatim*. Boulder, CO: Real People Press.

Pope Francis (2015). *Laudato Si: Caring for Our Common Home*. Rome: The Vatican. Available at goo.gl/Ggy5FM.

Rod, A. & Fridjhon, M. (2015). *Creating Intelligent Teams: Leading with Relationship Systems Intelligence*. Randburg, South Africa: KR Publishing.

Rogers, C. R. (1961). *On Becoming a Person: A Therapist's View of Psychotherapy*. New York: Houghton Mifflin.

Rumi, J. (2007). *The Mathnawi of Mawlana Jalaluddin Rumi*. II 2094. Nicholson, Reynold A. & Kayadibi. Konya, Turkey: Saim Euromat Printing House.

Stolorow, R. & Atwood, G. E. (1992). *Contexts of Being: The Intersubjective Foundations of Psychological Life*. Hillsdale, NJ: Analytic Press.

Tudor, K. (2013). From humanism to Humanistic Psychology and back again. In R. House, D. Kalisch & J. Maidman (Eds), *The Future of Humanistic Psychology* (pp. 136–48). Ross-on-Wye: PCCS Books.

Weil, S. (1952). *Waiting for God*, trans. E. Cauford. New York: Putnams.

25

HUMANISM

The fourth wave

John Heron

The first three waves of humanism

In the history of civilization in the Western world, there have so far been three main waves of humanism. The first wave arose in Greece in the fifth century BC when the Sophists and Socrates 'called philosophy down from heaven to earth', as Cicero put it, by introducing social, political and moral questions.

The second wave, the Renaissance, was well under way in the fifteenth century in Florence. Through the recovery of the classical culture of Greece and Rome, it affirmed the worth and dignity of human achievement – the unique genius and extraordinary ability of the human mind – over against the Christian pre-occupation with human sin. However, while Renaissance humanists made humanity the centre of interest, they were far from being atheists, for God still remained as creator – though more remote. And the artists of the Renaissance had an important spiritual declaration to make about our relation with our world, as we shall see.

The powerful third wave began with the Enlightenment of the eighteenth century, and became the rational, scientific, secular and atheistic humanism of modern times.

Humanistic Psychology and the third wave of humanism

Humanistic Psychology, when it emerged in the USA in 1961, had a clear affiliation with this third wave of humanism, as exemplified by two of its primary protagonists. Abraham Maslow insisted that he was an atheist, and as such regarded the peak experiences of his self-actualizing exemplars as simply an expression of the best of their selfhood:

> I want to demonstrate that spiritual values have naturalistic meaning, that they are not the exclusive possession of organized churches, that they do

not need supernatural concepts to validate them, that they are well within the jurisdiction of a suitably enlarged science.

(Maslow, 1964: 3)

Carl Rogers was selected in 1964 as humanist of the year by the American Humanist Association, which promotes humanism as 'a progressive philosophy of life that, without theism and other supernatural beliefs, affirms our ability and responsibility to lead ethical lives of personal fulfilment that aspire to the greater good of humanity'.

A full-on humanist declaration from Rogers (1961: 23–4) reads as follows:

> It is to experience that I must return again and again; to discover a closer approximation to truth as it is in the process of becoming in me. Neither the Bible nor the prophets – neither Freud nor research – neither the revelations of God nor man – can take precedence over my own direct experience.

A late turn to the spiritual

However, Maslow apparently took a turn toward the non-naturalistic spiritual – 'beyond humanistic' – as he got a bit older. Stan Grof (2004: 2) reports that:

> In spite of the popularity of humanistic psychology, its founders Maslow and Sutich themselves grew dissatisfied with the conceptual framework they had originally created. They became increasingly aware that they had left out an extremely important element – the spiritual dimension of the human psyche.

In 1967 they joined up, says Grof, with him and others to create

> a new psychology that would honour the entire spectrum of human experience, including various non-ordinary states of consciousness. During these discussions, Maslow and Sutich accepted Grof's suggestion and named the new discipline 'transpersonal psychology'. This term replaced their own original name 'transhumanistic' or 'reaching beyond humanistic concerns'.

(Grof, 2004: 3)

Soon afterwards the Association of Transpersonal Psychology was launched. Maslow died in 1970.

Rogers kept the spiritual out of his psychology for a long time. But finally, in the last decade of his life, he turned toward it in terms of presence, inner spirit and self-transcending relationship:

> I find that when I am closest to my inner intuitive self, when I am somehow in touch with the unknown in me then whatever I do seems full of healing. Then simply my presence is releasing and helpful to the other. When I can

relax and be close to the transcendental core of me it seems that my inner spirit has reached out and touched the inner spirit of the other. Our relationship transcends itself and becomes a part of something larger.

(Rogers, 1980: 129)

Rogers died in 1987.

What I find prescient – albeit conjectural – about these two late turns is that they appear to embrace three fundamental spiritual dimensions: Maslow turns to the Beyond (the transpersonal), and Rogers turns to the Within (the intrapersonal) and the Between (the interpersonal), opening to the Beyond (for more on this triad, see Heron, 2006, 2007; and for related notions, see Ferrer, 2011; Shirazi, 2005; Chaudhuri, 1977). And these three are basic *spiritual* elements contributing to, and interdependent with, but not reducible to, the *humanism* of the fourth wave, as I will discuss after a brief look at the issue of separation.

The humanistic–transhumanistic separation

The existence of two Associations, one humanistic and the other, in Maslow's choice of a title, transhumanistic – the first dealing with the personal, and the second dealing with what is beyond the personal – tends to condone a separation between the spiritual and that which is distinctively human. Their co-existence also implies that neither of them is giving an integrated account of the full range of human experience.

Lajoie and Shapiro (1992) reviewed 40 definitions of Transpersonal Psychology in the literature between 1969 and 1991. They found five key themes: states of consciousness, higher or ultimate potential, beyond the ego or personal self, transcendence, and the spiritual. This clear emphasis on the higher, the ultimate, the beyond, the transcendent, echoes the historical fact that spiritual traditions, beliefs and practices for the past 3,000 years have been predominantly transcendent in their orientation. And as several commentators have pointed out (e.g. Walsh & Vaughan, 1993), this has led to definitions and declarations of Transpersonal Psychology being invaded by the ontological assumptions, belief systems and practices of the traditions.

Some of these early definitions, declarations and demarcations have been modified in recent years, but the whole movement is still dogged by the implicit transcendental focus of the 'trans', the beyond, in its title. This can be confirmed by scanning through the titles of all the articles published in the *Journal of Transpersonal Psychology* over the 43 years between 1969 and 2012. They are listed on the journal's website.

John Rowan (2005) maintains that Humanistic Psychology has a place for the spiritual, but then he also makes it plain that those who concern themselves with the spiritual aspects of Humanistic Psychology do so under the aegis of 'a separate *Journal of Transpersonal Psychology*'.

On its website, the Association for Humanistic Psychology in the USA makes a brief mention of 'the interaction of body, mind and spirit', but otherwise focuses on a third-wave humanist account of Humanistic Psychology as 'a value orientation that holds a hopeful, constructive view of human beings and of their substantial capacity to be self-determining'. It ends with a problematic statement to the effect that because Humanistic Psychology has spread into many other areas of society, it is no longer Humanistic Psychology, and that, although it is still represented by the AHP, it is also represented in Transpersonal Psychology and in many other movements.

Wilber has long since adroitly stepped away from the humanistic–transpersonal divide and commandeered 'integral' to name his attempt to present an all-inclusive psychology (Wilber, 2000). But it too has suffered invasion, in his case by the non-dual traditions, and it has no adequate model of spiritual inquiry, only consensus within a school or tradition (Heron, 1998).

I myself thought for a while, in the context of writing about the Institute for the Development of Human Potential, that it would be wise to reunite Humanistic Psychology and Transpersonal Psychology under the name Holistic Psychology (Heron, 2001). However, I now rescind that view, while putting some of the ideas advanced in that paper to better use. Rather than a simple name change, today I think it is more fundamental and fruitful radically to reconstruct the meaning of 'humanism', and thus, by its extension, the meaning of 'humanistic'. My reconstruction is both radical and tentative in its first expression. In later sections of the chapter I sketch out some of the recent background to the fourth wave, and the possible role of collegiality in its future.

The fourth wave of humanism

Inaugural statement

The fourth-wave paradigm, as I conceive it, is fully committed to the self-determining capacity of humans, and believes that the development of this capacity presupposes a dynamic context of spiritual animation/inspiration in which persons can actively participate. This animation has three interdependent immediate dimensions – intrapersonal, interpersonal and transpersonal. It can move deep *within* the psyche in the case of autonomous decision-making; centrally and crucially in the energetic relation *between* collaborating persons; and in the potent field of universal mind *beyond* and including personal mind. The paradigm proposes that humans become more fully human when exercising their self-determination in a co-creative relation with these three kinds of spiritual animation in ongoing dynamic interaction with each other.

In truth, I think it is Carl Rogers who implicitly launches the fourth-wave paradigm in the 1980 quotation cited above, which, in my reading of it, gives a deeply *human* account of his helping relationship in terms of the spirit *within* reaching out to the spirit *between*, which in turn opens to the spirit *beyond* – 'becomes a part of something larger'.

Some primary features

Here are some of the initial working assumptions underlying the inaugural statement:

1. The 'personal' in each of the three dimensions always refers to a person in their local and wider eco-system, including all other forms of life.
2. The dimensions are *sui generis* with respect to their shared ontological status as spiritual. They engage fully with the naturalistic, but are not reducible to it.
3. They are mutually supportive in their interactions with each other and in co-creative relations with humans, in whom they may elicit self-determining capacity, collaborative capacity including eco-effective capacity, and multi-dimensional awareness capacity.
4. They provide a dynamic context for ongoing human action research into the greater emergence of the breadth, depth and height of intrinsically human flourishing, within flourishing eco-systems, and as such:
5. They are part and parcel of the practice of Humanistic Psychology.

What is culturally unusual about this strange declaration – which I elaborate further in the section headed 'More on primary features' below – is that it makes human action research and essential human flourishing central to the measure of all things spiritual. For reasons of space, I will look at only three areas of my personal experiential inquiry which have a bearing on this thesis.

Co-counselling experience

I first encountered – experientially and phenomenologically – what I now realize is the fourth wave of humanism when I was fully engaged with applied Humanistic Psychology in the 1970s and 1980s. In my own co-counselling sessions, there were three quite distinct and interrelated phenomena. I will describe these in terms of 'animation', by which I mean a spiritual stimulation of a co-creative human response. So when I write below of an animation eliciting something, I mean that the person is making an instantaneous micro-choice to engage creatively with the eliciting process.

As a self-directing client, when engaging with the free attention of my counsellor, I would feel (1) an animation of the shared field of awareness *between* us, eliciting a living liberating interest, which in turn released (2) an animation deep *within* my psyche eliciting an impulse to attend to, and work creatively with, an emerging emotion, image, memory, felt sense to move or breathe in a particular way, or give voice or sound, etc. This in turn, when followed through, would release a whole series of further intrapsychic animations eliciting and sustaining a clearing and healing process. After a pause to re-enter fully the shared field of awareness *between* myself and my counsellor, there would suddenly occur (3) an animation like a discreet light from *beyond* my mind, eliciting spontaneous insights and realizations, cognitively restructuring the life-experience I had been dealing with.

In my micro-world as client, the developmental series went from an animation *between*, to a series of animations *within*, to a pause in the *between*, to an animation as if from *beyond*. The *beyond* in a session can cover a wide range, from illuminations of cognitive restructuring as above, to the following:

> I was giving free attention to a self-directing client who was repeating the phrase 'I am a loving person' to contradict a deep-seated self-deprecation distress pattern. This brought forth various degrees and kinds of emotional discharge. After a longish pause, she looked up and quietly and simply declaimed 'I am', and between further pauses repeated this with ever greater fullness and radiance. In reporting on this afterwards, she said it was as if the declaration 'I am' brought her to a threshold where personal consciousness is open to consciousness that is anywhere and everywhere. She has long since given me permission to share this story with others.

The inquiry group experience

'The inquiry group' is the simple name of a group meeting regularly here in New Zealand, in the early years every three weeks, in recent years every fortnight, since 1994. The description that follows amplifies the account given in Heron & Lahood (2008). The group's original purpose is to celebrate together through charismatic sound and movement our individual and interactive coming into being, and to carry this arousal forward into individual practical behaviour in everyday life and work. The core method is collaborative action inquiry, an innovative variant of Torbert's individual action inquiry (2001). We often start with a check-in round, in which each person is animated from *within* to share anything about their current inner and outer life. There is no comment on, nor interaction with, what each person shares, because the check-in is offered to the presence *between* us. There might then be a period of verbal silence, or this plus someone stroking the rim of a Tibetan bowl with a stick of wood to produce a tone.

At a certain point there is a distinct, spontaneous animation of the energy field *between* us, which elicits a further animation *within* each person, expressed in idio-syncratic improvised posture and gesture, movement, toning, rhythmic sounding of a diversity of instruments. This co-created orchestration is both an enlivenment by the spirit *within* us, and a resonant engagement with the animation *between* all our individual enlivenments. It is also both a heart-felt communion with the living presence *within* and *between* us, and an aware inquiry into its nature and credentials – a dynamic marriage of appreciation and experiential research.

This dynamic, charismatic, inquiring opening goes on for a considerable period – on average about 45 minutes – with series of crescendos and diminuendos which are potently co-created with the rhythmic life *within* us and *between* us.

There is an unmistakable final diminuendo. We become entirely still. We draw together and hold hands, or sit silently apart, and for a long period feast on, and probe with the soul, the extraordinary depths of the spiritual presence *between* us, also aptly named by one of our members as 'the band of golden silence'. This also has a clear ending. It might, or might not, be followed by a sharing, an affirmation, and an inquiring review, of what has been going on. Then we close the meeting, and people depart for their homes.

A very important outcrop of what is generated in the depths of the *between* is that, at varying intervals, we plan a co-operative inquiry into some specific human-spiritual activity undertaken in everyday life between our fortnightly meetings. Then we make space during the session for each person to report on and review the previous two weeks of activity, and, in the light of that, plan the next two weeks.

In summary of the primary process, the check-ins from *within* arouse, and engage with, the build-up of presence *between*, which, in the following period of silence, deepens to the point at which enlivenment *within* each bursts forth, further intensifying the charismatic resonance *between* all. It is also clear that the deeper the presence *between* us, the more intrinsically open it is, out of the intensity of its subtle passion, to the *beyond* – like the deep resonance between trees in a forest participates in the glory of the overarching sky beyond them and including them. The beyond is also always within and between.

Daily living experience

It also seems to me that these three kinds of animation are also available for co-creating my daily living – if and when *I* am available, and not forgetful and distracted, not caught up in self-perpetuating maladaptive attitude and action. In this context, the interpersonal widens out into the situational, a felt dynamic resonance with the presence *between* myself and the other persons and the place here where I am now. The intrapersonal is the ongoing play of animations deep *within* my psyche, each animation arousing a creative adaptation to, and interaction with, the immediate presenting situation. The transpersonal is an animation from the *beyond*, arousing me from the sleep of limited awareness, and inviting me to open the margins of my mind to an all-embracing awareness, in the light of which everything integrally possible is appropriate.

Animations *within* and *between* are in continual interplay with each other, in the light of the *beyond*. And this is especially so in a close personal relationship, where the *between* is clearly central, enriched by the *within* and the *beyond*.

More on primary features

There are several further provisional points I would like to share from my experience of these animations, to elaborate further the five key points presented above:

6. Depending upon the human structure of the situation – session, group or daily life – they come and go in their own rhythms; they both call, and can be called up; and their sequencing can vary, they can interweave and interrelate in diverse ways.

7. They are micro-gifts of living grace and discreet congeniality, three dynamic spiritual dimensions, which, when given human space to interact *together*, supportively enhance the essential humanity of our nature. And it is inherent in each animation that while it calls to be recognized as a spiritual gift, it also honours the liberty of humans to ignore it. Indeed, the animations respectfully allow for agnosticism and atheism, since anyone is free to regard any of them as naturalistic.

8. Most importantly, these gifted animations invite humans to be co-creative with them: they elicit and facilitate autonomous, intentional, innovative adaptations and initiatives. Intrapersonal animations in particular cultivate the emergence of self-determining capacity in humans. Spirited self-determination is one primary feature of the intrinsically human.

9. I have an overall sense that the *between* and the *within* provide the best conditions for effective and appropriate human co-creation with the *beyond*. I also believe, as a fourth-wave humanist, that spiritual animations between persons, *and between persons and place including other kinds of beings in that place*, are central, and that this centrality is serviced by animations both within and beyond (Heron, 2006).

10. These or any other propositions about the animations can be researched by collaborative phenomenological action research (Heron, 1996, 1998, 2006; Heron & Lahood, 2008). This kind of inquiry can establish the intentional human conditions within which these spiritual animations may occur, and clarify their distinguishing characteristics. Practical wisdom also suggests the benefits, for any such inquiry – whether individual or collective – of times of wise suspension, in which every dimension is abandoned for a period in favour of not-knowing – the paradoxical way of intentional nescience.

Sacralization

My impression is that the spiritual deeply values the unique nature of the human, delights in co-creatively enhancing and expanding it, and does this in a way that sacralizes and exalts the embodied realm of individuated persons who are creatively interacting in regenerating their world. The notion of humanism as a sacralizing force is certainly not new, for it was brilliantly foreshadowed in the second wave of humanism.

The Renaissance was an awakening of the senses: its artists rediscovered the lushness, beauty and exuberance of nature. But they did not just reproduce nature in a humdrum manner: 'They brought sanctity to nature. Renaissance landscapes are alive precisely because they are infused with spiritual energy. Beneath the visible currents of the sensuous forms of life, a deep process of re-sacralization is going on' (Skolimowski, 1994: 130).

The artists of the Renaissance showed through their own achievements that the human being is an imaginal co-creator of the world. It was not just the person as the measure of all things, but the person as the measure of a sacral reality, of a spiritually co-generated world. However, as Skolimowski points out, the world-transforming potential of this aesthetic achievement was interrupted by the dominance of the mechanistic–materialistic worldview of Bacon, Galileo, Descartes, Newton – and the third wave gradually took over.

There is indeed a sense in which the fourth wave of humanism completes and carries forward the work of the second phase, which is perhaps why I lived for ten years in the triangle between Florence, Pisa and Siena – cities of the Renaissance – where I wrote four books central to my fourth-wave worldview.

The recent background of the fourth wave

Let us start with Carl Rogers, for whom personality was governed by an innate actualizing tendency, the inherent tendency of the organism to develop all its capacities in ways which serve to maintain or enhance the organism. This organismic tendency, he believed, is selective, directional and constructive. It affects both biological and psychological functions. Psychologically, it guides people toward increased autonomy and self-sufficiency, expanding their experiences and fostering personal growth. The connotation of organismic tendency construed self-actualization as a naturalistic drive, and affirmed a grounding element of third-wave humanism in the humanistic approach (Rogers, 1959, 1980).

Eugene Gendlin, following in Rogers' footsteps, developed experiential focusing as a method for making quite explicit, within the body-mind, the selective and directional guidance of the actualizing tendency. You create a relaxed space within the body-mind, take an issue of concern into that space, let it take shape in appropriate symbolic form, and attend to the form, with all its associated affect, within that pregnant space. You focus until there is an emergent resolution of the issue in imagery and/or words, the hallmark of resolution being a subtle liberating release of somatic energy. Once again the action of the actualizing tendency was seen as organismic, i.e. somatic (Gendlin, 1981).

The spiritual animation breakthrough comes with McMahon & Campbell (1991), practitioners of experiential focusing, who re-categorize Gendlin's somatic release as a bio-spiritual event, an experience of grace in the body. Letting go into the body-feeling about an issue, Gendlin's felt shift, is now sensed as a movement of the indwelling life-giving presence and power of the spirit.

Here returns Schelling's *deus implicitus*, not only in this form, but also in several other related versions: the entelechy self, the root self, the ground of one's being, and the seeded coded essence which contains both the patterns and the possibilities of one's life (Houston, 1987); the dynamic ground (libido, psychic energy, numinous power or spirit) of somatic, instinctual, affective and creative-imaginal potentials (Washburn, 1995); Eros as spirit-in-action, the indwelling divine drive at the root of human aspiration (Wilber, 1995). Human motivation is grounded in the spiritual life-potential within. The organismic actualizing tendency becomes reconfigured as, replaced by, a process of spirit-human becoming and co-creation (Bruteau, 1997; Hubbard, 1998; Heron, 1992, 1998, 2006, 2007).

This spiritual animation within people appears to have a basic polarity, a radical and dynamic complementarity: there is the impulse to realize individual distinctness of being, and the impulse to realize interactive unity with wider fields of being (Heron, 1992). The same basic principle is found in Hindu psychology: Bhagavan Das postulates a polarity of the primal Shakti, or divine creative power within the psyche, as a will to live as an individual, and a will to live as the universal (Das, 1953). It is a subtle balance: too much individualism leads to egocentric narcissism; too much universalism leads to spiritual fascism, authoritarianism and subtle oppression.

Collegiality in the fourth wave

I think a guiding principle for balance is that of collegiality – a collegiality of unbound mutuality and *co-inherence* of distinctness of being without separation of being, the flowering of individual diversity in free unity. Berdyaev (1937) gives a good account in terms of *sobornost*: the creative process of spirit manifest through the self-determining subjectivity of human personhood engaged in the realization of value and achieved in true community. The co-inherence of persons in such a community is an interpersonal true unity-in-diversity, a dynamic, developing social form of diune awareness (Heron, 1998: 14, 99; Heron & Lahood, 2008; on the non-dual, compare and contrast with Wilber, 2000: 181).

Translated into my conceptual system, Berdyaev's account means that living spirit manifests as a dynamic interplay between, and animation of, autonomy, hierarchy and co-operation. It emerges through co-creation within and between autonomous people, each of whom can identify their own idiosyncratic true needs and interests; each of whom can also think hierarchically in terms of what values promote the true needs and interests of the whole community; and each of whom can co-operate with – that is, listen to, engage with, and negotiate agreed decisions with – their peers, celebrating diversity and difference as integral to genuine unity.

Hierarchy here is the creative leadership that seeks to promote the values of autonomy and co-operation in a peer-to-peer association. Such leadership is exercised in two ways: first, by the one or more people who take initiatives to set up such an association; and second, once the association is up and running, as spontaneous rotating leadership among the peers, when anyone takes initiatives that further enhance the autonomy and co-operation of other participating members.

The autonomy of participants is not that of the old Cartesian ego, isolated and cut off from the world. Descartes sat inside a big stove to get at his *cogito, ergo sum* – I think, therefore I am; and while his exclusively subjective self provided a necessary leverage against traditional dogmatisms to help found the modern worldview, it left the modern self alienated from the separated world it commands. The autonomy of those who flourish within *sobornost*, by contrast, is an autonomy that is rounded and enriched by a profound kind of inner animation that develops and flourishes only in felt interconnectedness, participative engagement, with other persons, and with the biodiversity and integral ecology of our planet (Spretnak, 1995).

This is the participatory worldview, which I see as the foreground of the emerging fourth wave of humanism. It is also expressed in an extended epistemology: our conceptual knowing of the world is grounded in our experiential knowing – a felt resonance with the world and imaginal participation in it. This epistemic participation is the ground for political participation in social processes that integrate autonomy, hierarchy and co-operation. What we are now about is a whole collaborative regeneration of our world through co-creative engagement with the spirit that animates it and us. For just a few of the many contributors to the early dawn of the participatory worldview, see: Abram (1996); Bateson (1979); Berman (1981); Ferrer (2002); Heron (1992, 1996, 1998, 2006); Merleau-Ponty (1962); Reason (1994); Reason & Rowan (1981); Skolimowski (1994); Spretnak (1991); Tarnas (1991); and Varela, Thompson & Rosch (1991).

A Humanism-4 account of Humanistic Psychology

What would Humanistic Psychology look like if it were an expression of this account of fourth-wave humanism? Primarily, it would take spirituality out of the 'transhumanistic' realm, and put it back where it belongs, in an enhanced, more rounded and grounded form at the very core of the human realm. It then manifests as collegiality, a collaborative regeneration of what it is to be a human being.

On this overall view, spirituality is located in the interpersonal heart of the human condition, where people co-operate to explore meaning, build relationship and manifest creativity through collaborative action inquiry into the integration and consummation of many areas of human development. One possible model of such collegial applied spirituality has at least eight distinguishing characteristics:

1. It is *developmentally holistic*, involving diverse major areas of human development; and the holism is both within each, and between them. Prime value is put on relational areas, such as gender, psychosexuality, emotional and interpersonal skills, communicative competence, peer communion, morality, human ecology, supported by the individualistic, such as contemplative competence, physical fitness.
2. It is *psychosomatically holistic*, embracing a fully embodied and vitalized co-creative expression with spirit. Spirituality is found not just at the top end of a developmental line, but is explored co-creatively with spiritual animations in the living root of its embodied form, in the relational heart of its current level of unfolding, and in the transcendent awareness embracing it.
3. It is *epistemologically holistic*, including many ways of knowing: knowing by presence with, by intuiting significant form and process, by conceptualizing, by practising. Such holistic knowing is intrinsically dialogic, action- and inquiry-oriented. It is fulfilled in peer-to-peer participative inquiry, and the participation is both epistemic and political.
4. It is *ontologically holistic*, open to the manifest as nature, culture and the subtle, and to spirit as immanent life, the situational present, and transcendent mind.

It sees our relational, social process in this *present human situation* as the immediate locus of unfolding human co-creative integration with immanent life and transcendent mind (Heron, 1998).

5. It is focused on worthwhile practical purposes that promote a flourishing humanity-cum-ecosystem; that is, it is rooted in an extended doctrine of rights with regard to social and ecological liberation.
6. It embraces peer-to-peer relations and participatory forms of decision-making. The latter in particular can be seen as a radical discipline in relational spirituality, burning up a lot of the privatized ego.
7. It honours the current progressive and widespread emergence of peer-to-peer forms of association and practice including the resurgence of the commons and the development of a post-capitalist worldview (Bollier & Helfrich 2016; Kostakis & Bauwens 2014; Mason 2015).
8. It affirms the role, as defined earlier, of both initiating leadership, and spontaneously surfacing rotating leadership among the peers.

In a sentence: it encourages us to inquire together, imaginatively and creatively, about how to act together in a spirited way to flourish on and with our planet.

References

Abram, D. (1996). *The Spell of the Sensuous.* New York: Vintage Books.

Bateson, G. (1979). *Mind and Nature: A Necessary Unity.* New York: Dutton.

Berdyaev, N. (1937). *The Destiny of Man.* London: Ayer.

Berman, M. (1981). *The Reenchantment of the World.* Ithaca, NY: Cornell University Press.

Bollier, D. & Helfrich, S. (Eds) (2016). *The Wealth of the Commons.* Amherst, MA: Levellers Press.

Bruteau, B. (1997). *God's Ecstasy: The Creation of a Self-Creating World.* New York: The Crossroad Publishing Company.

Chaudhuri, H. (1977). *The Evolution of Integral Consciousness.* Wheaton, IL: The Theosophical Publishing House.

Das, B. (1953). *The Science of Emotions.* Madras: Theosophical Publishing House.

Ferrer, J. (2002). *Revisioning Transpersonal Theory: A Participatory Vision of Human Spirituality.* Albany, NY: State University of New York Press.

Ferrer, J. (2011). Participatory spirituality and transpersonal theory: a ten-year retrospective. *Journal of Transpersonal Psychology*, 43: 1–34.

Gendlin, E. (1981). *Focusing.* London: Bantam Press.

Grof, S. (c. 2004). A Brief History of Transpersonal Psychology, available at www.stanislavgrof.com (accessed 30 March 2017); also published in the *International Journal of Transpersonal Studies*, 27, 2008: 46–54.

Heron, J. (1992). *Feeling and Personhood: Psychology in Another Key.* London: Sage.

Heron, J. (1996). *Co-operative Inquiry: Research into the Human Condition.* London: Sage.

Heron, J. (1998). *Sacred Science: Person-centred Inquiry into the Spiritual and the Subtle.* Ross-on-Wye: PCCS Books.

Heron, J. (2001). Holism and collegiality. *Self & Society*, 29(2): 17–19.

Heron, J. (2006). *Participatory Spirituality: A Farewell to Authoritarian Religion.* Morrisville, NC: Lulu Press.

Heron, J. (2007). Participatory fruits of spiritual inquiry. *Re Vision: A Journal of Consciousness and Transformation*, 29(3): 7–17.

Heron, J. & Lahood, G. (2008). Charismatic inquiry in concert: action research in the realm of the between. In P. Reason & H. Bradbury (Eds), *Handbook of Action Research: Participative Inquiry and Practice*, 2nd edn (pp. 439–49). London: Sage.

Houston, J. (1987). *The Search for the Beloved*. Los Angeles, CA: Tarcher.

Hubbard, B. M. (1998). *Conscious Evolution: Awakening the Power of our Social Potential*. Novato, CA: New World Library.

Kostakis, V. & Bauwens, M. (2014). *Network Society and Future Scenarios for a Collaborative Economy*. London: Palgrave Macmillan.

Lajoie, D. H. & Shapiro, S. I. (1992). Definitions of transpersonal psychology: the first twenty-three years. *Journal of Transpersonal Psychology*, 24: 79–98.

McMahon, E. & Campbell, P. (1991). *The Focusing Steps*. Kansas City, MO: Sheed and Ward.

Maslow, A. (1964). *Religions, Values, and Peak-Experiences*. New York: Penguin Press.

Mason, P. (2015). *PostCapitalism: A Guide to Our Future*. London: Allen Lane.

Merleau-Ponty, M. (1962). *Phenomenology of Perception*. London: Routledge & Kegan Paul.

Reason, P. (Ed.) (1994). *Participation in Human Inquiry*. London: Sage.

Reason, P. & Rowan, J. (Eds) (1981). *Human Inquiry: A Sourcebook of New Paradigm Research*. Chichester: Wiley.

Rogers, C. (1959). A theory of therapy, personality, and interpersonal relationships, as developed in the client-centred framework. In S. Koch (Ed.), *Psychology: A Study of a Science*, Vol. 3. New York: Penguin.

Rogers, C. (1961). *On Becoming a Person: A Therapist's View of Psychotherapy*. London: Constable.

Rogers, C. (1980). *A Way of Being*. Boston, MA: Houghton Mifflin.

Rowan, J. (2005). *A Guide to Humanistic Psychology*, 3rd edn. London: UK Association for Humanistic Psychology Practitioners (AHPP).

Shirazi, B. A. K. (2005). Integral psychology: psychology of the whole human being. In M. Schlitz, T. Amorok & M. S. Micozzi (Eds), *Consciousness and Healing: Integral Approaches to Mind–Body Medicine* (pp. 233–47). St. Louis, MO: Elsevier Churchill Livingston.

Skolimowski, H. (1994). *The Participatory Mind*. London: Arkana.

Spretnak, C. (1991). *States of Grace: The Recovery of Meaning in the Postmodern Age*. San Francisco, CA: Harper-Collins.

Spretnak, C. (1995). Embodied, embedded philosophy. *Open Eye* (California Institute for Integral Studies), 12(1): 4–5.

Tarnas, R. (1991). *The Passion of the Western Mind: Understanding the Ideas That Have Shaped Our World View*. New York: Ballantine.

Torbert, W. R. (2001). The practice of action inquiry. In P. Reason & H. Bradbury (Eds), *Handbook of Action Research* (pp. 207–18). London: Sage.

Varela, F. J., Thompson, E., & Rosch, E. (1991). *The Embodied Mind: Cognitive Science and Human Experience*. Cambridge, MA: MIT Press.

Walsh, R. & Vaughan, F. (1993). On transpersonal definitions. *Journal of Transpersonal Psychology*, 25: 199–207.

Washburn, M. (1995). *The Ego and the Dynamic Ground: A Transpersonal Theory of Human Development*. Albany, NY: State University of New York Press.

Wilber, K. (1995). *Sex, Ecology, Spirituality: The Spirit of Evolution*. Boston, MA: Shambhala.

Wilber, K. (2000). *Integral Psychology*. Boston, MA: Shambhala.

26

HUMANISTIC PSYCHOLOGY AND THE EVOLUTION OF CONSCIOUSNESS

Jill Hall

How are we, at this particular stage in the long, complex journey of unfolding consciousness, to do justice to the full spectrum of human experience? What I most value about Humanistic Psychology is not only its acknowledgement but its active exploration of this spectrum. Commitment to open-minded enquiry follows as an inevitable consequence, all the more salient as preoccupation with either desired or dreaded 'regulation' of 'professionals' in the field of psychotherapy and counselling fuels a contraction of perspective. How did this stealthy slippage toward reductionism come about?

In the 1980s and 1990s I spoke of the effects of what I termed 'Ego Imperialism' (see Hall, 1993). This not only energizes the blossoming of the Victim Archetype, but the concurrent creative urge toward individuation – enabling the taking of personal responsibility for one's choices in life – tends to be waylaid and hijacked into individual*ism*. The last thing acknowledged by ego is the uniqueness of each and every human being, as this makes comparisons between us redundant. An unintegrated ego, being fundamentally insubstantial, can only too easily be drawn beyond its necessary task of delineation which the ability to make comparisons is designed to serve. Comparison then feeds notions that go beyond that of being a differentiated entity: it enables the notion of being 'better' than others which, of course, carries the threat of being 'worse' than others. What was intended to boost a sense of security inadvertently undermines it, and a circularity results. Mechanisms that are necessary for the phenomenon of consciousness can only too easily be subverted and can, when this occurs, carry a heavy price.[1]

Is this not mirrored on the socio-political level by the spread of Western capitalism, with its emphasis on competition as prior to that of co-operation? Compelling but increasingly insubstantial as it loses its original grounding, capitalism has to adapt at a radical level or play itself out – just as life itself has eventually to respond to real conditions or else live itself to collapse or death. An ego-dominated psyche not only regards fellow human beings as competitors, but Nature as an object of exploitation, a resource from which to extract whatever we want and believe we need; and the more incomplete we experience ourselves to be, the more we feel driven, even justified, to continue in this vein. 'Ultimately neoliberal capitalism is self-destructive', Madeleine Bunting wrote in the *Guardian Weekly* of 10 October 2008. We could add – yes, and also destructive to the individual selves caught up in it.

A parallel surge in ego-level 'takeover' of religion is revealed both in ever-more ardent and reductive forms of fundamentalism or in a progressive diminution of energy – a sense of gradually fading out, as access to wonder and mystery is curtailed. Spiritual energy is often left somewhat rootless (unless still culturally entwined with its ancient timeless source), and thus moves and unfolds here and there, all over the world, within and through and between individuals.

What is the role of Humanistic Psychology in this 'story'? Not only its underlying philosophical base in an holistic metaphysics, but also its insistence on applying this on the experiential level of human exchange, is surely of crucial import.

As I see it, Humanistic Psychology evolved as an inspired expression of the creative impulse in those drawn toward self-development and/or involved in psychotherapy. It was about the individual, in commonality with other individuals, taking responsibility for their well-being, along with the healing of their woundings rather than being defined by the 'experts', with their rationalizations and theories about 'the other' (i.e. 'patients'). A flurry of fresh ideas and practices were born, developed and offered, tasted and tested, through active participation. A search toward greater consciousness and fulfilment ensued, courageously experimental, flawed and sometimes chaotic, but essentially liberating and life-affirming. An experiential and holistic approach established a place in the field of practical psychology, embracing body, mind and spirit with the built-in assumption that those engaging in such exploration would take responsibility for their choice to participate. The very idea of regulation would have appeared alien, and would have stifled the green shoots of what so many in the field now take for granted.

What are practitioners in the arena of therapeutic human exchange now bringing on ourselves if, or as, we begin to find ourselves tempted to claim and control, formalize and 'scientize' a relational activity that is closer to an art and cannot help but work differently for different people? Have not many who are drawn to Humanistic Psychology begun to let fear slip in, often dressed up as 'being responsible' or 'realistic', and thus found themselves sliding toward increasing professionalization, unaware of those aggregations of collective misplaced ego energy? Clients (or co-workers) fall into the background, as debates ensue about who should be included and who excluded among those who erstwhile were free to focus on them. If clients are seen as victims who need specialized 'protection' or 'direction', rather than sensitive respect, those who deem this necessary will inevitably, even if inadvertently, end up as victims of controlling systems themselves. What a diversion of energy. And who decides? By what criteria? Who judges? On and on and on, while the immediate urgent needs of actual clients recede into oblivion. What an ironic outcome of the rise in risk and safety rhetoric. Safe for whom?

And so I ask again, what is the role of Humanistic Psychology in this 'story'?

I believe it has a vital role to play, as new insecurities emerge in this time of uncertainty and transition to 'we know not what'. Rather than being dragged backwards, drawn by the energy of contraction, giving way to caution and fears of exclusion from controlling bodies that will subsequently be seen as blatantly inadequate and limiting, may we remember our roots. May we continue to embrace, in ourselves and in those with whom we work, all that it means to be a human being.

Only by acknowledging the whole of who we are – body, heart, mind, soul and spirit – can ego relax into a less dominant role. Only then can ego cease exacerbating our insecurity by over-reaching its necessary contribution of delineation on the three-dimensional plane. Only then can we give fitting attention and weight to the uniqueness and mystery of each human being. And only then can we become resilient enough to be able to respond creatively to the new and unknown challenges that lie ahead. For they are likely to be exacting.

As previously posited, we face the phenomenon of global capitalism fuelled by the essentially insubstantial but inflated energy of 'Ego Imperialism', and thus glorifying highly organized and yet anarchic competition, not just for natural resources but for what we do not actually need (other than to boost ego). It is not surprising that we eventually land up trading fictions – packaged figures with no material base whatsoever, deficit financing (which even the vast US arms industry cannot 'make good') with increasing reliance on elusive future 'growth' fanning active encouragement of more and more people taking on more and more debt.[2] The inherent vulnerability of non-holistic, ego-driven systems is all too evident, and it is fascinating to witness a political culture that so reveres rationality increasingly reduced to blind faith and the manipulation of 'facts' through the game of statistics. And all this relying on a climate of conscious or semi-conscious deception.

Our 'profession' is already tainted with this global pull to rationalize and ignore what it cannot deliver. This is evidenced in the proliferation of training courses for therapists and counsellors (and this includes those with a Humanistic Psychology orientation) in the full knowledge that there are not enough jobs for them all. The pretence that a university degree or two will solve the problem has become a means of 'upping the package' – a selling-point. The acceptance of students looking for a career and who have never had any therapy themselves, or shown an interest in focused self-development, is another worrying tendency. Clients' needs are easily marginalized if the agenda is dictated by forces outside them. It is not only the bankers who have been sliding into a loss of integrity. It could be any one of us, including people we value and respect.

I believe that we must wake up and stand aside from these defective trends, as we did some decades ago – although at that time the dangers and limitations we hoped to transcend appeared more specific to our field, then dominated by psychiatry, with its labelling and emphasis on pathology (Barnett, 1973). Humanistic Psychology recognized that a fundamental shift was necessary: an expansion in how we see ourselves as human beings.[3] This latter needs to be affirmed afresh. And the holding of a well-grounded space or context that is inclusive of the spiritual dimension experienced by human beings, and the integration of such experience in the lives of individuals, constitutes one of our greatest contributions to the field in which we work, and one of our most crucial tasks for the future, as we move toward an increasingly secularized Western world.

I myself arrived in the experimental and exploratory arena of early Humanistic Psychology days straight from the world of academic philosophy, having just completed an examination in formal logic. A few weeks earlier I had been visited by a most unsought and unwelcome intuition. While gazing at an avenue of trees in South London I suddenly knew I had to give up my studies. They had become an absorbing passion which at that time balanced domestic life and motherhood, and I knew in the same instant that I would fall into a state of depression if I were to give them up. However, since early childhood I had always known that I must follow such inner promptings. Sure enough, I dived into a place of internal darkness that my intense 'head' activity had held at bay – thinking about metaphysical matters had eased the pain of my reluctant atheism. I was rescued by a flier advertising Encounter Groups being dropped through our letter-box. A commitment to four evenings was required. I had never heard of such things, but signed up out of curiosity. Although stunned and amazed by this new mode of interaction, after two evenings I found I was 'working' in the centre of the group myself. Within a few weeks I tracked down and joined a one-year 'Intensive' course in Body Work. My whole world changed, and I was no longer depressed.

However, the lack of 'evidence-based data', let alone feasible argument, for the array of assumptions and spiritual notions that others took as truth astounded and taxed me greatly, in spite of becoming as passionate about bio-energetics as I had been about philosophy. What a liberation when, one day, I relieved myself of the burden of deciding whether someone else's views (or even my own) were *either* true *or* false. I decided to suspend this practice, and replace it with discerning if someone felt authentic to me. What mattered was making a real connection with the unique fellow human being they happened to be. Gradually, through my own incremental experience, sometimes somewhat startling and inexplicable in purely rational terms and yet undeniable as a lived reality, I could do no other than reclaim the immediacy of the spiritual 'knowings' that had sustained me as a child.

Ian McGilchrist, in his fascinating book *The Master and his Emissary: The Divided Brain and the Making of the Western World* (2009), makes a brilliantly compelling and informed case for the necessity of letting the right brain, with its all-inclusive intuitive consciousness, lead, while welcoming the necessary service of the left brain *as its emissary*. This is precisely what Humanistic Psychology stood for and practised in its initiating days. The powerful reign of left-brain dominance which began its ascendancy in the 17th century – what we call the Enlightenment – has served its time. It has both affirmed and encouraged the robust questioning of the independent rational mind, and brought about phenomenal advancement in the mechanical and technological arena; but it cannot handle a holistic appreciation of what it is to be a human being, nor see why the right brain is so essential for this purpose. The job of the left brain is to be selective and blot out anything extraneous to a particular focus. It literally does not see, or take account of, that which lies outside its selected task. It does not aim to know the whole picture, and is not set up to do so. All great scientists rely on flashes of right-brain intuition and creative thought, both to explore and actualize the possible. Mathematicians posit imaginary numbers to further the power of equations, which later result in effective applications on the material plane. The left brain cannot cope with mystery. It is not surprising, therefore, that its dominance gave birth to Literalism, Reductionism and Realism, without even being aware that these were perspectives only – mere 'ways of seeing' the world – enabling the illusion of 'having' the truth. Unfortunately, the clarity afforded by selection, or unacknowledged abstraction, from the intricate ever-mobile complexity of the whole supports this illusion. The left brain can never deal with, let alone apprehend, ontological unity.

Deprived of the means of acknowledging what we do not know, the prominence of this bias invited arrogance, and rendered understanding of our full humanity unavailable or radically diminished. It also left the field clear for the inflation of ego with the costly and dysfunctional repercussions previously described. Given that this can never serve workers in our field, Humanistic Psychology with its right/left brain balance has an important, and urgent, contribution to make at this point in the unfolding of consciousness.

I remember, when working in a residential group setting, the thrill and liberation of experiencing the mystery of the other – both the commonality and the inherent mystery. And then discovering the fruitfulness of honouring that mystery which also continually reveals itself, the more you honour it. We can never fully know another (although we know ourselves more fully through the other), and in the respectful wonder and fascination and appreciation of difference, we discover that more and more becomes evident, and we dare to find ways to communicate to that other what they reveal of who they are. And yet far from allowing the leadership of the right brain in this way, it seems that training courses in our field give ever-more prominence to left-brain preoccupations. Surely we betray all we once stood for if we move away from giving priority to in-the-moment utterly creative and unplanned occurrences of connection with another that no theorizing or writing of papers and getting of further degrees can win for us.

It is essential that we take stock and honour our genesis. The establishment of connection with the other, at whatever level they endeavour to offer of themselves, and responding, if possible, with that level in oneself; being in the living moment with them, knowing not where it can take us – from the ordinary, the petty, tainted or tragic, obscure or self-evident, or perhaps sublime. The bonus is that learning through connection with the other leads to a further unfolding of oneself, and to the discovery of new levels of consciousness.

Reciprocal learning; this is how I see the essence of Humanistic Psychology, and thus the seed for the continual regeneration of its future. All our work experientially based, inspired and structured by creative theorizing, but these hypotheses and theories elucidated in training as much as is possible face to face, and not primarily through the written word, nor the trainee's understanding of them primarily assessed through the written word. I am a great lover of theories, and enjoy exploring them, but had to learn to hold them lightly. (I believe it was Jung who urged us to 'Learn your theories well, but put them aside when you touch the miracle of a living soul' (Jung, 1928). He certainly had quite a lot to drop!)

Theories are like different intellectual 'species' which can illuminate different modes of psychic and energetic structure and expression. My foundational training was with Gerda Boyeson, who founded the Institute of Bio-dynamic Psychology in London. She embodied what she taught, and thus communicated the reality of unfolding life energy, along with the means of accessing and regulating that life energy, and thus the bio-dynamic nature of being-in-the-world. Gerda herself did not advocate the practice of mixing different methods and approaches to therapy – what she called 'fruit salad'. However, such an approach could be viewed as exploring different 'fruits' for different people in different circumstances or on different occasions, and seeing if they bring forth illumination and greater well-being for that client. This is how I see that vital combination of inclusiveness and particularity expressed in the rich and comprehensive range of therapeutic practices that characterize Humanistic Psychology in its responsiveness to the diversity within our oneness.

It is the unique individual expression of our common nature that Humanistic Psychology endeavours to address. And the creativeness of the different approaches that have evolved under this title could be seen not as 'fruit salad' but as a bunch of flowers, each whole and distinct in itself and 'right' (i.e. therapeutically releasing and revealing) for different individuals in their particularity. It is of vital importance that we stand clear and firm, and resist the current pull toward more contained models with set numbers of sessions, while not excluding that such methods have some value for many people. We must be alert to the danger of any creeping resignation with regard to this trend as some sort of inevitable convergent reality.

If Humanistic Psychology is to have a vibrant future, it could do well to sustain the spirit of its vibrant past. It is not a call to mimic the past, but to reconnect with the source that enabled the courageous and innovative growth of the Humanistic Psychology movement. After a period of contraction and control, consciousness at some point will expand once more. After a 'season' of regulation and reduction to the measurable, continued out-of-date left-brain dominance and thus the prestige of numerical outcomes, tick boxes, caution and reductionist notions of experimentation, I feel confident that a fresh thrust of consciousness will surge forth yet again. I believe that Humanistic Psychology, if it holds to being truly humanistic, will then ride on a further tide of courageous innovation, based on the lived appreciation of the pain and wonder of being a human being.

We must endeavour neither to react nor capitulate to the disheartening backsliding that so often occurs within the underlying evolutionary expansion of consciousness, and I find it helpful to view this present state of contraction in our field within this wide-ranging context. Helpful because it allows an uncompromising short-term pessimism while embracing an irrepressible optimism and confidence in the thrust of life itself. It is not surprising that agonizing excursions and countless deviations occur, as we attempt to integrate the complexity of who we are. It appears that all life on earth evolved in this marvellous but hazardous process of becoming, and so we human beings are equally vulnerable – we who have the most complex journey to undertake. For we have many dimensions of being to integrate before we become free enough to enter into fully loving relationship with each other and All That Is.

I believe the time will come when ego relaxes into its necessary function as an instrument of delineation employed by the self, each individual active on a three-dimensional plane, but informed by the multi-dimensional awareness of soul (mediated by the phenomena of imagination, intuition and inspiration) and the promptings of spirit – the 'Whole' emanating as a dynamic all-embracing collective of unique sparks of conscious loving.

Humanistic Psychology has its tiny but significant part to play in all this. However depressing current trends may be, I have a deep confidence in the ultimate realization of humanity. Although shadowed now in somewhat ludicrous individualism resulting in inadequate, misleading and divisive forms of association or 'ego-collectives', do we not have glimpses of true connection between individuating beings, enabling the exchange of love and an empathetic sense of the underlying affinity of all beings in the universe? No matter if the fulfilment of what it means to be a human being takes eons, all the seeds and intimations are discernable, although not yet sustainable. May we hold faith and do our bit.

Notes

1   I ponder on the notion that this is what is meant by the 'forgiveness of sins' revealed by the multi-consciousness realized in the person called Jesus.
2   It is telling that Microloan – lending small sums to people to establish small enterprises to sustain themselves – truly does lead to growth. And being 'Person Centred', 99 per cent of the loans are repaid.
3   Our success is reflected in the 2002 report by The Royal College of Psychiatrists: 'Strict adherence to guidelines, for fear of risk, should not be allowed to stifle responsible innovative practice or the patient's choice of alternative therapeutic solutions to the same problem.'

References

Barnett, M. (1973). *People, Not Psychiatry*. London: Allen & Unwin.

Bunting, M. (2008). *Guardian Weekly*, 10 October.

Hall, J. (1993). *The Reluctant Adult: An Exploration of Choice*. Bridport, Dorset: Prism Press.

Jung, C. G. (1928). *Contributions to Analytical Psychology*; quoted in *Self & Society*, 27(1), 1999: 22.

McGilchrist, I. (2009). *The Master and his Emissary: The Divided Brain and the Making of the Western World*. New Haven, CT: Yale University Press (2nd edn, 2012).

EDITORIAL CONCLUSION

Richard House, David Kalisch and
Jennifer Maidman

I am not a mechanism, an assembly of sections . . .

(From D. H. Lawrence's poem, 'Healing')

It was some half a century ago when Humanistic Psychology first burst on to the scene in the USA, and then a little later in Britain, being widely hailed at the time as a 'Third Force' that would humanize what was seen as an increasingly *de*humanizing Psychology, helping to counterbalance the perceived shortcomings of behaviourism and psychoanalysis, and bring a much-needed holistic perspective to mainstream Psychology. In this book we have deliberately presented readers with a broad spectrum of views from right across the humanistic field; and as you will have seen, while there is some degree of consensus around core, defining humanistic values and practices, there is also a great deal of diversity, debate and even disagreement. That sort of open and vigorous exchange of ideas has surely to be a healthy sign, wherever the field might be headed – cf. William Blake's resounding 'Without contraries is no progression'!

It is certainly difficult to dispute the contention that Humanistic Psychology has already had a very significant impact on modern Western culture. Keith Tudor, for example, has highlighted just some of the ways in which Humanistic Psychology has been a big success story – namely, that it is 'a recognized "force" or tradition with a number of "schools", "modalities" or "approaches"'; that it has well-established training courses and programmes; that it has generated a considerable literature, including three professional journals, the *Journal of Humanistic Psychology*, *The Humanistic Psychologist* and *Self & Society*; and that it has a presence in mainstream organizations, including the American Psychological Association (APA) and as a College of the UK Council for Psychotherapy (UKCP).

One key question that arises from this is that of how important it is that Humanistic Psychology should work harder to provide a clear and unambiguous definition of its subject-matter, values and practices. Such a move (as suggested by Windy Dryden in his challenging chapter) can appear attractive and pragmatic. However, and as outlined at length in our Introduction, Humanistic Psychology has historically stood for counter-cultural values that challenge head-on the taken-for-granted assumptions of a modern technocratic society; and for many of its adherents, it would be in grave danger of abandoning its key cultural role of 'ideology-critique', if it were to collude with mechanistic 'audit culture' values and practices (King and Moutsou, 2010; cf. D. H. Lawrence's wonderful poem, 'Healing'). So, when Windy Dryden urges us to really 'get our act together', sharpen up our theory and self-publicity, publish some key texts, and, in the process, earn legitimacy and recognition within the mainstream, many will probably agree with him, but some humanistic folk at least will likely think long and hard before going down that path. Having said that, in his chapter Keith Tudor argues that Humanistic Psychology is, in many respects, *already* mainstream and institutional, if not institutional*ized*. So clearly, even within Humanistic Psychology itself there are very different views on the extent to which the approach has already become part of 'the mainstream', and how it might align or re-align itself going forward.

If it *is* the case that a somewhat ill-defined, and perhaps inherently 'un-definable', humanistic approach is floundering amid the current audit-obsessed *Zeitgeist*, is this perhaps an acceptable – indeed, unavoidable – price to pay for retaining Humanistic Psychology's integrity, humanity and counter-cultural edge, in a world that shows clear signs of movement, politically at least, in the opposite direction? For if Humanistic Psychology and its advocates were to embrace and merely 'fit in with' current cultural toxicities, who would be left to hold the counter-cultural space that many believe to be necessary for any healthy and growthful society? As postmodern theorist David Harvey poignantly shows, fitting in with the status quo can only ever generate what he terms 'status quo theory' (Harvey, 1973) – surely the very antithesis of what Humanistic Psychology represents and stands for.

So we certainly do not see any pat solutions or easy answers emerging from this book, and for the future of the Humanistic Psychology project. Indeed, those of us with some postmodern (see James T. Hansen's and Lois Holzman's chapters) and phenomenological and/or existential (Kirk J. Schneider) sympathies might well argue that it is actually vitally important *not* to close down or prescriptively define what Humanistic Psychology might be or become, or to fetishize the quest for clarity of identity and definition. From this perspective, an intrinsically indissoluble aspect of Humanistic Psychology is precisely that it *is* counter cultural, difficult to pin down and codify, with a fluid and ever-evolving identity whose very mutability is part of what the approach is all about. And if being somewhat marginalized relative to mainstream culture is the price we have to pay for staying true to core values, then, perhaps, some would say, 'So be it'. Richard Mowbray (1995) wrote eloquently about this issue over two decades ago in his seminal text *The Case against Psychotherapy Registration*. Referring to what he calls 'Preserving the fringe' (the title of his Chapter 27) – or a kind of 'counter-cultural space' – Mowbray wrote that Humanistic Psychology and the human potential movement must stay on the margin and not be 'absorbed', not be tempted by the carrots of recognition, respectability and financial security into reverting to the mainstream but rather remain – on the 'fringe' – as a source that stimulates, challenges convention and 'draws out' the unrealized potential for 'being' in the members of that society.

(pp. 198–9)

And he continued, 'A society needs a healthy fringe . . . *it must not be absorbed into the mainstream* – which would stultify it with "establishment" thinking and respectability' (p. 199, our italics).

A caveat here is that of course, the 'fringe' itself does not remain fixed. The 'cultural margins' are themselves always moving, and that which may have once seemed incontrovertibly radical and 'counter cultural' might be experienced as conservative and stuck-in-the-past by a younger generation. We cannot help wondering whether some aspect of this dynamic might account for the increasing average age of the humanistic community. If so, it is even more crucial that humanistic practitioners and academics be ruthlessly honest with themselves regarding taken-for-granted assumptions and potential blind spots. We hope this book might, among other things, facilitate reflection on such issues, because it is by no means unthinkable, in an age of increasing personal autonomy and 'service user' involvement, that Humanistic Psychology, at least in some of its more overtly professionalized and status-obsessed manifestations, could come to be perceived as *itself* part of an unhealthy and even redundant 'expert-driven' status quo, rather than the empowering, counter-cultural force which its traditional adherents would wish and believe it to be.

Editing this book has helped to remind us that there are also quite different humanistic *identities*, as between American, British and (no doubt) other Humanistic Psycholog*ies*; and that in a culturally relative world, it seems wholly apt that different cultures should indeed generate different manifestations of the humanistic impulse, and that therefore there never can be one, universal definition of Humanistic Psychology. Thus, John Heron (Chapter 8) reminds us that the founding fathers of Humanistic Psychology in the USA were self-proclaimed atheists; whereas in the UK, both of the Johns who are very much the respected Elders of British Humanistic Psychology, John Heron and John Rowan, see transpersonal and spiritual concerns as being central to the humanistic impulse (Chapters 25 and 19, respectively; cf. *Self & Society*, 2017). So the cultural struggle between secular and transpersonal humanism is one that is also playing itself out within Humanistic Psychology itself; and far from this being a problem or an unwelcome contradiction, one might ask why should Humanistic Psychology itself not faithfully reflect the cultural and evolutionary struggles and arguments that are preoccupying humankind at this juncture in the evolution of human consciousness? (e.g. see Hansen, 2012; Rowan, 2012; Jill Hall's Chapter 26 in this volume).

Might Humanistic Psychology, then, help to build a philosophical bridge between the transpersonal/spiritual and the secular? Certainly, at this time there appears to be a dire need for a counterbalance to the extreme and fundamentalist visions of both science and religion which increasingly predominate, and Humanistic Psychology, with its emphasis on mutual respect and diversity, appears well placed to facilitate some common ground (cf. Griffin, 1997, 2000). What sometimes seems to be absent amid the sound and fury of clashing ideologies is something that humanistic approaches have historically been very good at: fostering a sense of the significance and value of relationships and, crucially, the necessity for authentic, human encounter as a fundamental foundation for understanding, movement and creativity.

Another tension within Humanistic Psychology is that between modernity and postmodernity – that is, whether or not to embrace, or at least forge some kind of relationship with, the postmodern, post-structuralist and social constructionist thinking represented by theorists such as Nietzsche, Derrida, Foucault, Merleau-Ponty, Lacan, and others. Again, there are very different viewpoints on this within Humanistic Psychology, with writers like James T. Hansen (Chapter 7) and Manu Bazzano (Foreword) strongly supporting an engagement with postmodern thought, while others, such as John Rowan (2000), are sceptical of the value and the relevance of such engagements. Certainly, some hallowed Humanistic Psychology notions, like that of the unitary, actualizing 'self', are fundamentally problematized by both postmodern and Critical Psychology thinking (as Hansen argues; cf. Parker, 1999, 2007); yet our hunch is that many, if not most 'critical humanists' (Halliwell and Mousley, 2003; Moon, 2012) are actually instinctively drawn to such deconstructionist ideas, and are also open to having the 'shadow' side of our humanist ontologies and epistemologies subjected to a critical deconstructionist 'gaze' (Parker, 1999). Indeed, it might well be that – to coin a phrase (and with apologies to John Rowan) – 'Scratch a humanist and you'll likely find an incipient post-structuralist underneath' – and also, perhaps, vice versa!

Certainly, at the very least we should perhaps be open to building bridges with adjacent cosmologies such as these (embodiment and phenomenology being other notable examples – Felder & Robbins, 2011; Johnson, 2012; *Self & Society*, 2014), just as Humanistic Psychology has historically found, and is currently finding, a great deal of common ground with the existential and phenomenological thinking of the likes of Heidegger, Husserl, Merleau-Ponty, Buber, Levinas and even the later Wittgenstein (e.g. Loewenthal and Snell, 2003; Orange, 2009; Heaton, 2010), and with postmodern critiques of 'psychopathology' discourse (e.g. Levin, 1987; Fee, 2000).

Another key theme with which Humanistic Psychology today has to grapple is that of identity and (dare we use the term!) 'branding'. In an age where – rightly or wrongly – clear and unambiguous 'branding' increasingly seems to be a taken-for-granted, commonly unquestioned requirement, can Humanistic Psychology (and the therapeutic practices that have historically aligned themselves with it) effectively 'sell itself' without compromising its core values? Fundamentally, should Humanistic Psychology seek ways to establish its own place at the mainstream 'high table', or does intrinsically counter-cultural humanistic praxis still 'hold' something crucially important which is absent from other therapeutic and cultural discourses? – something that desperately needs preserving from the dead hand of bureaucracy, fear-driven regulation, and the professional 'status wars' that have characterized the therapy world for decades (House, 2010). Or as we have suggested in our Introduction to this book, and as several of our contributors have argued, is there in fact – in the huge changes that are now happening globally – a middle position opening up? As Peter Hawkins puts it 'Much of what Humanistic Psychology initiated and fought for has entered the mainstream, . . . the challenges of our time call for a new rhetoric of participation and co-responsibility'.

However, having said that, it might also be the case that as Dina Glouberman writes in Chapter 17, 'if we look closely at some of the areas where we [Humanistic Psychology] have been pioneers, we will see that the ideas might have been adopted, but the application has narrowed so that they no longer represent the original vision' (p. 209). For us this is a crucial point, for it is commonly argued that there is a very real sense in which 'we are all humanists now', and that most core humanistic ideas have long since been assimilated into the mainstream. Glouberman rightly cautions us to be aware that it can often look as if mainstream culture has been humanized, when in reality this is far from being the case. As Jean-François Lyotard might have said (Sim, 2001), echoing spiritual seer Rudolf Steiner from almost a century earlier (Steiner, 1914), the march of 'the inhuman' is always something that we have to be vigilant about.

Jill Hall, in this book offering an Iain McGilchrist-informed evolution-of-consciousness perspective (McGilchrist, 2009), also emphasizes the contemporary relevance of Humanistic Psychology. She writes that 'Humanistic Psychology recognized that a fundamental shift was necessary: an expansion in how we see ourselves as human beings. *This needs to be affirmed afresh*' (our italics). Hall goes on to highlight the importance of the 'holding of a well-grounded space or context that is inclusive of the spiritual dimension', with 'the integration of such experience in the lives of individuals [being] one of our . . . most crucial tasks'; and of a 'reconnect[ion] with the source that enabled the courageous and innovative growth of the Humanistic Psychology movement'. For Hall, then, if it can stay true to its core values, Humanistic Psychology 'will . . . ride on a further tide of courageous innovation'.

Notwithstanding these passionately held positions, with which we have much sympathy, in our view Humanistic Psychology should also strive to be a broad-enough 'church' to encompass a range of principled positions – for example, those who wish to reconnect with core values (e.g. Hall), those who really believe that we need to sharpen up our theoretical act (e.g. Dryden), and those who sincerely believe that it is possible to 'professionalize', codify and make Humanistic Psychology 'respectable' (e.g. Chalfont), without necessarily 'selling our soul' (Edwards, 1992). Here, perhaps, is where Andrew Samuels' perspective on pluralism becomes crucial (Samuels, 1997); for rather than seeing these as contradictory positions that somehow need to be resolved and extinguished, these ongoing dynamic tensions and conflicts are actually (and *healthily*) constitutive and emblematic of what Humanistic Psychology always has been and will be – indeed, they are arguably its very lifeblood.

On this view, then, perhaps we need to let the 'contraries continue to generate progression' (to misquote that quintessentially humanistic visionary, William Blake), and even to welcome The Other who disagrees with us, as they help us to both define our own position and also to imagine how it – and we – might conceivably be different. It can be challenging at times to hold open a space in which to honour diverse subjectivities and divergent opinions, to resist the temptation to either retreat into entrenched positions or expediently subsume our differences into an incongruent and false unity; yet what ultimately could be a more humanistic undertaking? That has been our driving ethos and overarching intent throughout the selection and editing process for this book; we hope that, at least to some extent, we might have succeeded.

Attempting to summarize a book such as this is a hazardous, even 'impossible' exercise. Some might say that Humanistic Psychology has 'had its day', others that it has been successfully assimilated into society. Whatever the case, it seems to us that a humanistic perspective remains, in its essence, a progressive and potentially emancipatory force. Without the existence of the 'healthy fringe' mentioned earlier, it is difficult to imagine how such promising counter-cultural innovations as the UK Independent Practitioners Network (or IPN; e.g. House, 2004; Totton, 2011), or Denis Postle's recent important work on what he terms the 'PsyCommons' (Postle, 2012, 2013) could have taken root and begun to flourish. These are just two of a number of important humanistic initiatives that certainly warranted greater coverage in this book. We do believe that we live in a time when humanistic values are urgently needed and under threat, and that therefore their explicit reaffirmation is essential.

So, to summarize, then: far from Humanistic Psychology having 'had its day', or having been successfully assimilated throughout modern society, we think that – and we are very strongly reinforced in this belief by recent global events – *never before has there been such an urgent need for humanistic values to be re-affirmed in modern culture.* Humanistic Psychology, at its best, provides us with some of the theoretical tools, the ideological commitment, and the practical means with which to challenge the dominance of the scientistic-technocratic, 'evidence-based', over-professionalized, expertise-fixated, pathologizing, instrumentalist, inauthentic and eco-abusive mentalities that are so prevalent in late-modern culture. And notwithstanding its arguable flakiness, its sometimes infuriating definitional fluidity, and its occasional lapses into self-satisfied moral superiority, Humanistic Psychology does offer an explicit privileging of authenticity, creativity and imagination, uniqueness, phenomenological experiencing, curiosity, irony and paradox, human potential, spontaneity, and the power of empathy and love – an extraordinary list of attributes, whose very existence, with all its richness and its contradictions, underscores the huge and largely hugely beneficial influence of Humanistic Psychology to the wider culture from its origins to the present time, and makes, we believe, a formidably compelling case for a very fruitful, growthful and exciting future for Humanistic Psychology in these highly challenging times.

Certainly it seems to us, as we contemplate a new and unprecedentedly fluid political and social landscape in which many of the values we have held dear appear to be under threat from the resurgence of an intolerant and anti-intellectual right-wing populism, that if Humanistic Psychology did not already exist, there is surely no doubt that we would urgently be needing to invent it.

References

Edwards, G. (1992). Does psychotherapy need a soul? In W. Dryden & C. Feltham (Eds), *Psychotherapy and Its Discontents* (pp. 194–224). Buckingham: Open University Press.

Fee, D. (Ed.) (2000). *Pathology and the Postmodern: Mental Illness as Discourse and Experience.* London: Sage.

Felder, A.J. & Robbins, B.D. (2011). A cultural-existential approach to therapy: Merleau Ponty's phenomenology. *Theory and Psychology,* 21: 355–76.

Griffin, D.R. (1997). *Parapsychology, Philosophy, and Spirituality: A Postmodern Exploration.* Albany, NY: State University of New York Press.

Griffin, D.R. (2000). *Religion and Scientific Naturalism: Overcoming the Conflicts.* Albany, NY: State University of New York Press.

Halliwell, M. & Mousley, A. (2003). *Critical Humanisms: Humanist/Anti-Humanist Dialogues.* Edinburgh: Edinburgh University Press.

Hansen, J.T. (2012). The future of humanism: cultivating the humanities' impulse in mental health culture. *Self & Society: International Journal for Humanistic Psychology,* 40(1): 21–5 (see also his Chapter 7, this book).

Harvey, D. (1973). *Social Justice and the City.* London: Edward Arnold (revised edn, 2009).

Heaton, J. (2010). *The Talking Cure: Wittgenstein on Language as Bewitchment and Clarity.* Basingstoke: Palgrave Macmillan.

House, R. (2004). An unqualified good: the IPN as a path through and beyond profession-alization. *Self & Society: International Journal for Humanistic Psychology,* 32(4): 14–22.

House, R. (2010). *In, Against and Beyond Therapy: Critical Essays Towards a 'Post-professional' Era.* Ross-on-Wye: PCCS Books.

Johnson, M. (2012). *The Meaning of the Body: Aesthetics of Human Understanding.* Chicago, IL: University of Chicago Press.

King, L. & Moutsou, C. (Eds) (2010). *Rethinking Audit Cultures: A Critical Look at Evidence-based Practice in Psychotherapy and Beyond.* Ross-on-Wye: PCCS Books.

Lawrence, D.H. (1993). Healing. In R. Bly, J. Hillman & M. Meade (Eds), *The Rag and Bone Shop of the Heart: Poems for Men.* New York: HarperPerennial.

Levin, D.M. (Ed.) (1987). *Pathologies of the Modern Self: Postmodern Studies on Narcissism, Schizophrenia, and Depression.* New York: New York University Press.

Loewenthal, D. & Snell, R. (Eds) (2003). *Post-modernism for Psychotherapists: A Critical Reader.* Hove: Brunner-Routledge.

McGilchrist, I. (2009). *The Master and his Emissary: The Divided Brain and the Making of the Western World.* New Haven, CT: Yale University Press (2nd edn, 2012).

Moon, L. (2012). Retro-review of Halliwell and Mousley, 2003. *Self & Society: International Journal for Humanistic Psychology,* 40(1): 74–5.

Mowbray, R. (1995). *The Case against Psychotherapy Registration: A Conservation Issue for the Human Potential Movement.* London: Trans Marginal Press; downloadable as a pdf file free of charge at: www.transmarginalpress.co.uk (accessed 31 March 2017).

Orange, D.M. (2009). *Thinking for Clinicians: Philosophical Resources for Contemporary Psychoanalysis and the Humanistic Therapies.* London: Routledge.

Parker, I. (1999). Deconstruction and psychotherapy. In I. Parker (Ed.), *Deconstructing Psychotherapy* (pp. 1–18). London: Sage.

Parker, I. (2007). *Revolution in Psychology: Alienation to Emancipation*. London: Pluto Press.

Postle, D. (2012). *Therapy Futures: Obstacles and Opportunities*. London: Wentworth Learning Resources.

Postle, D. (2013). The richness of everyday relationships. *Therapy Today*, 24(3): 30–2.

Rowan, J. (2000). Humanistic Psychology and the social construction of reality. *British Psychological Society Psychotherapy Section Newsletter*, 29 (December): 1–8.

Rowan, J. (2012). Letter to the editors. *Self & Society: International Journal for Humanistic Psychology*, 40(2): 64.

Samuels, A. (1997). Pluralism and psychotherapy: what is good training? In R. House & N. Totton (Eds), *Implausible Professions: Arguments for Pluralism and Autonomy in Psychotherapy and Counselling* (pp. 199–214). Ross-on-Wye: PCCS Books (2nd edn, 2011, pp. 221–37).

Self & Society (2014). Special theme issue on Maurice Merleau-Ponty. Volume 41(3).

Self & Society (2017). Special theme issue on 'Rudolf Steiner and the Psychological Therapies'. Volume 45(1).

Sim, S. (2001). *Lyotard and the Inhuman*. Cambridge: Icon Books.

Steiner, R. (1914). Technology and Art: Their Bearing on Modern Culture. Lecture given at Dornach, 28 December. Accessible at goo.gl/h0RH8B (accessed 11 December 2016).

Totton, N. (2011). The Independent Practitioners Network: a new model of accountability. In R. House & N. Totton (Eds), *Implausible Professions: Arguments for Pluralism and Autonomy in Psychotherapy and Counselling* (2nd edition, pp. 315–21). Ross-on-Wye: PCCS Books.

INDEX